Environmental Ethics

An Introduction
to Environmental Philosophy

FIFTH EDITION

JOSEPH R. DESJARDINS
College of Saint Benedict/St. John's University

WADSWORTH
CENGAGE Learning

Australia • Brazil • Japan • Korea • Mexico • Singapore • Spain • United Kingdom • United States

WADSWORTH
CENGAGE Learning

Environmental Ethics: An Introduction to Environmental Philosophy, Fifth Edition

Joseph R. DesJardins

Publisher: Clark Baxter

Acquisitions Editor: Joann Kozyrev

Associate Development Editor: Daisuke Yasutake

Assistant Editor: Joshua Duncan

Editorial Assistant: Marri Straton

Media Editor: Katie Schooling

Marketing Program Manager: Sean Foy

Design and Production Services: PreMediaGlobal

Manufacturing Planner: Mary Beth, Hennbury

Rights Acquisition Specialist: Shalice Shah-Caldwell

Cover Designer: Michelle DiMercurio

Cover Image: Getty Images

Compositor: PreMediaGlobal

For product information and technology assistance, contact us at **Cengage Learning Customer & Sales Support, 1-800-354-9706**

For permission to use material from this text or product, submit all requests online at **www.cengage.com/permissions**. Further permissions questions can be e-mailed to **permissionrequest@cengage.com**.

Library of Congress Control Number: 2011941646

ISBN-13: 978-1-133-04997-5

ISBN-10: 1-133-04997-4

Wadsworth
20 Channel Center Street
Boston, MA 02210
USA

Cengage Learning is a leading provider of customized learning solutions with office locations around the globe, including Singapore, the United Kingdom, Australia, Mexico, Brazil and Japan. Locate your local office at **international.cengage.com/region**

Cengage Learning products are represented in Canada by Nelson Education, Ltd.

For your course and learning solutions, visit **www.cengage.com**.

Purchase any of our products at your local college store or at our preferred online store **www.cengagebrain.com**.

Instructors: Please visit **login.cengage.com** and log in to access instructor-specific resources.

Printed in the United States of America
2 3 4 5 6 7 16 15 14 13

One summer morning, while driving through the countryside, my four-year-old son asked, "Daddy, what are trees good for?" Sensing a precious moment of parenthood, I began gently to explain that as living things they don't need to be good for anything, but that trees do provide homes to many other living things, that they make and clean the air that we breathe, that they can be majestic and beautiful. "But daddy," he said, "I'm a scientist and I know more than you because you forgot the most important thing. Trees are good for climbing."
I hope that I have not missed too many other such obvious truths in writing this book, which I dedicate to Michael and Matthew.

Contents

II Environmental Ethics as Applied Ethics   47

3 Ethics and Economics: Managing Public Lands   49

4 Sustainability and Responsibilities to the Future   74

Preface

One winter evening some years ago, I reread Aldo Leopold's *A Sand County Almanac*. This occurred a few months after I had moved to rural Minnesota from suburban Philadelphia. I came upon Leopold's entry for February:

> There are two spiritual dangers in not owning a farm. One is the danger of supposing that breakfast comes from the grocery, and the other that heat comes from the furnace. To avoid the first danger, one should plant a garden, preferably where there is no grocer to confuse the issue. To avoid the second, he should lay a split of good oak on the andirons, preferably where there is no furnace.

This passage struck me in a way that it never could have had I still been living in a metropolitan area. The fact that it was 27 degrees below zero outside, and I was sitting in front of a roaring oak fire might have had something to do with this. I recognized that there are more than just two spiritual dangers in not owning a farm; one other concerns divorcing your life from your work. That evening, I realized that teaching courses on environmental and ecological issues would mean more to me now, personally and professionally, than it could have in the city. This book grows out of a commitment to integrate more fully my life with my work.

The primary aim of this book is simple: to provide a clear, systematic, and comprehensive introduction to the philosophical issues underlying environmental and ecological controversies. At the beginning of the twenty-first century, it is fair to say that human beings face environmental challenges unprecedented in the history of this planet. Largely through human activity, the very climate of the Earth is changing, and life on Earth faces the greatest mass extinctions since the end of the dinosaur age sixty-five million years ago. The natural resources that sustain life on this planet—air, water, and soil—are being polluted or depleted at alarming rates. Human population growth is increasing exponentially. When the first edition of this book was begun in 1990, the world population was 5.5 billion people.

By 2012 it will have grown to 7 billion, a 27 percent increase in just over twenty years. The prospects for continued degradation and depletion of natural resources multiply with this population growth. Toxic wastes that will plague future generations continue to accumulate worldwide. The world's wilderness areas—its forests, wetlands, mountains, and grasslands—are being developed, paved, drained, burned, and overgrazed out of existence.

The tendency in our culture is to treat such issues as simply scientific, technological, or political problems. But they are much more than that. These environmental and ecological controversies raise fundamental questions about what we as human beings value, about the kind of beings we are, the kinds of lives we should live, our place in nature, and the kind of world in which we might flourish. In short, environmental problems raise fundamental questions of ethics and philosophy. This book seeks to provide a systematic introduction to these philosophical issues.

OVERVIEW

A significant amount of philosophically interesting and important research on environmental and ecological issues has been conducted during the past few decades. The structure of this book reflects the way the fields of environmental ethics and environmental philosophy have developed during that period.

Two initial chapters introduce the relevance of philosophy for environmental concerns and some traditional ethical theories and principles. Chapters 3 and 4 survey topics that essentially fit an "applied ethics" model. Traditional philosophical theories and methodologies are applied to environmental issues with the aim of clarification and evaluation. The applied ethics model, it seems to me, accounts for much of the early work in environmental ethics.

Philosophers soon recognized that traditional theories and principles were inadequate to deal with new environmental challenges. In response, philosophers began to extend traditional concepts and principles, so that they might become environmentally relevant. Chapter 5 examines attempts to extend moral standing to such things as individual animals, future generations, trees, and other natural objects. Within much of this thinking, traditional theories and principles remain essentially intact, but their scope and range are extended to cover topics not previously explored by philosophers.

Many philosophers working in this field have come to believe that ethical extensionism is an inadequate philosophical response to environmental issues and controversies. To many of these thinkers, traditional ethical theories and principles are part of a worldview that has been responsible for much environmental and ecological destruction. What is needed, in their eyes, is a more radical philosophical approach that includes rethinking metaphysical, epistemological, and political, as well as ethical, concepts. At this point, the field once identified as environmental ethics is better conceived of as environmental philosophy. The final seven chapters examine more comprehensive environmental and ecological philosophies. These views include biocentrism (the view that all living things deserve moral standing), ecocentrism (the view that shifts away from traditional environmental concerns to a more holistic and ecological focus), deep ecology, social ecology, and ecofeminism.

THE FIFTH EDITION

One strong temptation in writing a new edition is to create a much longer book. Keeping pace with new developments, including all the latest cases and environmental controversies, and embracing new ideas would all lead one to include more and more material. But one important lesson we learn from ecology is to recognize that not every change is an improvement and not all growth is development. My primary goal for this book remains what it was in the first edition, now nearly twenty years ago: to provide a clear and concise introduction to the philosophical issues underlying environmental controversies. This book has proved popular for use in courses taught outside of philosophy, which I take as some measure of success in achieving this goal.

This new edition attempts to respond to suggestions and advice from faculty and students who have been using this book. I owe a great debt to all the generous people who have contributed recommendations for this edition. The primary goal of this new edition is to keep apace of recent developments in the field, without sacrificing the original goal of writing a concise introductory text. I continue to seek a balance between philosophical depth and practical relevance. Admittedly, students do not always appreciate the details of philosophical debates and would rather we "get to the point." But if there is any lesson to be drawn from the present political climate of rancorous partisan disagreement, it is that the world needs more, not less, careful and considered judgment.

Changes to this edition include new or significantly revised and updated discussion cases at the start of most chapters. New material includes cases on global climate change, BP's Gulf of Mexico Oil Spill, Synthetic Biology, Animals and Food, Sustainability, Hunting, Environmental Refugees, and Carbon Mitigation. I hope this new material will keep the book fresh for students and faculty alike. But the same basic format remains. Previous editions developed what has proven to be a coherent structure for presenting and teaching the content of environmental ethics and, for the most part, I have kept that structure as is.

But I have also done some minor restructuring of this edition to achieve greater clarity and coherence. I have combined the previous Chapter 9 (Deep Ecology) and Chapter 11 (Ecofeminsim) into a single chapter. I agree with reviewers who believe that neither field has developed much in the past decade, and that the material was no longer as cutting-edge as it had been. But both deep ecology and ecofeminism present intriguing and philosophically interesting perspectives that deserve attention, and each has had a significant impact on contemporary environmentalism. I have combined them into a single chapter because each is an example of a type of environmentalism—what I call radical environmentalism—which rejects reform in favour of more dramatic, radical social change.

Careful readers will notice several other minor changes. The section on ethical relativism has been moved from the chapter on ethical theory (Chapter 2) into Chapter 1, so that it can be included in a new section on "Philosophy, Politics, and Ethical Relativism." Chapter 1 also discusses the present partisan political climate in that same context, and backs away from a previous concern with an over-reliance on science in setting environmental policy. If only that were now the case that I thought it was two decades ago.

Finally, what previously was an epilogue has become a more extended discussion of pluralism, pragmatism, and sustainability. When I first added the epilogue, issues of pluralism and pragmatism were just emerging as a serious topic among environmental philosophers. I have tried to extend this discussion to include some final reflections on sustainability. It seems to me that while theorists continue to debate the relative merits of various environmental philosophies, the issue that motivates us all—environmental destruction—marches on. The philosophical debates concerning pluralism and pragmatism, in my opinion, share with the issue of sustainable development an urgent need that something be done in the meantime. Those who address these three topics seek a reasoned way to proceed even when a unified consensus on more theoretical issues remains elusive.

TO STUDENTS AND TEACHERS

Writing a book like this carries two intellectual dangers. One is the danger of supposing that students are as motivated by and interested in abstract philosophical issues as their teachers. The other is that in pointing to the immense practical relevance of environmental ethics, I ignore or understate the importance of careful and rigorous conceptual analysis. I have tried to address these dangers in a number of ways.

Each chapter begins with a description of a contemporary environmental controversy that can be used as an entry into the philosophical discussion that follows. These discussion cases describe issues that are at the forefront of the contemporary environmental scene, and they implicitly raise fundamental ethical and philosophical questions. My hope is that after some directed reflection and discussion, students will see the need to address philosophical questions in developing their own environmental and ecological positions. Each chapter also ends with a series of discussion questions that can be used either as the basis for a chapter review or as the basis for further study.

To avoid the second danger, I have tried to follow the philosophical debates far enough to provide an accurate example of how philosophers reason and how reasoning can make progress. There can be no substitute for a careful study and reading of the many primary sources that I have used in this book. But the nature of this book requires that these debates not be so comprehensive that readers get lost in, or bored by, the detail.

I have not always been successful in my own teaching at balancing a relevant introduction to the issues with an in-depth analysis. Without a clear context to motivate the need to know, students often get lost in philosophical analysis. On the other hand, without depth, students can become convinced too easily that they now know all the answers. Class time spent providing context, of course, takes away from time spent developing analysis; time spent following through on the debates prevents the forest from being seen for all the trees.

I wrote this book to address that tension. I suspect that for many teachers, the book provides a context and introduction, allowing them to use class time for fuller development of selected issues. They might do this in a number of ways: by reading classic or contemporary primary sources; by studying more empirical resources such as the Worldwatch publications; by keeping current on environmental controversies on the Web; by using some of the many excellent videos on environmental topics that are now available; and by addressing the claims of more activist groups ranging from the Sierra Club to Earth First!. However individual instructors choose to develop their courses, I hope that this book can provide a context to ensure that students remain as connected to the important philosophical issues as they so often are to the practical environmental ones.

ACKNOWLEDGMENTS

I owe my greatest debts to those thinkers who are doing the original research in this field. I have tried to acknowledge their work at every turn, but if I have missed someone, I hope this general acknowledgment will suffice.

Through the years many reviewers have provided thorough, insightful, and tremendously helpful advice. Some have been willing to help on more than one occasion, and I must especially acknowledge Claudia Card of the University of Wisconsin, Arthur Millman of the University of Massachusetts in Boston, and Ellen Klein of the University of North Florida. Although their advice improved this book immeasurably, the usual disclaimers of responsibility apply. I have especially benefited from advice offered by Holmes Rolston and Ernie Diedrich. My thanks also to previous edition reviewers Mary Brentwood, California State University, Sacramento; Douglas Browning, University of Texas, Austin; Larry D. Harwood, Viterbo University; Ned Hettinger, College of Charleston; Donald Hubin, Ohio State University; Dale Jamieson, University of Colorado; Kathie Jenni, University of Redlands; Sheldon Krimsky, Tufts University; Donald C. Lee, University of New Mexico; Eugene G. Maurakis, University of Richmond; Jon McGregor, Arizona State University; Greg Peterson, South Dakota State University; Wade Robinson, Rochester Institute of Technology; Arthur Skidmore, Kansas University; William O. Stephens, Creighton University; Charles Taliaferro, Saint Olaf College; Eugene Troxell, San Diego State University; and Charles Verharen, Howard University. And thanks to the new edition reviewers Benita Beamon, University of Washington; Joseph Chartkoff, Michigan State University; Johnna Fisher, University of British Columbia; Andre Goddu, Stonehill College; Gail Grabowsky, Chaminade University; Benjamin Hale, University of Colorado; Susan Mooney, Stonehill College; Paul Ott, Loyola University, Chicago; Kyle

Powys, Michigan State University; Patrick Walsh, University of Manitoba; Wei-Ming Wu, Butte College; and Jason Wyckoff, Marquette University.

My students at the College of St. Benedict and St. John's University worked through early versions of this text. We were all students in those classes, and their comments helped substantively and pedagogically. The College of St. Benedict provided financial support for research during the writing of this book. Everyone associated with Wadsworth Publishing has once again provided generous, skillful, and intelligent support.

Global Environmental Ethics Watch

Updated several times a day, the Global Environmental Ethics Watch is a focused portal into GREENR—our Global Reference on the Environment, Energy, and Natural Resources—an ideal one-stop site for classroom discussion and research projects. This resource center keeps courses up-to-date with the most current news on environmental ethics. Users get access to information from trusted academic journals, news outlets, and magazines, as well as statistics, an interactive world map, videos, primary sources, case studies, podcasts, and much more. Please contact your Cengage Learning Representative for information on how to get your students access to the Global Environmental Ethics Watch.

PART I

Basic Concepts

1

Science, Politics, and Ethics

DISCUSSION: Global Climate Change

Scientists have long known that carbon dioxide is one of several atmospheric gases, along with water vapor, ozone, methane, and nitrous oxide which are responsible for maintaining stability in the Earth's temperature. These so-called "greenhouse gases" function much as the glass in a greenhouse, which admits warming sunlight while preventing the warmer air from radiating back outside. This greenhouse effect is the reigning scientific explanation for how the atmosphere regulates the Earth's temperature.

For over a century it has been understood that human activities, primarily those associated with burning fossil fuels in automobiles and industry, have been adding significant amounts of carbon dioxide to the atmosphere. Carbon dioxide is a major by-product of burning fossil fuels such as coal, oil, and gasoline, and as human use of such fuels has increased, so too has the amount of carbon dioxide increased. By the 1980s,

some observers were claiming that increases in greenhouse gases could lead, and likely was leading, to an increase in global temperatures, or "global warming." Many people predicted that an increase in global temperatures would cause considerable environmental damage and human suffering and, as a result, recommended policy changes to minimize the use of fossil fuels and otherwise limit the discharge of greenhouse gases.

The natural process associated with global warming is straightforward. Sunlight strikes the Earth's surface and is radiated back as heat into the atmosphere. The Earth's atmosphere is composed primarily of nitrogen (78 percent) and oxygen (21 percent). But many of the remaining trace elements, especially carbon dioxide, water vapor, methane, and ozone, have molecular structures that absorb the radiated heat and reflect it back into the atmosphere and back onto the Earth. The initial global warming hypothesis claimed that because green-house gases trap heat in the atmosphere, an increase in the amount of greenhouse gases will result in an increase in the heat reflected back, thus increasing global temperature. In turn, an increase in global temperature could lead to such conse-quences as a rise in ocean levels due to melting of snow and ice in the Earth's polar regions, climatic shifts, worldwide droughts and famine, shifts in oceanic currents, and massive extinctions of plant and animal life as a result of ecosystem disruptions.

Given such dire predictions, many environmentalists have advocated for significant policy and lifestyle changes, particularly involving reduction in CO_2 emissions. Many recommended that countries should reduce their reliance on fossil fuels and support international treaties mandating CO_2 reductions. Gov-ernments should create incentive pro-grams to reduce the use of carbon-based fuels, including taxes and carbon-trading credits. Governments should also provide incentives and subsidies for alternative energy sources. Institutions such as busi-nesses and universities should pledge to become "carbon-neutral." Virtually every aspect of modern industrial economies would be affected by policies aimed at reducing carbon emissions.

Critics have challenged each step in this line of reasoning. While some early critics challenged the very idea of a greenhouse effect or the reality of increasing global temperatures, more recent critics have focused on the role of human activities in increasing the green-house effect and affecting climate change. While any cold spell or blizzard will be cited by some as evidence against global warming, scientific data has increasingly persuaded most observers that average overall global temperatures are increasing, even if not everyone agrees on the significance of the increase. Skeptics tend now to suggest that fluc-tuations in CO_2 and other greenhouse gas levels are within normal limits when viewed over the long range. They suggest that the Earth's climate has always fluc-tuated, and there is nothing to show that any changes presently occurring are not

within this normal range or that they are caused by humans. Many critics also dispute the catastrophic predictions based on the alleged fact of global warming. For example, increased temperatures could result in greater cloud cover due to increased evaporation, thereby reducing the overall amount of sunlight that reaches the Earth's surface, thus reducing temperatures. Increasing temperatures could simply shift global climate making previously inhospitable areas more tem-perate and livable. The bottom line is that no one knows for certain what slightly increased global temperatures will bring about. Whatever changes occur will occur slowly, thereby giving the ever-adaptable human species plenty of time to adapt.

Further, critics reject many of the pro-posed policy changes that are offered by defenders of global warming. Less devel-oped countries argue that the costs of any reduction in worldwide CO_2 levels will fall disproportionately on the poor. Having achieved high standards of living through fossil-fuel based economies, the rich now want to limit economic development of poorer countries in the name of reducing their carbon footprint. Furthermore, the economic changes required by a massive shift away from fossil fuels are likely to create as many new problems as would be avoided and, frankly, there really is no viable alternative to coal, natural gas, and oil to power the Earth's economies.

As these debates developed, there has been a shift away from the language of "global warming" in favor of the lan-guage of "global climate change." The rationale is that global warming refers to the average mean surface temperature, while global climate change refers to a broad range of climatic changes that would result from an increase in the average global temperature. Predictions made decades ago that increasing atmo-spheric carbon dioxide would lead to an increase in global temperatures have been proven true. But the consequences of those increased average temperatures are still evolving. An increase in greenhouse gases and an increase in overall average surface temperature does not necessarily result in warmer temperatures every-where and at all times. The complex relationships between air temperature, rainfall, ocean temperature, ocean currents, and ocean levels could result in weather patterns that include lower temperatures in some places and fiercer winter storms. Defenders of this language change claim that greater clarity and precision can be brought to these debates by speaking of global climate change rather than global warming.

Critics see this as a rhetorical ploy to shift attention away from lack of evidence for warming and allow environmentalists to claim that any change in the weather or climate is evidence for the result of increased CO_2 emissions. If every weather event can be claimed as evidence of global climate change, then this alleged problem can never be tested and this suggests that it is not a scientifically validated empirical claim after all. In addition, while "global climate change" rhetorically suggests major and catastrophic changes, the fact is that the global climate is constantly changing and always has. Global climate change is the norm, not the problem it is made out to be.

At first glance, it might appear that debates about global warming are primarily scientific debates. The greenhouse effect would seem to involve questions about such phenomena as solar radiation and the structure of certain molecules in such science disciplines as atmospheric science, physics, and chemistry. Science would also seem to be the proper domain for determining the degree to which human activity is causing an increase in CO_2 and other greenhouse gases. By measuring and comparing such things as the amount of CO_2 at various levels of the polar ice cap or the growth rate found in the rings of old or fossilized trees, scientists can determine the degree of correlation between the amount of atmospheric CO_2 and global temperatures in earlier periods of Earth's history. Using such correlations, science predicts future temperatures based on anticipated CO_2 levels. Over shorter terms, science can also trace trends in global temperatures, relative size of glaciers, ocean levels and temperatures, and habitat change, especially in northern climates.

In other words, resolving debates about global warming would seem to be a matter of determining the facts, and facts, as we usually understand things, are the proper domain of science. If we simply do more and better science, gather more data, establish greater patterns of correlation and causality, and confirm more predictions, we will arrive at stronger conclusions and reach consensus on policy options. Many also conclude that if there is a scientific consensus on the facts of global warming and climate change, the practical conclusions for what we ought to do about it logically follow.

But despite increasing scientific study, disputes remain, and they remain because debates about global warming are not simply about the science and facts. Especially within the United States, global warming has emerged as something of a political litmus test, as partisan as debates over big government, taxes, and abortion. One's view on global warming seems to be determined as much by one's political beliefs as by the facts. A 2008 Gallup poll reported that the gap between Democrats and Republicans has steadily increased during the past decade on such statements as "the effects of global warming have already begun," "global warming is due more to human activities than natural causes," and "global warming is occurring." In each case, Republicans are much less convinced by the science of global warming than Democrats. The Congressional elections of 2010 produced Republican leaders who made skepticism about global warming a central political tenet. Within a month of becoming the new chairman of the House Energy and Commerce Committee, Congressman Fred Upton denied that climate change is human caused. Republican Congressman John Shimkus, who sits on both the House Energy and Commerce Committee and the Subcommittee on Energy and Environment, expressed his skepticism about climate change in terms of his belief in God's promise to Noah that the Earth would not be destroyed by a flood for a second time.[1]

The prospect of global warming and global climate change raise fundamental questions concerning what we ought to do, both individually and as a society, about what we value, and about how we ought to live our lives. That is, they raise fundamental questions not only for science but for ethics as well. Knowledge of the facts alone does not determine what should be done. Political debates about global warming also raise important questions on what we should believe, and the degree to which we should rely on science when making policy decisions. In other words, the prospect of global warming, like so many other environmental issues, requires us to ask fundamental philosophical questions: What should we believe and why? What should we do, both as individuals and as a society? What do we value? What should we do when beliefs and values conflict? How should we live our lives?

DISCUSSION TOPICS:

1. Individuals seldom have the ability to evaluate by themselves the validity of a scientific claim and often have to trust the judgments of experts. Consider how often you must trust the judgments of doctors and engineers for example. What evidence would persuade you to trust those scientists who claim that global warming or global climate change is a factual event? What evidence would cause you to doubt those scientists? Where do you get your own information about global warming? Is this a reliable source? Are the advocates on both sides of these debates equally worthy of trust? How would you distinguish between scientific "experts" who are persuaded by global warming and those who are skeptical?

2. Hundreds of college and university presidents have signed the "Presidents' Climate Commitment," which pledges their schools to achieve "climate neutrality as soon as possible." (http://www.presidentsclimatecommitment.org/) Has your school's president signed this commitment? Why or why not? What steps, if any, has your school taken to reduce greenhouse gas emissions? Do you support this commitment by your school?

3. Do you think that more developed countries such as the United States, Canada, England, and Germany have a greater responsibility for reducing greenhouse gas emissions than developing countries such as China, India, and Brazil? What arguments can be offered for each side of this debate?

4. Would you support a tax on carbon emissions, and therefore higher prices for electricity and gasoline, as a means to reduce greenhouse gases? Why, or why not?

1.1 INTRODUCTION: WHY PHILOSOPHY?

In the early decades of the twenty-first century it is fair to say that human beings face environmental challenges unprecedented in the history of this planet. Largely through human activity, life on Earth faces the greatest number of mass extinctions since the end of the dinosaur age 65 million years ago. Some estimates suggest that more than 100 species are becoming extinct every day and that this rate could double or triple within the next few decades.[2] The natural resources that sustain life on our planet—the climate, air, water, and soil—are being changed, polluted, or depleted at alarming rates. Human population growth is increasing exponentially. World population reached 7 billion people in 2011, just 12 years after reaching 6 billion. Although it took all of human history until 1804 for world population to first reach 1 billion people, the most recent *increase* of 1 billion took just 12 years. The rate of population increase is slowing somewhat. It is estimated that it may take 15 years to add the next

1 billion people. Unfortunately, however, disease, famine, poverty, and war are among the factors contributing to this decline in the rate of growth. The prospects for continued degradation and depletion of natural resources multiply with population growth. Not only are there more people using more resources, but the lifestyles of that growing population place increasing demands on the biosphere. Toxic wastes that will plague future generations continue to accumulate worldwide. Some forms of nuclear waste will remain deadly for tens of thousands of years. The world's wilderness areas—its forests, wetlands, topsoils, mountains, and grasslands—are being developed, paved, drained, burned, and overgrazed out of existence. Destruction of large areas of the ozone layer and a significant increase in greenhouse gases that could result in global warming demonstrate that human activity threatens to disrupt the very atmosphere and climate of the planet Earth.

Complicating matters is the fact that many environmental topics, from global warming to land use, from energy policy to food production, have become embroiled in bitter partisan politics, especially within the United States. The days in which a Republican President (Richard Nixon) and a Democratic Congress could be unified in passing sweeping environmental legislation such as the Clean Water Act, the Clean Air Act, and the Endangered Species Act within a three-year period, are a distant memory.

Faced with such a potentially catastrophic environmental future, we are challenged with momentous decisions. But how do we even begin making the right decisions, especially in such a political climate as the present? We should also acknowledge that many of our present environmental challenges are the result of decisions made, not by thoughtless or dishonorable people, but in good faith by previous generations. In fact, many of those decisions had very beneficial consequences to both prior and present generations in the form of adequate food, affordable energy, and increased life expectancy. But these decisions have had devastating consequences as well. How can we be sure that the decisions about energy policy, population, and food production that we likewise make in good faith will not have equally ambiguous consequences? Before making such momentous decisions, it seems only reasonable that we should step back to reflect on the decision-making process itself.

In many ways, philosophical ethics is just this process of stepping back to reflect on our decision making. Philosophical ethics involves a self-conscious stepping back from our own lives to reflect on what type of life we should live, how we should act, and what kind of people we should be. This textbook will introduce environmental ethics by working across two levels of thought: the practical level of deciding what we should do and how we should live, and the more abstract and academic level of *stepping back to think about how* we decide what to do and what to value. As used in this book, philosophical ethics involves elements of practical normative ethics—deciding what one ought or ought not do—and critical thinking—evaluating the reasoning used to justify and defend such practical decisions.

Philosophical ethics in the West is exemplified by Socrates's questioning of Athenian society and an individual's role within it. When speaking with a self-proclaimed authority on what the gods expect of humans, Socrates set the standard of philosophical reasoning 2,500 years ago by refusing to accept a conclusion based solely on the words of an authority. When the religious authority Euthyphro claimed that he knew many things about the gods' desires of which most people were ignorant, Socrates responded with what is perhaps the most crucial philosophical call: "Let us examine what we are saying" so that we might all come to learn for ourselves what is true.

This textbook invites you on a similar Socratic journey with respect to environmental topics. Let us examine what is being said so that we might think for ourselves and better understand what is true and what we ought to do. This text introduces the many ways in which ethics and philosophy can contribute to the creation of a sane and judicious environmental policy. Environmental challenges such as global warming raise fundamental scientific and political questions, but they raise important philosophical questions as well. Ethics is the branch of philosophy that addresses questions on fundamental values, and these will be the primary focus of this book. However, as we shall see, engaging in a full analysis of environmental issues will require that we also address a wide range of questions from other branches of philosophy. Topics such as the allocation and distribution of environmental benefits and dangers raise important questions of social justice and political philosophy. Issues of moral standing for future generations, animals, and other nonhuman forms of life and the nature of such abstract entities as species and ecosystems raise important questions in epistemology and metaphysics.

A basic assumption of this book is that environmental policy ought to be decided in the political arena and not by experts in scientific laboratories, corporate boardrooms, or government bureaucracies. But to say this is not to say that all political opinions are equal. In an era when name-calling, shouting matches, and demonization of those with whom one disagrees passes for political debate, the need for critical thinking—careful, logical examination of controversial issues—has never been greater. Philosophical ethics will ask you to put aside what you hear from political pundits and commentators on Fox News or the Daily Show, suspend your assumptions and what you think you already know, and think carefully in as unbiased and balanced way as you can.

Thus an implicit goal of this textbook is to empower citizens to become full and thoughtful participants in these critical public policy debates. Familiarity with the ethical and philosophical issues involved in such debates is an important first step in this direction. Every position staked out in an environmental controversy will involve philosophical assumptions. Your challenge is to separate the good arguments from the bad, the rational conclusions from the unproven. Join with Socrates to examine what we are saying so that we might come to know what is true.

1.2 SCIENCE AND ETHICS

Environmentalists have long had an ambiguous relationship with science and technology. On one hand, science provides exactly the type of unbiased and rational source of information that citizens need for informed and rational policy making. Trusting science seems a reasonable strategy. Technology offers hope for addressing most, if not all, environmental challenges. On the other hand, science and technology have also played a major role in bringing about some of the worst environmental problems that we face. Blind trust of science and technology can appear as unreasonable as blind trust of political pundits. Surely science and technology must be a major partner in addressing environmental challenges, but it is important that we not abdicate decision-making responsibility to science alone and that we think carefully about the proper role of science and technology.

One of the pivotal events of the modern environmental movement was the publication of Rachel Carson's *Silent Spring* in 1962. This book focused international attention on the deadly effects of DDT and other chemical pesticides. The continued indiscriminate use of these "elixirs of death" would, according to Carson, lead to a time when death and poisoning would silence the "voices of spring." This book profoundly influenced the public's attitude toward chemical pollution and environmental protection. For the first time, widespread public doubt was raised about the safety and desirability of technological solutions to environmental problems.

Although chemical agents have been used to control pests and fertilize crops since the beginning of agriculture, the decades immediately after World War II witnessed tremendous development in the discovery, production, and use of synthetic chemical pesticides and fertilizers. Increasing population growth and a corresponding increase in demand on agriculture, along with a decrease in the number of farmers, led to intense pressures to increase agricultural productivity. One large part of this effort involved the use of chemicals to limit crop loss from pests and to enhance the growth of crops. Before the publication of *Silent Spring,* the only question generally asked about chemical pesticides and fertilizers, by both scientists and the public, concerned their effectiveness: Do they eliminate undesirable pests without harming humans or their crops? Do they increase yield? After Carson's work, the long-term consequences to both humans and the natural world, as well as the political and ethical implications of chemically enhanced agriculture, came to the forefront.

Even seemingly innocuous issues such as fertilizer and pesticide use can raise philosophical questions. For example, do we have any ethical responsibility to preserve the various life forms around us? Is there anything wrong with defining some living organisms as pests and working to eradicate them? Philosophical assumptions are involved wherever we stand in this debate. Should pesticides be proved safe before they are used, or should the burden of proof rest with those who predict danger? Answering this question also involves issues in ethics and political philosophy.

Relying on science or technology (or on economics or the law) without also considering the ethical and philosophical issues involved can raise as many problems as it solves. Leaving environmental decisions to the "experts" in science and technology does not mean that these decisions will be objective and value-neutral. It means only that the values and philosophical assumptions that do decide the issue will be those that these experts hold.

Whereas this book relies on philosophical ethics for guidance, many people look instead to science and technology for answers. If only we could develop safe, inexpensive, and effective chemical pesticides. If only we could engineer a carbon sequestration process to contain the carbon dioxide produced by burning fossil fuels. If only we could engineer more efficient solar panels or harness the energy potential of geothermal, wind, or tidal power. If only we could develop hydrogen fuel cell technology as an alternative to the internal combustion engine. If only we could master cold fusion.

For many people in our culture, and especially for many in policy-making positions, science and technology offer the only hope for solving environmental problems. Because environmental problems often involve highly technical matters, it is only reasonable to turn to experts in these technical areas for answers. Who better than meteorologists to tell us about the effects of global climate change? Who better than chemists to tell us about the safety and effectiveness of pesticides? Because science offers objective and factual answers in an area in which emotions run high and controversies abound, many believe that science is the obvious place to turn for help with environmental concerns. The only alternative to looking to science seems to be a pessimistic surrender to the type of controversy and disagreement so typical of talk television.

As Rachel Carson's writing suggests, we take risks when we treat environmental problems merely as technical problems awaiting solution from some specialized discipline. This is partly because the dimensions of environmental issues are seldom limited to the specific boundaries of any one particular discipline. Pesticide pollution, for example, involves agriculture, various branches of biology and chemistry, medicine, economics, politics, and law. Global climate change involves an equally diverse group of disciplines. But it is impossible to find an environmental issue that does not raise basic questions of value. Approaching any serious environmental issue with the hope of finding a technical quick fix guarantees only a narrow and parochial understanding of what is at stake. Carson's *Silent Spring* testifies to the dangers inherent in this approach. As seen in these examples, technological or scientific "solutions" have often inflicted as many new problems as they have solved.

Turning to science for help in understanding how the world works is a hallmark of a reasonable and educated citizen. But turning to science and technology for solutions to problems that are fundamentally ethical and political may not be. For example, in response to increasing levels of CO_2 and global warming, some have proposed technological and geo-engineering solutions on a massive scale. Manipulating the biophysical processes of both the atmosphere and the ocean have been proposed means to lessen the effects of increasing atmospheric CO_2. Skepticism about such grand experiments seems, as someone like Rachel Carson might advise, to be the mark of a reasonable and educated citizen.

But the danger in over-reliance on science and technology extends well beyond this technological complexity. Science is not as value-neutral as many assume. Our culture has a profound belief in science as the ultimate authority on questions of knowledge and truth. Although it is important not to overstate this point (science, of course, does have tremendous potential for helping us to understand and solve environmental problems), science is not always the purely objective and value-neutral resource that so many assume it to be.

For example, economics plays a dominant role in many environmental controversies. It is fair to say that economics is the primary tool relied on in making most major public policy decisions concerning the environment. The rationale for this reliance is that the social science of economics provides an objective methodology for analyzing social costs and benefits. Chapter 3 in this book, however, offers an in-depth analysis of the role of economics in environmental policy and demonstrates that the supposedly value-neutral science of economics is heavily value-laden. That chapter will show how such economic concepts as utility, happiness, costs, benefits, and self-interest involve controversial assumptions in philosophy and ethics.

This is not the place for a full discussion of the issue of scientific objectivity, but several points should give us pause when we are tempted to turn solely to science and technology for solutions to environmental problems. In some ways, science is nothing more than a detailed, careful, verified, and documented approach to knowledge. Science demands that its practitioners minimize assumptions, seek to eliminate bias, verify results, and limit conclusions to what the evidence supports. In this sense, the scientific method has a real "ethic" that aims to ensure arrival at an impartial, accurate, and rational result. To the degree that scientific practice measures up to this ethic, we can have confidence in the rationality of its results. This unbiased approach to knowledge also provides a vital alternative to the vitriolic rhetoric so common in contemporary political debates.

Nevertheless, this method may have hidden assumptions that can influence scientific practice. For example, Chapter 9 considers the claim that modern science is dominated by models imported from physics. In that view, we best understand something (a physical object, for example) when we reduce that object to its simplest elements (such as atoms and electrons) and investigate the forces that work on those elements (for example, gravity and electromagnetism). According to critics, however, that reductionist approach is inappropriate for other fields. Social sciences such as economics, sociology, and political science may well distort reality if they reduce "society" to a mere collection of individuals mechanically driven by the forces of self-interest.[3] What is more relevant to our concerns is that some biologists believe that the physics model is particularly misleading in the study of ecosystems. The reductionist tendency can ignore or distort the complex relations that exist within an ecosystem. Reductionism literally fails to see the forests for the trees.

Likewise, a commitment to mechanistic explanations can distort our understanding of ecological relationships. For example, debates that concern our understanding of animal behavior are sometimes framed in mechanistic terms. *Either* animal behavior is caused by environmental conditioning, *or* it is controlled by genetic programming. Either way, the explanation can be stated as invariable, deterministic, mechanistic "laws of nature." Again, for many biologists this represents a distorted and oversimplified account of animal behavior.

Even the simplest organism is capable of changing its environment as much as it and its progeny are changed by the environment.

Biological and environmental changes seem to occur as much through random chance as according to deterministic laws.[4] Accordingly, a policy of wildlife management based on a mechanistic model of animal behavior would have different consequences and recommendations from a policy that assumes that change rather than constancy is the norm. Thus, despite the commitment of science to the values of impartiality and objectivity, the practice of science is not always the unbiased procedure it is taken to be.

Science is also sometimes understood not as a method or procedure but as a body of information or facts. Surely facts are objective, and if science discovers the facts, scientific knowledge must be objective, or so the myth of scientific objectivity would have us believe. How comfortable should we be when we rely solely on scientific information to meet environmental challenges? Even when the facts are established through a careful, methodical, and verified procedure, we need to recognize that the facts seldom tell the whole story. Reliance on well-established scientific information can be risky if that information fails to give us a complete explanation. Perhaps the greatest obstacle to getting the whole story is not science's inability to get answers but science's limits in asking questions. Before relying on scientific answers to solve environmental problems, we need to know what questions the scientists are asking, and the questions they ask are often determined by factors that lie outside the realm of science.

For example, political leaders in my hometown have recently been faced with a proposal to build a four-lane road through a major wetland and rare and environmentally sensitive oak woodland. Before debating the specifics of this proposal, the local city council requested that the city engineer conduct a study and provide a recommendation. The city engineer returned with a recommendation that the road should be built because the facts demonstrated that a road was needed. Thus the public received a recommendation for what we *should* do based on the *facts* determined by a scientific study. What "facts" led to this conclusion? The city engineer produced a report full of graphs and numbers reflecting projections about population growth, housing density, traffic counts, and construction costs. The engineer admitted that environmental and neighborhood concerns were not included because they could not be measured in a scientific and objective manner.

Recognize what happens in such a situation. Society is faced with a decision that raises several concerns. Some of those concerns can be measured and quantified scientifically while others cannot. Given this, policy makers have two options. They can ignore the concerns that cannot be measured scientifically and decide solely on the basis of "scientific fact," or they can reject science as the appropriate basis for decision making. In this all too common situation, public officials nearly always defer to the judgment of science.

Amory Lovins, an internationally recognized energy scientist, makes a similar point when he reminds us that the "answers you get depend on the questions you ask."[5] Lovins uses an example from energy policy to develop this point.

If we define our energy problem as a supply problem, we can easily conclude that we are running out of energy and need new energy sources. Science can document the facts of resource depletion; calculate the known reserves of coal, oil, and uranium; compare the technological advantages of various energy sources; and predict the costs and efficiencies of coal, oil, nuclear-powered generating plants, and so forth. We might thus imagine collecting a significant amount of relevant scientific data on the various alternatives of energy production. We can also imagine that, given these facts, one alternative (for example, nuclear reactors) might emerge as the most reasonable option. This decision, we can well imagine, is based on the objective, neutral facts of science.[6]

But if we define our energy problem as a question of demand, we come up with different answers. We begin to ask questions about energy use, matching energy sources with energy use, energy efficiencies, appropriate technologies, and the like. A scientist who asks these questions is more likely to focus on such issues as home heating, insulation, efficiency of electric motors, lighting, appliances, fuel-efficient cars, mass transportation, hydrogen fuel cells and solar power. Clearly, the information emerging from efforts to answer these questions, which is every bit as factual and objective as the information coming from supply questions, will suggest different energy policies. These facts might well prove that heating homes with electricity is quite unreasonable, even if the source of that electricity is safe and efficient compared to alternative sources.

Thus we have a situation in which two sets of facts, each equally valid and objective from a scientific standpoint, lead to quite different policy recommendations. One set supports building new power plants, and the other set supports a greater emphasis on appropriate technologies. In such a scenario, the scientific facts alone tell us nothing about which alternative we ought to choose.

Later chapters will examine the more general difficulties involved with reasoning from facts to values. Philosophers have long recognized that descriptions of the world do not, in themselves, commit us to particular conclusions about how the world should be. Simply acknowledging the gap between statements of fact and statements of value is enough to caution us about an over-reliance on science and technology. We need to be especially careful in determining which questions the environmental scientists are asking. If the questions are limited, the answers will also be limited, and so will the policy recommendations that society adopts on the basis of those answers.

Where, then, do scientists get their questions? The answer is that scientific questions are formed to a large degree by the people who pay for scientific research. Contemporary, state-of-the-art scientific research is an expensive enterprise. Typically, it is funded by government and private industry. The projects that get funded are those that answer the questions being asked by government and industry. We should not be surprised, for example, when scientists working for the chemical industry respond to the problem of resistant strains of insects by recommending the use of new (and typically more expensive) chemical pesticides. Science conducted under these conditions may not always supply the answers that government and industry want, but the likelihood of its supplying radically different answers is seriously restricted. Continuing with the Lovins energy example, most of what is known about nuclear energy is derived from research supported by the U.S. government. Specifically, the Department of Defense has spent billions of dollars developing nuclear weapons. In fact, the standard design for a nuclear power plant is a modified version of the nuclear reactor that powers submarines. Thus the knowledge that we possess about nuclear energy is directly traceable to political decisions made in a quite different context. (So too is our knowledge about chemical pesticides. Much of that research began during the world wars with research on chemical weapons.)

This is not to suggest that such knowledge is somehow less reasonable or valid than it might be. However, we need to acknowledge that the environmental decisions we make are dependent on the information, technology, and financial resources we have available and that these depend on the types of questions the scientists are asking. Imagine the knowledge and technology that we would have in the area of solar power, for example, if the money spent on nuclear weapons and nuclear research in the last sixty years had been spent instead on solar energy research.

A reasonable caution is that we not over-generalize the expertise of scientists. We should not deceive ourselves into thinking that because science demands objectivity and neutrality, all its uses are objective and value-neutral. Even if the scientific enterprise is committed to impartial and objective methods, and even if its findings are valid, the practical *uses* that we make of scientific information may not be reasonable. We also should not deceive ourselves into thinking that because many environmental problems involve technical issues, they do not raise ethical questions as well. The myth of objectivity that sometimes surrounds science can obscure these points. One role of environmental philosophy is to make explicit the hidden value assumptions of alternative environmental policies. Sometimes this will require examining the value assumptions implicit in science and technology.

Nevertheless, it also would equally be a mistake to think that some abstract ethical theory can resolve environmental controversies. Ethical and philosophical analysis done in the abstract, ignorant of science, technology, and other relevant disciplines, will not have much to contribute to the resolution of environmental problems. Looking to philosophical ethics for a quick fix is just as short-sighted as over-reliance on science.

How we understand our world and, therefore, how and what we value are significantly shaped by what science tells us about that world. The best approach is to recognize that both science and ethics are essential if we hope to make meaningful progress in meeting the environmental challenges that confront us. We can capture this perspective by adapting an old philosophical adage: "Science without ethics is blind; ethics without science is empty." This textbook is a survey of the variety of ways in which philosophers attempt to provide such a vision for environmental science and environmental policy.

1.3 PHILOSOPHY, POLITICS,
AND ETHICAL RELATIVISM

If environmental decisions should rightfully be made in the political realm rather than left exclusively to scientific experts, it might seem naïve for a person to hold out much hope for environmental progress from politics. Given the present partisan political climate in the United States, perhaps it is naïve to think that environmental challenges can be rationally resolved in the political arena. But the only alternative to rational political discourse, seems to be to leave such decisions to those who shout the loudest, pay the most for lobbyists, and manipulate the media the best. Can we trust politics to make sane environmental decisions?

Let us return to Socrates for a philosophical perspective on this issue. Early in Plato's *Republic*, Socrates and his companions are engaged in a philosophical examination of justice. After several speakers offer their account of justice, the sophist Thrasymachus breaks into the discussion and offers a cynical answer: "Justice is nothing other than the advantage of the stronger." In other words, right and wrong, justice and injustice, is whatever those who have power say they are. Or as we might say, might makes right. All talk of ethics, justice, morality, according to this skeptic, is but a smokescreen for what really is happening behind the scenes. Political decision making is nothing other than power politics— competing interest groups asserting their own preferences and the winners defining what is right and wrong. There is no independent, rational, objective means for determining right and wrong. In modern political terms, this view would be called political realism. In philosophical terms, this is a version of what is called ethical relativism, and it is worth examining at the start of this book.

Thrasymachus's assertion represents the most serious challenge to any study of ethics. Underlying the view of people who agree with Thrasymachus, ethics is futile because ethical values are, ultimately, a matter of personal opinion and belief. For this reason, they believe, ethical controversies cannot have rational answers. Ethics is simply a matter of personal opinion and, therefore, political disagreements can only be resolved through the exercise of power: political, economic, military, and physical. He who shouts the loudest wins the debate. "Justice is the advantage of the stronger."

According to *ethical relativism* it is not possible to make unbiased, objective ethical judgments. The relativist holds that ethical standards depend on—that is, are *relative to*—an individual's beliefs, feelings, culture, religion, and so forth. Because those beliefs, feelings, cultures, and religions differ, there is no rational way to resolve ethical disagreements. A relativist would deny the existence of independent rational norms by which we can evaluate ethical judgments and reach an unbiased conclusion.

Is there an alternative to this? Are we unrealistically naïve to think that civil dialogue can lead to reasoned conclusions and an unbiased consensus? Socrates rejected Thrasymachus's skepticism and argued that careful, logical, reasoned dialogue can distinguish, on rational grounds, right from wrong, justice from injustice. Let us follow the Socratic model and examine this skeptical position.

First, we should not confuse the *fact* that people disagree about ethical issues with the philosophical *claim* that objective agreement is impossible. People in different cultures and from differing backgrounds hold different beliefs about many things, including—but not limited to—questions of ethics. But it would be a mistake to conclude that there is no right answer simply because two cultures hold different beliefs. For example, some people may believe that the planet Earth is flat and lies at the center of the universe. But we have no reason to conclude that because people disagree, there are no objective standards for evaluating these beliefs. So, too, is it a mistake to reason that because cultures disagree about values, no correct answer exists. Believing that the planet Earth is flat does not make it flat, and believing that murder is right does not make it right.

We should also be careful not to ask too much of ethical reasoning. Few controversies that are examined in this book can be resolved with moral certainty. It is tempting to think that if ethics cannot "prove" a conclusion beyond doubt, then no objective conclusion exists. But this standard of proof, though it may be applicable in mathematics and a few other areas, is surely inappropriate in ethics. Just as sciences such as medicine, ecology, and meteorology offer rational and objective judgments without proving these judgments beyond any doubt, so too does ethics involve standards of reasoning that are different from those found in mathematics.

Finally, we should point out the implications of relativism. A consistent relativist must believe that there is no objective basis for praising friendship, love, freedom, and democracy, while condemning hatred, murder, slavery, and totalitarianism. The relativist must accept the conclusion that no objective grounds exist for denouncing a tyrant or praising a hero. A consistent ethical relativist must deny that rational persuasion and dialogue in ethics are possible. A consistent relativist is left with Thrasymachus's position, that right and wrong is defined by those with power, and those without power have no (rational) recourse when they disagree. We are left with power versus power. Although some people may talk like ethical relativists, few of us could live our lives as consistent relativists. Perhaps this practical contradiction is the most telling refutation of the relativist position. If we don't want to leave all political disagreement to power conflicts, we must assume, naïvely perhaps, that rational dialogue and progress is possible.

1.4 ENVIRONMENTAL ETHICS: AN OVERVIEW

Perhaps the only way to truly resolve the question of relativism and rationality in ethics is in the practice of ethics. Is there a rational way to resolve ethical disputes? Is ethical progress possible? Can we trust the political realm to approach, if not reach, ethically valid and responsible outcomes? Or, should we be content with Thrasymachus and try to become the strongest so that we might be able to impose our views on others? Let us engage in the practice of environmental ethics and work through a wide variety of ethical issues concerning the environment to see if rational progress is possible.

In general, environmental ethics is a systematic account of the moral relations between human beings and their natural environment. Environmental
ethics assumes that ethical norms can and do govern human behavior toward
the natural world. A theory of environmental ethics, then, must go on to explain
what these norms are, to whom or to what humans have responsibilities, and
how these responsibilities are justified.

Different theories of environmental ethics offer various answers to these questions. A brief survey of some of the answers will serve as an overview of this textbook. Some philosophers argue that our responsibilities to the natural environment
are only indirect—that the responsibility to preserve resources, for example, is best
understood in terms of the responsibilities that we owe to other humans. Anthropocentric ("human-centered") ethics holds that only human beings have moral value.
Thus, although we may be said to have responsibilities *regarding* the natural world,
we do not have direct responsibilities *to* the natural world.

Many issues that arose in the early decades of the environmental movement,
such as air and water pollution, toxic wastes, and the abuse of pesticides, grew
out of anthropocentric ethics. Pesticide-contaminated food and polluted drinking
water pose direct threats to human well-being. Thus anthropocentric environmental ethics involves simply applying standard ethical principles to new social
problems. Chapter 3 provides some examples of this approach.

One extension of anthropocentric ethics is to consider future generations of
human beings as objects of our moral responsibilities. This approach remains
anthropocentric in that only human beings count morally, but it extends our
responsibilities to include some to humans who do not yet exist. This extension
requires that we ask not only ethical questions but also epistemological and
metaphysical. It makes sense to ask about my responsibilities to other people,
but does it make sense to say that I have a responsibility to people who do not,
and may never, exist? For example, do people in the present have a responsibility
to people who might be alive in 100,000 years, such that we should change the
way we store nuclear wastes? Various problems highlighted by the early environmental movement, such as resource conservation and nuclear waste disposal,
were regarded from this ethical perspective. Chapter 4 addresses various philosophical and ethical issues concerning our responsibilities to future generations.

Other philosophers have argued that, in addition to our responsibilities to
other human beings, we have direct responsibilities to natural objects. Nonanthropocentric ethics grants moral standing to such natural objects as animals and
plants. Typically, this approach requires further extensions and revisions of standard ethical principles. Controversies surrounding the ethical treatment of animals and the threatened extinction of many plant and animal species are among
the best-known issues of nonanthropocentric ethics. Chapters 5 and 6 examine a
variety of nonanthropocentric systems of ethics. A further development of environmental ethics occurs by shifting from a focus on individual living things—for
example, spotted owls or redwood trees—to a focus on collections or "wholes"
such as species, populations, or ecosystems. Holistic ethics holds that we have
moral responsibilities to collections of (or relationships between) individuals
rather than (or in addition to) responsibilities to those individuals who constitute

the whole. For example, holistic environmental ethics might allow selective hunting of individual animals so long as the population of that species is not endangered. Holism, greatly influenced by the science of ecology, raises more serious philosophical challenges than do more individualistic ethics. For example, standard criteria for moral standing—that something is alive, can feel pain, is conscious, and so forth—apply plausibly to individuals but less plausibly to collections. The presentation of holistic, nonanthropocentric ethics in Chapters 8 through 11 considers how recent environmental philosophers have met these challenges. Typically, the development and justification of these environmental ethics require defenders to move more fully into the areas of epistemology, metaphysics, and political philosophy. The later chapters introduce these broader environmental philosophies.

One final caution is in order before we leave this discussion. It is fair to say that many philosophers think of ethics as providing the same general type of practical guidance as science and technology. Many believe that the role of ethics is to provide a general principle or theory that can be applied in specific cases and from which we can deduce specific practical conclusions. Thus, for example, an ethical principle might direct us to act in such a way as to maximize the overall happiness. Ethical behavior, therefore, involves determining which of two acts, A or B, will in fact maximize overall happiness. Once we have made this determination, we can deduce the ethically responsible act. From this perspective, ethics is capable of offering the same kind of objective and unambiguous conclusions as science. But be forewarned. Ethical issues of any type, including environmental issues, are seldom open to such unambiguous resolution. The world is not as simple as we might like it to be. This text will not provide a list of ethically correct answers. With luck, it will help you think more carefully and systematically about a range of ethical and philosophical issues involving the natural environment.

1.5 SUMMARY

This textbook tells a story within a story. Its primary objective is to survey the wide variety of contributions that philosophers have made to environmental debates. These represent the philosophical "visions" being offered to environmental scientists and policy makers. The goal of this story is to empower citizens to become full participants in a civil debate about environmental issues by helping readers develop a more complete understanding of the issues at stake. The hope is that environmental challenges can be successfully addressed through rational, civil discourse.

But within this story is a description of how philosophical ethics itself is challenged and extended by its encounter with the contemporary environmental and ecological crisis. For many philosophers, traditional philosophical theories have proved inadequate for resolving environmental problems. Accordingly, this textbook introduces philosophical ethics as an ongoing intellectual activity in which readers are encouraged to become active participants rather than passive observers. The goal of this story is to engage you in the practice of philosophy, rather than simply learning about philosophy.

NOTES

1. Riley E. Dunlap, "Climate-Change Views: Republican-Democratic Gaps Expand: Sharp divergence on whether the effects of global warming are yet evident," Gallup May 29, 2008. http://www.gallup.com/poll/107569/climatechange-views-republicandemocratic-gaps-expand.aspx. (Accessed March 13, 2011.); Judith Warner, "Fact-Free Science," *New York Times Magazine*, February 25, 2011; "Shimkus: No more water but the fire next time," *Chicago Tribune*, November 11, 2010.

2. E. O. Wilson offers estimates like these in a number of places. See, for example, "Threats to Biodiversity," *Scientific American* 261 (September 1989): 108–116.

3. Jane Mansbridge, *Beyond Self-Interest* (Chicago: University of Chicago,

1990), is a helpful collection of essays on this topic.

4. See, for example, Daniel Botkin, *Discordant Harmonies* (New York: Oxford University Press, 1990), for a critique of a mechanistic view of science from an ecological perspective.

5. Amory Lovins, "Technology Is the Answer (But What Was the Question?)" published as a guest essay, pp. 56–57, in G. Tyler Miller, *Environmental Science*, 3d ed. (Belmont, Calif.:Wadsworth, 1991).

6. For an example of such an approach to energy supply, see an address on energy policy by then Vice President Richard Cheney to the Associated Press on April 30, 2001. Available from various online sources.

DISCUSSION QUESTIONS

1. When evaluating the effects of greenhouse gases or the safety of chemical pesticides, who should determine levels of acceptable risk? Is "risk" a matter of scientific fact, or is it a matter of value? What makes an issue a value issue?

2. Do a quick Internet search for "global warming" and review some of the most popular sites. Which ones would you describe as generally unbiased and objective, and which would you

describe as biased, partisan, and unreasonable? On what grounds did you make your decisions? Do your classmates agree with your judgments?

3. Identify as many different uses of the words *natural* and *nature* as you can. Which, if any, have value connotations? Are all things that are "natural" also good? What about "human nature"? What is not natural about human beings? What would be the difference

between "natural" fertilizers and "nonnatural"? Could there be such a thing as a "natural" pesticide?

4. Is there a difference between good science and bad science? We often hear that science should be value neutral. Is this true? Can you think of any values involved in the practice of good science?

5. How is reasoning about ethical matters different from reasoning about scientific matters? How do scientists evaluate controversial claims in science? How would we evaluate controversial ethical claims?

6. What makes a belief or statement objective? Contrast this with subjective beliefs or statements. What statements about a tree, for example, are objective? What statements about a tree are subjective?

GLOBAL ENVIRONMENTAL ETHICS WATCH

For more information on Environmental Ethics, please see the Global Environmental Ethics Watch. Updated several times a day, Global Environmental Ethics Watch is a focused portal into GREENR—our Global Reference on the Environment, Energy, and Natural Resources—an ideal one-stop site for current events and research. You will have access to the latest information from trusted academic journals, news outlets, and magazines as well as access to statistics, primary sources, case studies, videos, podcasts, and much more.

To gain access please use the access code that accompanies your book. If you do not have an access code, visit cengagebrain.com to purchase one.

2

Ethical Theories and the

Environment

DISCUSSION: Why Protect Endangered Species?

Much of the most significant environmental legislation in the United States was enacted during the 1970s. The Clean Air Act of 1970 (amended and renewed in 1977), the Federal Water Pollution Act of 1972 (amended and renewed as the Clean Water Act of 1977), and the Endangered Species Act of 1973 grew out of a national consensus for addressing environmental problems. Each law was originally enacted by a Democratic Congress and was signed by a Republican president.

From almost the very beginning, critics have charged that these environmental regulations have gone too far. Criticism has focused on two charges: that environmental legislation fails to consider the full consequences of regulation, including the economic costs, and that this legislation violates the rights of private property owners.

Critics point out that environmental legislation has been expensive for individuals and business. Regulations require expensive pollution control technology, prohibit economic development, control land use, and so forth. Many major public and private projects have been delayed or derailed in the name of such obscure and insignificant creatures as the snail darter, the spotted owl, the American burying beetle, and the valley longhorn elderberry beetle. Critics acknowledge that species preservation is one public goal but maintain that it needs to be balanced against the values of economic growth and development. The goal of environmental policy should be to maximize all public benefits and minimize all public costs.

Further, according to these critics, much environmental regulation violates individual rights. In this view, government has an obligation to protect the rights of its citizens and, when this cannot be done, to compensate those whose rights have been violated.

In recent years, various states and Congress have considered takings legislation (from the so-called takings clause of the Fifth Amendment: "nor shall private property be taken for public use without just compensation") that would require compensation for the loss of property value arising from government regulation. Thus, for example, if developers are prohibited from building a housing project in an area that provides habitat to an endangered species, the government might owe those developers the profits they would have made had they been allowed to develop the land. Defenders of such legislation argue that if government action denies people that to which they are entitled, fairness demands that the government compensate them for their loss.

The Endangered Species Act (ESA) in particular has been extensively criticized and modified through the years. There has generally been strong public support for protection of such major species as bald eagles, humpback whales, grizzly bears, California condors, salmon, and the gray wolf. But there is less support for lesser-known species, particularly relatively unknown and unseen plant and insect species. These controversies raise the question: Why preserve any plant or animal species?

Defenders of the ESA offer three general answers to this question. First, many argue that preservation of species contributes to human well-being and satisfaction. A version of this argument often cites future benefits, especially agricultural and medicinal uses, which might be lost with the extinction of a species and the corresponding reduction in the gene pool. A second approach argues that plants and animals themselves have a right to life that should be respected, even if they are of little or no use to humans. A third approach appeals to the natural order of things and argues that plant and animal species have an intrinsic value, or serve a higher purpose, that humans ought to respect. Sometimes this argument is made in terms of the role, such as that of predator or prey, which a particular species plays within an ecosystem. Another version of this argument appeals to religious or spiritual understanding of the value of each species as resting in its unique status as a creature of God. Because humans have not created the diversity of life on Earth, humans ought not to destroy this creation.

DISCUSSION TOPICS:

1. Some people defend the Endangered Species Act on the grounds that it protects the beneficial consequences that humans can derive from diverse species. But critics point out that protecting species can also have harmful consequences. How would you determine if a particular species has, on balance, more or less beneficial consequences? What benefits and costs should be included in your calculation? How would you determine what a species is worth?

2. Are some species more valuable than others? Is it a good thing that the smallpox virus is extinct? Shouldn't we aim to eradicate the HIV virus or disease carrying mosquitoes? Where, and on what grounds, would you draw the line between a species that should be protected no matter what, and one that should not be protected?

3. Is there an ethical difference between species that exist naturally and those that, via breeding or cloning, are created by human technology? Would it be a good thing if an extinct species could be regenerated via cloning? What is your opinion of human-created or engineered life forms?

2.1 INTRODUCTION

Chapter 1 asserted that unbiased, rational decision making in the political realm is the most responsible alternative to leaving environmental controversies to be decided by scientific experts or by partisan politics. This chapter will introduce several ethical theories that can provide guides to rational decision making in ethics. I suggest that you can understand ethical "theories" as reasoning patterns about ethics that have been systematically developed and evaluated by generations of philosophers. They are patterns of reasoning that are deeply embedded in the ways in which we already think about ethics and what philosophers have said about them can help us judge the validity of our own environmental decision making.

It would be difficult to examine environmental controversies without using the fundamental categories and language of ethics: rights, fairness, justice, and utility. People who oppose environmental regulation often appeal to property rights, fairness, and social benefits. Environmentalists likewise appeal to the rights of nature, the values of wilderness, and the harms of pollution. Implicit within the three general answers given to the question "Why preserve endangered species?" are three major ethical theories that this chapter introduces. Each answer presupposes a different pattern of reasoning about ethical issues.

One approach to ethics advises us to make decisions in terms of the consequences of our actions and to act in ways that maximize overall social benefits. Utilitarianism is an ethical theory that determines right and wrong in terms of the overall consequences of our actions. Preserving species because they provide beneficial consequences fits this pattern of ethical reasoning. A second approach reasons in terms of rights and principles and tells us that we have certain fundamental duties that require us to act in certain ways and to refrain from acting in others. What we will call deontological approaches to ethics begin with fundamental ethical principles that guide behavior. Preserving a species because it has a right to live, or restricting the application of the Endangered Species Act because it violates someone's property rights, fits this pattern of ethical reasoning. A third approach argues that there are natural rights and duties prescribed by nature laws which direct ethical behavior. In one important version of this approach, these natural laws are derived from God's laws. Natural law ethics derives standards of right conduct from the laws of nature. Preserving a species because it has an intrinsic value, or play an important role in the balance of nature, would fit this pattern of reasoning.

Before turning to an examination of these theories, reflect for a moment on the challenge laid out in Chapter 1. A responsible approach to environmental issues, one that does not surrender decisions making either to scientific experts or to vitriolic partisan politics, requires us to reason carefully and rigorously. Fortunately, we do not start from scratch in this. Throughout history, philosophers have developed systematic and comprehensive accounts of the ethical life. The ethical theories that we examine in this chapter provide a basis from which we can begin to understand, analyze, evaluate, and make ethical decisions.

This chapter considers the relevance of such theories and briefly describes several that are important for much of what is discussed in this textbook.

2.2 PHILOSOPHIAL ETHICS: GETTING COMFORTABLE WITH THE TOPIC

The word *ethics* is derived from the Greek word *ethos,* meaning something like "customary" or "habitual." In this sense, ethics consists of *the general beliefs, attitudes, or standards that guide customary behavior.* Thus any society will have its own ethics in the sense that it will have certain typical beliefs, attitudes, and standards that determine what is customary. Whether consciously or not, the behavior of every individual is also guided by certain beliefs, attitudes, or standards. But from the earliest days of Greek philosophy when Socrates challenged Athenian authorities, *philosophical ethics* has not been satisfied simply to accept as right that which is customary. Ethics as a branch of philosophy seeks a reasoned examination of what custom tells us about how we ought to live. Indeed, it is fair to say that Western philosophy was born in Socrates's lifelong critical examination of the customary norms of Greek society.

This critical examination involves stepping back or abstracting ourselves from ordinary experience. (Perhaps this explains the common perception of philosophy as "too abstract.") We all hold certain beliefs, attitudes, and values about our ordinary, customary experience. Philosophy asks us to step back from this experience to reflect critically on it: Why do we believe the things we believe? Should we change our attitudes? Are our values justified? At this first level of abstraction, customary behavior is examined by appeal to some norm or standard of what *ought to* or *should* be done. The difference between ordinary experience and the first level of philosophical abstraction is the difference between what *is* done (or valued or believed) and what *ought to* be done (or valued or believed).

One of the first challenges in any study of ethics involves identifying an issue as an ethical issue. We all need to practice this stepping back in order to recognize ethical issues in our everyday experience. For example, in the classic environmental essay *The Land Ethic,* Aldo Leopold retells the story of Odysseus's return from the Trojan War.[1] Odysseus hanged a dozen women slaves whom he suspected of misbehavior. Because Greeks saw slaves as property, they apparently saw nothing ethically wrong with this action. Leopold uses this example to call for an "extension of ethics" to include human relations to the land. Just as Odysseus was ethically insensitive to the evil of killing slaves, we fail to notice the wanton destruction of the land. Leopold's point is that sometimes we need to work intellectually in order to be capable of noticing an ethical issue. The creation of the Endangered Species Act might be seen as another example of a previously unrecognized ethical issue coming to public attention. A major contribution of such notable environmental writers as Aldo Leopold and Rachel Carson was precisely this ability to get us to notice ethical and philosophical issues where previously we were limited by our customary beliefs, attitudes, and values.

Uncovering the limitations of our ethical and environmental consciousness is a regular theme in the chapters that follow. This may also turn out to be the cause of some of the frustration that characterizes ethical discussions and prevents us from following through on the careful thinking required in ethics. Many environmental controversies rest on different attitudes and values concerning our world. Few things are as frustrating as having our fundamental perspectives challenged. But we need to be open to the possibility that, like Odysseus, we might suffer from an ethical blindness. A primary goal of philosophical ethics is to stretch our understandings, shift our perspective and consciousness, and help us escape the limitations implicit in customary ways of thinking.

To make ethical judgments, give advice, and offer evaluations of what ought to or should be is to engage in *normative ethics*. This first level of abstraction is the type of ethical reasoning that most people associate with ethics. Normative judgments prescribe behavior. "We should reduce the level of carbon dioxide emissions." "Pesticide use should be reduced." "Endangered species ought to be protected." "Nuclear power plants should not be located in flood zones." Normative judgments implicitly or explicitly appeal to some norm or standard of ethical behavior. Many environmental controversies involve disputes of normative ethics. One side believes that the spotted owl ought to be protected even it this costs jobs in the timber industry, and the other side believes that jobs for human beings are more important than the life of some obscure bird. Each side cites evidence and appeals to certain norms to support its judgments. Normative disputes can be frustrating when ethical discussions are left at this level, with disagreements and controversies abounding.

However, philosophy insists that we not remain at the level of normative ethics. Resolving controversy requires us once again to step outside of, or abstract from, specific disagreements in order to examine the values in conflict and the competing factors that underlie the conflict. Moving to this more abstract level of thinking is moving from normative to philosophical ethics.

Philosophical ethics is a next level of generality and abstraction, at which we analyze and evaluate normative judgments and their supporting reasons. This is the level of the general concepts, principles, and theories to which we appeal in defending and explaining normative claims. This is the level at which philosophers are most comfortable and have the most to offer. The essence of philosophical ethics involves evaluating reasons that support normative judgments or seeking to clarify the concepts involved in such judgments. In this sense, environmental ethics is a branch of philosophy engaged in the systematic study and evaluation of the normative judgments that are so much a part of environmentalism.

As used here, the term *ethical theory* refers to any attempt to provide systematic answers to the philosophical questions raised by descriptive and normative approaches to ethics. These questions are raised from both an individual moral point of view and the point of view of society or public policy. Individual moral questions include: What should I do? What kind of person should I be? What should I value? How should I live? Questions of social philosophy or public policy include: What type of society is best? What policies should we follow as a group? What social arrangements and practices will best protect and promote individual well-being? What should be done when individuals disagree? From the earliest days of Western philosophy, ethics has included questions of both individual and social morality. Thus, in this broad sense, ethical theory includes philosophical analyses of moral, political, economic, legal, and social questions.[2]

Four general considerations make theory relevant to the study of environmental ethics. First, ethical theories provide a common language for discussing and understanding ethical issues. Environmental ethics is characterized by deep and numerous controversies. Clearly, a necessary first step in examining and resolving controversy is to understand these disputes fully and accurately. The basic concepts and categories of ethics—rights, responsibilities, utility, the common good, and the relationships among these concepts—can provide a basis for mutual understanding and dialogue. Ethical theories make explicit and systematize the common beliefs and shared values that are often implicit in specific controversies. By learning the language of philosophical ethics, we become better able to understand, evaluate, and communicate. This, in turn, can empower us to become full participants in environmental debates. Philosophical ethics can contribute to the common language that is essential to reasoned dialogue.

Second, because various ethical theories have played a major role in our traditions, they tend to be reflected in the ways in which many of us think. By learning about ethical theories, we become more aware of the patterns in our ways of thinking and the assumptions reflected therein. Thus we become better able to articulate our views and better able to defend them. Of equal importance, we gain a philosophical perspective that makes possible a critical examination of our ways of thinking. Having made these patterns explicit puts us in a better position to see and understand issues as ethical issues.

Third, one traditional function of an ethical theory is to offer guidance and evaluation. We can apply theories to specific situations and use them to generate specific recommendations. The long history of ethics gives us a reasonable and strong basis from which to analyze and offer advice. As we work our way through environmental controversies, it will be helpful if we do not have to reinvent the wheel at every step. People reason about ethics in standard ways, many of which match standard ethical theories. Because philosophers have spent considerable time pondering these theories and uncovering their strengths and weaknesses, knowledge of theory is an important resource for the debates that follow.

Finally, familiarity with ethical theories is important because some commentators claim that these theories, embedded as they are in common ways of thinking, have actually been responsible for some of the environmental problems we face. That is, the practice of environmental ethics occasionally involves challenging the very theories of ethics that philosophers have been busy defending. Some argue that these theories are part of the problem and have misled us. Thus an important part of environmental ethics is examining philosophical theories about ethics. In this way, environmental ethics not only benefits from traditional ethical theory but also contributes to the development of this branch of philosophy.

2.3 THE NATURAL LAW TRADITION— TELEOLOGY AND VIRTUES

One of the oldest ethical traditions relevant to environmental ethics is the *natural law* or *teleological tradition*. We can trace the ethical views associated with this tradition to Aristotle (fourth century B.C.) and Thomas Aquinas (thirteenth century C.E.).

Aristotle did not distinguish between ethics and science as clearly as we distinguish between them today. Aristotle thought that the study of biology and psychology was an essential part of ethics, because it required, at a minimum, knowledge of basic human needs, common capabilities and potentials, and motivation. Further, Aristotle placed the biological sciences at the forefront of knowledge, whereas in the twenty-first century, physics and math seem to hold sway. This interesting blend of biology and ethics is one reason why this ethical tradition can be relevant to environmental issues.

For Aristotle, to understand something scientifically was to understand the *causes* for its being the way it is. Science involves more than simply describing what exists, it also requires that we be able to explain *why* something is what it is. Aristotle reasoned that this "Why?" question can be answered in four different ways—what he called the four causes of an object's existence—the *material, formal, efficient,* and *final causes.*

An object's material cause is what an object is made from, its matter. The formal cause explains how that matter is organized or structured so that this material is what it is rather than something else that is made from the same material. Thus, a tree and a table have the same material cause, wood, which exists in two different forms. We might say that ice, water, and steam have the same material cause, but have different structures or forms. An efficient cause explains how something comes to be what it is. A carpenter would be the efficient cause for some lumber becoming a table. Last, a final cause explains the purpose or characteristic activity of the object; heat would be the efficient cause by which ice becomes water and water becomes steam. The final cause of the table is to provide a place at which to sit and eat. The final cause or characteristic activity of a tree would be that activity that trees do that other living things do not do. No doubt, Aristotle would be happy with the type of explanation that modern biology offers: trees take nutrition from their environment and convert it into wood, bark, and leaves in a process of growth and reproduction.

Aristotle's science differed in part from a more modern version of science in holding that we have not fully understood an object until we understand its final cause, or its characteristic or natural activity. On the basis of his observations of nature, Aristotle believed that all natural objects do have a natural and distinctive activity. The goal of this activity—what it is aiming for (sometimes called its purpose or function)—was identified in the Greek language as the object's *telos*. Hence Aristotle's science and his ethics are often called *teleological*. To understand some object fully, according to Aristotle, we must understand its natural function or activity, as well as its matter, structure, and the forces at work upon it.

For example, suppose that we seek a scientific explanation of a heart. In Aristotle's view, we do not fully understand the heart until we understand its characteristic activity. A teleological explanation of the heart answers these questions: What is the distinctive activity of hearts? What functions do hearts perform that distinguish them from other bodily organs? We understand the heart when we understand its function in the circulatory system. A teleological explanation would describe the heart as an organ that pumps blood throughout the body.

A more modern explanation might instead explain the heart in terms of its composition (or matter): muscle tissue, cells, and the like. A modern tendency is to reduce the object to be studied to its more simple elements and to investigate their structure (form) and the physical, mechanical, and chemical forces (efficient causes).[3]

Aristotle distinguishes two basic types of natural objects: those that are alive and those that are not. The characteristic activity of living things, what we might call the principle of life itself, is called the psyche, or, as it was later translated, the soul. Thus, to say that some body has a soul is just another way of saying that it is alive. Aristotle describes three fundamental activities of life: nutrition, sensation, and thinking. Some living things possess only one (the "nutritive soul"), whereas others possess two (the nutritive soul and the "appetitive" or "sensitive" soul), and some possess all three types (the nutritive, appetitive, and thinking souls). Plants are living things that possess only the nutritive soul. This means that their characteristic activities include only the powers of nutrition, growth, and reproduction. Animals possess appetitive powers in addition to the nutritive soul. This means that their natural activities include the powers of sensation, desire, and motion. Finally, only humans possess the three life activities of nutrition, appetite, and thought.

With this admittedly brief characterization, we can now see how the distinction between scientific fact and ethical value was not as obvious for Aristotle as it sometimes seems today. When we understand the characteristic activity of a heart, for example, we also come to understand what a *good* heart is. A good heart is one that pumps blood through the body in a regular, stable, and continuous manner and does so over a long period of time. A good heart is one that performs its characteristic activity well.

Aristotle believed that this teleological framework could be applied to all natural objects, including humans. All things have a natural activity or function. Things are good when they fulfill this function, or, in terms more common to this tradition, when they actualize their potential. In general terms, every living thing can be said to have a good of its own. The good of any living thing is to attain fully its natural activity (or fully actualize its soul). Thus the good of a plant is to accomplish the nutritive functions of taking in nutrition, growth, and reproduction. The good of animals includes these functions, as well as attaining its desires and fulfilling its appetites. The human good includes all these ends, as well as living a thoughtful and deliberative life.

This teleological system was further developed in the writings of Thomas Aquinas in the thirteenth century. Aquinas attempted to synthesize Christian theology with Aristotle's science and ethics. The ethics of natural law and teleology has perhaps had its greatest influence on Western thought through Aquinas's writings and this integration of Christianity and science.

Aquinas interprets the scientific and ethical teleology of Aristotle as evidence that a divine plan operates in nature. The laws of nature that were discovered in the Aristotelian tradition, when combined with a religious worldview, become the laws established by the creator of the natural world. The characteristic activity of all natural objects results from God's plan. As science comes to understand the natural telos of each living thing, science helps us understand God's purpose. Because God is assumed to be supremely good, and because the purposes discovered in nature are God's purposes, the natural order can be equated with the moral order. Nature itself has a purpose, and the harmonious functioning of nature reveals the goodness of God's plan. In this theory, the laws of nature include both descriptive regularities that we discover in nature and, because these regularities are part of the divine plan, the normative and prescriptive rules that we ethically ought to follow. In this ethical tradition, fulfilling our natural potential—a potential implicitly in harmony with the rest of nature—is the highest form of ethical activity for an individual.

A final aspect of this tradition that is worth mentioning is the role played by the virtues. Much of modern ethical thinking (particularly utilitarianism and deontological ethics, which are described in the following sections) is rule-based and focuses on human actions. The goal of ethics is to provide the rules and principles that we should follow in order to live a good life. In this view, the basic questions of ethics are "What should I do?" and "How should I act?" Virtue ethics emphasizes not action so much as character and habits. Virtue ethics asks, "What kind of person should I be?" In the ethical tradition stretching from Aristotle and Aquinas, the virtues are understood as those character traits or habits that describe the ethically good person. For Plato, the major virtues were courage, moderation, justice, and wisdom. Aristotle adds many others, including generosity, pride, good temper, truthfulness, friendliness, and modesty. Christians promote such virtues as faithfulness, hopefulness, and charity.

Perhaps the major difference between virtue ethics and more modern rule-based ethics emerges when we consider how each understands the role of self-interest, particularly how self-interest and ethics are related. For most modern rule-based theories, self-interest is the major barrier to ethical responsibility. Ethics and self-interest generally conflict. The rules and principles of ethics act to restrict self-interest and coerce people to do what they should do, even when they do not want to do it. But self-interest is neither so narrowly understood nor so troubling in virtue ethics. A generous person does not struggle with selfishness and decide to act generously only because some rules require it. From the perspective of virtue ethics, there is no conflict between what ethical people should do and what they want to do, no conflict between ethics and self-interest. A good person wants to be generous, truthful, just, charitable, and modest. These characteristics are not barriers to self-interest. Ethics and self-interest coincide rather than conflicting. Because both qualities actually describe who I am—describe my "self"—the apparent conflict between ethics and self-interest collapses. I act ethically because that is what I want to do, and I want to do it because that is just the kind of person I am. Given this emphasis on character formation, virtue ethics is particularly interested in questions of moral education and moral psychology. How one develops the right sort of habits and character traits is a central focus of virtue ethics.

2.4 CONTEMPORARY PERSPECTIVES ON TELEOLOGY

Several themes in modern environmentalism are reminiscent of this ethical tradition. For example, we shall examine several issues in which ethical virtues play a central role. Care for future generations, reverence for life, respect for all living things, and even love of nature are all issues in which virtuous behavior will play a role.

The key natural law idea of a naturally good order also plays a role in environmental debates. Basing their views on the findings of some ecologists, many environmentalists assume that natural ecosystems are well ordered and harmonious. All parts of an ecosystem, and especially all of its biotic members, have a distinctive place in the overall scheme. Each contributes to the natural order in its own way. Nature undisturbed is good. Ecological problems arise when humans interfere with the natural order and treat other natural objects as having value only insofar as they serve human purposes. In this view, the way the world is (or would be if humans did not interfere), is the way the world should be. This ethics would prescribe a general policy of preservationism and nonintervention.

Other environmentalists emphasize the ethical status of all living things and base this status on the fact that every living thing has a good of its own. A version of this view is presented in the examination of biocentric ethics in Chapter 6. Although the Aristotelian system allows for a moral hierarchy with humans "higher" than animals and animals "higher" than plants, it nevertheless also allows for the possibility of seeing that all living things have a good of their own. Thus the natural world possesses a good and purpose that are independent of human interests and uses. Finally, we shall also see a virtues-based approach to such issues as caring for future generations, domesticated animals, all living beings, and ecosystems.

Unfortunately, several major objections to the Aristotelian tradition weaken its relevance to contemporary debates. The first objection denies that natural objects have one definite and distinctive telos. It seems true that some objects have a definite purpose or function. Human artifacts, such as chairs and computers, are obvious examples. Some *parts* of a natural whole, such as a heart or a chromosome, also seem to have natural functions. But for a thing to have a function within a system is not the same as its having a good of its own. Besides, it does not seem obvious that these wholes or systems themselves have a purpose. What, for example, is the characteristic activity or function or purpose of a human being? What is the characteristic activity of a spotted owl? Many philosophers and scientists in the modern era have thought that they could fully understand and explain natural objects without having to assume some natural purpose or plan.

A second objection denies that we can conclude that something is good simply because it is natural. Because some natural occurrences seem evil—for example, pain and suffering caused by death, disease, and natural disasters— some reason other than the appeal to nature must show why something is good. It would be a giant leap, for example, to reason from the characteristic natural activity of the HIV virus to the conclusion that this virus is good. In the natural law tradition, the explanation most often given for the connection between natural and good lies in a divine plan. However, this appeal effectively ends the philosophical discussion, because it provides a reason only to those people who already assume a divine creator. To people of other religious traditions or to people who do not believe in a supremely good creator, this reason carries little rational weight.

The claim that one cannot justify normative judgments solely on the basis of natural fact is most commonly associated with the eighteenth-century Scottish philosopher David Hume. Hume, explicitly modeling his own method on the work of Sir Isaac Newton, thought that only careful empirical observation could distinguish between reasonable beliefs—what Hume called matters of fact—and "sophistry and illusion." He concluded that although science can tell us all that we can know about nature, it cannot provide the basis for drawing normative conclusions from nature. Empirical science can provide a rational basis for judgments about matters of fact, but there can be no scientific or empirical justification for normative judgments themselves. The claim that normative conclusions cannot be inferred from natural facts has come to be called the "is/ought" or "fact/ value" gap, and it is one of the most serious challenges to teleological ethics.

Finally, modern evolutionary science provides a significant and perhaps insurmountable challenge to the natural law tradition. The process of natural selection offers an account of the apparent design found in nature without appealing to any purpose or telos. The order that is found in nature comes not from a divine plan but from the process of species adapting to their environment, typically through a process of random mutation and natural selection. For example, a defender of natural law might explain the long neck of the giraffe by claiming that the long neck exists (or was designed) in order to enable the giraffe to reach food high off the ground. The defender of natural selection, on the other hand, would claim that the giraffe did not develop a long neck *in order to* reach the leaves high in a tree but, rather, that giraffes that happened to have longer necks than other giraffes survived more reliably than shorter-necked giraffes, because they could reach these leaves more readily and were thus better adapted to their environment. The long neck is itself the result of random evolutionary change. Thus the purposive language of teleology can be reduced to the more mechanistic language of the physical sciences. In this view, nature as we find it today is the result of hundreds of millions of years of random evolutionary change. Nature is neither good nor bad; it just is.

But the appeal of the natural law tradition remains. Contemporary biologists are very comfortable using teleological categories when speaking about the natural world. Even within a Darwinian framework, such teleological concepts as function, purpose, goal, and design are used regularly by scientists and philosophers.[4] The biological sciences commonly refer to an object's purpose, goals, or function. Consider the following examples: "The purpose of the kidney is to remove waste from the blood." "The goal of brightly colored plumage on male birds is to attract females." "The function of a predator species is to control the population of a prey species." "Wetlands function as flood control and water-filtration systems." In the Aristotelian and natural law traditions, it is a logical and reasonable inference from such teleological ascriptions to a value or normative conclusion: "This is a healthy kidney." "This is a successful male." "Predators ought to be preserved." "Wetlands ought not to be destroyed." The contemporary challenge is to determine whether such inferences are legitimate and what the ethical and normative significance of this would be.

Many observers continue to resist any inference from natural facts to any value claim. One approach is to claim that the functional language that is common and appropriate in the biological sciences can be fully explained in terms of antecedent causes. Thus, although kidneys, plumage, predators, wetlands, and even long necks might perform a function, they do not do so out of a prior purpose or design. The functions themselves are simply the result of previous evolutionary and biochemical processes. Inferring a value conclusion from these facts would require an implicit value component already built in. For example, only by assuming that adaptation and survival are good could one infer that bright plumage is a good thing for male birds or that long necks are good for giraffes.

Even so, it does seem reasonable to assume that adaptation and survival *are* good and therefore that it is reasonable to reach normative conclusions from biological facts. It seems reasonable to conclude that the adaptive capacity a species has developed to outrun or hide from its predators is good for that species. It is good for the giraffe to have a long neck, and a kidney that does not filter blood effectively is bad kidney. Chapter 6 will examine a version of such teleological reasoning developed in biocentric ethics.

The contemporary debates continue. Assessing these debates would require us to distinguish carefully among such concepts as function, purpose, design, and goal. When used in science, each of these concepts involves explaining some phenomenon (kidneys, long-necks, bright plumage, predators, and wetlands) in terms of some future state or activity (filtering blood, reaching high food, attracting a mate, controlling prey populations, and absorbing flood water). This is the essence of any teleological explanation. But the questions remain: Are such forward-looking explanations scientifically valid? If so, is it always a good thing to attain this future state or perform this activity? Is value built into any concept involving aiming for and attaining some future state? If so, is this value necessarily an ethically good thing?

Much modern science, particularly as it developed under the influence of physics and mechanics, argues that the only legitimate scientific explanations are those that refer to some antecedent causes. Thus some challenge the legitimacy of any teleological explanation in the biological sciences. Other skeptics argue that even though some teleological explanations are legitimate, no value conclusions can be drawn from this. Still others argue that although value conclusions might be drawn from biological facts, the values are always qualified and conditional. *If* it is assumed that survival is good, or *if* it is assumed that adaptive fit is good, then one can conclude that certain traits are good for certain species. But, as the HIV example shows, survival and adaptability are not always *ethically* good things. Good-for-a-species, or good-for-an-individual, is not always identical to an ethical good. As we shall see in the section on deontological ethics that follows, many philosophers argue that ethical norms and goods must be unconditional or categorical.

Thus, although the natural law tradition provides a framework for thinking and reasoning about relations between nature and ethics, it is not without significant philosophical challenges. This brief review will help us evaluate later occasions when we see various insights from this tradition applied to contemporary environmental issues.

2.5 THE UTILITARIAN TRADITION

Utilitarianism is a second ethical tradition that is helpful in the study of environmental ethics. This is a philosophical theory that develops the common sense insight that the consequences of our decisions should play a significant role in deciding what to do. Although the classical statements of this tradition are found in the writings of Jeremy Bentham and John Stuart Mill in the nineteenth century, and it has roots in Adam Smith's economic thinking in the eighteenth century, utilitarianism continues to be an extraordinarily influential theory today.[5] Utilitarian reasoning is especially influential in the areas of economics, public policy, and government regulation, and this means that it has also played a significant role in environmental policy.

In general terms, utilitarianism directs us to maximize the overall good or to produce the greatest good for the greatest number. Thus utilitarian theory rests on two elements: an account of the good and a rule for judging all acts and decisions in terms of that good. The rule tells us to look to the *consequences* of any particular act and judge the ethical status of that act in terms of those consequences. If the act tends to maximize good consequences, the act is ethically right, and if it does not, the act is ethically wrong.

Consequently, utilitarians distinguish between two basic types of value: the good, which is valued for its own sake, and all other things, which are valued because of their relation to the good. Thus all acts or decisions are judged in terms of their utility, or their usefulness in producing good consequences. This distinction is sometimes made in terms of *intrinsic* and *instrumental value*. Utilitarians defend some view of intrinsic value (for example, pleasure or happiness) and then judge the value of all other things and activities in terms of how well they serve to achieve the optimal amount of that value.

The challenge to utilitarians, of course, is to successfully defend an account of the good that can serve as the basis of all other values. If this good is to function in this way, it should be *objective* (good in a way that is not dependent on particular human interests) and *universal* (good for all people at all times). Different versions of utilitarianism can then be distinguished by how they describe the good.

Two versions of utilitarianism are important for the environmental issues that we examine in what follows. One type of utilitarianism takes pleasure, or at least the absence of pain, to be the only good valued for its own sake. Pleasure and the absence of pain are universally desired. People who desire pain or avoid pleasure are typically suspected of acting unreasonably. Pleasure would seem to be a plausible candidate for something that is objectively good and universally valued. This outlook is called *hedonistic utilitarianism,* and it has played a role in recent thinking about the ethical status of animals.

A second version of utilitarianism understands the good as the happiness that results from the satisfaction of our desires. In this view, people are happy when they have what they want—when their desires are satisfied. A world in which as many people as possible have as much of what they desire as possible would be the ethically best world. Contemporary defenders of this version often fine-tune it by adding the requirement that individuals are best left to choose and rank their desires. Sometimes called *preference utilitarianism,* this version would direct us to satisfy as many individual preferences as possible. As presented in Chapter 3, this ethical theory is closely associated with free-market economic theory, and in that way it has significant implications for environmental policy.

A number of standard objections are raised to utilitarian thinking, and reviewing several of them will prove helpful. We can group together one set of such challenges as *measurement* problems. Utilitarianism essentially involves a process of measurement and comparison. Phrases such as "maximize the overall good" and "the greatest good for the greatest number" necessarily require measuring, comparing, and quantifying. However, a tension exists when we attempt to quantify that which is primarily qualitative. The good is taken by utilitarians to be that which has intrinsic value. Yet intrinsic value may not be the sort of thing that can easily be counted, measured, or compared.

These considerations lead to several serious philosophical problems. The first challenges the very possibility of quantifying such things as pleasure, happiness, desires, and so forth. Are we to assume that all pleasures or desires are qualitatively the same? Are all pleasures created equal? Is the pleasure that I receive from breathing clean air equal to the pleasure that you receive from smoking? If not, how can we measure them? What scale can we use? In part, preference utilitarianism attempts to overcome this problem, because preferences, unlike desires, are ranked. I want both a vacation and more time to finish my work, but I *prefer* the vacation to work. However, although this approach may overcome some problems of comparing an individual's desires, it does not help us compare the pleasure (or other value) experienced by two people with conflicting desires.

A second problem follows from this. Because "the good" is difficult to quantify, utilitarians have a tendency to substitute for the good something that can be quantified. For example, suppose we take good health to be the social goal we seek to maximize. How can we measure and compare the health consequences of various pollution control decisions? In practice, it could become easy to substitute for health some quantifiable considerations, such as life expectancy, infant mortality, injury rate, per capita expenditures on health care. But although such factors may well give us an indication of health, they surely do not tell us the whole story. Moreover, in practice it becomes easy to forget the primary goal of health and simply identify these quantifiable factors as the final goal. This problem raises significant questions when we realize that the most easily quantifiable substitute for the good is money.

Critics claim that this is exactly what occurs when environmental regulation is subjected to cost–benefit analysis. Because regulators seem unable to measure the value of health itself, they instead measure various economic factors associated with health and then decide cases by comparing the costs of health to the costs of closing down the source of pollution.

A final measurement problem arises when we consider the *scope* of the people involved and the *range* of what counts as a person. In theory, the utilitarian should be concerned with all the pleasure or happiness that is affected by the particular act. In practice, this is next to impossible. We can never know all the consequences of any act. The tendency among utilitarians is to restrict consideration to the expected consequences to people in the immediate vicinity. Further, an act's effects on future generations, or on people in other countries, or on animals (who do experience pleasure and pain) are often ignored. Each of these limitations has significant environmental implications.

The criticisms raised so far could be countered by adjusting the application of utilitarian principles. Other criticisms raise more direct challenges to the theory itself and call for abandoning utilitarianism rather than reforming it.

One such challenge begins with the provisional nature of utilitarian judgments. According to the utilitarian, no particular act, in and of itself, is ever right or wrong. The ethical status of any act always depends on something else: its consequences. Right and wrong always depend on the context and, therefore, always depend on factors outside the individual's control. But this reasoning seems to miss an important area of ethical concern: those occasions when the ethically correct decision is to act on principle, regardless of consequences. There can be times when we judge an act to be wrong in principle, even if the overall consequences turn out to be good. There are times when we judge an act to be ethically right in principle, even if the overall consequences turn out to be bad. Because utilitarianism seems unable to account for such notable cases, critics charge that this theory is at best incomplete.

Two examples may help illuminate this point. Imagine a situation in which significant and good consequences would result if only I would betray a friend. Imagine also that this friend would never know that I was responsible for the betrayal. In such a scenario, the utilitarian decision would be to betray the friend. However, critics would claim that this betrayal violates an important ethical principle ("do not betray friends") and ought not to be done, even if the consequences of not betraying the friend were bad.

A second example can be developed from a well-known environmental controversy. In recent years, many environmentalists have fought to prevent logging in the old-growth forests of the Pacific Northwest. Logging activities were threatening to destroy the habitat of the spotted owl, an endangered species. The spotted owl was threatened with extinction if the logging continued. On the other hand, significant social benefits would follow from a growth in the logging industry. Because the owl has no known *use* and because it does not contribute to society in any obvious way, a utilitarian calculation might suggest that the logging should be allowed. However, environmentalists charged that causing the extinction of a species is wrong in principle, even if doing so would result in a net increase in beneficial social consequences.

2.6 CONTEMPORARY PERSPECTIVES ON UTILITARIANISM

At the beginning of this chapter, we suggested that ethical theory should be studied because, among other reasons, some standard theories are embedded in common ways of thinking and reasoning. This is perhaps most true of utilitarianism.

In many ways, utilitarianism is the unofficial ethical theory of public policy in much of North America and Western Europe and, increasingly, for much global policy as well. Time and time again, environmental debates are framed in utilitarian terms. Recent political debates about the Clean Air Act, the Clean Water Act, and the Endangered Species Act are clear examples of this, as is the public policy decision making surrounding nuclear power plants and protection of the spotted owl.

We shall explicitly examine utilitarian reasoning in two major areas of this text. In the following chapter, we look at the significant impact of market economics on environmental matters. Implicit in most market-based policy is the utilitarian commitment to maximize overall happiness. As we shall see, such claims are not without controversy. In Chapter 5 we will examine a utilitarian analysis of ethical consideration for animal welfare. Inspired in part by Jeremy Bentham, some contemporary animal welfare advocates argue that the pain and suffering of animals must be included in any utilitarian calculation of the greatest good for the greatest number.

Beyond these two specific issues, utilitarian thinking is deeply embedded in many environmental issues, especially in matters of social policy. In any situation in which there are competing interests and in which every interest is treated as equally deserving, a utilitarian desire to balance competing interests so that an optimal outcome is achieved seems an obvious ethical approach. Public officials who are charged with serving the public interest almost inevitably set policy on utilitarian grounds. This brief introduction to utilitarianism should help you recognize this reasoning when you come across it. The goal of this section is to sensitize you to the implicit strengths and inherent dangers of this common public philosophy and to make you better able to assess environmental policy that is based on this traditional ethical theory.

2.7 DEONTOLOGY: AN ETHICS
OF DUTY AND RIGHTS

The final ethical tradition considered here emphasizes the notion of acting on principle rather than in terms of consequences. In this view, the central concepts of ethics involve duties and rights. (This approach to ethics is sometimes called *deontology* from the Greek word for "duty.") The classic philosophical defense of this view is found in the writings of the eighteenth-century German philosopher Immanuel Kant.[6]

Recall one of the central criticisms of utilitarianism: that it seems to make the ethical status of our acts depend on factors over which we have no control. My acts are judged by their consequences, yet surely I can neither anticipate nor control all the consequences of my actions. Thus utilitarianism seems to hold people responsible for things that they cannot control. This would seem to violate a fundamental maxim of ethics. People can be held responsible only for those things within their power, or, in the words of an often-used phrase, *ought* implies *can*.

Kantian ethics begins with the claim that we can be held responsible only for those things that we can control. This, argued Kant, means that the focus of ethics should be on those principles (he called them maxims) on which we freely and autonomously choose to act.

We can think of these principles as expressing the intention of our action, and the Kantian principle is that we can be held ethically responsible for our intentions. Assuming that we are rational beings and do not act merely as a result of instinct or conditioning, we can be held responsible because we have freely chosen, or have intended, our actions. Thus Kant held that we are ethical beings because we are rational beings, who can freely form intentions and deliberately choose to act on them. Our standing as moral beings is derived from our nature as free and rational beings.

But how do we determine which intentions are ethically correct and which are unethical? Kant argued that we are acting ethically whenever the principle or maxim on which we act is a rational one. A rational principle in ethics, like rationality in other areas, would be found acceptable and binding by all other actors. That is, a rational principle is one that is categorical and universalized. The fundamental ethical duty, which Kant called the *categorical imperative*, is to act only in those ways that all rational beings could find acceptable.

Kant believed that this fundamental ethical duty could be expressed in a number of different ways. The categorical imperative also requires that we treat people as *ends* and never simply as *means* or as *subjects,* and never simply as *objects.* Thus we are ethically obligated to treat people as rational and autonomous beings. We should never treat a person as a mere thing to be used for our own purposes. People are subjects who have their own purposes and intentions, and we have a moral obligation to respect them as capable of making their own decisions.

The categorical imperative, then, establishes our fundamental ethical duties: Treat people as ends and never as mere means or as objects. However, because other people are equally obligated to treat me in this manner, the categorical imperative can also be seen as establishing our fundamental ethical *rights*. Like all people, I have the right to be treated as an end, not as a means. I have the right to be treated as a free and rational being, who has his own purposes and goals. I have the right to pursue those goals, so long as I do not myself treat others as a means to my ends. Following from these considerations, this ethical tradition places primary value on the duty to treat other people with respect and on the rights of equality and freedom. These basic rights and duties all follow from our nature as beings capable of free and rational action.

This discussion of duties and rights gives us another way to understand the major deficiency in utilitarian thinking. Given its focus on consequences, utilitarianism neglects the important role that moral principles can play in ethical decision making. According to Kant, to act on principle is to act in accordance with the categorical imperative. The principle of justice, for example, requires us to fulfill our duties to other people. Justice requires that we respect the rights of others at all times and under all conditions. (That is what it means to call this imperative "categorical.") Utilitarianism, on the other hand, requires us to fulfill our duties and respect others' rights *only* when doing so maximizes the overall good consequences. But this, argues the Kantian, is the perfect example of injustice: fulfilling duties and respecting rights only when doing so has beneficial consequences.

Thus rights can trump social utility.[7] If I have a right to some good (or a right to be protected from some harm), denying me this good (or not protecting me from that harm) would be wrong, even if doing so would contribute to the overall social good. This is one way to understand the recent debates concerning the Endangered Species Act. If I have a right to private property, taking this property from me simply to provide habitat for an endangered species, even if doing so would satisfy the desires of the wider community, would be wrong. Proponents of takings legislation claim that many environmental laws violate the rights of individuals simply to serve the utilitarian goal of maximizing overall happiness. In this view, such acts violate principles of social justice.

Such ideas have had a profound influence on Western ethical and political thought. They are reflected in the central notions of democracy and civil liberties. An ethical theory that does not take seriously the dignity of each person as a free and rational agent would need significant philosophical defense.

2.8 CONTEMPORARY PERSPECTIVES ON DEONTOLOGICAL ETHICS

Despite the intuitively clear importance of an ethics of rights and duties, contemporary deontological ethics is not without controversy. Some critics claim that the Kantian ethical tradition offers no practical basis for making substantive value judgments. So long as I am treating other people correctly (which I might accomplish simply by leaving other people alone), no ethical basis exists for evaluating those choices that I make. In that view, value questions become merely a matter of personal choice or preference.

According to some critics, this deontological tradition offers no account of what is good, valuable, or worthy. A life of conspicuous consumption, if autonomously chosen and if lived without violating the dignity of other autonomous agents, is ethically no better or worse than a more ecologically sound lifestyle. A life spent competing with others or a life spent in solitude and loneliness is ethically no worse than a life of friendships, caring, and community.

A version of this criticism holds that talk of rights amounts to little more than a disguised way of talking about "wants." That is, if people want something strongly enough, they attempt to legitimize their wants by identifying them as rights. One result is an explosion of rights, as society becomes a collection of numerous interest groups, each claiming rights against the greater public interest and overall social good.

Other critics see a strong human-centered, or anthropocentric, bias implicit in this tradition. It seems a short step from treating humans as ends because they are rational, to treating nonrational things as mere means. There appears to be little basis in this tradition for ethical obligations to anything that is not free and rational. Thus it would seem legitimate to treat other living beings and the environment simply as means to our ends. These things are, after all, the perfect example of objects, not subjects. Some of these criticisms are developed at greater length in later chapters.

Earlier in this chapter, I suggested that ethics has traditionally included both individual moral questions (What should I do? What kind of person should I be?) and questions of social justice or public policy (How should we arrange our society? Which political and economic institutions are just?). We should recognize that the ethical traditions of natural law, utilitarianism, and Kantian deontology have had a significant influence on the development of modern political thinking. Indeed, it is fair to see these philosophical theories as providing the intellectual and ethical framework of most modern social and political arrangements.

Both classical utilitarianism and Kantian deontology are especially influential in the development of democratic forms of government that provide strong protections of individual freedoms and individual rights. The political arrangements of a constitutional democracy are a useful example of the connections between these ethical traditions and contemporary politics. A commitment to majority rule can be seen as serving the utilitarian goal of maximizing happiness. If we seek to attain the greatest happiness for the greatest number, we do not go far wrong by taking a vote and following the will of the majority. On the other hand, constitutional protections of civil rights and civil liberties can be seen as serving the Kantian goal of respecting individual autonomy. Thus constitutional rights serve as a check on, and a limit to, the majoritarian decisions of legislatures.

The greatest challenge to this Kantian tradition is to specify and defend "rights claims." What rights do we have? Where do they come from? Who or what has rights? To whom and to what do we owe duties? How do we reconcile conflicting rights claims? In many ways, such questions foreshadow numerous significant environmental controversies. A brief review of issues involving claims of rights and duties indicates how prevalent this approach to ethics is and why it is important to understand this ethical theory. Pollution is thought wrong, because it violates the rights of innocent people. Wilderness preservation is disputed, because it violates private property rights. We ought to conserve resources, because we have a duty to future generations. Do humans have any duties to animals and other living beings? Does a consumerist lifestyle violate our duties of social justice toward people living in less developed regions?

2.9 ENVIRONMENTAL ETHICS
AND RELIGIOUS PRINCIPLES

Increasing environmental awareness has extended beyond philosophical ethics and has given rise to a significant amount of reflection on theological and religious approaches to the environment. Religious traditions throughout history have addressed the ethical relationship between humans and their natural environment, and significant common ground exists among a variety of religious traditions. Historically, however, the record of religion on the environment is mixed, and some observers claim that certain religious attitudes have been among the root causes of environmental destruction.[8] Nevertheless, an increasing number of theologians and religious believers are re-examining religious traditions to find the intellectual and ethical resources for a new, more responsible environmental ethics.

There is a long tradition of distinguishing *philosophical* from *religious* ethics that would advise caution about using religious ethics to promote political dialogue. From at least the time of Socrates, philosophers in the Western tradition have been hesitant to base ethical claims on religious beliefs. The primary hesitation is that religious-based ethics would appear to leave the analysis one step short of rational resolution. Philosophical ethics seeks to universally persuade any and all rational people, whereas religious ethics seems persuasive only on those who share the underlying religious assumptions. If a religion-based ethics provides justification only for those who already accept the religious starting points, then religious ethics would seem unable to resolve conflicts between and among religious believers, and we would be left with no universal and unbiased basis for ethical conclusions. As Socrates argued in the dialogue *Euthyphro*, if religious believers can justify their beliefs to the nonbeliever, then the appeal to religion is irrelevant; if the believer cannot justify those beliefs, then the nonbeliever has no good reason to accept them. Either way, basing ethical conclusions on religious beliefs seems incomplete.

It would, of course, be a mistake to think in terms of a single "religious environmental ethics." There are countless religions and denominations, and any attempt to survey the rich variety of religious approaches to environmental concerns would be well beyond the scope of an introductory philosophy textbook. Nonetheless, religious ethics has a role to play in thinking about environmental ethics. Religion can provide an important context for helping us to understand different perspectives on the natural environment. Religious ethics also appeals to deeply held ethical values and principles, and civil dialogue is advanced when we find common ground from which to begin discussions. Equally important, religious ethical principles are a resource for environmental motivation. Ethics, after all, seeks to provide reasons both to *justify* ethical beliefs and to *motivate* ethical actions. These reasons warrant a brief consideration of some themes from religion in a philosophical text in environmental ethics. Five themes that appear in various guises later in this text are worth mentioning here.

The Good of God's Creation

Any religious tradition that understands the natural world as the creation of a good and beneficent God will be inclined to value that natural world as a good in its own right and independent of human valuation. In the biblical story of creation, for example, after creating all living creatures, God "saw that it was good" (Gen. 1:25) and "God saw everything that he had made, and indeed, it was very good" (Gen. 1:31). Thus, the world's goodness was established before humans were even created. This religious theme would tend to work against any view that the natural world has merely instrumental value or becomes valuable only when humans conceive it as such. The natural world is good objectively and independently of human judgments. From this perspective, one shows respect for God by treating the divine creation with respect.

Such a religious perspective would be compatible with an interpretation of natural teleology as the natural law of God. Assuming a purposive, intelligent, and beneficent God, one can easily assume that there is a natural order to creation and that this order is good. This perspective would also support the preservation of natural areas, and urge vigilance when we appropriate parts of creation for our own uses.

Finding the Divine in Nature

A second theme from religious ethics suggests that human beings come closest to the divine when they separate themselves from human culture and civilization. From Buddhist monks living at high altitudes in the Himalaya Mountains, to early Christian ascetics, to nineteenth-century romanticism, to Native American practices, to John Muir's description of a sequoia grove as cathedrals, there are many traditions that understand a withdrawal from human society as a path to God or enlightenment. Because God created the natural world, and humans created society, one can most closely approach the divine by retreating from society to experience creation. Oftentimes, these views are associated with religious spirituality, an approach to religion that is more focused on religious experience and living than on religious doctrine and theology. This spiritual perspective thus would be sympathetic to the preservation of nature as a refuge and as a haven for religious experience.

There are both religious and secular approaches to spirituality. Both share a common belief that there is more to existence than the immediate and material physical world. Both value communion with this spiritual side of existence as what brings most meaning and value to life. While some strands of spirituality can lead some to an ascetic life, in which the physical environment is almost irrelevant, other strands of spirituality promote a deep interconnectedness of all creation that calls human beings to greater empathy, if not identification, with nature. For many, spirituality is an aspect of religious experience that brings human into a closer relationship with God, and this experience can often best be found in communion with God's natural creation.

The Ultimate Respect for and Value of Life

Many religious traditions are re-examining their commitments to the value of life to expand "pro-life" from an exclusive human focus to the realization that any and all life forms have intrinsic worth. Although much of Christianity, for example, emphasizes a life-centered ethic, much of the tradition has understood this only in terms of human life. But many believers, both Christians and others, argue that *all* life is to be valued. The early Christian Francis of Assisi, for example, proclaimed a life-affirming ethics that explicitly included plants and animals.

For many religious traditions, the dignity of life itself is the ultimate value. It is the deepest mystery and greatest expression of God's love. For many religions, the principle of life—whether it be called spirit or soul—is that which is closest to the creator. Increasingly, many religions are extending their recognition of the sacredness of life to include nonhuman life as well. Chapter 6 will consider philosophical versions of such a life-centered, or biocentric, ethics.

Social Justice Ministries

There is an aspect of many religions that calls believers to serve the common good and to bear witness to a beneficent God by speaking out against oppression and working for the disenfranchised. Many Christians, for example, emulate Christ by serving the poor and advocating social policies that protect and help the least fortunate. This social justice tradition within religious ethics has implications for environmental issues in two major ways. As the discussion of environmental justice in Chapter 10 will explain, all too often the people who suffer the greatest harms from environmental pollution and degradation are exactly the people least able to defend their own interests. The world's poor endure the greatest environmental burdens and receive the fewest environmental benefits. Those who answer a religious calling to serve the poor often find themselves acting for environmental justice and environmental causes such as clean air and water, fertile farmland, healthful food, and open space.

Second, within this social justice tradition, many observers conclude that social oppression and environmental destruction result from common social practices and attitudes. Environmental philosophies such as deep ecology, social ecology, and ecofeminism cite various contemporary attitudes such as materialism, industrialism, consumerism, and patriarchy in their analysis of the causes of environmental destruction. According to some observers, these same attitudes are part of a general worldview that fosters the dominance of one class—wealthy, male, privileged—over another—poor, female, disenfranchised. Thus a commitment to social justice will address the root causes of both social oppression and environmental destruction.

Stewardship

Finally, there is an approach common to many religions that understands human responsibility toward the natural word in terms of stewardship of resources that have been entrusted to humans by a creator. From this perspective, the natural world is valued for the resources that it can provide for human use. But this world should be treated with the appreciation, reverence, and respect that are due a gift from the creator. Destruction, desecration, or waste of resources is an affront to the generosity and beneficence of God. The idea of stewardship calls on humans to nurture and protect God's creation and not to destroy it. The metaphor of the shepherd, common in Judeo-Christian traditions, is often used to explain the concept of stewardship. The good shepherd nurtures, sustains, and protects the flock, while still using it as a source of food and wool. A shepherd cares for the sheep. So, too, must humans care for the natural world. Humans have dominion over the world but are not entitled to destroy or ruin it. Dominion is not domination. This stewardship tradition would be sympathetic to conservation of natural resources and sustainable economic development, two topics that we examine later in this text.

2.10 SUMMARY AND CONCLUSIONS

We might think of this textbook as presenting a continuing conversation among philosophers, scientists, environmentalists, and citizens. The conversation has been going on for some time, but it clearly has a long way to go before reaching any conclusions. These initial chapters provide an introduction to some of the main participants in the conversation and to some of the motivation that initiated it. We have also introduced some of the language that the participants are using and reviewed some of what has been said in the past.

By no means have the philosophers had the final word. Do not think that all that is now required is simply to apply these philosophical theories and concepts to environmental problems. Rather, now that the introductions have been made, you should see yourself as a participant in this conversation. Join in, learn as you go, contribute what and when you can, and do not end the discussion too soon.

NOTES

1. Aldo Leopold, "The Land Ethic," in *A Sand County Almanac with Essays on Conservation from Round River*, pp. 237–64 (New York: Oxford University Press, 1949).

2. For an insightful critique of a standard understanding of the role of ethical theory and principles in environmental ethics, see Ken Sayre, "An Alternative View of Environmental Ethics," *Environmental Ethics* 13 (Fall 1991): 195–213. Sayre argues against what he calls the inferential view of ethical theory, a view similar to what we will be calling applied ethics. Like Sayre, this textbook suggests that the inferential/applied view of ethical theory is at best incomplete when addressing environmental issues.

3. For Aristotle's account of the four causes, see his *Physics*, book 2, ch. 3. For a critique of the abuse of the more mechanistic model in environmental science, see Daniel Botkin's *Discordant Harmonies* (New York: Oxford University Press, 1990).

4. Readers interested in pursuing these debates are advised to consult Colin Allen, Marc Bekoff, and George Lauder, eds., *Nature's Purposes: Analyses of Function and Design in Biology* (Cambridge, Mass.: MIT Press, 1998); David Buller, ed., *Function, Selection, and Design* (Albany, N.Y.: SUNY Press, 1999); and David Hull and Michael Ruse, eds., *The Philosophy of Biology* (New York: Oxford University Press, 1998). In particular, readers of the Hull book should consult "Teleology Revisited" by Ernst Nagel and "Where's the Good in Teleology?" by Mark Bedau.

5. For the classic statements of utilitarianism, see Jeremy Bentham, *Introduction to the Principles of Morals and Legislation* (Oxford: Clarendon Press, 1781) and John Stuart Mill, *Utilitarianism*, ed. by George Sher (Indianapolis, Ind.: Hackett, 1979). For a contemporary defense of utilitarianism, see J. J. C. Smart and Bernard Williams, *Utilitarianism: For and Against* (Cambridge, England: Cambridge University Press, 1973).

6. For Kant's views on ethics, see especially his *Groundwork for the Metaphysics of Morals*, ed. James Ellington (Indianapolis, Ind.: Hackett, 1993).

7. For a thorough presentation of this view, see Ronald Dworkin, *Taking Rights Seriously* (Cambridge, Mass.: Harvard University Press, 1977).

8. See especially Lynn White, Jr.'s claims in "The Historical Roots of Our Ecological Crisis," *Science* 155 (March 10, 1967): 1203–1207. White's views are treated in more depth in Chapter 5.

DISCUSSION QUESTIONS

1. Given that society receives benefits from nuclear power, how should we determine the distribution of the burdens that go along with these benefits? Should nuclear waste storage facilities be located where the energy is generated? Or should they be located where the energy is used, even if that means within a large urban center? Or should they be located in an area where the risks are

lowest, even if the people living in that area do not benefit from nuclear energy?

2. Aristotle suggested that all natural objects could be distinguished in terms of a natural and character-istic activity. Can we apply this approach to an ecosystem? Do different elements of an ecosystem perform different functions within that system? Could you reason from such ecological facts to nor-mative conclusions about what should be? Why or why not?

3. Many environmental controver-sies are seen as a debate between jobs and environmental protec-tion. For example, the spotted owl controversy in the Pacific Northwest is often framed in terms of owls versus jobs. Are such utilitarian tradeoffs reasonable? Are tradeoffs possible?

4. The biblical story of creation speaks of a God who creates humans "to rule the fish in the sea, the birds in the sky, the cattle, all the wild animals on earth and all the reptiles that crawl upon the earth" and who grants humans "dominion over" all other living things. Some have interpreted this to mean that humans may rightfully "domi-nate" and control the natural world. Others have argued that humans should act as stewards, or caretakers, of what is, after all, God's creation. What reasons do you see for either view?

GLOBAL ENVIRONMENTAL ETHICS WATCH

For more information on Ethical Theories and the Environment, please see the Global Environmental Ethics Watch. Updated several times a day, Global Envi-ronmental Ethics Watch is a focused portal into GREENR—our Global Reference on the Environment, Energy, and Natural Resources—an ideal one-stop site for current events and research. You will have access to the latest information from trusted academic journals, news outlets, and magazines as well as access to statistics, primary sources, case studies, videos, pod-casts, and much more.

To gain access please use the access code that accompanies your book. If you do not have an access code, visit cengagebrain.com to purchase one.

PART II

Environmental Ethics as Applied Ethics

3

Ethics and Economics:
Managing Public Lands

DISCUSSION: BP's Deepwater Horizon Oil Spill

Six hundred million acres of land within the United States, nearly one-third of the total land area, is classified as public land. Fully 83% of the land area of Nevada and 44% of California, for example, is public land. Approximately 240 million acres, or 65% of all the land in Alaska, is owned by the federal government. Public lands are managed by public agencies which are charged with serving the public interests and therefore must balance competing and conflicting claims concerning the proper use of public land. But how should we decide what the public interest is? How should public lands be used? How should government agencies decide what to do when public interest groups disagree?

The ocean waters bordering the country are one area of public property with significant environmental implications often overlooked in public policy debates. Consistent with a United Nations convention governing the world's oceans, the

United States claims a border of its territorial waters of 12 nautical miles and 200 nautical miles as its exclusive economic zone. This means that an ocean area extended 12 miles out from its borders is considered the sovereign property of the United States, and is treated under international law as land within its borders. The exclusive economic zone gives countries exclusive rights to exploit marine resources within 200 miles of its shore.

The public agencies that manage the oceans are as diverse as the ways in which these waters are used. At the federal level, what happens in, on, under, and around the oceans is managed by, among others, the Coast Guard, the National Oceanic and Atmospheric Administration, the Army Corps of Engineers, the National Park Service, the U.S. Fish and Wildlife Service, the Department of Defense, the National Marine Fisheries Service and the Environmental Protection Agency. In addition to federal agencies, a variety of state and local government agencies also have a role in managing public waters. Perhaps no use of coastal waters has created as much controversy over how public waters should be managed as oil drilling. There is no better example of these controversies than what occurred with BP's Deepwater Horizon.

The need for oil, and for domestic sources of oil, are well-known. The United States uses more than 21 million barrels of oil each day, which at a prevailing cost of $100 per barrel, amounts to $2 billion each day. Gasoline, heating oil, jet fuel, and diesel fuel are the leading uses of oil. Less than one-third of the oil consumed in the United States is produced domestically, and the area surrounding the Gulf of Mexico is largest source for domestic oil production.

On April 20, 2010, an explosion seriously damaged the Deepwater Horizon oil rig operated by BP in the exclusive economic zone about 40 miles off the coast of Louisiana. Eleven men were killed in the explosion and fire, and within two days the entire rig sank in 5,000 feet of water. For three months, as millions of people watched daily updates on the evening news, all efforts to stop the flow of oil into the Gulf failed. Estimates are that a total of 5 million barrels of oil was spilled in the Gulf of Mexico. By comparison, the Exxon Valdez, perhaps the most famous previous oil spill, dumped a total of 260,000 barrels of oil into Prince William Sound in Alaska.

The spill caused significant environmental and economic damage throughout the Gulf region. Despite massive clean-up efforts, oil washed ashore along more than a thousand miles of the Gulf Coast, and underwater oil plumes drifted throughout the Gulf. Thousands of animals died as a direct result of the spill, and the habitat of thousands of species, including many migratory species, was disrupted and poisoned. The area was closed to fishing for many weeks, severely damaging the commercial fishing, shrimp, crab, and sport fishing industries. The tourist industry lost substantial business as beaches from Texas to Florida were closed.

BP acknowledged responsibility for the spill and, in addition to paying for clean-up efforts, established a fund of $20 billion to compensate victims. By July 2011, almost $5 billion in claims had been paid, mostly for clean-up costs and compensation for lost wages and loss of business income.

Within a month of the disaster, the U.S. Department of Interior issued a moratorium on all off-shore drilling pending inspection of all drilling rigs. In response to a lawsuit, a federal judge overturned that moratorium a month later, concluding that the government had not proven that a moratorium was warranted by the potential harms. Critics of the moratorium argued that the oil industry would be forced by a moratorium to lay-off thousands of workers, a major problem with the United States' economy still suffering from the effects of the 2008 recession and the Gulf region already facing the loss of jobs caused by the oil spill.

DISCUSSION TOPICS:

1. Economists define costs as "opportunities foregone"; every decision imposes costs in the sense that every decision abandons other choices. What are the economic costs of deciding to ban deepwater oil drilling? What are the non-economic costs?

2. What are the pros and cons of government ownership of large tracks of land? Do you support public ownership of land? Why or why not? Should all public lands be privatized? If so, should all public lands be sold to the highest bidder?

3. What role should consumer demand for such resources as oil and pristine beaches play? Should such decisions simply be left to the market to determine which resource is most valued by the public?

4. How do you compare the values associated with such diverse goods as wildlife habitat and inexpensive gasoline? How would you recommend a public resolution of conflicts between such values be made?

5. Is it always possible to compensate for the loss of such things as habitat, wildlife, jobs, clean beaches, and family-owned businesses?

3.1 INTRODUCTION

Chapter 1 introduced ethics in terms of both individual moral decisions and broader questions of social justice and public policy. In this chapter, we will examine the ethical and philosophical basis of economic analysis, one of the most influential and widely used frameworks used in public policy. Faced with controversial environmental issues, policy makers are challenged to make decisions in a way that is fair to all parties and that relies on reasonable, unbiased, and objective criteria. In this context, policy analysts, government decision makers, and private sector experts most often rely on economic criteria. Economics offers a way to take the interests of all interested parties into account, and it offers an objective and measurable decision-making procedure. As we will see, economics also has important ethical values embedded in its methodology, and therefore economic decisions also reflect some strongly held ethical views as well. Using examples involving the conservation of natural resources and pollution of air and water, this chapter will examine how economic analysis plays a central role in environmental debates.

It is not surprising that economics would play a major role in environmental debates. Economics is often defined as the science that deals with the production and distribution of finite goods and services. Understood in this way, an environmental controversy such as BP oil spill appears to be fundamentally an economic problem involving the distribution of scarce resources, the allocation of risks and benefits, the balancing of competing interests, the production of desired goods, the meeting of consumer demand, and so forth. Debating the relative merits of a copper mine versus a salmon fishery calls for an unbiased method for measuring and comparing costs and benefits. It would seem that an ideal solution would be one that optimally satisfies as many competing interests as possible, which in many ways is exactly the goal of efficient economic markets. This chapter provides a philosophical examination of the role of economic analysis in resolving environmental debates.

3.2 CONSERVATION OR PRESERVATION?

A pivotal moment in the history of American environmentalism occurred during the first decade of the twentieth century. A growing population and consumer demand put environmental protection at odds with the economic need for natural resources. The specific debates concerned a proposal to build a dam and reservoir in the Hetch Hetchy Valley adjacent to California's Yosemite National Park. Demand for water in San Francisco led to the plan to flood the Hetch Hetchy, which would destroy thousands of acres of pristine forests. This debate has often been cast as a debate between economic interests and environmental interests. Two of the most prominent early American environmentalists, Gifford Pinchot and John Muir, were at the center of this debate, which has come to symbolize two major competing worldviews.

Gifford Pinchot, head of the U.S. Forest Service, was one of the first professionally trained foresters in the United States, and a close friend and adviser to President Theodore Roosevelt. Pinchot was a founder and leader of the conservation movement, which held that forestlands are to be conserved, so that they might be wisely used and controlled by all citizens. He was an early defender of the scientific management of national forest lands. Pinchot's guiding principle was that public lands exist to serve the needs and uses of the public:

> The object of our forest policy is not to preserve the forests because they are beautiful ... or because they are refuges for the wild creatures of the wilderness ... but ... the primary object is the making of prosperous homes.[1]

He also said:

> Forestry is the knowledge of the forest. In particular, it is the art of handling the forest so that it will render whatever service is required of it without being impoverished or destroyed.... Forestry is the art of producing from the forest whatever it can yield for the service of man.[2]

Pinchot supported San Francisco's plan to build the reservoir. Damming the Hetch Hetchy would provide much needed water to millions of people and it would represent the most efficient and economical use of this natural resource.

John Muir was the founder of the Sierra Club and the best-known representative of the preservation movement. Muir argued against Pinchot's plan to build the dam, and he worked to preserve the Hetch Hetchy valley. He thought that the conservationist view, which treated natural resources as commodities to be used for human consumption, was a serious mistake. Muir defended the spiritual and aesthetic value of wilderness, as well as the inherent worth of other living things.[3] In his view, the Hetch Hetchy should be preserved—protected from human activity that would degrade and spoil it.

This early debate symbolizes the worldviews of two dominant strains of American environmentalism. Conservationists seek to protect the natural environment from exploitation and abuse so that humans can receive greater long-term benefits from it. Preservationists seek to protect the natural environment from any human activity that would disrupt or degrade it. Their goal is to preserve the wilderness in its natural, unspoiled state. Importantly, debates between conservationists and preservationists, as we see in Hetch Hetchy, are very often played out in economic terms.

The ethical justification for the conservationist program is fairly straightforward and reflects a standard utilitarian approach. The natural environment is valuable as a means for serving human interests. Thus natural resources have instrumental value and should be managed in whatever way best serves the greater overall good. Pinchot argued that these resources were being wasted when they were left undeveloped. The biggest question for conservationists is how to decide which policy option best serves the overall social good.

Preservationists, on the other hand, appealed to two different types of reasons to support their goals. One was the instrumental value of wilderness as a source of religious inspiration, refuge from modern life, location for aesthetic experience, and so on. In this sense, leaving the wilderness undeveloped also served human interests. But some preservationists also argued that the wilderness should be recognized as having an intrinsic value of its own. We have a duty to preserve the wilderness not only for its human uses, but also for its own sake. Thus preservationists appealed to both utilitarian and deontological considerations to defend their conclusions.

Contemporary observers could easily cast Muir as the environmentalist and Pinchot as the environmental villain in this dispute. But this would be a mistake. Pinchot's position was quite progressive at the time, and it will be worthwhile to consider this claim briefly.

For much of American history, the forests and wilderness areas represented a threat to be overcome, an enemy to be conquered. The images are common throughout the first 400 years of European settlement of North America—man against nature. The frontier was to be pushed back, and the wilderness was to be conquered. Life in the wilderness was difficult, and if humans were to survive, they needed to fight and defeat the forces of nature. Nature was seen as the enemy to be subdued and exploited.

By the late nineteenth century, the United States had largely succeeded in these tasks, and most of the American landscape lay open for human use. During this period of tremendous industrial growth and urbanization, nature was generally thought to be less an enemy to be conquered and more a resource to fuel the U.S. economy. In some ways, this brought American attitudes towards the natural environment more in line with the older cultures of Europe and Asia. But this also often meant that natural resources contributed to the extraordinary wealth of the privileged few, who monopolized much of American industry.

Pinchot's conservationism was part of a more general progressive movement fighting the laissez-faire, monopolistic social Darwinism characteristic of much of nineteenth-century American economic life.[4] Along with President Roosevelt and other progressives, Pinchot held that natural resources should benefit all citizens, not just the wealthy few who privately owned vast amounts of property. Government policy should serve this goal by preventing waste, limiting monopolistic control, providing economic opportunity for the many, and keeping prices low.

Pinchot's progressive conservation was in line with the progressivism of nineteenth-century utilitarians such as Bentham and Mill. Government policy, including economic policy, should aim to provide maximum benefit to all citizens, not just to a privileged few. Consistent with thinking of many classical utilitarians, Pinchot believed that experts, in this case those trained in scientific forestry, were best situated to decide how to maximize overall benefits. In Pinchot's words:

> The central idea of the Forester, in handling the forest, is to promote and perpetuate its greatest use to men. His purpose is to make it serve the greatest good of the greatest number for the longest time.... The idea of

applying foresight and common sense to the other natural resources as well as to the forest was natural and inevitable.... It was foreseen from the beginning by those who were responsible for inaugurating the Conservation movement that its natural development would in time work out into a planned and orderly scheme for national efficiency, based on the elimination of waste, and directed toward the best use of all we have for the greatest good of the greatest number for the longest time.[5]

Thus Pinchot's conservation movement fits squarely within the utilitarian tradition. Public policy should be directed to "serve the greatest good of the greatest number for the longest time." Acting in a manner consistent with much in the utilitarian tradition, Pinchot encouraged the use of experts who could manage policy so that it might achieve this goal. Utilitarians begin with the maximum satisfaction of public welfare as the goal, and then promote reliance on experts, especially scientists, to calculate, measure, compare, predict, and influence the consequences of various policy options. Decision makers should rely on professional managers to determine which of the policy options will result in consequences most closely approaching this goal. This is precisely the role that Pinchot saw for the professional forester, and it is fundamentally the same role played by economists and other social scientists in many of today's environmental policy debates.

3.3 MANAGING THE NATIONAL FORESTS

By 2010, Pinchot's U.S. Forest Service was managing more than 150 different national forests containing 190 million acres of land. It is the largest agency in the U.S. Department of Agriculture, employing more than 34,000 people.[6] In the more than 100 years of its existence, the U.S. Forest Service has gone through a number of changes. For its first 50 years, the U.S. Forest Service accomplished its mission "to furnish a continuous supply of timber" through fire suppression, research, and other custodial duties aimed at simply conserving a reserve of forest lands. In the years after World War II, an increase in demand for housing and a decrease in the supply of privately owned timberlands led to a greater focus on timber sales. Later, in 1960, Congress enacted the Multiple-Use Sustained Yield Act, which broadened the mission to require that the U.S. Forest Service manage the forests for "outdoor recreation, range, timber, watershed, and wildlife and fish purposes." It is easy to understand how this expanded mission addresses the utilitarian demand that all of the consequences of policy decisions be taken into consideration when making a decision. Multiple use remains the primary legal mission of the service and this continues to reflect how deeply public policy has been influenced by utilitarian thinking.

Of course, a government bureaucracy responsible for administering a multiple-use policy is likely to be the focus of criticism from its competing constituencies. The timber industry believes that not enough high-quality forests are open for its use. Environmentalists argue that too much wilderness is being sacrificed to timber interests. Ranchers would like to see more forestland open for grazing. Hunters and anglers decry the loss of habitat. But some of the most vocal contemporary critics argue that public policy should not be set by government bureaucrats at all. Instead, these critics argue that public policy decision making should be taken from government and left to the workings of a competitive marketplace.

As we have noted, the primary responsibility of the U.S. Forest Service is to serve the oftentimes competing interests of various constituencies. As is consistent with the goals of utilitarianism, it seeks to balance these interests in a manner that makes as many people as happy as possible. In this sense, the end or goal is a given, and the challenge is to find the best means for attaining the goal.

Two alternative means compete to answer this challenge. On one hand, acting in a manner consistent with Pinchot's practice, the U.S. Forest Service could rely on the informed judgments of public policy and forestry experts. These people would use their expertise and training in such fields as forestry and economics to resolve conflict, balance competing interests, and maximize the overall good. On the other hand, the U.S. Forest Service could rely on the workings of a free market with open competition to achieve the most efficient uses of the forests. Examining this debate will provide insight into the philosophical and ethical foundations of the use of economics in environmental policy.

According to classical free-market economics, markets alone, with minimal government regulation to prevent fraud and coercion, are sufficient to ensure attainment of the utilitarian goal of maximizing overall good. While this remains the ideal for many economists, the real world does not always match the standards of free and competitive markets. Many contemporary economists recognize that, in practice, markets can fail to reach the goals envisioned in theory. Thus a new type of expert, one who is trained in economics and can determine what should be done to mimic the workings of an idealized market, should shape environmental policy. Although ideal markets do not exist in the real world, environmental economists can develop policies that help actual markets approximate the results of ideal markets. One such environmental economist is Randal O'Toole.

O'Toole has written a sustained critique of U.S. Forest Service management and has been a leading voice in the movement to take environmental policy from the hands of government and foster greater reliance on the marketplace. In his book *Reforming the Forest Service,* O'Toole summarizes his five years of analyzing the activities of the U.S. Forest Service.

> I've visited national forests in every part of the country and have seen costly environmental destruction on a grand scale. Money-losing timber sales are costing taxpayers at least $250 to $500 million dollars per year. Many of these sales are reducing scarce recreation opportunities, driving wildlife species toward extinction, and polluting waters and fish habitat.[7]

Although the U.S. Forest Service manages assets estimated by some to be worth in excess of $42 billion, the agency is not only unprofitable, it actually costs taxpayers more than $1 billion per year in subsidies. O'Toole explains:

> In terms of assets, the agency would rank in the top five in *Fortune* magazine's list of the nation's 500 largest corporations. In terms of operating

revenues, however, the agency would be only number 290. In terms of net income, the Forest Service would be classified as bankrupt.[8]

Nevertheless, O'Toole remains optimistic in offering his recommendations.

> My economic research has convinced me that Americans can have all the wilderness, timber, wildlife, fish, and other forest resources they want. Apparent shortages of any of these resources are due solely to the Forest Service's failure to sell them at market prices.[9]

O'Toole's diagnosis of the U.S. Forest Service's problems is consistent with much economic analysis and is a clear example of how economic analysis is used in environmental debates.

The U.S. Forest Service is a large government bureaucracy with little or no incentive to balance revenues and expenses. Economic and environmental problems created by the policies of the U.S. Forest Service can be attributed "not to ignorance or maliciousness but rather to a lack of incentive to be concerned." O'Toole attempts to show that "inefficient management and environmental controversies are not problems in themselves but are merely symptoms of major institutional defects within the Forest Service."[10] In general, the major institutional defects all stem from the fact that the U.S. Forest Service does not operate according to the economic laws that would guide a private, for-profit business operating within a truly free market.

O'Toole's analysis is based on "the fundamental economic assumption that people's decisions are strongly influenced by the incentives affecting the decision makers."[11] The current structure of the U.S. Forest Service provides incentives only to "maximize its budget" and provides little or no incentive to supply Americans with "all the wilderness, timber, wildlife, fish, and other forest resources they want." The laws of economics tell us that if we "change the incentives, the decisions change."

What are the sources of U.S. Forest Service mismanagement? Essentially, there are two. The U.S. Forest Service is primarily responsible to Congress. Like Congress, its decisions reflect an attempt to balance the demands of competing and sometimes contradictory interest groups. Recent debates concerning protection of the spotted owl in the Pacific Northwest demonstrate the type of controversial decisions the U.S. Forest Service faces. Thus the primary incentive for the U.S. Forest Service is to satisfy these interest groups as much as possible, even if doing so means that the agency cannot devise and consistently enforce a long-range, rational, and efficient policy. Like Congress, which measures its success not in terms of the quality of legislation but in terms of re-election rates, the U.S. Forest Service is left with no measure of its success other than its budgetary retention rates. If its budget is maintained or increased, the U.S. Forest Service must be properly balancing the demands of its constituencies.[12]

The second source of U.S. Forest Service mismanagement lies in its budget, much of which comes from revenues retained from timber sales. An example is the Knutson-Vandenberg Act of 1930, which allows the U.S.

Forest Service to retain money collected from timber sales to fund reforesta-
tion. Congressional thinking seems to have been that this would accomplish
desired goals without costing taxpayers money. However, because this made
the U.S. Forest Service's budget dependent on the timber revenues
collected, including those collected from unprofitable sales of timber, the
practice provides an incentive to sell timber at any price. The service has
no incentive either to balance revenues and costs or to balance timber sales
against other uses of the forests.

Thus classical economic analysis has uncovered the underlying cause of the
U.S. Forest Service's inability to manage national forests in an ecologically sound
manner. The bureaucracy is organized in such a way that managers have incentives only to maximize their budget. In short, the U.S. Forest Service does not
exist within a free-market framework. This is the diagnosis of U.S. Forest Service
ills. Now, what is the cure?

The recommendation of environmental economics calls for the "marketization of the Forest Service." That is, the decisions of the U.S. Forest Service
should mimic those decisions that would be made by private sector business
managers seeking profits in a competitive market. The economic laws of the
marketplace would lead to decisions that would best satisfy the diverse demands
of the public. The market would "ensure efficient production of most forest
resources and an efficient allocation of forestlands." The market would give
Americans "all the wilderness, timber, wildlife, fish, and other forest resources
they want."

It is interesting to contrast this recommendation with Pinchot's views of the
U.S. Forest Service. Both approaches agree on the desirable outcome: using forestlands to provide the greatest good for the greatest number of people. In this
way, both apparently accept the utilitarian goal of maximally satisfying individual
preferences. The forests should be used to give people as much of what they
want as possible. These approaches differ, however, on the correct means for
attaining this goal. Whereas Pinchot left it to scientific foresters and other experts
to determine the correct policy, O'Toole trusts the workings of a competitive,
free, and open market to achieve this goal. Unlike Pinchot's forester, the role of
the economist is not to make substantive policy decisions but to help eliminate
barriers to the operation of the market. The economic marketplace is the most
appropriate means for attaining the utilitarian goal of maximal satisfaction of
wants.

O'Toole cites the work of environmental economists, especially John Baden
and Richard Stroup, to support his recommendations.[13] According to these
economists, it is a mistake to treat natural resources as "public goods" to be managed for the public welfare by experts. Instead, we should recognize that not
"every citizen benefits from his share of the public lands and the resources found
thereon." In leaving resource decisions to government bureaucrats and asking
them to make decisions for the public good, we assume that "culture can rewire
people, so that the public interest becomes self-interest."[14]

These economists argue that a market would be the most equitable and reasonable means for making these decisions. The market requires only those people

affected by a decision to participate in it, which makes it more equitable. Assuming that every person is motivated by self-interest, it is more reasonable. Ignoring the laws of the market has "caused most of the environmental destruction the United States has seen in this century."[15]

Specifically, how should U.S. Forest Service decisions mimic the market? The U.S. Forest Service should manage resources the way a private owner would seek to manage private property. Private owners use their property to maximize their self-interest. Baden and Stroup explain:

> If the buffalo is not mine until I kill it and I cannot sell my interest in the living animal to another, I have no incentive—beyond altruism—to investigate others' interest in it. I will do with it as I wish. But if the buffalo is mine and I may sell it, I am motivated to consider others' value estimate of the animal. I will misuse the buffalo only at my own economic peril.[16]

The U.S. Forest Service should seek to make a profit from its use of the national forests. According to the laws of economics, a profit is evidence that a decision is satisfying demand in an efficient manner. Maximum profit reflects the fact that those people who most value a resource—those who are willing to pay the most for it—have control of that resource. Thus O'Toole recommends that all U.S. Forest Service activities should be funded out of the profits, not the gross receipts, generated by those activities.

This would imply, first, that timber no longer would be offered for sale below cost. Selling timber rights to national forests on the open market would increase the cost of those rights. Following the economic law of supply and demand, this would decrease demand for timber, thereby increasing the amount of forestland available for wilderness, wildlife preservation, and recreation uses. Individuals who wish to use the national forests as wilderness areas or for recreational use will, of course, be required to pay for that use. These "user fees," in effect, will mean that competing users of the forests—timber, wilderness, and recreation—will be bidding against each other for access rights. By seeking to maximize the profits generated by the forests, the U.S. Forest Service will attain equilibrium between these competing interests. The group that most values the resource will be willing to pay the most for it, thereby achieving the most efficient use. The market optimally satisfies competing consumer demand. It provides Americans with "all the wilderness, timber, wildlife, fish, and other forest resources they want."

Consider how a free market analysis would decide the controversy over drilling for oil in the Gulf of Mexico. The likely result would be that the right to drill would be sold, ideally through an auction among competing oil companies. As in all auctions, presumably, the winning bid would be made by those who most value the property, and this would be the company that thinks it can best profit from the drilling by most efficiently managing it. Rights to harvest fish in the surrounding waters, if not the fish themselves, would also be auctioned, and ownership would likewise go to those who think they could best profit from it. So far, it would seem that the public is getting all the resources that they want.

But what of those people who do not want the oil drilling at all? Some oppose the drilling on aesthetic or other preservationist grounds. Environmental economists would argue that those people ought to enter the auction and try to purchase the land themselves. The fact that it is highly unlikely that preservationists could compete financially with oil companies demonstrates clearly that the use of the land as a resource for oil is more highly valued than alternatives, because the public is willing to pay more for oil than for yet more undeveloped shoreline. Consistent with utilitarian principles, drilling would seem the best way to create the greatest good for the greatest number.

Other opponents to the mine argue that it will create unreasonable risks to their fishing and recreational rights. Environmental economists have a straightforward answer to this concern as well. If fisheries are harmed by drilling operations, then the oil companies would owe the fishing owners compensation for their loss, as happened in the BP case. This compensatory requirement provides an incentive for the oil company to avoid polluting the Gulf of Mexico. The private property rights of the fishing community create restrictions on how the oil companies can use their land. In all cases, market forces work to ensure that natural resources are being used so that all interested parties get as much of the resources as they want, or at least, as much as they are willing to pay for.

This demonstrates, according to defenders of the free market, that the most efficient means for allocating scarce resources (that is, the way to give as many people as much of what they want as possible) is to rely on the workings of a competitive, open, and free market. Before analyzing these issues, let us turn to another environmental issue that also provides a common example of the use of economics in environmental policy.

3.4 POLLUTION AND ECONOMICS

Water and air pollution are among the most pressing environmental problems that we face. Few people anywhere in the world have not, at least at one point in their lives, been adversely affected by polluted water or air. But although people may be in wide agreement about the problem, they are in wide disagreement about the solution.

Part of the challenge in pollution issues lies with specifying the goal. Everyone wants clean water and clean air. But what exactly counts as *clean,* and what would we need to give up in order to attain it? Pure water with absolutely no contaminants exists in laboratories but nowhere in nature. What is clean air? The atmosphere contains nitrogen (78 percent) and oxygen (21 percent) and trace amounts of many other gases, water, and solids. How clean is clean?

Perhaps the only answer is that water and air are clean if they are safe for human consumption. But safety is not an all-or-nothing proposition. To determine safety, we need to identify, describe, and assess risks. To determine safety, we need to balance risks with benefits—something we do in many contexts every day. Is crossing a busy street safe? Is driving a car safe? Is it safe to eat food containing chemical preservatives?

It would seem that something is judged to be safe if its risks are judged acceptable—if its benefits outweigh its potential costs. When we express the issue in this way, we can see why treating pollution problems as economic problems is so tempting. How should resources be allocated so that maximum benefits are received from minimum costs? What are the costs and benefits of various levels of pollution?

In what has become a classic in environmental economics, William Baxter's *People or Penguins: The Case for Optimal Pollution* presented a market-based economic analysis of pollution.[17] In Baxter's words:

> To assert that there is a pollution problem or an environmental problem is to assert, at least implicitly, that one or more resources is not being used so as to maximize human satisfactions. In this respect at least environmental problems are economics problems, and better insight can be gained by application of economic analysis.[18]

Baxter begins his analysis by reviewing some of its basic assumptions. He values individual freedom so long as one person's actions "do not interfere with the interests of other human beings." He assumes that "waste is a bad thing" and, therefore, any resources that are "employed so as to yield less than they might yield in human satisfactions" are wasted.[19] He also assumes that human beings are the source of all value and that environmental policies ought to be "people-oriented."

He explains this point while discussing the threat posed to penguins by use of the pesticide DDT.

> My criteria are oriented to people, not penguins. Damage to penguins, or sugar pines, or geological marvels is, without more, simply irrelevant. One must go further, by my criteria, and say: Penguins are important because people enjoy seeing them walk about rocks…. I have no interest in preserving penguins for their own sake.[20]

With these assumptions, Baxter turns to an economic analysis of pollution. Denying that there is any "naturally good" state of air or water, he explains that "there is no normative definition of clean air or pure water, hence no definition of polluted air or of pollution, except by reference to the needs of man."[21] In a vein similar to the earlier discussion of risks, Baxter argues that "clean" air and water are whatever is judged acceptable by human beings. Too much pollution would be judged unacceptable by society, but so would too little pollution. Air and water that were totally free of any contaminants *could* be desirable, but their costs would be too high. In essence, society aims at a proper balance of risks, an "optimal level of pollution." This optimal level is "just those amounts that attend a sensibly organized society thoughtfully and knowledgeably pursuing the greatest possible satisfaction for its human members."[22] Reasoning consistently with much economic thinking, Baxter believes that the functioning of a free and competitive market would yield this "greatest possible amount of human satisfaction." How would this work?

Baxter reminds us that most decisions that we make involve tradeoffs. If I choose to do one thing, I give up something else. Every opportunity pursued involves other opportunities forgone. This captures the classic economic meaning of *costs*. The cost of something is equivalent to what must be given up to attain it. In Baxter's example, if we choose to build a dam, the resources that are used in building the dam cannot be used to build hospitals, fishing poles, schools, or electric can openers. Thus the cost of the dam is equivalent to alternative uses of those resources—labor, building materials, technological skills, capital, and energy—that have been forgone.

Accordingly, the costs of reducing water and air pollution should be understood in terms of those other goods that we would need to give up to accomplish this goal. In short, we need to make tradeoffs. Every resource devoted to reducing pollution is a resource not devoted to washing machines, hospitals, schools, B-1 bombers, and so forth. Left alone, markets would continue to make these tradeoffs so long as the result was a net increase in human satisfaction, and the benefits gained outweighed the additional costs. The optimal level of pollution is that point of equilibrium, at which the next trade-off made to reduce pollution results in a *decrease* in overall satisfaction. This is the point at which the resources used to fight pollution would have a higher value to society if used elsewhere.

Consider the following example of how this process might work. Suppose a community's drinking water showed contamination levels slightly above those recommended by health officials. Lowering the contamination below recommended levels would involve certain costs. In other words, tax monies diverted to this project could not be used to build a new school, fund road construction, and undertake other public works projects. Assume that this community decides that the benefits of reducing contamination outweigh the costs. The residents would rather have cleaner drinking water than newly paved roads, and they decide to make this trade-off. This decision results in a greater satisfaction of the community's desires than either the status quo or other alternatives.

Now, this community might also desire to have drinking water that is absolutely pure—water that is totally free of contaminants. The costs for this goal would be much higher. Other community projects would have to be sacrificed and tax rates raised. Eventually, the community must decide when to stop making these tradeoffs. This is the point at which water quality that is slightly improved is not worth the costs—not worth those other goods that would have to be given up to achieve this goal. At that point, any decision to obtain cleaner water would result in a net *decrease* in community satisfaction.

According to classical economics, arriving at this point of equilibrium between diverse and competing community desires should be the goal of public policy decisions. This is the point at which optimal satisfaction is achieved. People have more of what they want than they would have under any other allocation of resources. This is the "optimal level of pollution."

Baxter acknowledges that this may sound "so general and abstract as to be unhelpful."[23] However, this abstraction has accurately described just what results, at least in theory, from the workings of a free, open, and competitive marketplace. Economic analysis tells us that when people have the opportunity to exchange goods and services freely, when competition ensures that alternative choices exist, and when these individuals seek to maximize their own welfare, the result is an optimal satisfaction of desires. More people get more of what they most want through this process than they would under any other economic arrangement. According to Baxter, if individuals in a society are free to engage in whatever exchanges of resources are mutually satisfactory for themselves, then, at least in theory, every resource in society will be deployed in the way that yields the greatest possible human satisfaction.[24]

Thus Baxter's solution to the pollution problem, like O'Toole's solution to forest conservation problems, rests in the working of the free market. In both cases, economic analysis and methodology offer a diagnosis of environmental ills. Each case offers a particular economic prescription to cure those ills. A society that structures its economy to follow the principles of the free market will successfully meet all its environmental challenges.

3.5 ETHICAL ISSUES IN ECONOMIC ANALYSIS

Before turning to an analysis of these claims, we need to be clear about the issues involved. A first step of applied ethics is to identify and clarify the ethical issues at stake. As we saw in Chapter 1, turning to technical and objective disciplines such as economics can be an attractive option when one is faced with controversial environmental problems. Part of the reason for this lies in the belief that scientific and technical disciplines possess an objectivity that ethical and political discussions lack. According to this view, the scientific method offers precise and objective answers to our problems. Sciences such as economics are, in this view, value-neutral. A helpful starting point for our ethical analysis, therefore, is to show how these economic analyses are heavily influenced by value assumptions and to show that economic analysis is a value-laden analysis.

The ethical framework of classical economic analysis can be understood in terms of *ends* and *means*. The end of economic policy is the maximum satisfaction of individual desires or maximum happiness. The functioning of a free and competitive market is believed to be the ethically best means for attaining that end.

Economic analysis of environmental problems, as represented by the work of people like O'Toole and Baxter, thus assumes an essentially *utilitarian* ethics. The ultimate policy goal implicitly or explicitly assumed throughout these analyses is the utilitarian goal of maximizing the overall good. The specific understanding of that good and the specific means defended to attain that goal locate these views as a version of *preference utilitarianism*. Let us examine these claims more closely.

Perhaps Gifford Pinchot was most explicit in stating the utilitarian goals of his policies. Forest management, he said, sought the "greatest good for the greatest number for the longest time." O'Toole is less explicit but no less utilitarian. His recommendations aim to provide the American people with the maximum satisfaction of their wants in this regard. Baxter's recommendations seek to ensure that resources are "used so as to maximize human satisfactions." Thus, they all judge environmental policies in terms of their ability to produce certain beneficial consequences.

Pinchot believed that scientific management techniques could best lead us to this goal. O'Toole and Baxter argue that the workings of the marketplace are the most efficient means available. Their reasons for relying on the market suggest further value assumptions. Markets give priority to the wants that people actually express, as opposed to those interests that other people (for example, professional foresters) determine or assume that they have. That is, the market version of utilitarianism assumes that the best way to determine what is good for someone is to figure out what that person wants, and that the best way to learn this is to see what that person is willing to pay for in the marketplace.

To say that the market is the best way to determine what people want is to claim that it is not only the most efficient way (although for economists it certainly is that) but also the best way ethically. Why *should* public policy give priority to those preferences expressed in the market? We can find at least three philosophical answers to this question in O'Toole and Baxter.

First, market utilitarianism is thought to promote individual freedom. Baxter takes it as a "basic tenet of our civilization" that "every person should be free to do whatever he wishes in contexts where his actions do not interfere with the interests of other human beings."[25] He acknowledges that his market solution to environmental problems "stems from" this criterion. O'Toole explains that the market "preserves individual freedom since those who support and wish to participate in each activity may do so on the basis of willing consent."[26] The market is preferable to government regulation, for example, because the government "is based on coercive activity." Thus O'Toole and Baxter would reject Pinchot's reliance on experts as a threat to individual freedom of choice.

A second reason for supporting market solutions rests with a commitment to the value of private property rights. O'Toole tells us that "the marketplace is centered around the notion of private property.... For the market to work, private property rights to resources must be easily transferable.... The market works when rights are both privately held and easily transferable." Indeed, "most environmental problems, such as lack of protection for wildlife, air pollution, and poor water quality, are due to the lack of transferable property rights."[27] Therefore, market solutions to public policy questions will be reasonable only within a society that recognizes and values private property rights.

Finally, market solutions are consistent with certain philosophical assumptions about human nature. O'Toole identifies a major problem with the U.S. Forest Service as the "lack of incentive to be concerned." "The fundamental economic assumption," he tells us, is that "people's decisions are strongly influenced by the incentives affecting the decision makers" and that if we "change the incentives, the decisions change." As it stands, this seems trivially true. But what are these incentives? The answer can be found when O'Toole quotes the reasons offered by the new resource economists, Baden and Stroup, for rejecting Pinchot's nonmarket version. The national forests, for example, were created with the idea that "scientific foresters" employed by the public could objectively determine the method of management that best meets the public interest. But to assume that managers will be altruistic, say Stroup and Baden, it must be assumed "that culture can rewire people so that the public interest becomes self-interest." Instead, "Property rights theorists assume that the decision maker will maximize his own utility ... in whatever situation he finds himself."[28]

The fundamental assumption about human nature is that human beings act, primarily if not solely, on the basis of self-interest. Self-interest then is understood in the classic utilitarian sense of maximizing our own satisfactions or "utilities." Altruism, or acting for the best interests of others, would require that human nature be "rewired." In Baxter's words:

> It may be said by way of objection to this position, that it is very selfish of people to act as if each person represented one unit of importance and nothing else was of importance. It is undeniably selfish. Nevertheless I think it is the only tenable starting place for analysis for several reasons. First, no other position corresponds to the way most people really think and actually corresponds to reality.[29]

Thus, underlying the economic analyses described in this chapter are commitments to the values of individual freedom and private property rights and philosophical assumptions about human nature. Along with the clear utilitarian goal of providing the greatest good for the greatest number, these commitments clearly show the ethical and philosophical nature of economic analysis. Despite the popular misconception that they do so, economic analysis and methodology do not claim to offer us ethically neutral answers to environmental controversies.

These recommendations clearly make philosophical assumptions concerning several value issues. Thus this type of analysis lies within the domain of philosophical ethics. We now need to ask whether these analyses offer justifiable answers and recommendations.

3.6 COST-BENEFIT ANALYSIS

Cost-benefit analysis, a technique for deciding among alternative courses of action, is one essential aspect of much economic analysis. It is implicit in the evaluations of both O'Toole and Baxter. It is also at the center of recent public policy debates concerning such environmental controversies as global warming and oil drilling. Many critics argue that the environmental laws all need to be revised in ways that require government regulators to incorporate cost-benefit analysis into their decisions. For example, critics of the Endangered Species Act argued that before banning logging to protect the spotted owl, government regulators should have been required to prove that the benefits of protecting the owl outweighed the costs to loggers, timber companies, local communities, and others.

To its defenders, cost-benefit analysis requires an obvious and simple step: Before deciding on some course of action, we should determine that the benefits of that act outweigh the costs. It is simply unreasonable to do something if the costs are greater than the benefits. But cost-benefit analysis is neither as simple nor as value-neutral as it may seem.

Cost-benefit analysis differs from what is sometimes called cost effectiveness, and the distinction is important. Cost effectiveness directs us to pursue the most effective means to a given end. Thus, to use a simple example, if we are seeking to reduce the amount of contaminants in drinking water, a cost-effective analysis might compare the relative costs of a centralized water treatment plant to the installation of filters on home faucets. We should pursue whichever is more effective—that is, the alternative that achieves our ends at lower cost.

Cost-benefit analysis directs us to determine whether a given end is worth pursuing in light of its costs. In this strategy, both the means and the ends of our decisions are subjected to economic analysis. When we distinguish cost effective-ness from cost-benefit analysis, we can see that much of the commonsense appeal of the latter may actually be the result of confusion with cost effectiveness. Consider the following example.

Imagine that a child is diagnosed with an illness for which a variety of equally effective treatments are available. Cost effectiveness would direct us to follow the lowest-cost treatment (for example, choosing a generic version of a name-brand prescription). On the other hand, a cost-benefit approach would require that we compare the benefits (the child's health) with the costs and pursue whichever strategy maximizes net benefits. We would need to ask whether the child's health is worth the cost. Now, although (sadly) this question must sometimes be asked, asking it is by no means the obvious and commonsense way to proceed.

This raises a second major challenge to cost-benefit analysis. It is far from clear that all our values or goals can be or should be expressed in economic terms. Cost-benefit analysis requires that we compare the "benefits" with the costs. To avoid the old "apples and oranges" problem, the benefits and costs must be in the same category. That is, they must be expressible in economic terms. Ultimately, this means that we must express both in terms of dollars and cents. Despite some clever work by economists, it is not at all clear that this is possible.

For example, several years ago I was on a canoe trip in Canada's Quetico Park. To preserve this wilderness area, entrance is by permit alone and motorized boats are prohibited. As we checked in with a park ranger, we were asked to fill out a short questionnaire that would be used to help determine future park policies, including price and availability of permits. Among other things, this questionnaire asked what we would be willing to pay for permits if we could be assured of such benefits as seeing bald eagles and moose or not seeing other campers. Because no free and open market exists for such goods as permits, eagles, or moose, and because a cost-benefit analysis requires that these goods be assigned a price, someone must devise an elaborate scheme to figure out (some might say create) a cost for these benefits.

This only hints at the difficulty in trying to establish the costs for those benefits that are not traded on economic markets. But it also hints at another danger. Because markets do not exist for many environmental goods, such as clean air and water or an endangered species, the use of cost-benefit analysis seems to require that we rely on economists and other social scientists to tell us what the cost would be if there *were* markets for such goods. Note that in determining forest policy, for example, this means that we still rely on the decisions of "experts" rather than markets. However, this time the experts are economists (usually working in universities and industry), rather than foresters trained in science and ecology. Thus one alleged benefit of economic analysis—that it takes decisions out of the hands of "experts" and government bureaucrats and gives them back to individual citizens—is soon violated when economists are required to determine a price for nonmarket goods.

Finally, apart from the issue of whether we can establish the cost of many environmental benefits, there is a serious question about whether we should be doing this at all. As the example of the child's health suggests, there are some values that should not be reduced to their economic costs. Imagine conducting a cost-benefit analysis of democracy, or of friendship, or of the Grand Canyon. Further, cost-benefit analysis is usually totally anthropocentric. You will seldom hear economists speak of either the costs or the benefits to animals or to other natural entities. Perhaps we should not. But to adopt cost-benefit analysis without addressing these questions is to ignore important value-laden questions.

3.7 ETHICAL ANALYSIS
AND ENVIRONMENTAL ECONOMICS

To the degree that contemporary economic analyses of environmental problems reflect a utilitarian ethics, philosophers have much to offer in the evaluation of this ethical theory. Several standard criticisms, mentioned briefly in Chapter 2, are a useful starting point for this evaluation.

Utilitarians face several problems when they attempt to quantify and measure consequences. These problems arise again in the use of cost-benefit analysis. One aspect involves the attempt to quantify qualitative goods. We have seen, for example, the challenge posed by trying to determine standards for clean or safe water and air quality. These qualitative goods find no place in the economic approach, because they cannot be easily quantified. A second problem is the resulting tendency to translate qualitative goods into categories that can be measured. Thus we find Baxter translating discussions of cleanness and safety into a discussion of risks, the probabilities of which can be quantified and calculated. We find O'Toole, in a manner consistent with typical applications of the cost-benefit method, translating qualitative goods into economic terms. The value of wilderness or recreation areas is understood as measurable by the willingness of users to pay for them. A final measurement problem involves the tendency to artificially restrict the range of relevant subjects. As presented in the chapters that follow, some critics claim that this tendency systematically ignores the well-being of animals, future generations, trees, the biosphere, and the like. We examine the charge that the economic approach is overly anthropocentric, or human centered, in greater detail elsewhere. The general point of these measurement problems is to raise the possibility that economic analysis seriously distorts or ignores important environmental issues.

In the book *The Economy of the Earth,* Mark Sagoff develops an insightful and convincing case against the use of economic analysis as the dominant tool of environmental policymakers.[30] In the remainder of this chapter, we will use Sagoff's evaluation as an example of the best that applied ethics has offered. Although his book offers a variety of subtle and powerful arguments, we concentrate on three major challenges to the use of economic analysis.

Sagoff argues that much economic analysis rests on a serious confusion between wants or preferences, on the one hand, and beliefs and values on the other. Economics deals only with wants and preferences because these are expressed in an economic market. The market can measure the intensity of our wants by our willingness to pay (by price), measure, and compare individual wants (through cost-benefit analysis), and determine efficient means for optimally fulfilling wants. But markets cannot measure or quantify our beliefs or values. Because many environmental issues involve our beliefs and our values, economic analysis is beside the point. When economics is involved in environmental policy, it treats our beliefs as though they were mere wants and, thereby, seriously distorts the issue. In an early article, Sagoff makes the following claims:

> Economic methods cannot supply the information necessary to justify public
> policy. Economics can measure the intensity with which we hold our
> beliefs; it cannot evaluate those beliefs on their merits. Yet such evaluation is
> essential to political decision making. This is my greatest single criticism of
> cost-benefit analysis.[31]

What exactly is the distinction between wants and beliefs, and why is it important?

When individuals express a want or personal preference, they are stating something that is purely personal and subjective. Another person has no grounds to challenge, rebut, or support my wants. Wants are neither true nor false. If I express my preference for chocolate ice cream, someone cannot challenge that and claim, "No, you don't." I have a certain privileged status with regard to my wants. In the public sphere, they are taken as a given. This is the way economists treat human interests. Willingness to pay measures the intensity with which I hold my wants (I will not pay more than a few dollars for a dish of chocolate ice cream), but willingness to pay says nothing about the legitimacy or validity of that want.

Beliefs, on the other hand, are subject to rational evaluation. They are objective in the sense that reasons are summoned to support them. Beliefs can be true or false. It would be a serious mistake (a "category mistake" in Sagoff's terms) to judge the validity of a belief by a person's willingness to pay for it. To put a price on beliefs is to profoundly misunderstand the nature of belief.

Sagoff reminds us that when environmentalists argue that we ought to preserve a wilderness area or an Alaskan fishing ground for its aesthetic or symbolic meaning, they are not merely expressing a personal want. They are stating a *conviction* about a public good that should be accepted or rejected by others on the basis of reasons, not on the basis of who is most willing to pay for that public good. Because economics has no way to factor them into its analysis, beliefs and convictions are either ignored or treated as though they were mere wants.

Essentially, O'Toole's marketization solution to environmental problems does exactly this. Remember that O'Toole's goal is to provide all the wilderness and the like that the American people "want." But he equates this goal with what the American people (in their roles as timber users, hikers, hunters, and so forth) are willing to pay. If recreational users are unwilling to pay a user fee that is economically competitive with the fees paid by the timber industry, then by definition they must not want recreation as much as timber users want the lumber. Returning to the discussions at the beginning of this chapter, if preservationists in the Gulf of Mexico area are not willing to pay as much for the land as are the oil companies, then they must not want the wilderness as much as consumers want oil. Likewise, if a community is unwilling to spend any more tax money to reduce air and water pollution, its residents must not want cleaner air and water as much as they want lower taxes or other public projects.

This tendency to reduce all beliefs and values to wants and preferences also seriously distorts the nature of the human being. That distortion treats people at all times as *consumers*. People, at least insofar as the economist or policy maker is concerned, are simply the locations of a given collection of wants. People care only about satisfying their personal wants, and the role of the economist is to determine how to maximally attain this end.

The alternative that is ignored by economic analysis treats humans as thinking and reasoning beings. The market leaves no room for debate, discussion, or dialogue in which we can defend our beliefs with reasons. It ignores the fact that people are active thinkers, not merely passive "wanters." Most important, by ignoring the distinction between wants and beliefs, economic analysis reduces the most meaningful elements of human life—our beliefs and values—to matters of mere personal taste or opinion. To the degree that they are held with equal intensity, all desires equally deserve to be satisfied, no matter what the desire is.

This leads to a second major challenge to economic analysis. By ignoring the distinction between wants and beliefs, market analysis threatens our democratic political process. By treating us as always and only *consumers,* market analysis ignores our lives as *citizens.* As consumers, we may seek to satisfy personal wants. As citizens, we may have goals and aspirations that give meaning to our lives, determine our nature as a people and a culture, and define what we stand for as a people. Ours is a liberal democratic society—liberal in the sense that we value personal liberty to pursue our individual goals, but democratic in the sense that collectively we seek agreement about public goods and shared goals. Thus our political system leaves room for both personal *and* public interests. We are all, at one and the same time, both private individuals and public citizens. Market analysis ignores this public realm and thereby undermines our democratic political institutions.

According to Sagoff:

> Our environmental goals—cleaner air and water, the preservation of the wilderness and wildlife, and the like—are not to be construed, then, simply as personal wants or preferences; they are not interests to be "priced" by markets or by cost-benefit analysis, but are views or beliefs that may find their way, as public values, into legislation. These goals stem from our character as a people, which is not something we choose, as we might choose a necktie or a cigarette, but something we recognize, something we are. These goals presuppose the reality of public or shared values that we recognize together, values that are discussed and criticized on their merits and are not to be confused with preferences that are appropriately priced in markets. Our democratic political processes allow us to argue our beliefs on their merits.[32]

Economic analysis seems to assume a particular view of democracy wherein representatives passively follow the demands of the electorate, seeking to balance competing demands in a manner that satisfies the majority. The role of the politician in this model is to read the public opinion polls and act accordingly. But this neglects the more participatory nature of democracy in which citizens exchange views, debate their merits, learn from each other, and reach agreement.[33] The participatory model encourages a view of elected officials as active leaders rather than passive followers. We are committed not only to the personal freedom that Baxter's analysis assumes, but also to a system in which we mutually define and pursue a vision of the good life. A healthy, beautiful, undeveloped, and inspiring environment may not benefit me as a consumer, but it may be quite valuable to me as a citizen. This participatory model of democracy would reject the views of the new resource economists that O'Toole approvingly quotes: "It is a common misconception that every citizen benefits from his share of the public lands and resources found thereon."[34]

Many economists reject the notion of a public welfare or public good, because they view people solely as consumers. Not every citizen "consumes" the Alaskan wilderness, for example. But this fails to recognize that we are citizens as well as consumers and that we can benefit from the environment as citizens. The Alaskan wilderness can be valuable to us as citizens because of what it means to us, because of what it says about our self-image and self-respect. These benefits are not and cannot be priced in the market, so they are ignored by the type of economic analysis offered by O'Toole, the new resource economists, and Baxter.

A final challenge denies that economic analysis has any ethical basis at all. Despite the appearance that markets are committed to utilitarian ends, in actuality the goal of efficiency lacks any coherent and substantive ethical basis. Remember the role that economic analysis plays in many contemporary environmental issues. Unquestionably, economic and cost-benefit analyses are the major public policy methodologies used in reaching environmental decisions. Economics tells us as individuals, as a society, and as a government what we should do. Why should we follow this advice? Presumably because doing so will lead us to a better state of affairs. At first glance, this better state of affairs— economic efficiency—appears to be the utilitarian goal of providing the greatest good for the greatest number. But does economic efficiency provide the greatest good for the greatest number? Again, Sagoff is persuasive in claiming that it does not.

What is the goal of economic efficiency? As suggested earlier, efficiency implies optimal satisfaction of consumer preferences. An efficient market is one in which more people get more of that for which they are most willing to pay. But why should we, as a society and especially when we are concerned with environmental issues, take the satisfaction of individual preferences as our over-riding goal? Why should this be the goal of public policy, when we recognize the obvious and acknowledge that many individual preferences are silly, foolish, vulgar, dangerous, immoral, criminal, and the like? Why should we think that satisfying the preferences of a racist, criminal, fool, or sadist is a good thing?

What is so good about satisfying preferences? The only options seem to be that satisfying preferences is good in itself or that it is a means to something that is good. In terms that we used in describing utilitarianism in Chapter 2, prefer-ence satisfaction is either intrinsically good or instrumentally good. Given the wide variety of harmful, decadent, and trivial preferences that exist, surely no one could claim that satisfying preferences is good in itself. Surely it is not good in itself that child molesters or rapists have their preferences satisfied. If not good in itself, what other good is brought about instrumentally by satisfying preferences?

Typically, this economic approach uses such terms as *utility, welfare, well-being,* or *happiness* to explain the goal of satisfying preferences. However, to explain the value of preference satisfaction by simply defining it in these ways is to beg the question by offering a trivially true explanation. On the other hand, if utility, welfare, happiness, and well-being are more thoroughly defined, the claim that preference satisfaction always leads to these goods is false. Satisfying my preference for a cigarette does not always make me happy in a nontrivial sense. Sometimes having my preferences frustrated can be in my best interest by teaching me patience, diligence, or modesty. Sometimes satisfying preferences is disappointing. Sometimes I might have all that the market can supply, but I might still lack what is important ("What would it profit a man to gain the whole world if he loses his soul?"). The economic methodology assumes that all other things being equal, for people to get what they want is a good thing. A more realistic and honest assump-tion would seem to be that whether what I want is a good thing depends on what it is that I want.

Thus, even if (and it is a big *if*) economic analysis could overcome the mea-surement problems and all the other problems associated with applying market analyses to the real world, and if the market succeeded in attaining its goal, we still would have no reason for accepting preference satisfaction as an ethical goal. An efficient allocation of resources is not itself an ethical goal at all.

3.8 SUMMARY AND CONCLUSIONS

As we struggle with great environmental controversies, we must look beyond the economic market for a vision to guide policy decisions. Economic analysis cannot answer the fundamental ethical and philosophical questions that these controversies raise. The solution, according to Sagoff, is do the following:

> Recognize that utopian capitalism is dead; that the concepts of resource and welfare economics, as a result, are largely obsolete and irrelevant; and that we must look to other concepts and cultural traditions to set priorities in solving environmental and social problems. To set these priorities, we need to distinguish the pure from the polluted, the natural from the artificial, the noble from the mundane, good from bad, and right from wrong. These are scientific, cultural, aesthetic, historical, and ethical—not primarily economic—distinctions.[35]

Sagoff encourages us to do the hard thinking required to explain and justify environmental policy. We must explain why we value clean air and water, and we must justify why we value the preservation of wilderness areas. We must move beyond simply saying that these are things that we want or prefer and offer reasons that show their value and meaning.

But even Sagoff's alternative is restricted to the important interests of living human beings. The "scientific, cultural, aesthetic, historical, and ethical" values and beliefs tend to keep the environmental debate focused on the claims of the current generation of humans. In Chapter 4, we will see how environmental concerns lead us away from this narrow focus.

NOTES

1. Samuel Hays, *Conservation and the Gospel of Efficiency* (Cambridge, Mass.: Harvard University Press, 1959), pp. 41–42.

2. Gifford Pinchot, *The Training of a Forester* (Philadelphia: Lippincott, 1914), p. 13.

3. See Michael Cohen, *The Pathless Way* (Madison: University of Wisconsin Press, 1984), for a helpful study of John Muir. Chapters 6 and 7 especially provide an insightful introduction to many ethical aspects of Muir's thinking.

4. This may be too simple an interpretation of the conservation movement. An alternative view is defended by Samuel Hays in *Conservation and the Gospel of Efficiency* (Cambridge, Mass.: Harvard University Press, 1959). Hays argues that American business supported the conservation movement, recognizing that supporting it as a more enlightened, long-term economic self-interest served them better than fighting it. Pinchot's writings seem to me to suggest a strong anti-corporate sentiment. For an interpretation that supports my reading of Pinchot, see James Bates, "Fulfilling American Democracy: The Conservation Movement, 1907–1921," *Mississippi Valley Historical Review* 44 (June 1957). Whether early twentieth-century corporate America supported the conservation movement is irrelevant to the more general

point, however. Pinchot's progressivism was directed against a common nineteenth-century view that resources are there for the benefit of immediate economic exploitation. A more pragmatic interpretation, which seeks a common ground for environmentalists, is Bryan Norton, *Toward Unity among Environmentalists* (New York: Oxford University Press, 1991), especially Chapter 2.

5. Pinchot, The Training of a Forester, pp. 23–25.

6. http://www.fs.fed.us/aboutus/ meetfs.shtml (Retrieved March 20, 2011.)

7. Randal O'Toole, *Reforming the Forest Service* (Washington, D.C.: Island Press, 1988), p. 14.

8. Ibid., xi.

9. Ibid., xii.

10. Ibid., xi, 7.

11. Ibid., 101.

12. O'Toole quotes a more detailed study to support this claim. See Ronald Johnson, "U.S. Forest Service Policy and Its Budget," in *Forestlands: Public and Private*, ed. Robert Deacon and Bruce Johnson (San Francisco: Pacific Institute for Public Policy Research, 1985), pp. 103–33.

13. See especially Richard Stroup and John Baden, *Natural Resources: Bureaucratic Myths and Environmental Management* (San Francisco: Pacific Institute for Public Policy Research, 1983). The new resource economists offer policy analyses and recommendations based on neoclassical economics. They attribute most environmental problems to market failures and recommend policies that would mimic the workings of a competitive free market.

14. Ibid., 7, 29.

15. O'Toole, *Reforming the Forest Service,* p. 190.

16. Baden and Stroup, *Natural Resources: Bureaucratic Myths and Environmental Management*, p. 14.

17. William F. Baxter, *People or Penguins: The Case for Optimal Pollution* (New York: Columbia University Press, 1974).

18. Ibid., 17.

19. Ibid., 5.

20. Ibid.

21. Ibid., 8.

22. Ibid.

23. Ibid., 27.

24. Ibid.

25. Ibid., 2.

26. O'Toole, *Reforming the Forest Service,* p. 189.

27. Ibid., 188–90.

28. Ibid., 190.

29. Baxter, *People or Penguins: The Case for Optimal Pollution*, p. 5.

30. Mark Sagoff, *The Economy of the Earth* (New York: Cambridge University Press, 1990).

31. Mark Sagoff, "Economic Theory and Environmental Law," *Michigan Law Review* 79 (1981): 1393–1419.

32. Sagoff, *The Economy of the Earth*, pp. 28–29.

33. For an examination of representative and participatory democracy, see Jane Mansbridge, *Beyond Adversarial Democracy* (New York: Basic Books, 1980).

34. O'Toole, *Reforming the Forest Service,* p. 189.

35. Sagoff, *The Economy of the Earth*, p. 22.

DISCUSSION QUESTIONS

1. Review the distinction between *conservation* and *preservation*. In the debate concerning Hetch Hetchy, would you support Pinchot's conservationist policies or Muir's preservationist policies? What values underlie your decision?

2. The Rolling Stones used this lyric, "You can't always get what you want." Is that a bad thing? Should government policy always seek to supply people with what they want? Should government play a role in teaching citizens which wants are of value and which are not, or should government remain neutral on such questions?

3. Should government agencies such as the U.S. Forest Service aim to make a profit? Why or why not? If you were director of the U.S. Forest Service, how would you understand your role of serving the public?

4. It has been suggested that one way to protect endangered species such as the blue whale would be to sell them to the highest bidder. In this view, only unowned species are threatened with extinction. Species that are owned, such as chickens and cows, seldom face extinction because people (their owners) have a strong incentive (profit) for keeping them around. Property rights would ensure a similar protection for all endangered species. Do you think it would be wise to sell exclusive whaling rights to Norwegian, Russian, or Japanese whalers?

5. Baxter claims that "penguins are important because people enjoy seeing them." Do you agree? Is this the only reason why penguins should be protected?

6. Is human nature "undeniably selfish," as Baxter claims? Can you think of any situations in which people do not act selfishly? In answering this question, be careful to distinguish between a *reason* for acting and the *feelings* that follow from acting.

GLOBAL ENVIRONMENTAL ETHICS WATCH

For more information on Environmental Ethics as Applied Ethics, please see the Global Environmental Ethics Watch. Updated several times a day, Global Environmental Ethics Watch is a focused portal into GREENR—our Global Reference on the Environment, Energy, and Natural Resources—an ideal one-stop site for current events and research. You will have access to the latest information from trusted academic journals, news outlets, and magazines as well as access to statistics, primary sources, case studies, videos, podcasts, and much more.

To gain access please use the access code that accompanies your book. If you do not have an access code, visit cengagebrain.com to purchase one.

4

Sustainability and Responsibilities to the Future

It would be difficult to find almost any institution in contemporary culture that has not in some way attached itself to the idea of sustainability. We find "sustainable" used to modify: agriculture, architecture, business, buildings, construction, communities, consumerism, development, economics, ecosystems, forestry, marketing, investing, transportation, and on and on. The concept of sustainability is everywhere. Thousands of corporations, for example, have replaced the traditional corporate annual report with an annual sustainability report. But one should be leery when any idea is so ubiquitous, especially when it was originally introduced as a critical alternative to the status quo. Has "sustainability" lost its meaning? Is it only a passing fad; or worse, is it a smokescreen behind which anything goes?

As most commonly used today, the concept of sustainability is about 30 years old. It is traced to a United Nations

commission that studied questions of economic development, environmental protection, and future generations in the 1980s. Named for its chairman, former Norwegian Prime Minister Gro Harlem Brundtland, the Brundtland Commission focused on long-term strategies that might help nations achieve economic development without jeopardizing the earth's capacity to sustain all life. The Brundtland Commission published its findings in 1987 in a book titled *Our Common Future*, which offered what has become the standard definition of sustainable development: "sustainable development is development that meets the needs of the present without compromising the ability of future generations to meet their own needs." Beginning with this report, the concept of sustainability and sustainable development has guided much of the world's thinking about global economic growth and development.

In some ways, sustainability is an intuitively clear idea. A practice is sustainable if it can continue indefinitely. A simple example comes from finance. Putting money into savings and spending only the interest generated from those savings exemplifies a sustainable budgeting practice. Spending down the principal, as well as spending the principal and the interest, is unsustainable. The income will decrease as the savings are spent, and thus the income will run out eventually. Aesop's fable about the goose that laid the golden egg captures a similar insight. Limiting your consumption to the golden eggs is sustainable; eating the goose itself is not.

Sustainability also has a certain ethical intuitiveness. As discussed in Chapter 2, rights are sometimes explained in terms of protecting those central human interests that we identify as needs. In this sense, we might explain human rights in terms of every person having a right to what she needs. Therefore, the Brundtland Commission's definition of sustainability seems simply to assert that this same human right should be extended not only to every person presently alive, but to future generations as well. Sustainability in this sense seems just another way to say that equal opportunity should extend to people not yet living.

Similarly, the Brundtland Commission's economic goal had a certain intuitive appeal. Economic development as practiced throughout the twentieth century, if not throughout most of human history, treated the productive capacity of the earth as if it were infinite. But in the late twentieth century, all signs are that human consumption is approaching the limits of that productive capacity. It is as if we are beginning to look hungrily at the goose itself rather than just at its eggs. The Brundtland Commission's call for sustainable development, rather than simple unrestricted growth, was a call for us to dial back on both the quantity and quality of our consumption.

Sustainability is thus often characterized in terms of three fundamental categories, frequently called the "three pillars of sustainability" or the "triple bottom line." Sustainability has an economic dimension that concerns production and distribution of goods and services to meet human needs. Economic sustainability implies that we not use productive resources, such as capital, labor, and natural resources at rates faster than those at which they can be replenished. But sustainability also has both an environmental dimension and ethical dimension that restricts this economic activity to activities that do not degrade the biosphere in such a way that people are denied in the future an equal right to meet their own needs. There are three pillars of sustainability: economic, environmental, and ethical.

From one perspective, the explosion of attention now paid to sustainability is good news. The optimistic view is that people worldwide have understood the call to sustainable practices and that global economic development is evolving in a way that is promising for the future. The hopes that were implicit in the Brundtland report seem to be coming to fruition. But skeptics remain unconvinced.

Some who are sympathetic to the goals of Brundtland Commission, interpret the universal attention to sustainability and the explosion of businesses and countries that now identify with sustainability as an indication that something is amiss. To understand this skepticism we should ask, "What is being sustained?" It seems clear that some who have jumped on the sustainability bandwagon believe that the status quo is what we should sustain. To commit to sustainability means that I commit to finding ways to keep doing what I am doing. But, if sustainable development was introduced as an alternative to the status quo, if the present patterns of consumption, production, and growth are what has led to the present predicament in which we find ourselves bumping up against the limits of growth, then it should be clear that not everything that we are presently doing can be "sustained." Some critics, for example, would argue that sustainability cannot be applied to the consumption patterns of industrial societies such as the United States, or to an energy industry built on fossil fuels. Finding consumer giants such as Walmart, or oil companies such as BP, claiming allegiance to sustainability convinces these critics that the concept has been severely corrupted.

In a similar vein, other critics claim that sustainability is unjust if it implies that the path to economic development enjoyed by the western industrialized countries is no longer open to the developing world. If sustainability means sustaining the status quo for the present alignment of the world's economies, then countries such as China, India, Brazil, Pakistan, Russia, and Indonesia decidedly are not in favor of sustainability. These critics interpret the West's call for sustainable development as the rich telling the poor that they should be satisfied with what they have and find another way to prosperity.

Other critics doubt the very foundations of the sustainability movement. Sustainability is built on the assumptions that there are limits to growth, that we have a responsibility not to put future generations at a disadvantage in meeting their needs, and that the best way to fulfil that responsibility is to adopt policies that limit growth. Each of these assumptions can be challenged.

The sustainability movement takes as a given the assumption that resources are limited. But some argue that this misrepresents the nature of resources. Human beings do not value natural resources for their own sake, but for the services that they provide to us. There is no value in oil itself, for example; oil is valued only in so far as it can be used to provide us with energy for transportation, electricity, and heat. If we discover some substitute for oil, solar power for example, then all the oil reserves in the world will lose their value. In economic terms, natural resources are fungible; their value is equal to whatever substitute they can be traded for. Economics teaches us that as the supply of one resource declines, its price will increase which, in turn, will provide greater incentives for human creativity to find a substitute. For example, as the supply of oil declines, its price will rise, which will make alternative energy sources such as solar power more competitive. Eventually, the cost differential will shift demand from oil to solar, which will create a market for solar, which in turn will creative efficiencies that will drive down the price of solar.

From this perspective, the only resource we should value without hesitation is human creativity and ingenuity. Importantly, these human characteristics are likely to flourish more in a society which is prospering, a society in which education and technology are expanding, a society which uses its resources for today, rather than saving them for tomorrow, so that we create added incentives and opportunities for creative solutions to today's problems. In short, we could best serve future generations by using our resources at present to support the most vibrant and creative society possible.

DISCUSSION TOPICS:

1. Can you think of a business or industry that is not sustainable? Why do you think it is not? How could it be made sustainable?

2. Should present generations sacrifice for the well-being of future generations? Why or why not? Does posterity have rights, and do we have duties to people who do not even exist?

3. Do all presently living people bear the same degree of responsibility to future generations, or does that vary depending on such things as wealth or citizenship?

4. Do you consider your own lifestyle, or the lifestyle of your family, sustainable?

5. It is obvious that people can have such emotions as love, empathy, and compassion, and that they can be motivated to help, their children and grandchildren. It is also understandable that we might feel such emotions for, and be motivated to help, people living in distant lands, even if we don't know them personally. But can we feel such emotions for, and be motivated to help, people living in distant future generations?

4.1 INTRODUCTION

As mentioned in the opening discussion case, the Brundtland Commission defined sustainable development as: "development that meets the needs of the present without compromising the ability of future generations to meet their own needs." Beginning with this U.N. report, the concept of sustainability and sustainable development has guided much of the world's thinking about global economic growth and development. Since that time, it has been taken as a given within environmental circles that the present generation does have ethical responsibilities to future generations.

Thus, sustainable development raises important ethical questions that are both *intra*generational, and *inter*generational. That is, meeting the needs of the present generation requires that we make judgments about the ethical legitimacy of how economic and environmental benefits and burdens are distributed across presently living people and societies. For example, in addressing global climate change, should developing countries be held to the same CO_2 emission standards as industrialized countries? Is it fair that less developed countries be denied the opportunity to attain the consumerist lifestyle of the developed world? But sustainability also raises ethical questions about the distribution of economic and environmental benefits and burdens across generations. Do we have an ethical obligation to help posterity meet their needs, even if that means that we need to sacrifice some of our own interests in doing so?

But thinking about responsibilities to future generations can quickly become puzzling. First, any discussion of future happiness or the rights of people of the future forces us to consider who those future generations might be and what they will be like. Because those people do not exist and because we do not know which people will ever exist, it is difficult to understand how we can even talk about responsibilities to them. Yet we must talk about such responsibilities, if we are to ask present generations to make significant sacrifices for the benefit of future generations. Thus an initial philosophical challenge concerns the plausibility of the very concept of having responsibilities to people who do not now and may never exist. Only after having established that we do have responsibilities to future generations can we address the question of what those responsibilities are. This chapter will examine a range of ethical issues that arise as we think about responsibilities across generations.

Beginning in the late 1960s, population growth became a major focus of environmental concern. *The Population Bomb,* a 1968 best-selling book by Paul Ehrlich, argued that exploding population growth was responsible for widespread environmental destruction. Others, such as Barry Commoner in his 1971 book *The Closing Circle,* argued that the consumption-driven lifestyle of industrial societies, rather than population size *per se,* was more responsible.[1] These debates are summarized in a formula that is still widely used in environmental discussions: $I = PAT$. This formula acknowledges three major variables affecting environmental impact. I (environmental impact) depends on population (P), consumption patterns and affluence (A), and technology (T).

In some obvious ways, growth in population does increase the environmental damage caused by humans and makes present lifestyles less sustainable. An increasing *number* of people requires providing more energy, homes, food, and jobs, and this creates more trash, pollution, and development. All other things being equal, the more people that exist, the greater the challenge will be to meet the needs of the present and the less likely future generations will be able to meet their own needs. More people means that a greater number will suffer from, and contribute to, pollution, resource depletion, and global warming.

Environmental devastation is intensified when the economic growth required by these increasing populations includes a consumerist lifestyle and environmentally destructive technologies. In industrialized countries such as the United States, environmental damage per capita is higher than in many less developed countries. For example, with less than 5 percent of the world's population, the United States uses 33 percent of the world's nonrenewable energy and mineral resources and contributes more than 20 percent of the carbon dioxide emissions. As less developed countries pursue the higher standard of living attained by the industrialized countries, threats to the environment increase significantly.[2]

Given clear signs that environmental impact, *I,* already is approaching a crisis stage, the ethical challenge of sustainability is to address each of the three major variables *P, A,* and *T.* Is there some ethically preferable population goal? If so, what are the philosophical grounds for establishing this goal, and what policies should be promoted to attain it? Do humans have an obligation to refrain from having babies? Do people in the industrialized countries of the world consume too much? Is it unjust that the richest 16 percent of the world's population consumes 80 percent of the world's resources? Do people in the industrialized world have direct ethical obligations to the world's poor? Does the present generation have responsibilities to preserve resources for future generations? Do we have a responsibility to avoid technologies such as nuclear power that might put future generations at risk?

4.2 DO WE HAVE RESPONSIBILITIES
TO FUTURE GENERATIONS?

Several arguments have been offered against the view that we do have responsibilities to future generations. The two major arguments are called the "argument from ignorance" and the "disappearing beneficiaries" argument. Because one assumption underlying many environmental issues, and in particular the idea of sustainability, is that it is meaningful and reasonable to talk about the needs of, and our obligations to, future generations, it will be helpful to consider these arguments in depth.

The "argument from ignorance" stresses that we know little about people of the future.[3] We do not know *who* they will be, *that* they will be, *what* they will be like, or what their needs, wants, or interests will be. Because we know so little about them, it makes little sense to try to specify any obligations to them that we might have. Because we are ignorant of their needs, we should not be expected to sacrifice our real needs for future assumed needs.

However, it is difficult to see why we should draw this conclusion. Surely we have a fairly good idea about what people of the future will need and what their interests will be if they are to have a reasonably good life. Minimally, this would include an adequate supply of clean air and water, a moderate climate, protection from poisons and disease, and so forth. For example, we know the science behind radiation and how it affects living beings. We also know that nuclear waste will remain toxic for many thousands of years. Thus, for as long as human biochemistry remains the same, exposure to nuclear radiation will pose a danger to human beings and future generations, whoever they are, will need to be protected from nuclear wastes.

Further, we already acknowledge responsibilities that parallel those to future generations. In civil law, we hold people responsible for actions that result in unintended but foreseeable harms to others. For example, imagine that someone establishes a toxic waste dump on a piece of property. Imagine that a few years later, escaping toxins poison neighbors of the dump. Imagine that the polluter offers a defense based on the argument from ignorance: "I did not know who would be hurt, I did not even know for certain that anyone would be hurt, and I surely did not know that these people would have a particular interest in health. How can I be said to have had an obligation to them?" Just as in cases of legal negligence, where we hold people liable for unintended but foreseeable and avoidable harms that occur in the future, it is meaningful to talk about foreseeable but unknown harms to future generations.

A second argument against the view that we have responsibilities to future generations has been called the argument from "disappearing beneficiaries." This perspective argues not only that we have no responsibility to bring future generations into existence but also that it is meaningless even to talk about ethical obligations to future generations.[4] The short version of this claim holds that we can have no obligation (based on either the utilitarian "maximum happiness" principle or deontological duties to respect the rights of future generations) to bring a generation into existence, because there are no particular people to whom that responsibility is directed.

Consider the following policy debates about global warming. In 1997, representatives from 160 of the world's nations met in Kyoto, Japan, to consider proposals that would significantly limit the amount of greenhouse gases discharged into the atmosphere. This conference followed a 1992 agreement at the "Earth Summit" in which industrialized countries pledged to reduce greenhouse gas emissions to 1990 levels. At the Kyoto conference, the United States proposed a plan that would not meet the 1990 levels, arguing that a significant reduction of greenhouse gases would have disastrous economic repercussions.

Many environmentalists argued that we ought to accept these short-term consequences in order to protect the interests of future generations. Many people argued that we need to reduce our reliance on fossil fuels to ensure a world protected from global warming in the future. Intuitively, we might say that reducing greenhouse emissions is the ethically preferable decision because those people born into that world will be better off than they would have been if we had maintained the status quo and continued our heavy reliance on fossil fuels. "Better off than they would have been" assumes that these very same people would have existed if we had chosen the alternative. The moral intuition underlying this decision is that one set of people of the future will be either harmed or benefited by our decisions.

But alternative policy decisions, especially those as significant as what would be required to achieve major reductions in carbon dioxide emissions, will surely result in *different* people being born. According to this objection, the existence of any one person is dependent on a remarkable number of contingencies. (Imagine all the events that might have prevented your parents or great-grandparents from meeting or caused them to postpone the moment of conception by a year, a month, or even a minute.) Thus alternative policy decisions will result in two sets of people of the future, not one: those who will be born if we choose policy A, and those who will be born if we choose policy B. (Of course, this simplifies the issue. Alternative policies adopted at Kyoto would be only a few of the many factors that determine who is born.) Because the group that would be harmed by one choice would not exist unless we made that choice, it makes little sense to say that they would be better off, if we had made the other choice (hence they are "disappearing beneficiaries"). Because different policy decisions result in different future generations, there simply is no one single future generation that would be made better or worse off by either decision.

Consider the following two responses to the "disappearing beneficiaries" argument. Philosopher Annette Baier argued that we can make sense of the claim that someone is made worse off by our actions even if, under the alternative action, that person would not have existed at all. On the one hand, we can acknowledge the significance of a "wrongful life," a life in which the person can say, "I would have been better off not being born."[5] We can imagine a world so polluted and so miserable that a population would acknowledge that its members would have been better off had they not lived and suffered at all. Further, the concept of moral rights provides us with a way to explain "worse off" even when the alternative is nonexistence.

If we acknowledge that all humans have and will continue to have rights to certain goods or to have certain interests protected, then our actions today may violate the rights of people of the future. Thus, if we continue to dump massive amounts of pollutants into the atmosphere, we harm people of the future not by making them worse off than they would have been but by violating their rights. That is, we have failed in our duty to provide those people, whoever they turn out to be, with a certain moral minimum. These people can say that they were harmed, not because *they* would have been better off in some other future but because, in the future in which they do exist, our actions jeopardized certain central interests of theirs (for example, health). In this sense, our obligations are not to any particular people of the future but to the interests that those people, whoever they turn out to be, will have. These interests do not disappear with alternative decisions.

Philosopher Mary Anne Warren developed a somewhat different response.[6] Warren distinguished between "possible people," those people who could but do not necessarily exist, and "future people," those people who will exist in the future. Warren acknowledges that it is absurd to suggest that we have obligations to merely "possible" people. Because the number of possible people is infinite, that view makes little sense. But we can meaningfully compare the happiness or suffering of "future people." We can do this because we can compare "types of human life" and recognize that a life of suffering is worse than a life of happiness. Thus, although any one particular potential beneficiary may "disappear" under alternative decisions, the relative amount of suffering or happiness does not. Our obligations to future generations, in this view, are not obligations to specific possible people but are obligations to "recognize certain *minimal requirements of moral responsibility*." As Warren sees it, "It is irresponsible, and contemptuous of the welfare of future persons, to deliberately bring into being persons who will almost certainly be unhappy. It is wrong because it results in unnecessary suffering in the future, suffering on the part of individuals [future people] who in the timeless perspective are no less real than we are."[7] Thus, following Baier and Warren, it can be meaningful to talk about responsibilities to future generations. We have good grounds for believing that our actions today can be restricted by ethical obligations that we owe to people of the future.

Thus, although the view that the present generation has responsibilities to future generations raises some real puzzles, it does seem that we can meaningfully talk about such responsibilities. We have good reason to believe that people will exist in the future and that they will be similar enough to us that we can have a good idea what their well-being requires. Knowing this and knowing that our present actions can influence their future well-being, it is reasonable to conclude that presently living humans must give ethical consideration to future people. Let us now consider the content of those responsibilities.

4.3 WHAT DO WE OWE FUTURE GENERATIONS?

Assuming that we can meaningfully be said to have responsibilities to future generations, what do we owe them and how do we decide where those responsibilities lie? What is the ethical basis of these responsibilities? This section answers the question from the perspective of three ethical traditions: utilitarian ethics, a rights-based approach, and an ethics of care.

As we saw when we discussed Warren's position, one way to answer these questions is to focus on minimizing unnecessary suffering. A utilitarian and intuitively plausible view would suggest that we minimally have an obligation to reduce the suffering of future generations and optimally an obligation to maximize their happiness. The attempt to specify this obligation further has led to some problems, however.

Might someone argue on utilitarian grounds that although we do have responsibilities to people of the future, those responsibilities are overridden by the interests of people presently alive? Certainly, if we were concerned with the basic interests of people of the present generation—their interests in life, health, and liberty for example—and with the less basic interest of future people to live a comfortable life, then it would be reasonable for present interests to override future interests. But what of cases in which the basic interests of future people are jeopardized by less important interests of the present? Some argue that present interests always override future interests because, being uncertain about the latter, we must discount them.

The idea of discounting the interests of people of the future has roots in the classical utilitarianism of Jeremy Bentham. Bentham argued that uncertain or remote pleasures count for less than certain and immediate ones. This practice of discounting future interests finds a contemporary expression in the economic concept of discounting the present value of future payments. In this view, one dollar held now is worth more than one dollar held at some time in the future, because we could invest that dollar today, earn interest on it, and therefore have more than one dollar at that future date. Thus future dollars must be "discounted" in order to be equivalent to present value. As a result, the practice of discounting future interests is common in economic analyses of environmental issues.

As we noted in Chapter 3, economic analysis is the methodology most commonly used in deciding public policy. Thus what may seem like an abstract and arcane concept ends up playing a significant role in environmental policy. One implication of this practice, for example, might require us to maximize the present value of our resources by using them now and discounting their value to later generations. Thus we actually fulfil our responsibility to future people by getting the most we can out of our resources now.[8]

Two immediate considerations cast doubt on the logic of discounting future interests. First, no matter how small the discount rate, any discounting eventually reduces future values to nothing. Eventually, we would be committed to saying that future people do not count at all. Second, it would seem that some values, such as health and life, should not be discounted in any case. A single dollar possessed by my great-great-grandchild may be worth less (in purchasing power) than a single dollar that I possess, but it would be peculiar to claim that my great-great-grandchild's life (assuming that my children and their children's children have children) will be worth less than my life.

Philosopher Mary Williams has developed a strong case against the discounting of future interests on utilitarian grounds.[9] Williams argues that discounting the future value of resources can be consistent with utilitarian goals, so long as those resources remain to produce value in the future. In that case, maximizing present value also maximizes the total overall value, because in the future these resources will continue to produce value. However, when resources with future value can be removed from production, as happens when current generations deplete nonrenewable resources (or deplete renewable resources at a rate below sustainability), the total overall good is not maximized.

Thus Williams's argument provides a utilitarian basis for the type of sustainable development described by the Brundtland Commission. The essential point of this argument, for our purposes, is this: In calculating the future consequences of our current environmental policies, policy makers have a tendency to rely on the economic practice of discounting future values (costs and benefits). As we saw in Chapter 3, the ethical basis of this approach is a version of utilitarianism. However, even on utilitarian grounds, discounting social value in environmental cases oftentimes frustrates rather than promotes maximum total happiness. This occurs because those resources that would produce the future value are being depleted to the point of extinction by our current policies. Williams's claim is that rather than living off the interest of our "investments," we too often are spending our savings so that, eventually, we will have no savings left to generate interest payments. This point is reminiscent of the lesson of golden goose fable described in the opening discussion case.

Her alternative is to defend an environmental policy of "maximum sustainable yield." That is, we should seek to maximize the present return on our investments (for example, our environmental and agricultural resources) without jeopardizing the investments themselves. We should, in economists' parlance, live off our interest, not our capital. To use an agricultural image, we should seek to maximize the yield of our croplands in a manner that guarantees that the cropland will continue to be productive for the indefinite future. Sustainable practices enable us to maximize overall well-being into the indefinite future, clearly the optimal utilitarian result. By discounting future values, we make it too easy for the current generation to spend its capital as well as its interest and thereby fall short of long-term optimal happiness.

A second problem with utilitarian accounts of our responsibility to future people is less easily overcome. Suppose we adopt a utilitarian view and argue that we have a responsibility to maximize the happiness of future generations. Should that "maximal happiness" commit us to increasing the *total overall* happiness or the *average* happiness?[10] This distinction is not as important to utilitarianism when we restrict our concerns to today, because given a constant population, total and average happiness amount to the same thing. However, when we recognize that one of our decisions regarding future generations concerns *how many* future people there will be, we see that the distinction between total and average happiness is quite important.

For example, suppose we elect the total happiness view and adopt environmental policies aimed at increasing total future happiness. One implication of this view may well commit us to *increasing* future population size. This seems to commit us to what Derek Parfit has called the "repugnant conclusion."[11] So long as overall world happiness is increased, we ought to create as many people as possible. Thus we might be obligated to create a world with billions and billions of marginally happy people rather than a world with a much smaller population of much happier people. (Or suppose we were committed to a world in which *total* suffering was minimized. Might such a future world contain *no* human beings? Might our obligation under this view be to refrain from having any children?)

The total happiness alternative does not appear to be attractive. It seems to commit us to sacrificing the happiness of individual people of the future to an abstract notion of some total overall happiness. Is it permissible to cause the existence of countless people who will suffer, so long as the overall amount of world happiness increases?

On the other hand, the average happiness view also might place us on a slippery slope to a particularly repugnant conclusion. It might be argued that because people living in impoverished, non-industrialized countries will produce future generations that would probably not increase average happiness, population policy ought to restrict the reproductive freedom of the world's poor. Those countries with relatively high standards of living, and with access to plentiful and affordable food, health care, education, resources, and energy, would have an ethical claim to reproductive priority. Those countries in which a person's life prospects are relatively low (even if still moderately happy) should be required to lower birth rates. Minimally, this appears to imply assigning an unfair priority to the status quo. The rich get richer, and the poor get contraception.

It would seem that defenders of the average happiness view need to say more about the *distribution* of both happiness and the resources necessary to achieve happiness. Note that this problem is a version of the justice criticism raised against utilitarianism in Chapter 2. This criticism, along with problems of discounting the lives of future people, suggests that perhaps a deontological and rights-based account of responsibility to future people will be more satisfactory.

As we have seen, discounting the interests of future people allows us to override their interests in life and health with our interests in a comfortable lifestyle. Ordinarily, we would think that life and health are rights that should trump mere comfort. Philosophers who take seriously the rights of future generations (or our obligations to them) deny that we can override the central interests of future people. The distribution challenge to the total happiness and average happiness views also suggests that we violate the rights of future people to equal treatment and equal opportunity. Thus the question has become "Can future generations be said to have rights and, if so, what rights do (would) they have?"

Is it meaningful to say that future generations have rights *now*? If we tend to think of rights as some sort of attribute that belongs to people and exists in the world to be discovered, it is difficult to see how that claim could be defended. If the rights-holders do not exist, how could they have rights? But if we think of rights in terms of their *function,* assigning rights to future generations becomes more logical. Rights function to limit the behavior of other people. My rights limit your behavior by imposing certain obligations on you. Rights limit behavior in order to protect certain basic interests of the rights-holder.

But the attempt to specify the rights of people of the future would seem to encounter serious difficulties. Let us use the example of conserving resources. By definition, any use of nonrenewable resources means that others will have less available for their use. But if present generations have a duty to conserve out of respect for the rights of the near future generations, ought they not to conserve out of respect for the rights of even more distant future generations? If the near future has the right to use these resources, why do not we?

Philosopher Brian Barry provides an interesting response to these problems.[12] Barry's position is to allow current generations to continue to use nonrenewable resources, even if this means placing future generations at a relative disadvantage, so long as we compensate those people for causing them this disadvantage. Barry holds that, at a minimum, justice requires equal treatment. When we use nonrenewable resources, we are denying future generations the equal opportunity to use those resources.

Justice demands that denials of equality be compensated. We cannot compensate future generations for the loss of resources by returning those things to them, but we can compensate them for the loss of those opportunities and choices that require those resources. The central human interest lies not in the resources themselves (for example, oil, gas, and coal) but in those uses to which we put energy resources. They and we use natural resources to produce the goods and services that we need. Barry says it is the loss of an equal opportunity to use these goods (the loss of this "productive capacity") that requires compensation.

We can now venture a statement of what is required by justice toward future generations. As far as natural resources are concerned, depletion should be compensated for in the sense that later generations should be left no worse off (in terms of productive capacity) than they would have been without the depletion.[13] Interestingly, such a conclusion closely parallels the more utilitarian conclusions concerning maximum sustainable yield defended by Mary Williams, and it closely matches the responsibility to the future advocated by the Brundt-land Commission. Our responsibility to people of the future is not to provide them with specific goods or resources but, rather, to provide them with equal and fair opportunities. Future people should have the same opportunity that we have had to live healthy, happy, and satisfactory lives. The basic interests of future people are no more, and no less, importantly ethical than our own.

Barry acknowledges that many practical difficulties are involved in specifying what would be required to offset the loss of productive capacity. Nevertheless, we can infer some implications. Because the resources that we are using are relatively accessible, we owe future generations capital and technological investments that will pay future dividends in terms of their ability to find and extract natural resources. Presumably, we also owe them an investment in research and development of alternative energy sources and sustainable agriculture. It would also seem reasonable to say that we owe them as large an inheritance of natural resources as is practical. Wasting any resource is a particularly callous violation of their right to equal opportunity.

What other conclusions might we draw from this discussion of our responsibilities to future generations? I offer three. First, we have the responsibility to make a sincere and serious effort to develop alternative energy sources. The risks of continued reliance on fossil fuels and nuclear power are real. We can reasonably foresee the dangers that follow from reliance on these energy sources, and it is within our power to minimize them. Failing to take steps to avoid these dangers is on a par with criminal negligence.

Second, we have the duty to conserve resources. At current rates, we will use up the known reserves of fossil fuels and uranium within two hundred years. Wasting these resources, especially when known technology can increase efficiency, so that we can conserve without significant sacrifice of convenience, denies people of the future a fair opportunity to attain a lifestyle commensurate with our own. The principle of eco-efficiency is a good starting point for conservation.

Finally, we owe future people a reasonable chance for happiness. The earth cannot continue to support an exploding population. We need to limit population growth, so that we do not bring people into the world who will have little chance to live a minimally decent life. Additionally, we need to recognize that poverty is a major factor that both contributes to and exacerbates overpopulation.

Thus future generations would seem to have strong claims to our use of a variety of resources that are essential for their well-being. Clean air and water, a stable atmosphere and climate, fertile agricultural lands, and clean and available energy are all tied in obvious ways to the central interests of people of the future. But what about other, less essential resources? Do future generations have a right to undeveloped shorelines, wilderness areas, wetlands, and mountainsides? Do we have a duty to preserve animal and plant species for future generations? Is the preservation of these resources more akin to acting out of charity than to acting from a duty? Do future generations have a *right* to such resources?

We can understand that future generations, like us, might enjoy such resources. But then again, they might not. This issue is even more difficult when we recognize that what future generations will enjoy or desire depends largely on the type of world they inherit from us. Will a world miss an extinct blue whale? Will future generations that have never experienced a wilderness area, rain forest, or grizzly bear care about such things? Do we miss the dodo bird? The passenger pigeon? Would we really miss the snail darter or the California condor?

We can make several arguments that we have a duty to preserve wilderness areas and plant and animal species. We might argue that the biological diversity protected in wilderness areas and represented by plant and animal species has the potential to benefit humans greatly. The agricultural and medical potential of biological diversity provides strong and prudent reasons for their preservation.

As we will see in the chapters that follow, a number of philosophers have argued that animals, plants, and ecosystems should be the direct beneficiaries of our responsibilities. In this view, we should preserve them for their own sake. Before turning to these questions, however, consider a defense of preservation that has nothing to do with prudence or self-interest. This defense claims that we should preserve such natural resources because we *care* about future generations. We care about the type of people they will become, and we believe that a life lived in a world in which wilderness areas and rare species are preserved is a better, richer life than the alternative.

Consider how parents might think about their responsibilities to children. Part of being a good parent involves providing those things that children need and want. These responsibilities parallel the utilitarian and rights-based approaches just described. Future generations are like our children, and we should use our resources frugally so that they will have a reasonable chance to get what they need and want. But another part of being a responsible parent involves trying to shape and develop *appropriate* wants so that children will not only get what they want but will also want what is good and appropriate. This part of parenting involves moral education and moral development. If we care about future generations, we should be concerned with the type of life they might live and the type of people they might become.

But can we care about people who do not exist? Can our concern for the interests of future generations—for the type of life they will face and the type of people they will become—provide a reason for us to act today? Can it provide a reason that can override our personal interests? Put in this way, the question would seem easy to answer. Reasonably strong empirical evidence suggests that people are often motivated to act out of a concern for the interests of people of the future. On the political level, decisions to protect wilderness areas, to establish national and state parks, forests, and shorelines, to build museums and libraries, and to fund research and development in medicine, industry, and national defense make sense only if we recognize that the beneficiaries of these decisions will be generations as yet unborn. On a private level, decisions to endow charitable and educational foundations and to fund artistic, cultural, and social organizations also seem obviously motivated, at least in part, by a concern to provide people of the future with a decent and humane world. On a personal level, a decision as simple as planting an oak tree (one of countless varieties of plants that mature over long periods of time) suggests that individuals are motivated by a concern for the distant future.

Against this empirical evidence, however, lies a strong philosophical tradition that holds that humans are motivated solely by self-interest. This view, which is called psychological egoism, is associated with a tradition of thought running from the Sophists of Greece through Hobbes and contemporary economics. That philosophical tradition holds that rational people act only when they believe that doing so is in their self-interest. (Remember the economists mentioned in Chapter 3, who suggest that the alternative would require that we rewire human nature.)

Of course, this tradition does not deny that people act in ways that benefit others or manifest concern for them. It does not claim that all people are narrowly selfish. It claims only that our ultimate reason for acting to benefit others lies in self-interest. In this view, I help others, because I will benefit in turn. When we donate to charity or contribute to posterity, we seek the esteem, status, or tax deduction that follows from such gifts. Thus egoism interprets altruism or friendship on a contractual model: "I will benefit you, if you will benefit me." Accordingly, because people in the distant future can do nothing that serves my self-interest, it makes little sense to talk about caring for future generations. "Posterity never did anything for me."

But surely this is an impoverished understanding of caring for another. If we find that someone cares for us only because doing so is in that person's self-interest, we are justified in denying that any caring actually exists. Caring for others seems to exclude, rather than to be a form of, self-interest. Care requires that we take, as much as possible, the point of view of the other.

In an insightful analysis of the role of caring in ethics and education, philosopher Nel Noddings suggests that apprehending the other's reality, feeling what he feels as nearly as possible, is the essential part of caring from the point of view of the one caring. For if I take on the other's reality as possibility and begin to feel its reality, I feel, also, that I must act accordingly; that is, I am impelled to act as though on my own behalf, but in behalf of the other.[14]

To care for another is to take the other's point of view. It is not to ask, "What would *I* do if I were in that position?" but, insofar as is possible, to ask, "What would be best for this other person from her perspective?" As Noddings says, "When my caring is directed to living things, I must consider their natures, ways of life, needs, and desires. And, although I can never accomplish it entirely, I try to apprehend the reality of the other."[15] Thus the question of whether we can care about future generations asks whether we can view the world from their perspective. Can we replace our interests, needs, and desires with the interests, needs, and desires of people of the future?

At first glance, it would seem that we could. Friendship and parenting seem the two most obvious and familiar situations, in which people restrain their self-interests for the interests of others. If it were not possible to be motivated by the interests of others, neither friendship nor parenting could exist. "Rational egoism," as we can call it, would make loyalty, love, sacrifice, honesty, and a whole range of other virtues and attitudes rationally impossible.

But friends and children are actual people who have real interests and needs. Future generations do not exist, and perhaps this is a relevant difference. But why should it matter? Perhaps we could argue that we could take the point of view of and care for only people who are actually living. Yet many people (this may be more common in other cultures) seem to care deeply about their ancestors. People seem able to act in ways that would make their ancestors proud, honor their ancestors, and show respect for and pay homage to their ancestors.

Perhaps we would argue instead that because the interests and desires of people of the future will depend in part on the type of world they inherit from us, we have no way to know in advance what those interests and desires will be. But if we do not know this, we cannot view the world from their perspective and, hence, would find it impossible to be motivated by their interests and desires. We cannot care about them because we cannot know what would count in their behalf.

However, this argument fails to appreciate the true nature of the motivation to preserve nonessential resources for future generations. We do not seek to preserve a wilderness area or an endangered species because we believe people will desire these things in the future. The objection is correct in holding that if people of the future do not know of these things, they cannot desire (or miss) them. But the motivation to preserve for the future does not rest on the content of their desires. It rests with our judgment that a life lived with the possibility of knowing and desiring these things is fuller and more meaningful than one lived without them.

We can make a parallel argument by using the example of distinguished works of art. If we failed to preserve all Renaissance paintings, for example, and all records of this art were lost to future generations, surely they could not be said to miss them. If future generations knew nothing of these paintings, they could not feel their loss. But their lives would nonetheless be impoverished by that loss. It is our concern for this—our caring that they not live an impoverished life—that motivates us to preserve great artwork for the future.

Thus it does seem meaningful to care about future generations. To the degree that we can imagine ourselves in their position, we can recognize that such a life would be missing much were it not to know the wilderness or the rich complexity of biological diversity. We can care about the type of people future generations become and the types of lives they can lead. This care, I suggest, can and does motivate us to act.

In summary, a strong case can be made that we do have ethical responsibilities to future generations. Out of a respect for their rights, we have a responsibility to provide them with an opportunity equal to our own to live a healthful and happy life. In consideration of their future happiness, we have a responsibility to provide them with the resources that they will need to live a happy life. Because we care for them, we have a responsibility to preserve those natural and cultural resources that will make their lives meaningful.

4.4 CONSUMPTION AND SUSTAINABLE DEVELOPMENT

Given this discussion of the moral status of future generations, we should return to questions that were implicit in the formula $I = PAT$. Do present population, consumption patterns, and technologies create such an environmental impact that they violate the responsibilities that we have to future generations?

As an intellectual exercise, it can be helpful to make sharp distinctions and argue that either population *or* consumption is *the* major cause of environmental destruction. But surely the truth is that both are responsible. To various degrees in different circumstances, each contributes substantially to environmental distress. For any given finite ecosystem, increased population and increased consumption of resources will each create stress on the ability of that ecosystem to sustain life over the long term.

Nevertheless, into the near future we cannot expect anything other than an increasing world population. Although the *rate* of global population growth may be slowing, the overall *size* of global population continues to increase and will increase for the foreseeable future. Even at a significantly reduced 1 percent growth rate (the rate of population growth during the mid-1990s was approximately 1.7 percent), world population will double in 70 years. Considerations such as these have lead many people to focus on the remaining variables in the $I = PAT$ formula: consumption patterns and technology.

Many environmentalists promote the idea of sustainable development as a descriptive and normative framework for understanding an appropriate lifestyle for present generations. The model of sustainable development reminds us that the economy is a subset of the ecosphere and is limited by the productive capacity of that ecosphere. If either population size or economic growth and consumption become too large, the ecosphere will be unable to support human life. The only defensible public policy, from this perspective, is one that seeks an optimal level of both population and economic activity. In the longer term, sustainable development calls for population policies that aim for a stable population size. In the shorter term, sustainable development will require a shift away from the consumption patterns of modern industrialized societies. Sustainable development aims for the most productive and efficient use of resources compatible with the ability of the earth's ecosphere to provide consistent, stable, and long-term productivity.

In recent decades, an alternative to classical, market-based economics has emerged. Sustainable economics, which is also called ecological economics, offers a different way to think about economics in light of our current environmental challenges and the apparent failure of classical market economics to meet these challenges.

Economist Herman Daly is perhaps the best-known champion of sustainable economics. According to Daly, a distinction between *development* and *growth* is at the heart of sustainable economics.

> To *grow* means to "increase naturally in size by the addition of material through assimilation or accretion." To *develop* means "to expand or realize the potentialities of; to bring gradually to a fuller, greater, or better state." When something grows it gets bigger. When something develops it gets different. The earth ecosystem develops (evolves), but it does not grow. Its subsystem, the economy, must eventually stop growing, but can continue to develop. The term "sustainable development" therefore makes sense for the economy, but only if it is understood as "development without growth."[16]

Sustainable economics can be understood in contrast with traditional market economics. The traditional model addresses two fundamental questions: How are resources to be allocated (the production question), and how are the goods and services thus produced to be distributed (the distribution question)? Market economics answers the first question in terms of price; resources are to be allocated to those uses for which users are willing to pay the most. The distribution question is also answered in terms of the market; goods and services should be distributed according to consumer demand, with those willing to pay most getting the products.

Sustainable economics adds a third dimension to economic analysis. Beyond allocation and distribution, sustainable economics is concerned with the rate at which resources flow through this economy. We must first recognize that all the factors that go into production—natural resources, capital, and labor—ultimately originate in the productive capacity of the earth. In light of this, the entire classical model will prove unstable if resources move through this system at a rate that outpaces the productive capacity of the earth or exceeds the earth's capacity to absorb the wastes and by-products of this production.

Thus we need to develop an economic system that uses resources only at a rate that can be sustained over the long term and one that recycles or reuses both the by-products of the production process and the products themselves. We need to close the loop and pattern the economic system more on a circular ecosystem model than on the linear model of classical economics.

This alternative model would have significant social, economic, and commercial implications. Consumer demand would no longer be the overriding factor in production decisions. Production decisions involving renewable resources, such as those made in forestry and agriculture, would be limited by the rate at which these resources could be replenished. Decisions involving nonrenewable resources would be limited by the rate at which alternatives are developed or lost opportunities compensated. Finally, responsibility for products would extend beyond the life of the product. The "optimal level" of such things as wastes and pollution would be determined not by willingness to pay but by the earth's capacity to assimilate them.

Turning from the level of public policy to the level of personal morality, let us consider the responsibility of individual consumers. Do we consume too much? The answer to this question will depend on whom we mean by "we." Not all living people consume in the same way and amount. For example, one estimate suggests that worldwide, 1.2 billion people live on less that $1 a day, and 2.8 billion people live on less than $2 a day.[17] In contrast, the 12 percent of the world's population who live in North America and Western Europe account for 60 percent of worldwide consumer expenditures. The wealthiest 25 percent of the world's population consumes 58 percent of the energy, 45 percent of the meat and fish, 84 percent of the paper, and 87 percent of the vehicles, and accounts for 86 percent of the total private consumer expenditures. In contrast, the world's poorest 25 percent consumes 24 percent of the energy, 5 percent of the meat and fish, 1 percent of the paper, and less than 1 percent of the vehicles, and accounts for only 1.3 percent of the total private consumer expenditures. Over one-third of the world's population (approximately 2 billion people), live in Sub-Saharan Africa and South Asia. Taken together, they account for less than 4 percent of the total worldwide consumption expenditures.[18]

Accordingly, let us take the question to refer to those of us who are among the consumer class, living in economically developed societies. Does the consumer class of developed economies consume too much? Various environmental facts, considered in light of an ethical analysis of our responsibilities to future generations, suggest that we do.

Our analysis of utilitarian considerations, for example, suggests that long-term calculations of the greatest overall good require present generations to conserve the productive capacity of natural resources. Mary Williams's concept of "maximum sustainable yield" advises present generations to refrain from using resources at rates that cannot be sustained over the long term. Similarly, Brian Barry concludes that, at a minimum, future generations have a right to opportunities equal to those enjoyed by present generations. In this view, the present has an obligation to ensure that the future is no worse off with respect to the opportunities provided by natural resources than the present.

Do present consumption and population patterns, in fact, leave future generations a natural environment that is at least as productive as the one we inherited? Although air quality and water quality in some industrialized countries, including the United States, have improved over the last few decades, worldwide air and water quality remains a major problem. Global climate change is already underway. Accessing clean drinking water remains a challenge in many parts of the world. Many ocean fisheries are in decline, largely because of over consumption and pollution. Agricultural productivity has increased worldwide, but only at the cost of significantly increased reliance on chemical pesticides and fertilizers. The price of many nonrenewable resources has remained low, but little work is being done to encourage alternatives to our heavy reliance on fossil fuels. Loss of habitat as a consequence of human economic expansion has caused the greatest extinction event since the extinction of dinosaurs 65 million years ago. It would be difficult indeed to claim that present generations are doing all that they should to fulfil our responsibilities to our descendants.[19]

But this having been said, we need to mention three concerns that caution against accepting the sustainability paradigm uncritically. First, when we hear talk about sustainability, we should always be prepared to ask, "*What* is being sustained?" It seems clear that sustainability is often assumed to mean "sustaining the present patterns and levels of consumption." In this sense, defending a model of sustainable living means simply sustaining the status quo. Some have even spoken of "sustainable growth," which, as we saw in the quote from Herman Daly, is not possible. To the degree that present consumption patterns, particularly those found in consumer-driven industrial economies, are causing environmental deterioration, the status quo is exactly what we need to change. The type of economic growth that characterizes present economic models is not sustainable. Sustainable living and sustainable development will require a changed economy and a changed society. They will also require substantially closing the economic gap between wealthy industrialized countries and the poor developing world.

Mark Sagoff has raised a second concern about sustainability.[20] Sagoff warns against over reliance on economic and self-interested arguments to support environmentalism. Sagoff argues that the environmentalist perspective sometimes relies on misconceptions about the depletion and scarcity of natural resources and the danger posed by technology. Some evidence suggests that we are not running out of resources and that environmentally benign technologies may improve rather than harm the ecosphere. If the environmental perspective relies on such claims, and if it turns out that natural resources are plentiful and technological ingenuity very innovative, we may be powerless to counter continued environmental destruction.

Sagoff wants to de-emphasize scarcity and overconsumption arguments and to rely instead on a value-based approach that emphasizes spiritual, aesthetic, and ethical values. Consumerism may or may not be depleting natural resources at unsustainable rates, and therefore it may or may not be violating our responsibilities to future generations. But consumerism is a lifestyle in which material possessions are taken as a substitute for such goods as self-esteem, beauty, compassion, humility, and worth. Sagoff also warns against over-reliance on scarcity arguments, because these suggest that the primary value of nature is as a resource. This concern raises a third caveat.

Discussions of sustainable development and sustainable living are criticized by some as overly anthropocentric. Arguing against consumption and overpopulation on the grounds that they are depleting resources and threatening the well-being of present and future generations can ignore harms done to the natural world itself. This shift away from anthropocentric ethics will emerge as a central theme in the following chapters. Nevertheless, this consideration of present population and consumption patterns and the concept of ethical responsibilities to future generations do provide philosophical support for the concept of sustainable development. Sustainability may not be the complete environmental perspective, but it does offer a plausible model for where present lifestyles ought to be heading.

4.5 SUMMARY AND CONCLUSIONS

As philosophers turned their attention to environmental issues, it became clear that simply applying standard ethical theories would not yield satisfactory analyses of these issues. As this chapter shows, some of the most pressing environmental challenges force us to consider in detail the ethical effects of our actions on people of the future. Yet this issue was often ignored in much traditional philosophy, and groundbreaking work was required. Philosophical ethics needed to be extended beyond traditional boundaries.

Chapter 5 shows how these boundaries were extended even farther. Most of the issues we have considered thus far have focused on the effects that various environmental policies have on humans. Chapter 5 describes a fundamental shift in our philosophical perspective. Do we have direct responsibilities to other species? Although many philosophers considered this question, nearly all rejected the possibility that anything other than humans, and perhaps humans of the future, had moral standing. Primarily in response to environmental concerns, philosophers have in recent years sought to extend ethical consideration to things other than human beings.

NOTES

1. See Paul Ehrlich's classic *The Population Bomb* (New York: Ballantine, 1968) and the more recent *The Population Explosion* (New York: Doubleday, 1990). For a well-known criticism of the view that population growth is the key to environmental devastation, see Barry Commoner, *The Closing Circle* (New York: Alfred A. Knopf, 1971).

2. G. Tyler Miller, *Environmental Science*, (Belmont CA: Wadsworth Publishing, 1999) p. 13–15. Here these two issues are referred to as "people

overpopulation" and "consumption overpopulation." For further development of these claims, see Anne Ehrlich and Paul Ehrlich, *The Population Explosion* (New York: Doubleday, 1990).

3. See Gregory Kavka, "The Futurity Problem," in Sikora and Barry, eds., *Obligations to Future Generations*, (Philadelphia: Temple University Press, 1978), pp. 180–203, for a full analysis of this argument. Kavka cites Martin Golding, "Obligations to Future Generations," *Monist* 56 (1972): 97–98, as an "interesting variant" of the argument from ignorance.

4. For versions of this argument, see Derek Parfit, "On Doing the Best for Our Children," in Bayles, ed., *Ethics and Population Policy*, pp. 100–15, and Thomas Schwartz, "Obligations to Posterity," in Sikora and Barry, eds., *Obligations to Future Generations*, (Philadelphia: Temple University Press, 1978), pp. 3–13. The phrase "disappearing beneficiaries" is from Schwartz, "Obligations to Posterity," p. 3.

5. Annette Baier, "For the Sake of Future Generations," in *Earthbound: New Introductory Essays in Environmental Ethics*, ed. Tom Regan (New York: Random House, 1984), pp. 214–15. Baier compares this with the legal notion of "wrongful life" in, for example, *Curlender v. Bioscience Laboratories* (106 Cal. App. 3d 811 [1980]), in which a California court allowed a tort suit on behalf of a child born with Tay-Sachs disease after the parents had been told that they were not carriers of the Tay-Sachs gene.

6. Mary Anne Warren, "Future Generations," in *And Justice for All*, ed. Tom Regan and Donald VanDeVeer (Totowa, N.J.: Rowman and Allanheld, 1982), pp. 74–90.

7. Ibid., 154.

8. For a discussion of this economic approach, see Colin Clark, *Mathematical Bioeconomics: The Optimal Management of Renewable Resources* (New York: Wiley, 1976).

9. Mary Williams, "Discounting versus Maximum Sustainable Yield," in Sikora and Barry, eds., *Obligations to Future Generations*, (Philadelphia: Temple University Press, 1978), pp. 169–85. Another, more general review of criticisms of social discounting can be found in Derek Parfit, "Energy Policy and the Further Future: The Social Discount Rate," in MacLean and Brown, eds., *Energy and the Future*, (Totowa, New Jersey: Rowman and Littlefield, 1983), pp. 31–37.

10. Kavka, "The Futurity Problem," pp. 186–203.

11. Parfit, "On Doing the Best," p. 100.

12. Brian Barry, "Intergenerational Justice in Energy Policy" in MacLean and Brown, eds., *Energy and the Future*, (Totowa, New Jersey: Rowman and Littlefield, 1983), pp. 15–30.

13. Ibid., 23.

14. Nel Noddings, *Caring: A Feminine Approach to Ethics and Moral Education* (Berkeley: University of California Press, 1984), p. 16.

15. Ibid., 14.

16. Herman Daly, "Sustainable Growth: An Impossibility Theorem," reprinted in *Valuing the Earth*, ed. Herman Daly and Kenneth Townsend (Boston: Massachusetts Institute of Technology Press, 1987), pp. 267–268.

17. "Why Do We Consume So Much?" by Juliet Shor, in *Contemporary Issues in Business Ethics*, 5th ed., Joseph DesJardins and John McCall, eds., (Belmont, Calif.: Wadsworth Publishing, 2005), pp. 373–79.

18. *State of the World 2004*, Worldwatch Institute, Washington, D.C.

19. For some who disagree that we are in the midst of an environmental crisis, see Julian Simon, *The Ultimate Resource* (Princeton, N.J.: Princeton University

Press, 1981); Gregg Easterbrook, *A Moment on the Earth* (New York: Viking Penguin Books, 1995); and Joseph Bast, Peter Hill, and Richard Rue, *Eco-Sanity: A Common Sense Guide to Environmentalism* (Palatine, Ill.: The Heartland Institute, 1994).

20. Mark Sagoff, "Do We Consume Too Much?" In *Atlantic Monthly* 279, no. 6 (June 1997): pp. 80–96. For a response to Sagoff, see also "No Middle Way on the Environment," by Paul R. Ehrlich, Gretchen C. Daily, Scott C. Daily, Norman Myers, and James Salzman, *Atlantic Monthly* 280, no. 6 (December 1997): pp. 98–104, and Sagoff's answer as a letter to the editor in that same issue.

DISCUSSION QUESTIONS

1. Do you believe that Americans consume too much? Does more material wealth always lead to greater happiness?

2. Population policy raises fundamental ethical questions. Do all people have a right to have children? What restrictions, if any, should society place upon having children? What responsibilities do we have to our (not-yet-conceived) children? What benefits are attained by producing a child of one's own that cannot be attained through adoption?

3. Controversies such as those surrounding global climate change and nuclear waste involve long-term predictions and therefore cannot be resolved in the short term. In light of this uncertainty, is there one reasonable course of action? What does reason advise when we must make a decision with incomplete information?

4. Strong moral relations exist between parents and children, but can moral relations such as love and care exist between people separated by more than one or two generations?

5. Many indigenous cultures were destroyed when Europeans colonized the Americas and Africa. We can only guess what we have lost as a result of these conquests. Have we been hurt by this loss? Can people be harmed by the loss of opportunities and the loss of knowledge of which they will never be aware? Will future generations be harmed if they never know about the blue whale or never experience a wilderness area?

GLOBAL ENVIRONMENTAL ETHICS WATCH

For more information on Sustainability, please see the Global Environmental Ethics Watch. Updated several times a day, Global Environmental Ethics Watch is a focused portal into GREENR—our Global Reference on the Environment, Energy, and Natural Resources—an ideal one-stop site for current events and research. You will have access to the latest information from trusted academic journals, news outlets, and magazines as well as access to statistics, primary sources, case studies, videos, podcasts, and much more.

To gain access please use the access code that accompanies your book. If you do not have an access code, visit cengagebrain.com to purchase one.

5

Responsibilities to the Natural World: From Anthropocentric to Nonanthropocentric Ethics

Historians sometimes speak of three agricultural revolutions. The first occurred when humans first began establishing relatively permanent settlements in which domesticated animals and farming replaced hunting and gathering as the primary food production. The second was fueled by advances in crop rotation, mechanical technology, animal breeding, and land reform and resulted in great increases in productivity that provided food for growing the exploding urban centers of the industrial revolution. In each of the first two agricultural revolutions, the amount of land cultivated increased significantly to account for the growth in food production. The third revolution began in the latter half of the twentieth century when chemical fertilizers increased fertility, pesticides decreased losses, industrial production methods and technology increased efficiency, and genetics created higher yielding varieties of crops.

When thinking about these agricultural revolutions, we should recognize that they involved animals as well as plants. The shift from a hunter and gatherer culture included domesticating animals and plants. The second revolution significantly expanded animal production by changing how humans bred, raised, refrigerated, transported, and processed beef, poultry, pork, fish, eggs, and dairy products. The third revolution continues to increase food production through industrialized production techniques, technology, and genetics.

A wide range of philosophical and ethical questions are raised by the variety of ways in which humans relate to animals as food. A handy way to categorize these questions is to distinguish questions about which animals, if any, are used as food; what restrictions, if any, should be placed on how we treat animals generally; and what restrictions, if any, should be placed on how food animals are bred, raised, slaughtered, and eaten.

From the earliest days in which human domesticated animals, some were used as food and some as companions. Humans have developed deep emotional ties with some domesticated animals, not with others. Consider the taboos in many cultures against eating horses, dogs, and cats, yet not against eating cows, pigs, and chickens. A person who will think nothing of spending large sums of money for the medical treatment (and often burial) of a family pet, will think not at all about a dead squirrel on the side of a road. But even among non-domesticated wild animals, some are regularly treated as food and others not. Consider the difference between a salmon and a porpoise, or between a deer and a chimpanzee, or between a pheasant and a rat. Are these distinctions simply a matter of cultural practices that depend only on where one was born and raised?

A range of norms also establish appropriate ways to treat animals. Hunting and shooting animals is allowed virtually in every culture, but torturing animals is not. Animals are allowed to be owned, bought, and sold. People regularly euthanize frail and sickly pets because allowing them to die a natural death is seen as cruel. Pet owners are strongly urged to sterilize pets so that they not reproduce, yet pets are regularly bred according to human tastes, even if constant inbreeding has harmful effects on the animals themselves.

Perhaps no area has received as much attention among both ethicists and the general public than the ways in which food animals are bred, raised, and processed. In particular, high-density animal agriculture, often called factory farming, has come under more critical attention than perhaps any other aspect of food production. In the view of many critics, human treatment of animals in food production has been scandalous. We need only look at how food animals such as calves, pigs, and chickens are raised to see examples of such claims. In the words of philosopher Peter Singer, "It is here, on our dinner table and in our neighborhood supermarket or butcher's shop, that we are brought into direct touch with the most extensive exploitation of other species that has ever existed."[1]

Singer's book *Animal Liberation* did much to publicize the nature of modern factory farming. Singer's ethical analysis of these practices is examined in some detail in this chapter. Let us review just one well-known example, veal production.

Veal is the flesh of young cows. The dairy industry relies on female cows that are lactating, and this means that the cows must become pregnant. Typically, female calves are raised to become future milk producers, but other than a few select males that are raised for breeding purposes, most male calves are raised for veal. Veal tends to be an expensive cut of meat and, therefore, more likely to be found in expensive restaurants and gourmet cooking than on the dinner tables of middle-class families. Veal is especially prized when it is tender and pink.

Traditionally, calves are taken from their mothers when they are just a few days old. To prevent exercise, which would develop muscles and therefore make the flesh less tender, these young calves are confined in small wooden stalls. The stalls are so small that the calf typically is unable to turn around or even lie down. The calf spends its entire life, perhaps sixteen weeks, confined to this stall.

Normal flesh is red because of the iron in the blood. A cow gets iron from the grass and hay that it eats. Critics have charged that veal calves are systematically deprived of a diet containing iron. They are, in other words, intentionally made anemic. Of course, if they become too anemic they die, so they receive a dietary balance—just enough iron to keep them alive but not enough that their flesh and blood are red. All this is done even though pinkness adds nothing to the taste of veal. To speed up the calves' growth and control their diet, they typically are fed a liquid diet of powdered milk, vitamins, and growth-producing drugs. This may be all that they eat in their entire lives. To ensure that the calves take in as much of this formula as possible, calves are denied water and kept in warm buildings. Their only alternative is to turn to the formula to quench their thirst. Singer concludes his description of this process as follows. "If the reader will recall that this whole laborious, wasteful, and painful process of veal raising exists for the sole purpose of pandering to people who insist on pale, soft veal, no further comment should be needed."[2]

Of course, veal is not the only animal food product that has been subject to intense public scrutiny. Campaigns have targeted MacDonald's, Burger King, and KFC (formerly, Kentucky Fried Chicken) for the ways in which their suppliers raised and processed the beef and chicken used by their restaurants. Beef and hog producers have received significant criticism for the environmental damage caused by their feedlots, as well as for the cruel ways in which animals are treated. Egg and chicken producers have likewise been criticized for the inhumane ways in which chickens are treated.

The food industry, both the animal growers and food sellers, have responded by making significant changes in the ways in which they treat animals. A fair assessment is that many of the past practices of animal cruelty have been eliminated, especially in Europe, the United States, and Canada. But a certain irony has not escaped notice. Beef cattle, calves, hogs, and chickens are treated in more humane ways, subjected to less cruelty, better fed and housed, but nevertheless led into slaughterhouses where they are killed, less cruelly than previously, but still killed and butchered for human consumption.

More recently, public attention has turned not only to the ways in which animals are treated, but the ways they are, literally, created and bred. Much criticism has been directed at genetically modified food in general, but also at genetically modified animals. Animal breeding by humans has occurred since the first days of domestication. Indeed,

the very process of domesticating an animal species, or "breed," has involved humans manipulating, unintentionally perhaps, animal genetics. Dogs, cats, horses, and cows have been bred by humans throughout history. But contemporary genetic science allows breeders not only to choose desired traits from among those naturally occurring within a population, but also to create new traits that were not otherwise naturally occurring. Desired traits for genetically engineered animals include increasing growth and reproduction rates, resistance to disease, and increased nutritive value.

DISCUSSION TOPICS:

1. Are prohibitions against eating such animals as dogs and cats based on anything other than cultural practices? Under what conditions would you eat dog?
2. If it is justified to kill an animal for food, why should it matter how the animal is treated prior to slaughter?
3. Is there an ethics to hunting animals? Are there ethically better or worse ways to hunt?
4. Is it reasonable to use words such as "humane," "inhumane," "suffering," and "thinking" when discussing animals?
5. Are there important distinctions between different animal species? Are some animals deserving of greater ethical concern than others? Why or why not?
6. Is there an ethical difference between treatment of domesticated and wild animals?
7. Does genetic modification of food animals raise any ethical concerns? Do you hold similar beliefs about genetically modifying humans?

5.1 INTRODUCTION

As philosophers began to apply various ethical traditions to environmental issues, two fundamental questions guided their work. First, what is the proper ethical relationship between humans and the natural environment? Second, what is the philosophical basis for this relationship? In seeking to answer these questions, many philosophers found that the appeal to standard ethical theories was highly ambiguous. Traditional philosophical (and theological) views on the human relationship with nature seemed in many cases to have contributed to environmental destruction and degradation.[3]

For the most part, the Western philosophical tradition denies that any direct moral relationship exists between humans and the natural environment. According to most ethical theories within this tradition, only human beings have moral standing. In this sense, such ethical theories are anthropocentric, or human centered. Thus, when making an environmental decision, the ethical person needs to ask only how this decision will affect humans. To the degree that it can be said to exist, "environmental ethics" in these views are all anthropocentric and consequentialist: Environmental right or wrong depends on the consequences to humans. Although we have responsibilities *regarding* the natural world, we have no direct responsibility *to* the natural world. Environmental responsibility is, at bottom, a matter of prudence: We protect the environment for our own interests. (Of course, sometimes this can include such interests as aesthetic enjoyment or symbolic appreciation.) As described in Chapter 4, this perspective has been extended to include responsibility to future generations of humans.

In this chapter we examine a more radical shift in the philosophical perspective. In the late twentieth century, some philosophers began to argue that we have direct ethical responsibilities to nature, responsibilities that do not depend on the consequences to humans. This shift can be characterized as a shift from anthropocentric to nonanthropocentric theories of ethics.

5.2 MORAL STANDING IN
THE WESTERN TRADITION

Setting a historical context for these discussions reminds us how far traditional ethics is being extended. Chapter 2 suggests that the natural law tradition possesses resources that could make it particularly relevant to environmental issues. Nevertheless, the two philosophers most closely associated with this tradition defended views that betrayed little sympathy with the moral status of natural objects. Aristotle told us:

> Plants exist for the sake of animals ... all other animals exist for the sake of man, tame animals for the use he can make of them as well as for the food they provide; and as for wild animals, most though not all of these can be used for food and are useful in other ways; clothing and tools can be made out of them. If then we are right in believing that nature makes nothing without some end in view, nothing to no purpose, it must be that nature has made all things specifically for the sake of man.[4]

Sixteen centuries later, Thomas Aquinas picked up this issue and placed it in a theological context.

> We refute the error of those who claim that it is a sin for man to kill brute animals. For animals are ordered to man's use in the natural course of things, according to divine providence. Consequently, man uses them without any injustice, either by killing them or employing them in any other way. For this reason, God said to Noah: "As the green herbs, I have delivered all flesh to you."[5]

Aristotle and Aquinas could hold these positions, since they believed that only human beings have moral standing because only human beings possess an intellect (or "soul") capable of thinking and choosing. Because animals lack this capacity, they cannot be considered morally relevant in themselves. Any duties that we have regarding nature are explainable in terms of the needs or interests of human beings.

Kantian deontological theory is only a little less restricted. We have some evidence that Kant was sympathetic to duties to future generations, and the categorical imperative seems relevant to several environmental issues.[6] Nonetheless, in his *Lectures on Ethics*, Kant was quite clear in saying that our duties regarding nature are indirect; that is, they are duties to other humans. More generally, the Kantian analysis—which limits rights and moral standing to "subjects" and "ends," as distinct from "objects" and "means"—strongly reinforces the view that only humans have moral standing. In this view, only autonomous beings, capable of free and rational action, are moral beings. Again, because eighteenth-century Europeans believed that other living things lacked this capacity, they could exclude them from moral consideration. Nonhuman animals and plants were the clearest examples of objects, rather than subjects.

Another view that proved quite influential is traceable to the seventeenth-century philosopher René Descartes. Descartes argued that all reality is reducible to two fundamental types of substances, "minds" and "bodies." The realm of the mental includes all thinking, sensation, and consciousness. The realm of the body includes all things physical and spatial. This physical realm is the domain of physics, which was seen as purely mechanistic and devoid of consciousness. Although he did not deny that animals and plants are alive, Descartes nonetheless denied that they are anything other than machines or "thoughtless brutes." In the Cartesian view, therefore, the criterion for moral standing is consciousness. Anything not conscious is a mere physical thing and can be treated without concern for its well-being.

One of the few philosophers who did not unquestioningly exclude animals from moral consideration was the utilitarian Jeremy Bentham. In a passage that is famous because it is such an exception to the mainstream of Western philosophy, Bentham suggested that:

> The day *may come*, when the rest of the animal creation may acquire those rights which never could have been withholden from them but by the hand of tyranny. The French have already discovered that the blackness of the skin is no reason why a human being should be abandoned without redress to the caprice of a tormentor. It may come one day to be recognized that the number of the legs, the villosity of the skin, or the termination of the *os sacrum*, are reasons equally insufficient for abandoning a sensitive being to the same fate. What else is it that could trace the insuperable line? Is it the

faculty of reason, or perhaps the faculty of discourse? But a full-grown horse or dog is beyond comparison a more rational, as well as more conversable animal, than an infant of a day, or a week, or even a month old. But suppose they were otherwise, what would it avail? The question is not, Can they *reason*? nor Can they *talk*? but Can they *suffer*?[7]

True to his utilitarian views, Bentham expanded the realm of moral considerability to include all things that have the capacity to feel pleasure and pain. We will see a view similar to Bentham's developed and defended when we consider the writing of Peter Singer.

To summarize, for most philosophers in the Western tradition, human beings and only human beings have moral standing. Few philosophers ever considered the question of whether other beings have moral standing, and most of those who did denied any moral status to natural objects. Most often, the criteria used to draw the boundaries of the moral realm are in some sense intellectual—for example, the ability to think or reason in some particular way.

As a result, two strategies are available to critics. They can reject the philosophical basis for the exclusion of animals by arguing, for example, that rationality is an inappropriate criterion for moral standing. They might argue instead, following Bentham's suggestion, that sensation should be the criterion for moral standing. On the other hand, they can accept the philosophical basis but deny the conclusions drawn from it. With this approach, they can argue that rationality is an appropriate criterion but that animals, at least certain "higher" mammals, do in fact possess this capacity.

Thus, we can make a case that much of the Western philosophical tradition is unsympathetic to the idea of a direct ethical responsibility to the natural world. Indeed, a plausible case can be made that this tradition provides a rationale for the exploitation and dominance of the natural world and, thus, has been partly responsible for our present environmental predicament. But philosophers are not alone here. Some scholars have suggested that the Western religious traditions are equally culpable in this regard. One of the first people to make this claim was the historian Lynn White, Jr.

> These religious traditions are represented symbolically by the passage from Genesis, in which the Judeo-Christian God creates all living creatures and says, "Let us make man in our image and likeness to rule the fish in the sea, the birds in the sky, the cattle, all the wild animals on earth and all the reptiles that crawl upon the earth." So God created them in his own image and blessed them and said to them "be fruitful and multiply, and fill the earth and subdue it; and have dominion over the fish of the sea and over the birds of the air and over every living thing that moves upon the earth."[8]

The possibility that our Western theological traditions are at the root of our current environmental crisis is the focus of White's classic essay "The Historical Roots of Our Ecological Crisis."[9] White argues that many of our modern scientific and technological approaches to nature are an outgrowth of a particular Judeo-Christian perspective. That perspective, developing from biblical sources such as the passage taken from Genesis, is especially anthropocentric. In this view, humans occupy a privileged position in all creation. Being created in the "image and likeness of God," they have a moral and metaphysical uniqueness. Humans are separate from and transcend nature. God has created a moral hierarchy in which humans are superior to nature and have been commanded by God to subdue and dominate it.

White's claim is not that this is the only or the most reasonable interpretation of Christian theology. Indeed, he goes on to suggest an "alternative Christian view" that would support a much more harmonious relationship with nature. What is crucial is that this is the interpretation that many Jews and Christians have given to the biblical story of the Creation. Much of contemporary science and technology developed in a context in which this anthropocentric view of nature held sway. This, according to White, lies at the root of our current ecological crisis.

5.3 EARLY ENVIRONMENTAL ETHICS

Thus we find in Western philosophical and religious traditions the ideas that encourage viewing humans as superior to nature and therefore justified in dominating it. At the same time, these very traditions contribute much to philosophical theories that were being applied to solve environmental problems. In a very real sense, the tension between these two developments of mainstream Western philosophy mounts the biggest challenge to traditional ethical theories. Can the dominant ethical traditions provide the resources to resolve environmental controversies? A good example of this ambiguity appeared in one of the first philosophical examinations of environmental issues, John Passmore's *Man's Responsibility for Nature* (1974).

Using an image that characterizes much of applied ethics, Passmore understands his own philosophical role in terms first used by John Locke. In identifying issues and clarifying and analyzing arguments, the ethicist is "employed as an under-labourer in clearing ground a little and removing some of the rubbish that lies in the way to knowledge." The first role of the philosopher is to dispose of unhelpful, unreasonable, or dangerous alternatives. Passmore places all views that call for the abandonment of the "Western tradition," including "mysticism," the "nature-as-sacred" view, and animal rights among the "rubbish" to be removed.

Nevertheless, Passmore recognizes the paradoxical character of his appeal to Western traditions. On the one hand, he acknowledges that the dominant Western tradition "denied that man's relationship with nature is governed by any moral considerations whatsoever."[10] In this tradition, the human being is the "despot," who rules over nature with arrogance and hubris and treats nature as mere wax to be molded in whatever manner humans desire. On the other hand, Passmore believes that the Western tradition contains the seeds for an ethically appropriate relationship with nature.

> The traditional moral teaching of the [W]est, Christian or utilitarian, has always taught men, however, that they ought not so to act as to injure their

neighbors. And we have now discovered that the disposal of wastes into sea or air, the destruction of ecosystems, the procreation of large families, the depletion of resources, constitute injury to fellow-men, present, and future. To that extent, conventional morality, without any supplementation whatsoever, suffices to justify our ecological concern.[11]

Thus the call for a "new set of moral principles" is "not entirely wrongheaded." However, what is needed is "not so much a 'new ethic' as a more general adherence to a perfectly familiar ethic." For example, Passmore concludes that the ethical problems associated with pollution are not overwhelming but involve applying the generally accepted principle that "nobody ought to poison his neighbor." He also believes that the primary causes of our ecological disasters are "greed and short-sightedness," problems that can be overcome with an "old-fashioned procedure, thoughtful action."[12]

For the most part, Passmore's work follows the standard applied ethics model. Careful philosophical analysis has much to offer to environmental controversies. However, one aspect of his analysis calls for an extension of modern Western ethics. Lamenting the materialistic greed of consumerist societies, Passmore calls for a more "sensuous" attitude toward the world. The "puritan attack" on sensuousness, which he traces from Plato through Augustine and the Protestant Church to the modern Western world, leads to a denial of the beauty and love of nature. The "new ethic" that the environmental crisis demands must be one in which aesthetic value plays a prominent role. The denial of sensuousness contributes to the environmental threats caused by the population explosion by "restricting the publicizing of birth control methods and condemning all sexual relationships which do not have procreation as their aim."[13] It also fosters an easy acceptance of environmental degradation.

> A more sensuous society could never have endured the desolate towns, the dreary and dirty houses, the uniquely ugly chapels, the slag heaps, the filthy rivers, the junk yards which constitute the "scenery" of the post-industrial West.... Only if men can first learn to look sensuously at the world will they learn to care for it.[14]

Thus Passmore was willing to criticize much of the Western philosophical and religious traditions for encouraging "man to think of himself as nature's absolute master, for whom everything that exists was designed."[15] Nevertheless, like much of that tradition, his ethics remains anthropocentric. The natural world has no value in its own right. It is valuable because humans care for it, love it, and find it beautiful. We have responsibilities regarding the natural world, but the basis of these responsibilities lies in human interests.

For many philosophers like Passmore, standard ethical theory does contain the resources for articulating new environmental rights. Another early attempt at extending standard ethical theories was developed by William Blackstone.[16] Contrasting those things that we merely *desire* with those things to which we have *rights*, Blackstone argues for recognition of a new human right, the "right to a livable environment." To provide a context for this discussion, return to the framework presented in Chapter 3. One way to look at environmental problems is to view them as involving conflicting interests. One side (for example, the developers of the Pebble Mine) prefers one thing, and another side (for example, the salmon fisheries) prefers something else. The challenge to public policy makers is to resolve these conflicts in fair and impartial ways.

The economic model resolves the conflict by treating all competing preferences as equally deserving of satisfaction. The goal, therefore, is to satisfy an optimal number of these preferences. That is, the resolution of conflict is accomplished on utilitarian and quantitative grounds: More is better.

Traditionally, the concept of a moral right functions to protect certain important interests from being sacrificed for a net increase in the overall good. As described in Chapter 2, the Kantian ethical tradition holds that our strong moral obligation to respect the dignity of people has meaning only when we protect central human interests by granting them a status ethically superior to mere wants. When my wants conflict with your wants, the market goal of seeking the optimal satisfaction of wants is attractive so long as the conflict does not involve rights. For example, if you want to dump toxic wastes on your property, which is adjacent to my home, we have more than merely a conflict of wants. In this case, what you *want* conflicts with my *rights*. In this view, rights trump mere desires and should not be sacrificed, even if doing so would maximize the overall good.

In Passmore's view, standard ethical theory has the resources to handle such situations. But to other philosophers, the changing environmental conditions of our world make crucially important certain interests that were not previously recognized as such. The interest in clean air and water and the interest in preserving dwindling wilderness areas may be important today in ways that they were not a generation ago. They may have become so important that they now deserve protection as moral rights.

Blackstone's approach adopts a standard deontological defense of human rights that is similar to the Kantian view described in Chapter 2. Blackstone defends the general view that there are universal and inalienable human rights. These rights entail a "correlative duty or obligation" on the part of other people either to act or to refrain from acting in certain ways. Our moral duties in turn limit our liberties and the exercise of certain other rights. Thus, to use a well-worn example, the liberties that follow from my property rights to a hunting knife are restricted by those duties that I owe to you as a result of your right to live. That is, I cannot stab you with this knife.

The question that arises from this general framework is whether humans have a right to a livable environment. Blackstone argues that they do. In this view, each person possesses human rights for these reasons:

> in virtue of the fact that he is human and in virtue of the fact that those rights are essential in permitting him to live a human life (that is, in permitting him to fulfil his capacities as rational and free being).[17]

Blackstone further argues that we can realize none of those basic human rights that follow from our nature as free and rational beings—equality, liberty, happiness, life, and property—without a safe, healthful, and livable environment. Thus a right to a livable environment can be defended as necessary to fulfilling a human life. Because a livable environment is equally necessary to all humans, there is "no relevant grounds for excluding any human the opportunity" to live this life.[18]

Accordingly, we have a fairly standard philosophical framework. Human rights follow from basic interests that we have by virtue of our nature as free and rational agents. They are defended as being necessary for fulfilling our natural human capacities and on the ground that no relevant basis exists for denying these rights to anyone—that is, they can be universalized. But how is this a new human right? Blackstone reasons that "changing environmental conditions" require us to restrict traditional freedoms and rights, especially property rights, in the name of both the public welfare and equality. Thus, "what in the past had been properly regarded as freedoms and rights (given what seemed to be unlimited natural resources and no serious pollution problems) can no longer be so construed."[19] When the traditional ethical and political framework of natural rights is applied to the new environmental reality, some traditional rights must be modified and some new ones created.

Critics can raise several challenges to Blackstone's position, however. They might argue that talk of a new right is not useful and is true only in a trivial sense. At best, this right to a livable environment is a shorthand way of talking about more fundamental rights, such as life, liberty, and property. If I dump toxic wastes into a river, I have caused harm to or violated the rights of people living downstream from me. Standard property rights would seem sufficient to handle this issue. If I pollute the groundwater you drink or the air you breathe, I have harmed you in fairly standard sorts of ways. The generally accepted principle of which Passmore speaks, that "nobody ought to be allowed to poison his neighbor," suggests that talk of a right to a livable environment is unnecessary. In fact, this new right might even be detrimental to the environmental cause by creating a new layer of rights that hides the real harms caused by pollution and environmental destruction. An expansion of the number of rights might make it more, rather than less, difficult to specify the ethical and legal harms of pollution.

Another criticism holds that when properly understood, rights entail only *negative* and not *positive* duties. My duty that follows from your right to live involves only the negative duty not to kill you. It does not entail the positive duty that I supply you with all that you need to live, for example. From this perspective, the right to a livable environment either is unnecessary or requires too much of others. If it is understood as a *negative* right (for example, the right not to be harmed by pollution or, more generally, the right not to have my well-being threatened by your environmental actions), then it does nothing ethically or legally that is not already done by standard ethical and legal concepts. If it is understood as a *positive* right (implying, for example, a duty on the part of others to provide or produce a clean environment), then, like education or health care perhaps, it is a desirable state of affairs but not a right. Serious challenges could be raised about the extent of other people's duties that would follow from the positive right to a livable environment. Are my rights violated whenever anyone drives a car and thereby pollutes the air, for example? Or whenever anyone uses pesticides to grow vegetables? Or disposes of sewage sludge in the ocean? Surely this would result in a proliferation of rights and duties so great as to paralyze much of modern life.

There are, of course, responses to these concerns. A defender of the right to a livable environment might argue that this right involves only certain minimal and basic duties on the part of others. A parallel might be drawn to education or health care. The right to health care need not imply a universal right to any and all medical procedures, such as cosmetic surgery, but it should include a right to emergency care. A right to education need not imply a right to free tuition for a graduate degree at a private university, but it might imply free public education through high school. So, too, a right to a livable environment need not imply a right to pristine and pure air and water, but it would prohibit a laissez-faire policy in regard to dumping toxic wastes, polluting the oceans with municipal garbage and sewage, burning high-sulfur coal, and so forth.

5.4 MORAL STANDING

As we saw in Chapter 4, environmental issues provoked philosophers to extend ethical concepts beyond their traditional boundaries. Developing a philosophically adequate account of energy or population policy, for example, required that philosophers consider the moral status of something other than living human beings. The remainder of this chapter examines further extensions of ethics that require consideration not only of our duties *regarding* objects in our natural environment, but also of our duties *to* these objects.

Consider carbon dioxide pollution. In standard ethical views, such pollution would be wrong if it harmed other human beings, perhaps by threatening their health or property. If standard ethical practice does not adequately address the harms caused by pollution, we could argue, as William Blackstone does, for recognition of some new environmental rights. When we learn that some harmful effects of carbon dioxide pollution might not occur for generations, we extend our ethical concepts, such as duties and rights, to include future generations. This extension gives future generations a moral standing that they do not possess under more traditional ethical theories.

We can identify the practice of extending moral standing to include future humans or to develop new human rights as *anthropocentric extensionism*. Ethics is extended beyond traditional boundaries, but only human beings continue to possess moral standing. Our duties, such as not to pollute, are duties *regarding* the environment, but they are not duties *to* the environment. As this brief survey of representative philosophers suggests, mainstream Western philosophy and theology hold an anthropocentric view of moral standing. Human beings and only human beings have moral standing.

We now begin to consider *nonanthropocentric extensions* of ethics. That is, we will examine attempts to extend ethics and give moral standing to things other than human beings. Candidates for moral standing include animals, plants, and species; natural objects such as mountains, rivers, and wilderness areas; and even the earth itself. Throughout these debates two fundamental positions emerge: the position of those who extend moral standing to include animals and other natural objects and the position of those who believe that these extensions are too outlandish and that traditional ethical concepts are sufficient to address environmental concerns.

The general concern in this chapter is with our responsibilities *to* the natural environment. Much of the discussion will be in terms of the rights of animals, trees, wilderness, and so forth. However, not every philosopher is willing to attribute rights in every case in which we have responsibilities. For example, we have seen that some philosophers are willing to say that although we have responsibilities to future generations, it makes little sense to say of people who do not exist that they possess rights—or anything else, for that matter. More generally, utilitarians reject talk of rights, although they too are willing to talk about responsibilities.

For this reason, although many philosophers speak in terms of rights, it is preferable to think in terms of moral standing and moral considerability when we examine our responsibilities to the natural environment. These more general terms include, but are not limited to, cases in which animals or trees are said to have rights. The general philosophical question concerns what things have a moral claim on us, such that we have a responsibility to consider them in our moral deliberations. Who and what count morally? On what grounds do we recognize (or attribute) moral standing?

When we phrase the matter this way, we recognize that many other contemporary moral problems and public policy debates are located at the boundaries of moral standing. The abortion debate often focuses on the moral status of the fetus: Is a fetus a moral person? Does it have rights? Many debates in medical ethics concern euthanasia and treatment of seriously impaired patients. These issues force us to consider the moral status of patients in irreversible comas, patients who are brain-dead, frozen embryos, and severely impaired infants. We also have seen how concern for future generations further stretches these boundaries. Thus, in pursuing the question of our duties to the natural environment, it is helpful to begin by examining a more fundamental philosophical issue: Where do we draw the boundaries of moral consideration? Who and what should have moral standing? On what grounds do we make these decisions?

What, then, is the proper relationship between humans and other living things? One of the earliest contemporary discussions of the moral standing of animals and other living beings is Joel Feinberg's "The Rights of Animals and Unborn Generations."[20] Feinberg's 1974 essay was quite influential, and a brief review of his argument provides a valuable introduction to the more recent debates.

Feinberg begins with a common understanding of rights as involving a claim *to* some good, *against* some other person (who would therefore have some duty), that is socially recognized in some way—for example, by legal rules or an "enlightened conscience." For example, freedom of religion is the right to worship as you choose and it creates a duty for the government not to interfere with your religious worship. Feinberg's strategy is to begin with clear and unproblematic cases of moral standing and attempt to pull from them a criterion that best explains our intuitions. We then can apply this criterion to more problematic cases.

> In the familiar cases of rights, the claimant is a competent adult human being.... Normal adult human beings, then, are obviously the sorts of beings of whom rights can meaningfully be predicated.... On the other hand, it is absurd to say that rocks can have rights, not because rocks are morally inferior things unworthy of rights (that statement makes no sense either), but because rocks belong to a category of entities of whom rights cannot be meaningfully predicated.... In between the clear cases of rocks and normal human beings, however, is a spectrum of less obvious cases, including some bewildering borderline ones. Is it meaningful or conceptually possible to ascribe rights to

our dead ancestors? to individual animals? to whole species of animals? to planets? to idiots and madmen? to fetuses? to generations yet unborn?[21]

Turning to the case of individual animals, Feinberg recognizes that most people acknowledge that we have a duty not to mistreat or be cruel to animals. Some might argue that this duty derives from a duty to other humans—that is, to those who are offended by the mistreatment of animals. Others might argue that this duty is derived from a duty to ourselves—for example, a duty to avoid situations in which we might develop character traits such as callousness or cruelty. Feinberg argues that these explanations are disingenuous, that surely animals are the direct beneficiaries of this duty. We can owe a duty *to* animals, according to Feinberg, because animals have interests that can be promoted or harmed by our actions. In order for us to say that something has rights, this thing must have interests or a "sake" or a good of its own to be protected by rights. A mere thing, even a precious thing like the Taj Mahal or a beautiful natural wilderness, cannot be said to have rights because it cannot be said to have any interests of its own.

Feinberg focuses on the question of rights, rather than on the more general question of moral standing. But the point is significant. In order to meaningfully say that we have an obligation *to* some object, rather than merely an obligation *regarding* that object, the object of our obligations must have some welfare or good of its own. If I have a duty to something, my fulfilling my duty to this thing must be good for this thing. But to say that something has a "good" or a "bad" is to say that it has interests. For example, it is in a dog's interest not to be tortured. I can have a duty not to torture animals, if it can be said that it is good *for the dog* not to be tortured. But what things can have interests? In Feinberg's view, only things with a "conative life," with "conscious wishes, desires, hopes; or urges or impulses; or unconscious drives, aims, or goals; or latent tendencies, direction of growth, and natural fulfillments," can be said to have interests.[22]

Feinberg then applies this criterion to various objects of environmental concern. Individual animals, at least the higher animals, can be said to have rights, although those of lower orders can be treated as mere pests. Plants cannot be said to have rights, because they lack the "rudimentary cognitive equipment" necessary to possess interests. Neither can we say that species have rights, although we might attribute rights to individual members of that species. Thus, for example, we might say that an individual dolphin has an interest in not being drowned in fishing nets and, therefore, might be said to have a right not to be killed in a fishing net. But dolphins as a species have no corresponding right to survive. We might have a duty not to kill an individual animal, but we have no duty to a species to protect it from extinction. Our duties can be only to individual beings that possess the appropriate "cognitive equipment."

Finally, because we can say that future generations will have interests with as much certainty as we can say that they will exist, it makes sense for us to talk about their rights as well.

Feinberg's essay was groundbreaking in many ways. Read narrowly, it offers merely a conceptual analysis of what can and cannot meaningfully be said about rights. Yet this essay also symbolizes a liberation of sorts for philosophical ethics. Environmental concerns encouraged philosophers to expand greatly the realm of moral considerability. Essentially, philosophers for the first time considered the possibility that beings other than humans deserve moral consideration for their own sake, not merely because humans happen to be interested in them.

5.5 DO TREES HAVE STANDING?

Before turning to more systematic attempts to extend ethical consideration to animals, we should examine another early and influential attempt at extending rights to nonhuman natural objects. Law professor Christopher Stone argues to extend legal, if not moral, rights to "forests, oceans, rivers and other so-called 'natural objects' in the environment—indeed, to the natural environment as a whole."[23] Unlike many defenders of animal rights, Stone bases his claim for standing less on the characteristics of humans and more on the nature of legal rights.

The occasion for Stone's defense of the rights of natural objects was the legal dispute concerning Mineral King Valley. The Sierra Club had filed suit to prevent Walt Disney Enterprises from building a large ski resort in the Sierras. This suit was rejected in California courts because the Sierra Club lacked standing. That is, members of the Sierra Club could not show that they would suffer any legally recognized harm by the development of Mineral King Valley. As this case made its way on appeal to the U.S. Supreme Court, Stone wrote an essay titled "Should Trees Have Standing?" Stone hoped to support the Sierra Club's case by arguing that the natural objects, such as trees and mountainsides, that would be destroyed in this development should be given legal standing. The Sierra Club could then be seen as a legal guardian of these rights.[24]

Stone's analysis begins with an examination of the nature of legal rights. Implicitly rejecting the view that rights are somehow there in nature to be discovered, Stone emphasizes the evolutionary development of rights. Rights exist when they are recognized by "some public authoritative body [that] is prepared to give some amount of review" to violations of that right. Citing Darwin's observation that "the history of man's moral development has been a continual extension in the objects of his social instincts and sympathies," Stone shows how the recognition of legal rights is witness to a parallel development.[25] Rights function to protect rights-holders from injury, and the list of rights-holders has been continually expanded. He reminds us that at one time only landowning white adult males enjoyed full legal rights. Legal standing now includes people who do not own land, women, blacks, Native Americans, and such things as corporations, trusts, cities, and nations. It is time to extend this protection to natural objects.

Stone argues that recognition by some authoritative body alone is not enough to establish the existence of rights.

> As I shall use the term, "holder of legal rights," each of three additional criteria must be satisfied. All three, one will observe, go towards making a thing *count* jurally—to have a legally recognized worth and dignity of its own right, and not merely to serve as a means to benefit "us." They are, first, that the thing can institute legal actions *at its behest;* second, that in

determining the granting of legal relief, the court must take *injury to it* into account; and, third, that relief must run to the *benefit of it.*[26]

The proposal to give legal rights to trees and other natural objects satisfies all three criteria. How can natural objects "institute legal actions" on their own behalf? Noting that corporations and mentally incompetent humans have legal standing, Stone argues that a guardian or conservator or trustee could be appointed to represent the interests of natural objects. Just as a comatose person has a legal guardian, for example, or a corporation, a board of trustees, forests, streams, and mountains could be legally represented by humans who are charged with representing their interests.

But do natural objects have interests that (1) we can agree on and (2) can be harmed in a legally recognizable way? Stone thinks that they do. Again noting the parallel with corporations, Stone believes that we can "know" the interests of and acknowledge the injuries to natural objects with at least as much certainty as we do in corporate cases.

> The guardian–attorney for a smog-endangered stand of pine could venture with more confidence that his client wants the smog stopped, than the directors of a corporation can assert that "the corporation" wants dividends declared.[27]

Similarly, Stone believes that we can give meaning to the concept of a legal remedy that can provide relief to the injured natural object. As a guiding principle, we could adopt a common legal standard and aim to make the environment whole. Just as when a person is injured in an automobile accident and is compensated for medical costs to return that person to health, so we could require the responsible party to compensate the natural object by returning it to health. In this sense, "environmental health" would be the state in which the environment existed before the injury.

Consider how this proposal might work. During the summer of 2010, the British Petroleum (BP) deepwater oil drilling platform, the Deepwater Horizon, exploded sending millions of gallons of oil into the Gulf of Mexico. The three month-long oil spill affected coastlines from Florida to Texas, causing extensive damage to fisheries, wetlands, beaches, and wildlife habitats.

Under current legal guidelines, the door is open for injured humans to file for damages against BP, which was responsible for the oil drilling. Landowners along the coast or businesses that depend on tourism and fishing, for example, might argue that they deserve to be compensated for certain losses. Under Stone's proposal, representatives of the shoreline and of the fish and wildlife killed by the oil could also sue for damages. Thus, not only would humans be compensated for their injuries, but also the coast itself should be "made whole"—that is, returned to its pre-spill state.

There are, of course, challenges for this proposal to overcome. First, despite Stone's suggestions, it is not at all clear that we can agree on the interests of natural objects. For example, some believe that the Gulf of Mexico should immediately be restocked with fish from hatcheries. Others argue that the Gulf should be allowed to restock itself. Good reasons can be given to support both options. Which is in the best interest of the Gulf?

A second challenge follows from this. Perhaps Stone's response would allow the shoreline's guardians to make that decision in the same way that a legal guardian might decide what is best for an orphaned child. But who should this guardian be? The Wilderness Society would have one view of the shoreline's interests, and a local fishing industry might have another view. Choosing the guardian would also be to choose the theory of interests that is ascribed to natural objects. Should the Sierra Club represent the interests of Mineral King Valley or the Pebble Mine region? Should a lumber company or mining company?

None of this suggests that Stone's approach cannot work. But it does suggest that more work needs to be done to articulate and defend a view of nature's interests. Stone's proposal essentially relies on society's reaching a consensus about the extension of legal standing to natural objects. Legal standing is, after all, something that needs to be "recognized" by a public body. But it would seem that this consensus can be reached only after the public has already reached a consensus about the nature and value of natural objects. This consensus, regrettably, is still to be achieved.

5.6 PETER SINGER AND THE ANIMAL LIBERATION MOVEMENT

Reviewing the discussion case that opened this chapter, we could discuss many different arguments on why it is wrong to torture and kill animals for reasons of satisfying gourmet tastes. We can find many anthropocentric reasons to defend the position that we have ethical responsibilities regarding animals. After all, many people own animals and thus have property rights over them. Many people care about animals and thus would be affected by the mistreatment of them. Further, mistreating animals can have an adverse effect on the person doing the mistreating. Such actions make us callous and insensitive to suffering.

In short, people value animals for a variety of reasons. But can we say that we owe any moral consideration directly to the animals themselves? Do animals have moral standing? Do they deserve moral consideration? These questions are among the first ethical issues raised in connection with environmental concerns to have received close and developed philosophical attention.

Perhaps the person most closely associated with the extension of philosophical ethics to animals is Peter Singer. Since the 1970s, Singer has argued that our exclusion of animals from moral considerability is on a par with the earlier exclusions of blacks and women. Singer popularized the term *speciesism* to draw a parallel with racism and sexism.[28] Singer argues that just as it is morally wrong to deny equal moral standing on the basis of race or sex, it is wrong to deny equal moral standing on the basis of species membership.

Singer begins his argument with a "fundamental presupposition" of moral theory, the "basic moral principle" that all interests should receive equal consideration. Essentially, this is the formal principle that any being that qualifies for moral standing "counts for one and none for more than one." Even racists and sexists can accept this principle, although they would deny that blacks or women have equal moral standing. Singer must therefore explain the criterion for inclusion. What characteristic qualifies a being for equal moral standing? Here Singer cites the passage from Bentham referred to earlier: The question is not can they *reason*, nor can they *talk*, but can they *suffer*? Singer goes on to say,

> The capacity for suffering and enjoyment is a *prerequisite for having interests at all*, a condition that must be satisfied before we can speak of interests in a meaningful way. It would be nonsense to say that it was not in the interests of a stone to be kicked along the road by a schoolboy. A stone does not have interests because it cannot suffer. Nothing that we can do to it could possibly make any difference to its welfare. The capacity for suffering and enjoyment is, however, not only necessary, but also sufficient for us to say that a being has interests—at an absolute minimum, an interest in not suffering. A mouse, for example, does have an interest in not being kicked along the road because it will suffer if it is.[29]

Like Joel Feinberg and Christopher Stone, Singer focuses on the concept of interests to explain moral standing. Unlike Feinberg and Stone, however, Singer is not concerned with using interests as a basis for attributing rights to animals. He is sympathetic to Bentham's dismissal of rights as nonsense or at least as only a shorthand way of speaking about moral protections. Nor does he turn to cognitive elements as the essential aspect of interests. In Singer's view, the capacity for suffering (and enjoyment) is all that is needed to establish that a being has interests. Singer uses the term *sentience* to refer to the capacity to suffer and/or experience enjoyment. Sentience is *necessary* for having interests, in that an object without sentience—a rock, for example—cannot be said to have interests. But Singer also believes that sentience is *sufficient* for having interests. A being that is sentient has at least minimal interests—that is, the interest in not suffering.

Because any and only sentient beings have interests, any and only sentient beings have moral standing. We are required to treat all sentient beings with equal moral consideration. This does not mean that we are required to make no distinctions between humans and other animals. Humans are different from other animals. They have different interests. A "hard slap across the rump" of a horse will cause relatively little pain and therefore is not particularly unethical. But this does not mean that the principle of equal consideration would justify an equally hard slap across the face of a child. A horse's rump is solid and broad, usually muscled or fat, whereas a child's face is bony and small. Certain human mental capacities might cause humans to suffer more from certain actions and in different ways than other animals. Beings with sophisticated mental capabilities and the capacity for complex emotional and affective states have a greater range of interests, and thus a different moral standing, than creatures with simple cognitive and emotional capacities. But the essential point is that the capacity to suffer and the amount of suffering are what determine specific moral requirements. Because all animals above a certain neurological threshold are sentient, all such animals deserve direct moral consideration.

What are the implications of these views? Singer acknowledges that making comparisons of sufferings can be difficult, especially when these comparisons are made between species. Nevertheless, even if we were to restrict ourselves to those cases in which severe animal suffering was condoned for the sake of mere human convenience, we would be forced to make radical changes in our treatment of animals that would involve our diet; the farming methods we use; experimental procedures in many fields of science; our approach to wildlife and to hunting, trapping, and the wearing of furs; and areas of entertainment such as circuses, rodeos, and zoos. As a result, a vast amount of suffering would be avoided.[30]

As the references to Bentham and the emphasis on minimizing suffering suggest, Singer's approach is utilitarian. He provides an account of intrinsic good (enjoyment and the absence of suffering) and says that our ethical responsibility is to minimize the overall amount of suffering. Before examining the implications of Singer's views, let us turn to an alternative, nonutilitarian defense of animal rights.

5.7 TOM REGAN AND ANIMAL RIGHTS

Whereas Peter Singer has defended the moral standing of animals on utilitarian grounds, Tom Regan has developed a rights-based defense of animals. Regan explicitly argues that some animals have rights and that these rights imply strong moral obligations on our part. Like Singer, Regan condemns on ethical grounds a wide variety of human activities that affect animals. These activities include the use of animals in scientific and commercial research, the use of animals as food, and recreational uses of animals that include sport hunting, zoos, and pets. Regan believes that these practices are wrong in principle, but not because of the pain and suffering they cause. They violate animal rights by denying the intrinsic ethical value that some animals possess.

Imagine that Singer's criticisms convince veal producers to change their methods so as to minimize suffering (as, in fact, has happened). The calves get some exercise, fresh air, and a balanced diet, and perhaps they are even groomed regularly. Like the cows in the old advertisements, these are contented calves. Imagine also that human taste for veal increases so that many consumers have a real desire for veal. Consumers suffer (no one suffers *much*, but many do suffer) when they are denied veal. In such a situation, we could argue that Singer's utilitarian position allows veal production to continue. With these imagined changes in the farming practices of the veal industry, the calves suffer minimally while human enjoyment increases notably.

A defender of Singer's position could dispute this example, of course. However, the dispute would probably involve specific calculations of relative suffering, pain, and enjoyments. That is, we would need to measure and dispute the consequences of the alternative practices. In this view, raising, slaughtering, and eating the calf for food is not wrong in principle. It is wrong only when the suffering that it causes outweighs the resultant enjoyment. Note how different Regan's point of view is:

> The forlornness of the veal calf is pathetic, heart wrenching.... But the fundamental wrong isn't the pain, isn't the suffering, isn't the deprivation. These compound what's wrong. Sometimes, often, they make it much worse. But they are not the fundamental wrong. The fundamental wrong is the system

that allows us to view animals as our resources, here for us, to be eaten, or surgically manipulated, or put in our cross hairs for sport or money.[31]

How does Regan explain the principle that underlies this view? To understand this, we should consider why it would be wrong to subject humans to similar treatment. Suppose someone were to follow Jonathan Swift's satirical "Modest Proposal" and treat disadvantaged young children as food. These children would be raised in a manner that kept them content and relatively free from suffering. However, at a certain point in their lives (Swift proposed a well-nursed one-year-old), these humans were slaughtered, albeit painlessly, and "stewed, roasted, baked, or boiled." Presumably, we would all acknowledge the moral evil of these activities even if the overall balance of enjoyment over suffering were increased. Why?

Regan argues that the answer lies in our belief that humans possess what he calls "inherent value." We have seen this concept before in our discussion of ethical theories. Essentially, to have inherent value is to have value independent of the interests, needs, or uses of anyone else. Inherent value is to have value in and of oneself. It is to be contrasted with instrumental value, in which a thing's value is a function of how it might be used by others or what it might mean to others. Objects with inherent value are ends in themselves, not merely means to some other end. It is wrong to treat humans (and, as it will turn out, some animals) as mere means to other ends, even if this includes as an end maximizing the net amount of enjoyment over suffering, because to do so denies to these humans the inherent value that they possess.

So far, this approach sounds similar to the Kantian tradition in ethics, and clearly it is greatly influenced by that tradition. But Regan denies that the basis for inherent value lies in the capacity for autonomous action. To see why, we need to introduce a distinction between *moral agents* and *moral patients*. Thus far in our discussion of moral standing, we have taken competent adult human beings as the clearest example of things with standing. As we have noted, philosophers have disagreed about the criterion used to establish standing, but they all agree that competent adult humans meet it. These adults are full *moral agents* because they are free and rational. As such, they can understand their duties, can choose whether to act on them, and can be held responsible for those choices.

This characterization raises familiar problems with incompetent or immature humans, however. Infants and mentally incapacitated or comatose individuals lack the ability to understand and choose. Therefore, they cannot be said to be moral agents. They have no duties and cannot be held responsible for what they do or fail to do. Indeed, they are *moral patients*. This means that they have moral standing—we cannot do just anything to or with them—even though they are not full moral agents. They cannot *act* morally or otherwise, but they can be *acted on* morally or immorally.

When we understand this distinction and recognize that many things that are not full moral agents still have moral standing, we can figure out what is missing from much of the standard discussion of moral standing. Too many philosophers have focused exclusively on moral agents in establishing the criterion of moral standing. The class of all things with moral standing includes *both* agents *and* patients. We need to ask what it is about moral agents and moral patients that explains their inherent value. Why is it wrong, in principle, to treat either agents or patients as food, targets, entertainment, or slaves?

Regan's answer is that they are *subjects-of-a-life*. Having a life, as opposed to merely being alive, involves a fairly complex set of characteristics.

> To be the subject-of-a-life … involves more than merely being alive and more than merely being conscious. To be the subject-of-a-life is to … have beliefs and desires; perception, memory, and a sense of the future, including their own future; an emotional life together with feelings of pleasure and pain; preference and welfare-interests; the ability to initiate action in pursuit of their desires and goals; a psychophysical identity over time; and an individual welfare in the sense that their experiential life fares well or ill for them, independently of their utility for others.[32]

Regan argues that justice demands that we treat all individuals with inherent value in ways that respect that value. This "respect principle" identifies Regan's views as reflecting an *egalitarian* theory of justice. Justice demands that we treat individuals with respect. Because inherent value is not reducible to any other type of value, we fail to treat individuals who have inherent value with the respect they deserve when we treat them as though they were valuable only as a means to some other end. Individuals with inherent value thus have the *right* to be treated with the same respect due to all individuals with inherent value.

It remains for Regan to conclude that animals can be subjects-of-a-life. At least some mammals possess the characteristics required for "having a life." These animals therefore have inherent value, and justice demands that we treat them with respect. Minimally, this means that we have a strong prima facie obligation not to harm them. (Regan acknowledges that this obligation can sometimes be overridden. But it can be overridden only in the same sorts of cases in which we would override the rights of an innocent human being.)

5.8 ETHICAL IMPLICATIONS OF ANIMAL WELFARE

Both Singer and Regan have written extensively on the ethical implications of their views. Although each has addressed a variety of specific issues, we will limit ourselves to four topics that have received wide attention among environmentalists.[33] First, both would argue that we have a responsibility as a society to end most commercial animal farming. None of the considerations that might be used to defend animal farming—taste, nutrition, convenience, efficiency, and property rights—can justify treating animals as food. Similar arguments would not suffice to justify eating humans, and they cannot suffice to defend eating animals. Individually, we have an ethical responsibility to be vegetarians. As citizens, we should outlaw these practices.

Likewise, sport hunting and trapping are unjust. Killing and often torturing animals for sport and entertainment is more than cruel. It is a serious injustice. Similarly, abusing and mistreating animals for any form of human entertainment is wrong. Just as it was cruel and vicious for Romans to use Christians for a particularly brutal form of entertainment, it is wrong for us to use animals in zoos, rodeos, and the like. A third issue concerns the use of animals in science and research. Experimentation on animal subjects can be especially harsh. We ordinarily would conclude that experimenting on human subjects who have not given their consent is unjust at best and barbarous at worst. People have been convicted as war criminals for such behavior. So, too, should we judge experimentation on animals.

Finally, like Feinberg, Regan and Singer do not support moral standing for species. Regan's view protects individual animals from harm but does not recognize species as having rights. An individual animal can be a subject-of-a life, but a species cannot. Likewise, for Singer, although individual animals can suffer pain, a species cannot. Thus, although these views support efforts to save endangered species, they do so only because the remaining members of that species, as individuals, have a moral standing that we must respect. In this context, Regan raises an issue that will become the focus of important discussions later in this textbook. Let us introduce this issue within a general review of philosophical challenges to the views of Singer and Regan.

5.9 CRITICAL CHALLENGES

Let us step back at this point and consider some criticisms raised against the animal liberation/animal rights view. The work of Singer and Regan generated a significant response among philosophers, much of it critical. Many of these criticisms followed familiar lines. For example, some philosophers, including Regan, challenge the utilitarian basis of Singer's program. Singer, after all, makes no *in principle* case against causing animals to suffer. Other philosophers develop the debate about attributing rights to nonhumans. Some argue that the concept of interests is so vague that it would allow tractors and buildings to have moral standing.[34] Although a complete review of these debates would take us too far afield, looking at several challenges will help us make the transition to later chapters.

One type of criticism directed against Singer calls to mind the measurement problems discussed in the introduction to utilitarianism. On one level, the "equal consideration of interests" principle defended by Singer does suggest a helpful decision process. It directs us to take all suffering into consideration when deciding among alternative policies. However, any effort to apply this directive soon encounters enormous complexity in application. As Singer acknowledges, humans are different from animals, so equal consideration does not entail equal (or identical) treatment. Further, interests and suffering are not all alike. Not all interests deserve to be treated equally, and not all suffering is created equal. For example, some philosophers distinguish between *basic* and *peripheral* interests.[35] Life, food, water, clothing, and freedom from intense pain might be thought of as basic interests. Indoor plumbing, automobiles, fur coats, air conditioning, and gourmet cooking might be considered peripheral interests.

But how are we to sift through these diverse and competing interests? Would a human's interest in fencing off prairie for agricultural purposes (something that might be necessary if we follow Singer's and Regan's advice and become vegetarians) override a wild animal's interest in unobstructed habitat? How does the spotted owl's interest in old-growth forests in the Pacific

Northwest compare with human interest in lumber? Would the lumber's use make a difference? As moral agents, do we have a responsibility to interfere with the life of animals in the wild? Should we protect predators or prey?[36] Are the interests of a starving wolf equal to the interests of a single member of a large herd of caribou? Are the interests of pets equal to the interests of farm animals? Of wild animals? Do we really want to give the interests of a rat *any* consideration when they conflict with the interests of a child that it might bite?[37]

These questions suggest problems for any view that gives the interests of individual animals serious moral weight. The relationships among humans and animals, animals of different species, animals and their habitat, and humans, animals, and the land are many and diverse. Establishing equal moral standing for individual animals is really only the beginning of the debate. Indeed, it frames the debate as a conflict, as fundamentally adversarial. Without a clear and determinate decision procedure, the question that began this entire debate—What is the proper relation between humans and other animals?—remains unanswered, if not unanswerable. Although "minimizing suffering" seems clear and simple, it does not seem to be a practical guide in light of complex realities.

Other challenges, usually aimed at Regan, suggest that the boundary of moral considerability is too restrictive—that is, it omits too many animals. (Similar criticisms of Singer, who has suggested that the boundary of considerability be drawn somewhere "between shrimp and oysters," charge that he includes too many animals). Although Regan most often speaks in general terms of "animals," the subject-of-a-life criterion most clearly applies to "mentally normal mammals of a year or more."[38] According to many environmentalists, this interpretation neglects important members of the ecological community.

The influence of ecology underlies other important criticisms of the animal welfare movement. For example, Regan acknowledges that his rights-based ethics, like most traditional ethical theories, is *individualistic.* That is, ethics is concerned with protecting and promoting the well-being of individuals, not communities or societies or some one "common good." This puts him at odds with much environmental and ecological thinking, which is *holistic.* Many environmentalists emphasize "biotic communities" or "ecosystems" rather than individual members (including humans) of those communities. Alluding to a parallel issue in political philosophy, Regan warns us of "environmental fascism" in which individual rights are willingly sacrificed to the greater good of the whole. "Environmental fascism and the rights view are like oil and water: they don't mix."[39]

Further, as we noted earlier, Regan is unwilling to attribute rights to species. He acknowledges that his view is individualistic. Only individual animals can be said to have moral standing or, more specifically, to have rights. This is a controversial claim even within the ethical tradition of which Regan is a part. Corporations and nations are but two examples of collections of individuals that are taken to have rights (albeit legal rights) that are not reducible to the rights of individual members. But beyond this issue, the individualistic bias of both Regan and Singer seems to imply other consequences that many environmentalists find unacceptable.

In Regan's view, an animal that is a member of an endangered species has no special moral status. The last remaining pair of bald eagles or spotted owls have less of a moral claim on us than a single mammal such as a whitetail deer. Preservation of the endangered blue whales is ethically no more important than preserving cows. We have no greater duty to mountain gorillas and black rhinos than to a stray cat, and we certainly have no direct ethical obligation to the millions of species of plants and animals that are not subjects-of-a-life.

Singer's views would also suggest conclusions counterintuitive to many environmentalists. Given the amount of suffering that can take place with intensive farming techniques, any one of literally billions of chickens would have a stronger moral claim against us (to relieve its suffering) than would the last remaining members of a plant or invertebrate species. Thus, according to critics, whatever else it might be, the animal welfare movement is not a central part of the environmental movement.

The emphasis on individuals also leads to controversial suggestions for wildlife management. Singer, for example, recognizes that it is conceivable that human interference could improve the conditions of wild animals. Nevertheless, judging in part on the basis of past failures, he recommends a policy of leaving wild animals alone as much as possible. We do enough, he tells us, "if we eliminate our own unnecessary killing and cruelty toward other animals."[40] This is consistent with a standard utilitarian belief that we have a greater responsibility to reduce suffering than to increase happiness. Regan apparently endorses a similar laissez-faire attitude. So long as we protect the rights of animals (or again, at least of mammals), other ecological concerns will take care of themselves. In his rights view:

> assuming this could be successfully extended to inanimate natural objects [which he thinks is unlikely at best], our general policy regarding wilderness would be precisely what the preservationists want—namely, let it be! ...
> Were we to show proper respect for the rights of the individuals who make up the biotic community, would not the *community* be preserved?[41]

But there are problems with this laissez-faire approach. First, we would need to reverse the long history of destruction and habitat loss before we could preserve biotic communities. Next, complete noninterference with the environment is impossible. The idea that some "untamed wilderness," untouched by human activity, can exist is a mirage. No place on earth, no animal on earth, and no period on earth has escaped human influence for quite some time. If only through the pollutants that we dump into the air and water (and our influence is much greater than that), humans affect every corner of the earth. The question is not *whether* we should actively influence the wilderness but *how* we should do so.

Second, the answer to Regan's question would seem, in many cases, to be no. Showing proper respect for the rights of deer, for example, can have disastrous consequences for its ecological community.[42] As is the case in many areas, the population of these deer can often overwhelm the carrying capacity of their habitat. With abundant food, protective hunting laws, and loss of natural predators, deer populations wreak havoc on their habitat and with many other species that populate that habitat. The result is destruction of many other life-forms in that ecological community.

Similar consequences face wildlife managers in parts of Africa. In some protected refuges in East Africa, the elephant population grew so large that it threatened to outpace its food supply. Left alone, many elephants would die a slow death of starvation, but not before destroying much of the surrounding vegetation. One alternative seems to be selective killing ("thinning the herd" or "culling the herd," in less offensive terms).[43]

The point of these examples is that animals, like humans, are part of a complex ecological community. Although it is constantly changing, this community seems to involve a delicate balance of interdependencies. For many environmentalists, the equilibrium of natural ecosystems should be the goal of an environmental ethics. Giving special ethical protection to individual animals threatens to upset that balance and cause damage elsewhere in that system. A laissez-faire attitude in conjunction with animal rights may well lead to serious ecological harms. There simply is no guarantee that a species—or, more generally, an ecological community—would be preserved if only we "show proper respect for the rights of the individuals who make up the biotic community."[44]

Many challenges to animal welfare ethics arise from the individualistic approach characteristic of Regan and Singer. Defending individual animals may not be the most appropriate environmental strategy. Other criticisms suggest that the extension of moral standing to animals has remained, in a peculiar sort of way and despite its intentions, anthropocentric.

How could moral standing for animals remain anthropocentric? Consider the philosophical method used by Feinberg, Singer, and Regan. They all begin by taking human beings as the paradigm of beings with moral standing. They all then ask what is it about humans that gives them moral standing? Feinberg answers with interests, Singer answers with the capacity to suffer, and Regan answers with being a subject-of-a-life. But why draw the line here? In effect, Feinberg, Singer, and Regan all seem to say that the paradigms of holders of moral value are human beings. Thus, only animals that are enough like us can have (or acquire because we "give it to them") moral standing. Moral standing seems a benefit that is derived from human nature and that living beings receive only if they are enough like humans.

Consider the case of invertebrates, the "little things that run the world," in the words of biologist Edward O. Wilson.[45] In the view of many environmentalists, preservation of invertebrates (animals that lack a backbone, such as insects, jellyfish, and mollusks) should be an ethical concern. Yet in the most obvious reading of Singer and Regan, these animals lack the necessary criteria for moral standing. Singer suggests that sentience is both necessary and sufficient for moral standing. That is, without sentience, a being does not have moral standing (the necessary condition), and sentience alone is enough (sufficient) to qualify for moral standing. Regan argues that moral standing derives from the inherent value found in subjects-of-a-life. But although it may be plausible to say that sentience and subjectivity are sufficient, why must we say that they are necessary? Why restrict inherent value to pleasure/pain or subjectivity?

One early challenge to this view was developed by philosopher Kenneth Goodpaster. Goodpaster argues:

> Neither rationality nor the capacity to experience pleasure and pain seem to me necessary (even though they may be sufficient) conditions on moral

considerability. And only our hedonistic and concentric forms of ethical reflection keep us from acknowledging this fact. Nothing short of the condition of being alive seems to me to be a plausible and nonarbitrary criterion.[46]

Further, Goodpaster reasons that sentience seems to be an adaptive characteristic that contributes to the survival of the organism. Presumably, the same could be said for subjectivity. This, according to Goodpaster, "at least suggests, though of course it does not prove, that the capacities to suffer and to enjoy are ancillary to something more important rather than tickets to considerability in their own right."[47] This "something more important" is life itself. When we restrict the range of moral standing among all living things to those sentient or conscious beings, we are, in fact if not logically, restricting moral standing to those beings most like us. Without further argument (and, in fairness, both Singer and Regan have answers), this would be an arbitrary restriction with significant environmental costs.

Thus some critics have come to believe that the animal welfare movement is not an adequate environmental philosophy. At best, it addresses only some environmental issues. In these critics' view, an adequate environmental ethics must reject both the individualism and the narrowness of philosophers such as Singer and Regan.

5.10 SUMMARY AND CONCLUSIONS

Whether or not Singer or Regan falls victim to these challenges, an important point has been established. Environmental ethics requires more than a simple concern for individual animals of a certain type. At a minimum, we need to consider questions about the moral status of a diversity of plant and animal life, about ecological communities, and about our role in those communities. A shift to such holistic and truly nonanthropocentric ethics, however, would require a radical break from tradition.

Toward the end of *Animal Liberation*, Peter Singer tells us:

> Philosophy ought to question the basic assumptions of the age. Thinking through, critically and carefully, what most of us take for granted is, I believe, the chief task of philosophy, and the task that makes philosophy worthwhile. Regrettably, philosophy does not always live up to its historic role.[48]

In the view of many environmentalists, Singer himself, along with Tom Regan, is guilty of exactly this failure. All of what follows in this textbook implicitly takes up this challenge to "question the basic assumptions of the age."

NOTES

1. Peter Singer, *Animal Liberation*, 2d ed. (New York: New York Review of Books Press, 1990), p. 95; the emphasis is Singer's.

2. Ibid., 136.

3. Later in this chapter we see this claim developed at more length by Lynn White.

4. Aristotle, *The Politics*, book 1, ch. 8, p. 1256b, in *Basic Works of Aristotle*,

ed. Richard McKeon (New York: Random House, 1941).

5. Thomas Aquinas, *Summa Contra Gentiles*, ed. English Dominion Friars (London: Burns and Oates, 1924), book 3, pt. 2. See Gen. 9:2–3, for the command to Noah. See also John Passmore, *Man's Responsibility for Nature* (New York: Scribner's, 1974), p. 6, for a brief discussion of Aquinas's views on this passage from Genesis. Passmore remains an excellent source for understanding the philosophical roots of the "man-as-despot" view.

6. See Passmore, *Man's Responsibility for Nature*, ch. 4, for a discussion of Kant's concern for future generations, and Annette Baier, "For the Sake of Future Generations," in *Earthbound: New Introductory Essays in Environmental Ethics*, ed. Tom Regan (New York: Random House, 1984), pp. 214–46, for further discussion of this issue.

7. The italics are Bentham's. This passage appears in *The Principles of Morals and Legislation* (Oxford, England: Oxford University Press, 1907), ch. 17, sec. 1, footnote to paragraph 4.

8. Gen. 1:26–29.

9. Lynn White, Jr., "The Historical Roots of Our Ecological Crisis," *Science* 155 (March 10, 1967): 1203–1207.

10. Passmore, *Man's Responsibility for Nature*, pp. 186–87.

11. Ibid.

12. Ibid.

13. Ibid., 189.

14. Ibid.

15. Ibid., 13.

16. William Blackstone, ed., *Philosophy and Environmental Crisis* (Athens: University of Georgia Press, 1974). See Blackstone's contribution, "Ethics and Ecology," pp. 16–42.

17. Ibid., 31.

18. Ibid., 32.

19. Ibid.

20. Joel Feinberg, "The Rights of Animals and Unborn Generations," in Blackstone, ed., *Philosophy and Environmental Crisis*, pp. 43–68.

21. Ibid., 44.

22. Ibid., 49.

23. Christopher Stone, *Should Trees Have Standing? Toward Legal Rights for Natural Objects* (Los Altos, Calif.: William Kaufmann, 1974), p. 9.

24. For a brief account of this history, see Roderick Nash, *The Rights of Nature* (Madison: University of Wisconsin Press, 1989), pp. 128–31.

25. Stone, *Should Trees Have Standing?*, p. 11.

26. Ibid.; the emphasis is Stone's.

27. Ibid., 24.

28. Singer attributes the term "speciesism" to Richard Ryder's essay "Victims of Science," in *Animals, Men, and Morals*, eds. Stanley Godlovitch, Roslind Godlovitch, and John Harris (New York: Grove Press, 1973). This book was the subject of a 1973 review by Singer, "Animal Liberation," *New York Review of Books*, April 1973, pp. 17–21.

29. Singer, *Animal Liberation*, pp. 7–8; the emphasis is Singer's.

30. Ibid., 16–17.

31. Tom Regan, "The Case for Animal Rights," in *In Defense of Animals*, ed. Peter Singer (Oxford, England: Basil Blackwell, 1985), p. 13; the emphasis is Regan's.

32. Tom Regan, *The Case for Animal Rights* (Berkeley: University of California Press, 1983), p. 243.

33. These are the four that Regan considers in *The Case for Animal Rights*. For other discussions, see especially Tom Regan, *All That Dwell Therein* (Berkeley: University of California Press, 1982). Singer's *Animal*

Liberation remains the best single source for his views.

34. See, for example, R. G. Frey, "Rights, Interests, Desires, and Beliefs," *American Philosophical Quarterly* 16 (July 1979): 233–39.

35. See Donald VanDeVeer, "Interspecific Justice," *Inquiry* 22 (Summer 1979): 55–70.

36. For a detailed response to some of these questions, see S. F. Sapontzis, *Morals, Reason, and Animals* (Philadelphia: Temple University Press, 1989), especially ch. 13, "Saving the Rabbit from the Fox," pp. 229–48.

37. This example is from Singer's *New York Review* essay "Animal Liberation," p. 21.

38. See Regan, *The Case for Animal Rights*, especially pp. 77–78. Regan later expands this a bit, suggesting that although it is always difficult to draw such lines, it would not be unreasonable to give the benefit of the doubt to any animal that shares the "relevant anatomical and physiological properties" with mammals. His example of such a relevant property is the central nervous system.

39. Ibid., 361–62.

40. Singer, *Animal Liberation*, p. 226.

41. Regan, *The Case for Animal Rights*, p. 363; the emphasis is Regan's.

42. For a review of these and similar challenges, see J. Baird Callicott's "Review of Tom Regan's The Case for Animal Rights," *Environmental Ethics* 7 (Winter 1985): 365–72. Callicott also cites Mark Sagoff, "Animal Liberation and Environmental Ethics: Bad Marriage, Quick Divorce," *Osgoode Hall Law Journal* 22 (1984): 306, as a reference for this particular point.

43. For a good discussion of the Tsavo National Park dispute, see Daniel Botkin, *Discordant Harmonies* (New York: Oxford University Press, 1990), ch. 2.

44. For development of this claim, see Mark Sagoff, "Animal Liberation and Environmental Ethics," p. 26; J. Baird Callicott, "Review of Tom Regan"; and "Animal Liberation: A Triangular Affair," *Environmental Ethics* 2 (1980): 311–28.

45. E. O. Wilson, "The Little Things That Run the World," *Conservation Biology* 1 (December 1987): 344–46. Wilson gave this as an address at the opening of the invertebrate exhibit at the National Zoological Park in Washington, D.C., in 1987; it is reprinted in *The Environmental Ethics and Policy Book*, eds. Donald VanDeVeer and Christine Pierce (Belmont, Calif.: Wadsworth, 1994), pp. 84–86.

46. Kenneth Goodpaster, "On Being Morally Considerable," *Journal of Philosophy* 75 (1978): 308–25.

47. Ibid., 31.

48. Singer, *Animal Liberation*, p. 236.

DISCUSSION QUESTIONS

1. Throughout the world, many laws prohibit abuse of animals. List as many reasons for these prohibitions as you can. Do any of these reasons commit you to holding that animals have a moral standing in their own right?

2. Can natural objects be said to have interests? What are the interests of the Gulf of Mexico? Can certain things be said to be good for rivers, mountains, and forests? Is this the same meaning of "good" that we use when we

talk about the moral good for humans?

3. Christopher Stone argues that trees should be granted legal standing. If this happens, how should their interests be represented? In the well-known Dr. Seuss book *The Lorax*, it is the Lorax who "speaks for the trees." Can anyone truly speak for the trees?

4. Try the following mental experiment concerning what objects have moral standing. Assume that competent adult human beings are placed at one end of a continuum and a rock at the other. Where along that continuum would you place the following: a child, a brain-dead adult, a fetus, a dolphin, a dog, an insect, an alien, a bird, a species, and a tree? Have you used a single criterion either implicitly or explicitly?

5. How exactly would you distinguish between the actions satirically advocated in Jonathan Swift's "A Modest Proposal" and the modern factory farming of veal, cows, chickens, and pigs? What are the relevant similarities, if any? What, if any, are the relevant differences?

6. Do you see any morally relevant differences between domesticated and wild animals? Would Singer? Would Regan? Do you see any morally relevant differences between animals that are threatened with extinction and those that are not?

7. What kinds of arguments can you give for vegetarianism? Which are moral arguments? Are you convinced by any of them? Why or why not?

8. Recently, during a particularly harsh winter, the state of Minnesota delivered tons of feed to wild deer faced with starvation. Do humans have such responsibilities to wild animals, particularly those that are in no danger of extinction? Does it matter to you that this state's action was supported mainly by hunters who feared a dwindling deer population?

9. Does hunting or fishing raise any moral issues? If people eat the animals they kill, does that make a difference? In many areas, deer are overpopulating local habitats. Destruction of the habitat as well as mass starvation can occur in such circumstances. Would you favor selective hunting to thin overpopulated herds?

GLOBAL ENVIRONMENTAL ETHICS WATCH

For more information on Responsibilities to the Natural World, please see the Global Environmental Ethics Watch. Updated several times a day, Global Environmental Ethics Watch is a focused portal into GREENR—our Global Reference on the Environment, Energy, and Natural Resources—an ideal one-stop site for current events and research. You will have access to the latest information from trusted academic journals, news outlets, and magazines as well as access to statistics, primary sources, case studies, videos, podcasts, and much more.

To gain access please use the access code that accompanies your book. If you do not have an access code, visit cengagebrain.com to purchase one.

PART III

Theories of
Environmental Ethics

6

Biocentric Ethics and the Inherent Value of Life

DISCUSSION: Synthetic Biology and the Value of Life

Does life itself have inherent moral value? Several criteria for moral standing were examined in the previous chapter, including sensation and being conscious. For many observers, such attributes as sensation and consciousness themselves serve a higher end of life, and therefore they conclude that only life itself seems to be plausible candidate for the inherent value that moral standing implies. A "biocentric" ethics is an approach that begins with the inherent value of life as its foundational principle of value.

The diversity of life on earth is amazingly complex. Biological science has been categorizing animal and plant species since before Aristotle began his taxonomy of living organisms more than 2,000 years ago. Current estimates suggest that more than 1.4 million different species have been scientifically categorized.[1] But, these categorized species represent only a small percentage of the actual number of species that exist. On the basis of research conducted in tropical forests, some estimates place the number at more than 30 or 40 million species. Biologist E. O. Wilson estimates that invertebrate species alone may number as many as 30 million. Each species contains from a few members (for example, the California condor) to many billions of members (such as bacteria). Each species exists in an ecological niche in which its members interact with their environment to maintain life. Wilson tells of many highly specialized life-forms.

> One of my favorite examples of such specialists living in microniches are the mites that live on the bodies of army ants: one kind is found only on the mandibles of the soldier caste, where it sits and feeds from the mouth of its host; another kind is found only on the hind foot of the soldier caste, where it sucks blood for a living, and so on through various bizarre configurations.[2]

Each organism must take in nutrition from its environment to sustain its life and propagate its species. The ability to do this has evolved through millions of years of changing environments via natural selection. This ability, and every other function of living beings, is stored in the genetic code of each organism. Each organism contains 1 million to 10 billion bits of information in its genetic code, representing an enormous genetic library of information developed over billions of years. The diversity of life has inspired scientists, philosophers, and poets for millennia. It is a remarkable phenomenon.

But that diversity is being threatened at astonishing rates. Some scientists, including E. O. Wilson, estimate that over 100 species per day, almost 50,000 species each year, become extinct. Fossil records show that extinction has been a fact of life. But these same fossil records show that the rate of extinctions that are not related to human influence—what scientists call the background extinction rate—is significantly smaller than present extinction rates. Mammals, for example, are becoming extinct at 100 times the background rate. The present extinction rates for rain forest species and freshwater species are even higher. Without question, the earth is in the midst of the greatest single extinction episode since the one associated with the extinction of dinosaurs 65 million years ago. The difference, unfortunately, is that this episode is largely due to human factors. Further, estimates suggest that it may take more than 10 million years of life on earth for a natural return to the same number of species as had existed before human-caused extinctions.

But even as many natural life forms are facing extinction, human technology has reached a point where new life forms are being designed and created artificially. In the emerging field of synthetic biology, scientists and engineers are designing biological objects, ranging from small strands of DNA to entire genomes, cells, and organisms. This technology promises to transform medicine, energy, industry, and the environment while it also raises fundamental philosophical and ethical questions.

Broadly understood, synthetic biology is a field in which biology merges with engineering to design biological entities that otherwise do not exist in nature. In more traditional genetic engineering, naturally occurring genes are recombined and manipulated to create a genetically engineered organism, for example by repairing a genetic malfunction or transferring some biological function to another organism. In contrast synthetic biology involves the use of DNA, genes, cells, or organisms that have been synthesized by humans.

In May 2010, a team of scientists at the J. Craig Venter Institute announced the following:

> the successful construction of the first self-replicating, synthetic bacterial cell. The team synthesized the 1.08 million base pair chromosome of a modified *Mycoplasma mycoides* genome. The synthetic cell is called *Mycoplasma mycoides* JCVI-syn1.0 and is the proof of principle that genomes can be designed in the computer, chemically made in the laboratory and transplanted into a recipient cell to produce a new self-replicating cell controlled only by the synthetic genome.

The Venter Institute goes on to describe that this genome was "constructed from four bottles of chemicals that make up DNA."[3] To many observers, this announcement meant that humans had succeeded in creating life itself from four bottles of chemicals.

Various definitions of synthetic biology have been offered, including: "the design and construction of new biological parts, devices, and systems, and the re-design of existing, natural biological systems for useful purposes. (Synthetic Biology.org)" "Synthetic biology ... can broadly be described as the design and construction of novel artificial biological pathways, organisms or devices, or the redesign of existing natural biological systems. (UK Royal Society)." "Synthetic biology is the engineering of biology: the synthesis of complex, biologically based (or inspired) systems which display functions that do not exist in nature. This engineering perspective may be applied at all levels of the hierarchy of biological structures – from individual molecules to whole cells, tissues and organisms. In essence, synthetic biology will enable the design of 'biological systems' in a rational and systematic way." (European Commission)[4]

So, on one hand, life on earth is undergoing mass extinctions, most of which are strongly influenced, if not caused, by human activities. On the other hand, humans are on the verge of major breakthrough in creating life in the laboratory. These two phenomena challenge us to consider the proper stance that humans ought to take towards the natural world, and in specific towards other living beings.

The loss of biological diversity raises a variety of value questions. What does it matter, for example, that a mite living only on the mandible of the soldier caste of army ants becomes extinct? What is the value of life? Traditionally, many instrumental justifications have been given to support the preservation of this biodiversity. Tremendous medicinal, agricultural, economic, and scientific potential lies in the variety and diversity of life. However, such achievements are exactly the primary goal of synthetic biology. Thus, it may well be that we can achieve those goals "in a more rational and systematic" way through synthetic biology than by working with naturally occurring organisms. If such values could be better served by artificial life forms, then this instrumental justification for biological diversity loses much of its force.

But these instrumental values suggest an attitude towards the natural world that views other living objects as mere tools to be used for our own ends. As we discussed in the previous chapter, however, many have argued that living beings have a value that goes beyond the merely instrumental. Some environmental philosophers have argued that life itself possesses inherent value, it is to be valued for its own sake and not simply for how we can use it. But does your attitude towards the natural world and towards life change as a result of synthetic biology's success in creating life in the laboratory?

DISCUSSION TOPICS:

1. Are naturally occurring life forms more or less valuable than artificial ones? Is there an important ethical distinction to be made between life that occurs naturally and life that is created artificially?

2. Do you think that every living being possesses some inherent value simply due to the fact that it is alive? Why, or why not?

3. Was the creation of a biological organism from four bottles of chemicals more or less wondrous than the species of mite that exists only on the mandibles of ants?

4. Critics of synthetic biology sometimes assert that scientists are "playing God." What exactly do you think this means? Is it a persuasive criticism?

5. Do artificial organisms have a purpose or good of their own that is independent of the purposes for them that their designers intend?

6.1 INTRODUCTION

Chapters 3, 4, and 5 showed how standard ethical principles and concepts can be applied to environmental issues. With this chapter, our focus changes to consider more systematic attempts at developing comprehensive environmental philosophies. These approaches question the wisdom of simply *extending* traditional ethics, or what we have called ethical extensionism, in favor of more radical shifts in our ethical perspective. The problems with ethical extensionism revolve around three issues. First, despite the work of such philosophers as Singer and

Regan, the principles and concepts used in their application often remain narrowly focused. The criteria for moral considerability defended by many philosophers are most clearly found in adult human beings. Critics charge that ethical extensionism gives moral standing only to those animals that most closely resemble adult humans. As a result, these extensions remain fundamentally hierarchical and, according to critics, beg the question of the moral status of other living things. For example, both Singer and Regan attribute moral standing only to some animals, leaving out a majority of living species. Other living things remain outside the range of moral consideration. This omission strikes many environmentalists as both an ethical and a logical mistake.

Second, these extensions remain thoroughly individualistic. Individual animals have standing, but plants, species, habitat, and relations among entities have no standing in their own right. Yet so much of the science of ecology stresses the interconnectedness of nature. Ecology emphasizes such wholes as species, biotic diversity, ecological communities, ecosystems, and biological, chemical, and geological cycles. Relations, communities, systems, and processes play a major role in the science of ecology. Unfortunately, standard ethical theories have little room for such concerns. Indeed, we need only remember Regan's dismissal of the ethical focus on communities as "environmental fascism" to see how unreceptive these standard ethical views can be. To some environmentalists, this is the perfect example of a perspective caught in the grasp of a philosophical theory and ignoring the facts of science.

Finally, these extensions are not, nor were they intended as, comprehensive environmental ethics. Philosophers applied ethics to specific problems as the latter arose and as they were perceived, making little or no attempt to build a coherent and comprehensive theory of environmental ethics. This narrow focus has had two unhappy results. First, the extension of ethics to cover, for example, the rights of animals can provide no guidance for many other environmental issues, such as global warming and pollution. Second, extensionism tends to remain critical and negative. It often tells us what is wrong with various policies and actions but seldom offers guidelines about what the alternative "good life" should be.

The chapters that follow present a survey of attempts to develop more systematic environmental ethics. Much of the recent philosophical work on the environment breaks with standard ethical theory and strives to rethink the relationship between humans and nature. Indeed, some of these emerging schools of thought might more appropriately be described as environmental philosophies than as ethics. As philosophers seek a comprehensive account of the place of human beings in their natural environment, they must address more than merely ethical questions. The following topics become important when we begin to rethink ethics in this way: metaphysics (nature and the natural; the ontological status of systems, relations, species, and so forth), epistemology (the logical relation between descriptive and normative claims), aesthetics (beauty and intrinsic value), and political philosophy (civil disobedience and environmental justice).

Let us, then, put aside the role of the philosopher who approaches environmental problems armed with a previously articulated ethical theory. Instead, let us adopt the point of view of an environmentalist (or, more simply, of a concerned citizen) seeking to articulate, develop, and defend a coherent and comprehensive environmental philosophy.

No rational person can reflect on such challenges as global climate change and mass extinctions without some concern and distress. But to understand the goals of an environmental philosophy, we need to go beyond the stage of merely reacting. We need to examine the source of our concern. Why exactly are we troubled by these facts? Why *should* we be troubled by them?

These questions seem to have no single answer. In some cases, our distress grows from our awareness that such environmental destruction poses a clear danger to human beings and thus raises familiar ethical concerns. In other cases, the way we treat the environment offends spiritual, aesthetic, or cultural values. In yet other cases, we seem to be causing direct moral harm to natural objects themselves. The goal of many environmental philosophers is to provide a single systematic principle or theory that can account for these various concerns. Achieving such a goal would require work not only in ethics but also in metaphysics, epistemology, aesthetics, and political philosophy. Still other philosophers conclude that no such systematic account is possible and argue instead for a position called *moral pluralism*.[5]

6.2 INSTRUMENTAL VALUE
AND INTRINSIC VALUE

One way to understand the philosophical shift that is occurring among environmental philosophers is to contrast questions of morality with more general questions of value. Morality, narrowly understood, has always taken human well-being and the relationship between humans as its focus. Morality seeks to understand the rights and responsibilities of humans, human well-being, and the good life for human beings. Therefore, it is perhaps not surprising that philosophers have difficulty granting environmental concerns moral consideration. Environmental concerns simply do not fit within the traditional domain of morality.

But understood more broadly, philosophical ethics asks more general questions about the good life and about human flourishing. These questions involve wider concerns of *value*. From this perspective, environmental concerns are more legitimately ethical concerns, because they raise a wide variety of value questions that establish norms for how we ought to live. Not all value questions concern moral value (narrowly understood). We also recognize aesthetic, spiritual, scientific, and cultural values as worthy and deserving of respect.[6]

Thus, central to a comprehensive environmental philosophy is a consideration of the nature and scope of value. A full account of value determines the ethical domain by helping to define what objects have moral relevance or what objects deserve consideration. Ethics is concerned with how we should live, how we should act, and the kind of persons we should be. Defining the full scope of these "shoulds" is to give an account of all that has value or worth. Consider the example described in the preceding discussion case.

Uncounted species of insects are becoming extinct as a result of destruction of the rain forest. Many people find the wanton destruction of diverse life-forms offensive. But what exactly is wrong with causing the extinction of millions of insects? Insects do not feel pain, are not conscious, and are not subjects-of-a-life. They are not, in any obvious way, moral beings. What seems to be wrong is that something of value is lost—indeed perhaps wantonly destroyed—by human activity. Too often these values are lost for the sake of greed or out of sheer ignorance. A similar explanation might be given for the destruction of the rain forest itself, as well as for the loss of wilderness areas, wetlands, trees, lakes, oceans, fish, and plants. Why value insects? Why protect a wilderness area? Why care about plants? As we noted in Chapter 2, some religious traditions are exploring ways to answer these questions from theological starting points, but how are they to be answered philosophically? The shift from an ethics of animal welfare to a more holistic environmental philosophy can perhaps best be understood as a shift from a narrow conception of morality and moral value to a broader concern with value itself.

Philosophers often have discussed moral value in terms of interests. Among the philosophers considered in the last chapter, Joel Feinberg, Christopher Stone, Peter Singer, Tom Regan, and Kenneth Goodpaster all use the concept of interests to decide what sorts of things deserve moral consideration. To say that an object has interests is to say that it has a "sake of its own" (Feinberg), a "worth" in its own right (Stone), a "welfare" of its own (Bentham and Singer), "inherent value" (Regan), or its own "well-being" (Goodpaster). All this is to say that these objects have a value or worth that is independent of the value and worth ascribed to them by human beings. This implies that we do something wrong when we treat an object that has a value in itself and of its own as though it has value only in relation to us. This difference is typically expressed in the important distinction between instrumental and intrinsic value. *Instrumental value* is a function of usefulness. An object with instrumental value possesses that value, because it can be used to attain something else of value. A pencil is valuable, because I can write with it. A dollar bill is valuable, because I can use it to buy something. The instrumental value of an object lies not in the object itself but in the uses to which that object can be put. When such an object no longer has use, or when it can be replaced by something of more effective or greater use, it has lost its value and can be ignored or discarded.

Thinking of natural objects in terms of "resources" is to treat them as having instrumental value. For example, Gifford Pinchot's conservation movement emphasized the instrumental value of forests and wilderness areas. We should protect and conserve the wilderness, because it is the repository of vast resources that humans can use. Pinchot and other progressives argued that the value of national resources was too often unfairly distributed or wasted, which is to say improperly used. Many other environmental concerns rest on the instrumental value of the environment. Clean air and water are valued, because without them human health and well-being are jeopardized. The preservation of plant and animal species is valued by many because of the vast potential therein for medical and agricultural uses. Virtually any utilitarian or economic proposal is based on the instrumental value of nature. The stewardship tradition in religious ethics also has a strong instrumental predisposition. Likewise, synthetic biologists view the life forms that they are creating as valuable in this instrumental sense.

Appealing to the instrumental value of the environment can be an effective political strategy. Public opinion is often most responsive to claims of lost opportunities, wasted resources, and the like. Yet an environmental ethics that is based solely on the instrumental value of the environment may prove unstable. As human interests and needs change, so too will human uses for the environment. The instrumental value of the Colorado River as a water and hydroelectric power source for southern California will quickly override its instrumental value as a scenic wilderness or recreation area. Emphasizing only the instrumental value of nature means, in effect, that the environment is held hostage by the interests and needs of humans, and it immediately evokes the necessity to make trade-offs among competing human interests.

An object has *inherent or intrinsic value,* on the other hand, when it is valuable in itself and is not valued simply for its uses.[7] The value of such objects is intrinsic to them. To say that an object is intrinsically valuable is to say that it has a good of its own and that what is good for it does not depend on outside factors. Thus its value would be a value found or recognized rather than given. Not all things that we value are valued instrumentally. Some things we value, because we recognize in them a moral, spiritual, symbolic, aesthetic, or cultural importance. We value them for themselves, for what they mean, for what they stand for, and for what they are, not for how they are used.

Some examples can help explain this distinction. Think of friendships. If you value a friend only for her usefulness, you have seriously misunderstood friendship, and you would not be a very good friend. Consider also historical monuments or cultural and aesthetic objects. The Liberty Bell, the Taj Mahal, and Michelangelo's *David* possess value far beyond their usefulness. Clearly, many of our environmental concerns rest on the intrinsic value that we recognize in nature. Life itself, in the view of many, is intrinsically valuable, no matter what form it takes. Wilderness areas, scenic landscapes, and national parks are valued by many people, because, like the Liberty Bell, they are a part of our national heritage and history. (This is essentially the argument Mark Sagoff made, which we examined in Chapter 3.) Grizzly bears may have little instrumental value, but many people value knowing that the bears still exist in Yellowstone National Park. The symbolic value of the bald eagle transcends any instrumental value it might have. Undeveloped and unexplored wilderness areas are highly valued, even by people who will never visit, explore, or use these areas. John Muir's disagreement with Gifford Pinchot was a disagreement between one who saw an intrinsic value in wilderness (Muir) and one who did not (Pinchot). Muir spoke of the great sequoia groves as a cathedral, suggesting that they possess a spiritual and religious value far above their economic usefulness.

When we say that human activity degrades the environment, we are often referring to the loss of or disrespect for intrinsic value. When sections of the

Grand Canyon are eroded by flooding caused by water released from hydroelectric dams upriver, when acid rain eats away at ancient architecture in Greece and Rome, or when shorelines are replaced by boardwalks and casinos, human activity destroys some of the intrinsic goods that we find in nature.

For a number of philosophers working in environmental ethics, the greatest challenge is to develop an account of intrinsic value that can counter arguments based on instrumental values. As we saw in Chapter 5, John Passmore calls for an emphasis on the sensuous to offset the materialism and greed dominant in modern culture. After criticizing the dominant economic model (which recognizes only instrumental value), Mark Sagoff summons philosophers to articulate the cultural, aesthetic, historical, and ethical values that underlie our environmental commitments. These values, Sagoff tells us, determine not just what we *want* as a people but what we *are*.

The development of a more systematic environmental philosophy, then, often involves a shift from a narrow focus on moral standing or moral rights and responsibilities to a more general discussion of value, especially intrinsic value. Unfortunately, appeals to intrinsic value often meet with skepticism. We seem to lack the language for expressing intrinsic value. Many people think that such value is merely subjective, a matter of personal opinion: "Beauty is in the eye of the beholder." Thus, when a measurable instrumental value (such as profit) conflicts with intangible and elusive intrinsic value (such as the beauty of a wilderness), the instrumental value too often wins by default. The remainder of this chapter considers various views that reflect the conviction that life itself possesses intrinsic value and that, accordingly, humans have some responsibilities to it.

6.3 BIOCENTRIC ETHICS
AND THE REVERENCE FOR LIFE

The term *biocentric ethics* refers to any theory that views all life as possessing intrinsic value. (The word *biocentric* means life-centered.) Thus, although someone like Tom Regan is willing to attribute an inherent worth to some animals, his view is not biocentric, because it does not include all living things. Kenneth Goodpaster's focus on life itself as sufficient for moral considerability is biocentric.

An early version of a biocentric ethics is Albert Schweitzer's "reverence for life" principle. Schweitzer (1875–1965) wrote extensively about religion, music, ethics, history, and philosophy. He also, of course, devoted much of his life to bringing medical care to remote and isolated communities in Africa. His ethics, captured in the phrase *reverence for life*, is an extremely interesting precursor of contemporary biocentric ethics.

Schweitzer's was an active and full life committed to caring and concern for others. Yet he was also a prolific writer, who devoted many volumes to diagnosing the ethical ills of modern society and seeking a cure for them. Reverence for life was the attitude that he believed offered hope to a world beset with conflict. It is worth our while to examine briefly Schweitzer's diagnosis and cure.[8]

Modern industrial society had moved away from a worldview that connected the goodness of life with the goodness of nature. This belief, which Schweitzer called world-and-life-affirmation, is reminiscent of the natural law tradition in ethics. The rise of science and technology and the industrialized society that accompanied them severed the connection between ethics and nature by viewing nature as an indifferent, value-free, mechanical force. Modern science often views nature as a machine, governed by physical and mechanical laws. There is no good (nor, for that matter, any evil) intrinsic in nature itself. Set adrift in such a world, human ethics is left without foundation. Ethical value becomes no more than personal opinion or sentiment. Modern industrial society, with its wars, impersonal bureaucracies, meaningless work, and cultural decay, is the result of this separation.

Schweitzer's ethical thinking sought to re-establish the bond between nature and ethics. Yet, having spent time traveling in the most remote sections of Africa, Schweitzer did not deceive himself that nature is benign and gentle. He had been made more than aware of the destructive and arbitrary power of nature. He was nonetheless convinced that there was good in nature, an intrinsic value that could help provide a basis for human ethics. The idea that Schweitzer developed to solve this issue is captured by his phrase *reverence for life*.

Schweitzer describes in almost mystical terms the moment that this idea came to him. While riding on a barge traveling upriver in Africa, "at the very moment when, at sunset, we were making our way through a herd of hippopotamuses, there flashed upon my mind, unforeseen and unsought, the phrase *reverence for life*."[9]

What does reverence for life mean? Schweitzer's original German phrase was *ehrfurcht vor dem leben. Ehrfurcht* implies an attitude of awe and wonder. Although *reverence* perhaps connotes a religious tone that is not present in *ehrfurcht,* it seems clear that Schweitzer had something like this in mind. The etymological roots of *ehrfurcht* suggest a combined attitude of honor and fear. It would not be misleading to think of the attitude often inspired by majestic vistas from atop high mountains or the attitude inspired by violent storms.

Schweitzer held that the most fundamental fact of human consciousness is the realization that "I am life which wills to live, in the midst of life which wills to live."[10] Ethics begins when we become fully aware and fully in awe of that fact.

> The man who has become a thinking being feels a compulsion to give to every will-to-live the same reverence for life that he gives to his own. He experiences that other life in his own. He accepts as being good: to preserve life, to promote life, to raise to its highest value of life which is capable of development; and as being evil: to destroy life, to injure life, to repress life which is capable of development. This is the absolute, fundamental principle of the moral.[11]

In our terms, Schweitzer is claiming that all living things have an intrinsic value, a value that commands our awe and reverence. Life is not a neutral, value-free "fact" of the universe. Life is good in itself. It is inspiring and deserving of respect.

Critics are quick to caricature the "reverence for life" ethic. Is Schweitzer suggesting that the life of a virus or of bacteria is as worthy as human life? Does he suggest that we treat the life of an ant with as much respect as we treat human life? If not, does he offer any formula for resolving conflicts between human life and the life of, for example, the HIV virus? Would the existence of artificial synthetic life change one's attitude towards life?

Schweitzer lived his life in a manner that many people would find overly demanding. He would go to great lengths to avoid killing even mosquitoes, going so far as to carry them out of the room rather than swat them. Even when fighting disease-carrying mosquitoes, he was reluctant to kill. He resisted using DDT, for example, because he mistrusted the way it killed indiscriminately. Nevertheless, Schweitzer was not naive about the necessity of sometimes taking lives, especially out of reverence for other lives. To maintain life, other life must be sacrificed as food. He was also willing to take an animal's life to end its suffering.[12]

But this does not mean that Schweitzer defended some formula or rule to be applied in cases of conflict to establish priorities. Such a hierarchy would undermine the foundation of the "reverence for life" ethic, by suggesting that some rule or criterion is more fundamental than reverence itself. It would also downplay the serious dilemma that we often face when we must take life. A principle or rule that unequivocally resolves conflict would suggest that any ethical conflict is only apparent and not real.

Schweitzer did not envision reverence for life merely as some rule that we could apply to specific situations and, as it were, simply be read as the recommended decision. Reverence for life is more an attitude that determines who we are than a rule for determining what we should do. It describes a character trait or a moral virtue rather than a rule of action. A morally good person stands in awe of the inherent worth of each life.

But what does this say about those circumstances in which the good person must choose to kill? What about the doctor who kills a virus? The butcher who kills a pig? The farmer who cuts down a tree? Schweitzer denies that we can escape responsibility for these decisions. They must be made, but they should be made responsibly and consciously. Reverence for life is that character trait that sensitizes us to our responsibility for these decisions. It is an attitude that makes us aware of the full implications of these decisions. It makes us reluctant to take a life randomly, callously, or without remorse. In doing this, it helps us live an authentic and moral life.

It is an interesting exercise to consider how the creation of life forms in a laboratory might affect our attitude towards life. Natural life was created and evolved over eons, and any number of countless factors could have changed the course of history. Still, against all this, life does exist, life continues to evolve. In the face of such wonder, humans might take a more humble attitude towards their place in the universe. Yet, if these same humans can create life in a lab, perhaps life itself is not so special, not so valuable. And perhaps humans are more unique, and should be more proud, than otherwise thought.

Schweitzer's ethical views are richly textured and firmly based in the experiences of many years in the African wilderness. Yet these views never attained wide popularity among either the public or philosophers. Perhaps the tendency to see such a perspective as overly romantic or naive is too common and too great an obstacle. Schweitzer also never developed the type of scholarly defense of this position that professional philosophers demand. However, recent biocentric theories may be more persuasive.

6.4 ETHICS AND CHARACTER

Before moving to more recent biocentric views, it may be helpful to reflect for a moment on a philosophical issue that underlies this discussion. In the opening section of this chapter, we suggested that recent environmental philosophies represent a break with many traditional theories. Since that time, we have seen hints of what this might involve, and developing these hints at this point will prove useful.

As we discussed in Chapter 2, many defenders of traditional ethical theories, such as utilitarianism, deontology, and natural law, treat the fundamental question of ethics as "What should I do?" The goal of ethics is to articulate and defend rules or principles that can guide our behavior. The philosopher's job, then, is to justify those rules by demonstrating why all rational people should act in accordance with them. For most philosophers in these traditions, this task ultimately requires showing that obeying them is in a person's rational self-interest.[13]

Given this approach to ethics, we can understand why many people would have difficulty accepting Schweitzer's views on the reverence for life. If we do treat Schweitzer's view as a rule for guiding our actions, reverence for life might well commit us to the type of counterintuitive positions we mentioned at the end of the previous section. But Schweitzer did not offer reverence for life as an ethical *rule*. Reverence for life would be a fundamental *attitude* that we would take toward the world. In this sense, Schweitzer's ethics focused not on the question of what I should do but on what type of person I should be. His was not an ethics solely of rules as much as it was an ethics of character, seeking first to describe morally good people in terms of their *character,* dispositions, and values, rather than in terms of their actions.

This shift represents a return to the tradition of virtue ethics described in Chapter 2. An *ethics of virtue* emphasizes moral character or virtues rather than rules or principles. Ethical systems such as utilitarianism, deontology, and natural law focus on human *actions* and seek to defend some rule or principle that we use to judge whether those actions are right or wrong. Virtue-based ethics constructs a philosophical account of the morally good person, describing and defending certain character traits of that good person. Like Aristotle's, most virtue-based theories are teleological. Virtues are distinguished from vices (the opposite of virtues) by their connection with attainment of some human *telos,* or fulfillment. For Aristotle, the virtues were those character traits and dispositions that enable people to live a meaningful and fulfilling human life.

Keep this distinction in mind as we examine more recent environmental philosophies. Many of these emerging philosophies are not simply proposing alternatives to the rules or principles advanced by utilitarianism or deontology. Instead, they require us to make a shift in our philosophical perspective—a shift away from a concern with rules of behavior toward a concern with moral character.

These shifts require not only a different view of the environment but, at least as important, a different view of ourselves. Recall that Mark Sagoff tells us that a satisfactory environmental ethics must address not only those values that determine what we *want* but also those values that determine what we *are*. Implicit in this distinction is the recognition that our identity as a person is con- stituted in part by our values and attitudes. A person's character—those disposi- tions, relationships, attitudes, values, and beliefs that popularly might be called a "personality"—is not some feature that remains independent of that person's identity. Character is not like a suit of clothes that the self steps into and out of at will. Rather, the self is identical to a person's most fundamental and enduring dispositions, attitudes, values, and beliefs. Thus, when an environmental philoso- phy requires that we change our fundamental attitude toward nature, it is requir- ing quite literally that we change ourselves.

Note how this shift changes the nature of justification in ethics. If, as seems true in many traditional ethical theories, justification of some rule requires that it be tied to self-interest, we should not be surprised to find that this justification often fails. Ethical controversies often involve a conflict between self-interest and ethical values. Consider how we would "justify" the reverence for life. For a self that does not already include a disposition to treat life with reverence, the only avenue open for justification would involve showing how the disposition serves some other interest of the self. Why should I, if I have not already embraced the principle of treating life with reverence, do so now? The only way to answer this question appears to be to show how it is in my self-interest to adopt this attitude. But this means connecting the attitude to, in Sagoff's terms, those values that determine what we want instead of those that determine what we are. And this is to say that reverence for life must be reducible to some instrumental value. We should adopt the attitude of reverence because it, in some way, serves our purposes or satisfies our wants. Of course, this is exactly what the "reverence for life" ethic denies. Life has *intrinsic value*. It is much more than merely *instrumentally* valuable.

On the other hand, for the person already characterized by a reverence for life, the question of justification is less relevant. If one of my fundamental atti- tudes is a reverence for life, the question of why I should revere life ordinarily would not arise.[14] Thus, justification for an ethics that requires a fundamental shift in moral attitude involves something other than an appeal to self-interest.

6.5 TAYLOR'S BIOCENTRIC ETHICS

Paul Taylor's 1986 book *Respect for Nature* offered one of the most fully devel- oped and philosophically sophisticated contemporary defenses of a biocentric ethics. Although Schweitzer tried to explain what reverence for life means and what practical implications follow from this attitude, he never provided an adequate justification for adopting it. Part of the strength of Taylor's view lies in his careful exposition of why it is reasonable to adopt the attitude of respect for nature. For this reason, we will concentrate on his view as our example of biocentric ethics.

As a biocentric theorist, Taylor seeks a systematic and comprehensive account of the moral relations that exist between humans and other living things. Taylor sees this relationship as being based on the inherent worth of all life.

> The central tenet of the theory of environmental ethics that I am defending is that actions are right and character traits are morally good in virtue of their expressing or embodying a certain ultimate moral attitude, which I call respect for nature.[15]

Taylor's explanation and defense of this theory proceed through a number of steps. He first argues that it is meaningful to say that all living things have a good of their own. All living things can be said to have a good of their own because all living things are, in Taylor's phrase, "teleological centers of life." Taylor believes that this "good" is a simple fact that follows from living beings having a life. An entity's having a good of itself is necessary, but not sufficient, for us to conclude that humans have any responsibility to that entity.[16] To say that an entity has inherent worth is to go beyond the factual claim that it has a good and to make the normative claim that this entity deserves moral consideration and that moral agents have duties toward it. We move from the descriptive claim that a being has a good of its own to the normative claim that it possesses inherent worth when we come to understand and accept what Taylor calls "the biocentric outlook on nature." To accept this outlook and recognize the inherent worth of all living things is to adopt respect for nature as our "ultimate moral attitude." In turn, adopting this attitude means that we will act in morally responsible ways toward the natural environment.

To understand Taylor's views, we first need to distinguish things that have a good of their own from things that do not. Taylor cites a child as a being with a good of its own and a pile of sand as something to which it makes no sense to ascribe goodness. Parental decisions aim to promote the child's good. The child is benefited when that good is furthered and is harmed when that good is frustrated. On the other hand, it is meaningless to talk of the sand's own good, as though the sand itself could be harmed or benefited in any way.

Taylor next relies on a traditional philosophical distinction between *real* and *apparent* good or between what he calls *objective* and *subjective* value concepts. A thing's good is not always identical with what that being *believes* is its good. What *appears* to me (subjectively) to be good for me may not *really* (objectively) be good for me. This distinction allows Taylor to include in his biocentric ethics any being that has an objective good of its own. Because he ignores the concept of apparent or subjective goods, he need not include only those beings that possess the beliefs, interests, or desires presupposed in any account of subjective good.

What entities have an objective good of their own? Taylor's answer is to be found in the concept of a teleological center of a life. To understand this, it is helpful to draw some parallels with Schweitzer's "reverence for life" ethics and the natural law tradition of Aristotle. It also is informative to contrast what Taylor says with the concept of a subject-of-a-life as Regan uses it in animal rights ethics.

Let us begin with an example from Taylor.

> Concerning a butterfly, for example, we may hesitate to speak of its interests or preferences, and we would probably deny outright that it values anything in the sense of considering it good or desirable. But once we come to understand its life cycle and know the environmental conditions it needs to survive in a healthy state, we have no difficulty in speaking about what is beneficial to it and what might be harmful to it... . Even when we consider such simple animal organisms as one-celled protozoa, it makes perfectly good sense to a biologically informed person to speak of what benefits or harms them, what environmental changes are to their advantage or disadvantage, and what physical circumstances are favorable or unfavorable to them. The more knowledge we gain concerning these organisms, the better are we able to make sound judgments about what is in their interest or contrary to their interest.[17]

This is something that most of us, at least when we are not caught in the grip of a philosophical theory, would accept. It makes perfect sense to talk about the good of any living thing. This good is objective in the sense that it does not depend on anyone's beliefs or opinions. It is a claim that biological evidence can support. It is something that we can come to *know*. When we know an entity's good, we know what would be in that entity's interests, even if the being itself, such as a plant, has no conscious interests of its own. Thus even the weekend gardener can meaningfully talk about compost being good for tomatoes, pruning being good for an apple tree, drought being bad for vegetables, aphids being bad for beans, and ladybugs being bad for aphids.

All living things have a good, because living beings are teleological centers of life. Remember from the discussion of natural law ethics in Chapter 2 that the Greek word *telos* is translated as "purpose," or "goal," or "end." Aristotle was led by his biological observations to claim that all living things act toward some distinctive goal, or telos. Like Aristotle, Taylor claims that each species has a distinctive nature that determines the specific good for that species. Unlike Aristotle, he believes this nature need not be identified with the organism's essence or soul. For Taylor, this nature is more like the ecological niche or function fulfilled by that species.

As the aphid and ladybug examples suggest, however, the good of one species may not be good for another species. Each species has its specific end, but all living things do have ends. In general, that end is growth, development, sustenance, and propagation. Life itself is directional in the sense that it tends toward this end. Each living thing is the center of this purposive activity. Each living thing is the teleological center of a life.

Schweitzer's phrase in this context was "I am life which wills to live in the midst of life which wills to live." So long as we do not assume that all things that "will to live" must do so consciously, Schweitzer's thinking is similar to Taylor's on this point. Each living thing has its own good because, as a living thing, each life has direction, a goal, a telos. This is true whether or not the being itself is consciously aware of that fact. The will to live is manifested in the biological processes of growth, development, propagation, and sustaining life.

This view can be contrasted with Tom Regan's defense of animal rights. In Chapter 5, Regan argued that all beings that are subjects-of-a-life have the inherent value that qualifies them for moral standing. (Regan's use of "inherent value" functions for him as "inherent worth" does in this chapter.) To be a subject-of-a-life involves a complex set of characteristics that go beyond merely being alive and merely being conscious. In this way, Regan defends moral standing only for "mentally normal mammals of a year or more." Taylor's concept of a teleological center of a life is more inclusive than Regan's subject-of-a-life. According to Taylor:

> To say it is a teleological center of a life is to say that its internal functioning as well as its external activities are all goal-oriented, having the constant tendency to maintain the organism's existence through time and to enable it successfully to perform those biological operations whereby it reproduces its kind and continually adapts to changing environmental events and conditions. It is the coherence and unity of these functions of an organism, all directed toward the realization of its good, that make it one teleological center of activity.[18]

Like Regan, and unlike Aristotle and Schweitzer perhaps, Taylor is especially careful in moving from the *descriptive* claim that some being has a good of its own to the *normative* claim that we have ethical duties toward that being.[19]

According to Taylor, it is a matter of biological fact that living things have a good of their own. But it is not an ethical good in the sense that this fact alone does not commit us to any particular ethical stance toward living things. Having a good of its own does not by itself confer moral standing on a being.

Taylor's perspective explains the normative claims that all living things have moral standing and that we have duties toward them by reference to the concept of inherent worth. As he uses this phrase, inherent worth commits us to making two further normative judgments: Entities with inherent worth deserve moral consideration, and all moral agents have duties to respect that entity's own good.[20] What is the connection between a thing's having a good of its own and its possessing inherent worth?

Having a good of its own makes it possible for a living thing to be the object of human duties. That is, we can have duties to promote or preserve a being's good, only if it does, in fact, have a good of its own to be promoted. Having a good of its own is therefore necessary for a being to possess inherent worth. But it is not sufficient. The normative claim that living things have an inherent worth is to be explained and justified by reference to what Taylor calls the biocentric outlook. The biocentric outlook is a system of beliefs that conceptualizes our relationship to other living things. It is a system of beliefs that provides a fundamental view of the natural world and our relationship to it. Once we adopt this worldview, we see that treating all living things as possessing inherent worth is the only way of treating them that makes sense. Only this way of understanding them is consistent with the biocentric outlook.

The biocentric outlook on nature revolves around four central beliefs. First, humans are seen as members of earth's community of life in the same sense and on the same terms as all other living things. Second, all species, including humans, are part of a system of interdependence. Third, all living things pursue their own good in their own ways (the "teleological center of life" belief). Finally, humans are understood as not inherently superior to other living things.[21]

Taylor goes on to explain that the biocentric outlook is a way of conceiving of nature that all rational and factually informed people should adopt. It is an outlook that is firmly based on reasonable scientific evidence. Rejecting this outlook would require us to give up or significantly revise a good deal of what the science of ecology has learned. Once a person adopts this view, she or he will see that recognizing the inherent worth of all living things is the only perspective on life that is consistent with this outlook.

To regard living things as possessing inherent worth is to adopt the attitude of respect for nature. It is to adopt a fundamental attitude toward nature that establishes certain basic motivations and dispositions. To adopt this attitude is to be disposed toward promoting and protecting the good of other living things, simply because it *is* their good. It is to accept the good of other beings as a reason for one's own action.

Taylor's biocentric ethics addresses a number of philosophical issues that were missing in Schweitzer's "reverence for life" ethics. Taylor's account of how the biocentric outlook makes the attribution of inherent worth to all living things reasonable offers a rational basis for this belief that is lacking in Schweitzer's. Likewise, his description of inherent worth and a good of one's own adds much to the philosophical debate. It remains for Taylor to turn to issues of normative ethics and offer more practical advice.

6.6 PRACTICAL IMPLICATIONS

Taylor's normative ethics focuses on two basic issues: the general rules or duties that follow from the attitude of respect for nature, and priority rules for resolving conflicts between the ethical claims of humans and those of other living things. Let us briefly review these normative implications as an example of how more recent ethical thinking might be applied to environmental practice.

Taylor develops four general duties that follow from the attitude of respect for nature. They are the rules of *nonmaleficence, noninterference, fidelity,* and *restitutive justice.*[22] As the term suggests, the duty of nonmaleficence requires that we do no harm to any organism. Taylor understands this as a negative duty. That is, we have the duty to refrain from any act that would harm an organism with a good of its own. We do not, however, have the positive duty to prevent any harms that we are not causing. Nor do we have the duty to reduce suffering or aid the organism in attaining its own good. Finally, like all duties, this requirement applies only to moral agents. For example, except for humans, predatory animals cannot be required to refrain from harming their prey.

The rule of noninterference also establishes negative duties. By this rule, we are required not to interfere with the freedom of individual organisms or, in general, with ecosystems or biotic communities. Because humans can interfere with individual organisms in a variety of ways, a variety of specific duties follow from this general rule. We should neither actively prevent organisms from freely pursuing their good nor act in such a way as to deny them the necessities required to attain that goal. Thus we should not trap or enslave organisms or do anything that would deny them health or nutrition.

The duty of noninterference requires that we "not try to manipulate, control, modify, or 'manage' natural ecosystems or otherwise intervene in their normal functioning."[23] Finally, because this is a negative duty, we have no positive obligation to help such organisms fulfill their telos, *except* where our own actions are the cause of the harm.

Taylor applies the rule of fidelity only to animals that live in the wild. Respect for nature requires that we not deceive or betray wild animals. Most hunting, fishing, and trapping—and much of the enjoyment and challenge of these activities—involve the attempt to deceive and then betray wild animals. As in any case of deception, the deceiver assumes a superiority over the deceived. The deceived, whether an animal or another human, is taken to have a lower worth than the deceiver. Although hunting, fishing, and trapping also typically involve violating the duties of nonmaleficence and noninterference, breaking the rule of fidelity is yet another way of showing disrespect for nature.

The fourth rule, the duty of restitutive justice, requires that humans who harm other living organisms make restitution to those organisms. Justice demands that when a moral subject has been harmed, the agent responsible for that harm make reparations for the harm. In general, the first three duties establish the basic moral relationship between humans and other living organisms. When any of these rules is violated, the rule of restitutive justice requires that the moral balance between the two be restored. Thus, if we destroy an animal's habitat, justice demands that we restore it. If we capture or trap an animal or a plant, justice demands that we return it to its natural environment.

Finally, Taylor argues for a priority relation for these four rules. He believes that the duty of nonmaleficence is our "most fundamental duty to nature." He also believes that with careful attention, we can minimize conflicts involving the other three. However, when conflicts cannot be avoided and when significant good can result without permanent harm, restitutive justice outweighs fidelity, which outweighs noninterference.

Perhaps the greatest challenge to any biocentric ethics arises when human interests conflict with the interests of nonhumans. In many ways, this is the primary test of any environmental philosophy, and it is typically the major motivation behind any attempt to develop an environmental philosophy. What is to be done when important human interests come into conflict with the welfare of nonhuman organisms?

We need to recognize that in order to remain consistent with the fundamental principle of biocentric ethics, any resolution of such conflicts must not privilege human interests. That is, we cannot accept as a solution any decision that grants an in-principle advantage to humans. Any solution to conflict must respect the inherent moral worth of nonhumans.

We thus recognize that many moral conflicts and dilemmas would not arise within an anthropocentric framework. It is only after we acknowledge the inherent worth of other living things that a wide variety of conflicts can arise. Taylor mentions several as examples: filling in a wetland to build a marina, bulldozing a meadow of wildflowers to build a shopping mall, plowing a prairie to plant wheat or corn, and strip-mining a mountainside.

These activities raise moral problems only when we acknowledge that they create significant harm to other living organisms. But how do we resolve these conflicts without automatically favoring humans?

Following a long tradition in liberal political philosophy, Taylor argues for several formal or procedural rules to provide fair and impartial resolution of these conflicts. These rules are (1) self-defense, (2) proportionality, (3) minimum wrong, (4) distributive justice, and (5) restitutive justice. Self-defense would justify favoring human interests when the conflicting interests of nonhuman organisms threaten or endanger human health or life. Thus we would be justified in killing an attacking grizzly bear or exterminating an infectious organism or insect. As in the case of human self-defense, this principle holds only as a last resort.

The other four principles come into play when no serious harm to humans is threatened. They all rely on a distinction between *basic interests* and *nonbasic interests*. The principles of proportionality and minimum wrong govern those cases in which the basic interests of nonhumans conflict with the nonbasic interests of humans. In this case, if the nonbasic human interest is incompatible with the basic interests of nonhumans, the principle of proportionality prohibits us from satisfying the (nonbasic) human interests at the expense of the (basic) nonhuman interests. Thus, for example, human interest in killing reptiles to make fashionable shoes and handbags is prohibited, via the principle of proportionality, by the respect for nature.

When nonbasic human interests can be made compatible with the basic interests of nonhumans, even though they threaten or endanger the nonhumans, the principle of minimum wrong sets the conditions for satisfying human interests. Thus the respect for nature might allow damming a river for a hydroelectric power plant even, when this will adversely affect other living things.

The principle of distributive justice sets the conditions for resolving conflicts between the basic interests of humans and nonhumans. In general, fairness demands that burdens be shared equally and that the distribution of benefits and burdens be accomplished impartially. Finally, restitutive justice demands that restitution be made whenever a resolution of conflict fails to meet the conditions established by the principles of minimum wrong or distributive justice.

6.7 CHALLENGES AND DEVELOPMENTS

Even Taylor's careful defense of biocentric ethics faces serious challenges. First, there are several practical challenges to his conclusions. For example, the emphasis on noninterference as a major normative principle suggests a view of humans and nature that is questionable at best. To say that we ought not to "interfere with" nature implies that humans are somehow outside of or distinct from nature: Humans are separate from nature, so we should leave natural processes alone. Thus the claim is that environmental change—or even environmental destruction—is allowable (good?), if it results from natural processes. Change or destruction is wrong, if it results from human interference. But surely humans are as much a part of natural processes as any other organism. Accordingly, the fact that change is brought about by humans should not in itself have any ethical implications.

Other challenges center on Taylor's emphasis on individual organisms. Inherent worth resides only in individual organisms. We have no *direct* duty to ecosystems, nonliving objects, or species, for example. Thus, although Taylor's biocentrism is nonanthropocentric, it remains individualistic. Several problems follow from this.

First, Taylor's ethics tends to assume an *adversarial* relationship between individuals. By focusing on individuals, each pursuing its own telos, Taylor assumes that conflict and competition are the natural state of life. The challenge for biocentric ethics, in this model, is to find a procedure for resolving these conflicts impartially. We will see other philosophers suggest that a more holistic philosophy would emphasize cooperation and mutual dependencies rather than conflict.

Further, the focus on individuals seems to place Taylor in a serious dilemma. Consider one example. I am planning to dig up a small section of my front yard and replace the lawn with a concrete and brick patio. In the process, I will be destroying countless living things, from the individual blades of grass to millions of microbiotic organisms. Does this action raise a serious moral conflict?

As we have seen, Taylor cannot simply grant the human interest priority without abandoning his biocentric egalitarianism. Thus he would rely on the distinction between basic and nonbasic interests and the principles of proportionality, minimum wrong, and restitutive justice to resolve this conflict. Ultimately, I will either be allowed to build the patio, or I will not.

If I am not allowed to build the patio, Taylor's ethics may require too much of us. This is more than simply saying that it is counterintuitive. (Taylor argues that we have no reason to reject a conclusion solely because it is counterintuitive.) Rather, Taylor's standard would require a level of attention and care far beyond the abilities of most people. (Should I refrain from walking across my lawn, lest I create a path and thereby destroy countless blades of grass? Do I really need to provide an ethical justification for eating vegetables?) It is difficult to see how we could ever be justified in doing much of anything if we treated all nonhuman life-forms as deserving moral consideration.

On the other hand, if I am allowed to build the patio, Taylor must show exactly why such a nonbasic interest as this can override the basic interests of the grass and microorganisms. Clearly, we could never allow the mass killing of humans for the sake of a patio, so in order to maintain the nonanthropocentrism, we need strong justification for why patio construction is allowed in the case of plants. Taylor seems to suggest that, finally, the principle of restitutive justice comes into play. I can build the patio so long as I "restore the balance of justice between us and them." Because I unfortunately cannot restore the balance with those organisms that I have destroyed, this option seems to imply that my duty is to the organism's species. Perhaps I ought to replant some grass elsewhere in my yard. But this, of course, requires us to abandon the individualism on which Taylor's ethics rests.

A more general challenge returns to the discussion of teleology and biological designs and purposes introduced in Chapter 2. Taylor's view relies on inferring, from certain biological facts, the conclusion that teleological centers of a life have a good of their own. The biological sciences do commonly refer to an object's purpose, goals, or function, and in this sense, they also seem to adopt a teleological framework. But does all goal-directed activity imply that the goal must be understood as a "good." Such an inference was made in the Aristotelian and natural law traditions, but it is not obviously valid.

Consider the clear example of a human action that aims for some goal. Why do we assume that this goal is a good thing? One explanation is that we assume that any intentional act by conscious and rational agents is undertaken, because that agent believes that the goal is, in some sense, good. Almost by definition, a rational person wouldn't choose to do something, unless he or she believed that it was the good thing to do. Aristotle himself argued that all acts aim for some good. But if the subject is nonconscious and nonintentional, can we still conclude that its goal is a good?

In contrast, consider the following examples from Chapter 2: "The purpose of the kidney is to remove waste from the blood," "The goal of brightly colored plumage on male birds is to attract females," "The function of a predator species is to control the population of a prey species," and "Wetlands function as flood control and water-filtration systems." Assuming that kidneys, bright plumage, species, and wetlands do not consciously and intentionally choose the goals they serve, it is less clear that attaining the goals does accomplish even a perceived good. Only if some other value component is elsewhere assumed (for example, that blood free from waste is good, that attracting females birds is good, that controlling the population of a prey species is good, or that floods are bad), can one conclude that attaining the goal is good. The question is whether Taylor slips in such a value assumption with the concept of a biocentric outlook and the attitude of respect for nature.

We can take a broader perspective on these challenges to Taylor by considering the case of synthetic biology that was introduced in this chapter's discussion topic. For all practical purposes, scientists have created life, self-replicating, biological organisms, in a laboratory. The existence of such artificial, synthetic life raises questions for each of the four principles that Taylor identifies as comprising the biocentric outlook and entailing an ethical respect for nature. First, Taylor claims that this biocentric outlook assumes that humans are mere members, on equal terms, of the biotic community. But, this claim loses some credibility, if humans are also creators of other members of the biotic community. Second, Taylor claims that all life forms, having evolved together, are part of a single system of interdependence. Yet, this is not true for synthetic life, which has played no role in an interdependent system. Third, Taylor asserts that all living beings have a good of their own and are "teleological centers of life." Given that humans have designed and created artificial life, a more plausible claim would be that the good of synthetic life forms is confirmed, when they serve the purposes for which humans have designed them. Finally, Taylor suggests that the biocentric outlook asserts that human beings are not inherently superior to other life forms. However, as creators of some life forms, one could argue that humans are, at least for those organisms, inherently superior.

So, major challenge to any biocentric theory remains. Are we justified in attributing a good to all living beings? Clearly, some things (Taylor's example was a pile of sand) have no good of their own. Clearly, other things do. Autonomous human beings, who form and pursue their own purposes and goals, surely have independent goods of their own. But do all living things have an independent good? What distinguishes life from random change, such that interference with one is a harm and with the other is not? It seems that unless we retrieve an Aristotelian teleological biology in which living beings naturally move to fulfill some natural end or adopt a "divine plan" version of natural law in which natural functions are God's design, it is not obvious that life left alone is good. Nor is it obvious that artificial life has a good of its own. Some life (those beings with their own purposes, for example) qualify, but others may not. The challenge remains for biocentrists to explain and defend the sense that all living things have a good intrinsic to their own life.

6.8 SUMMARY AND CONCLUSIONS

The biocentric approach pushes the bounds of moral standing about as far as they might ever go. All living beings, simply by virtue of being alive, have moral standing. Biocentrists are surely right to focus attention on the value of all living things. But the question is whether the value of life is moral value in the sense of full moral standing or is a different, perhaps still anthropocentric value. Reflecting on Schweitzer's reverence for life calls to mind the spiritual, symbolic, and aesthetic values discussed by Mark Sagoff. Perhaps not every object with noninstrumental, intrinsic value should be included in the category of moral standing.

Biocentrists also face the challenge arising from a more ecological point of view. It is not at all clear that species or ecosystems can be incorporated into the biocentric theory, because neither is alive in any straightforward sense. According to many environmentalists, such ecological wholes should be the primary focus of environmental ethics. We turn to these concerns in the following chapters.

NOTES

1. See, for example, E. O. Wilson, "Threats to Biodiversity," *Scientific American* 261 (September 1989): 108–16; E. O. Wilson, "The Current State of Biological Diversity," in *Biodiversity*, eds. E. O. Wilson and Frances Peters (Washington, D.C.: National Academy Press, 1988); and John C. Ryan, "Conserving Biological Diversity," in *State of the World 1992*, ed. Lester Brown (New York: Worldwatch Institute, 1992), pp. 9–26. For estimates of extinction rates besides Wilson's, see Dick Bryany, Daniel Neilsen, and Laura Tangley, *The Last Frontier Forests* (Washington, D.C.: World Resources Institute, 1997), and United Nations Environmental Program, *Global Biodiversity Assessment* (New York: Cambridge University Press, 1995). The statement on recovery rates is taken from the work of James Kirchner, University of California-Berkeley press release, March 3, 2000, "New Study Suggests Humans Will Not Live Long Enough to See Earth Recover from Mass Extinction."

2. E. O. Wilson, "The Little Things That Run the World," address given at the opening of the invertebrate exhibit, National Zoological Park, Washington, D.C., May 7, 1987. Reprinted in *The Environmental Ethics and Policy Book*, eds. Donald VanDeVeer and Christine Pierce (Belmont, Calif.: Wadsworth, 1994), p. 84.

3. http://www.jcvi.org/cms/fileadmin/site/research/projects/first-self-replicating-bact-cell/press-release-final.pdf.

4. All definitions were taken from Synthetic Biology project website, http://www.synbioproject.org/topics/synbio101/definition/ accessed June 13, 2011. A helpful ethical analysis of synthetic biology is "The Ethics of Synthetic Biology and Emerging Technologies," Presidential Commission for the Study of Bioethical Issues, Washington, D.C., December 2010. Available at www.bioethics.gov.

5. See Christopher Stone, *Earth and Other Ethics: The Case for Moral Pluralism* (New York: Harper & Row, 1987). Moral pluralism is discussed in Chapter 12.

6. Perhaps the best philosophical account of the values that support a comprehensive environmental ethics can be found in the writings of Holmes Rolston. See especially *Environmental Ethics* (Philadelphia: Temple University Press, 1988).

7. The philosophical debate over the meaning and legitimacy of instrumental, intrinsic, and inherent value continues. The understanding of instrumental value is relatively trouble-free. In what follows, I adopt Susan Armstrong and Richard Botzler's suggestion that an "emerging consensus" is settling on the meaning of intrinsic and inherent value. In this view, intrinsic value is independent of the presence of a valuer. An object has intrinsic value when it has value both in and for itself. Inherent value, on the other hand, requires the presence of a valuer who confers the value on the object. Thus, although it may be valued for its own sake (its value does not come from its usefulness), it does not have value in itself (if there were no one around to value it, it would be without value). For example, children have intrinsic value (they are valued in and for themselves), whereas a family heirloom has inherent value (it is valued for itself and not for its economic worth) but would be valueless, if there were no family around to value it. If we accept this distinction as meaningful, the major question becomes whether natural objects and nonhuman living

beings have intrinsic value or inherent value. For the emerging consensus claim, see Susan Armstrong and Richard Botzler, *Environmental Ethics: Divergence and Convergence* (New York: McGraw-Hill, 1993), p. 53. For a defense of intrinsic value, see Holmes Rolston, *Environmental Ethics* (Philadelphia: Temple University Press, 1988). For a defense of inherent value, identified as intrinsic value in a "truncated sense," see J. Baird Callicott, "The Intrinsic Value of Nonhuman Species," in *The Preservation of Species*, ed. Bryan Norton (Princeton, N.J.: Princeton University Press, 1986), Ch. 6.

8.   The most comprehensive statement of Schweitzer's ethical views is found in his *Civilization and Ethics* (London: A. & C. Black, 1946). His autobiographical *Out of My Life and Thought*, trans. A. B. Lemke (New York: Holt, 1990), is also quite helpful. James Brabazon's biography, *Albert Schweitzer: A Biography* (New York: Putnam, 1975) is a good secondary source.

9.   Schweitzer, *Out of My Life and Thought*, p. 130.

10.   Ibid., 130.

11.   Ibid., 131.

12.   Brabazon, *Albert Schweitzer: A Biography*, p. 257, reports that Schweitzer was willing to kill his pelican when he recognized that its injuries were untreatable. The other anecdotes reported in this paragraph are also from Brabazon.

13.   See Kenneth Goodpaster, "From Egoism to Environmentalism," in *Ethics and Problems of the Twenty-First Century*, eds. Kenneth Goodpaster and Kenneth Sayre (Notre Dame, Ind.: University of Notre Dame Press, 1979), pp. 21–35.

14.   Of course, people do have moments in which their fundamental attitudes are questioned. Such moments of existential crisis, however, tend to reinforce rather than counter the view that no further justification can be given.

15.   Paul Taylor, *Respect for Nature* (Princeton, N.J.: Princeton University Press, 1986), p. 80.

16.   Here Taylor uses the phrase *inherent worth* in roughly the same sense in which I have been using *intrinsic value*. An object with inherent worth possesses a value that is independent of any (other) valuer. It is to be valued both in and for its own sake.

17.   Taylor, *Respect for Nature*, pp. 66–67.

18.   Ibid., 121–22.

19.   For Tom Regan's views on this "naturalistic fallacy," see *The Case for Animal Rights* (Berkeley: University of California Press, 1983), pp. 247–48.

20.   Taylor, *Respect for Nature*, p. 75.

21.   Taylor, *Respect for Nature*, especially Ch. 3, fully develops the biocentric outlook.

22.   Chapter 4 of Taylor, *Respect for Nature*, fully presents these duties.

23.   Ibid., 175.

DISCUSSION QUESTIONS

1.   We use the word *value* both as a noun and as a verb. Certain objects are said to possess value, and humans value numerous objects. If no humans were around to do the valuing, would anything of value remain?

2.   Compose a list of things that you value. Distinguish those things that you value instrumentally from those things valued for their own sake. How many different types of value can you think of?

3.   Like Aristotle, Taylor suggests that each species has a distinctive nature that can best be identified in terms of a characteristic activity. How else might you distinguish between species?

4.   Taylor relies on a distinction between basic and nonbasic interests to mediate conflicting interests. Do you find this distinction helpful? What are some basic human interests? What are some nonbasic human interests? Do basic interests always override nonbasic interests?

5.   In Taylor's account, does it make sense to attribute interests or goods to a wilderness area, to a river, or to other ecosystems? Can such things be teleological centers of life?

GLOBAL ENVIRONMENTAL ETHICS WATCH

For more information on Biocentric Ethics, please see the Global Environmental Ethics Watch. Updated several times a day, Global Environmental Ethics Watch is a focused portal into GREENR—our Global Reference on the Environment, Energy, and Natural Resources—an ideal one-stop site for current events and research. You will have access to the latest information from trusted academic journals, news outlets, and magazines as well as access to statistics, primary sources, case studies, videos, podcasts, and much more.

To gain access please use the access code that accompanies your book. If you do not have an access code, visit cengagebrain.com to purchase one.

Wilderness, Ecology, and Ethics

The Greater Yellowstone Area (GYA) encompasses nearly 12 million acres of mostly public land surrounding Yellowstone National Park and Grand Teton National Park. The GYA includes two national wildlife refuges and six national forests in Idaho, Wyoming, and Montana. The summer of 1988 was the driest in Yellowstone's recorded history; virtually no rain fell during June, July, and August.

Each year, many dozens of fires burn within the GYA. Many result from lightning, and most extinguish naturally after burning little more than an acre or two. But the summer of 1988 was different. A total of 248 fires burned in the GYA that year, 50 within Yellowstone National park itself. Through May and June, rangers routinely allowed numerous small fires to burn, and most soon extinguished naturally. But by mid-July, high winds and continued drought conditions had lent a growing intensity to the fires. By late July, the National Park Service declared all the fires "wildfires" and began a major effort to suppress them. Despite the efforts of nearly 25,000 fire fighters, hundreds of fire-fighting vehicles and airplanes, and personnel from the U.S. Army, Air Force, Marines, and National Guard and the expenditure of more than $120 million, the fires continued to burn out of control throughout August and into September. For nearly two months, Americans watched and read news accounts of the fire as it burned through Yellowstone National Park.

Only a snowstorm in September finally brought the fires under control. By that time, nearly 1 million acres inside Yellowstone and an additional half-million acres outside the park had burned. Wild landscapes that had appeared as lush green forest in the spring had become blackened, devastated terrain by early fall.

For one hundred years after the creation of Yellowstone National Park in 1872,

149

fire suppression was the guiding policy of wilderness management, in both national parks and national forests. Smokey Bear was the well-known symbol of the effort to fight fires wherever possible. This policy had almost universal support. Timber interests saw it as a means of preserving valuable resources. Recreationists saw it as protecting their varied uses of the land. Preservationists saw it as a way to preserve the natural beauty of the wilderness.

As early as the 1940s, the U.S. Forest Service had begun to use fire as a tool for managing some forests. Through the 1950s and 1960s, the National Park Service experimented with controlled burns in certain areas. But the people charged with managing national forests and parks began to recognize the natural and beneficial function that fires can play within an ecosystem. Fires contribute to biotic diversity and natural plant succession. Seeds of some species (the giant sequoia and the jack pine, for example) can germinate only after exposure to the intense heat of fires. Some animal species, such as the Kirtland's warbler, in turn depend on such "fire species" of trees for habitat.[1] Fire can help litter decompose and can aid in recycling soil nutrients. Fires also help maintain habitat for larger species and allow access to food sources that sprout after a burn.

By the early 1970s, many parks, including Yellowstone, had adopted a fire policy that would allow certain naturally occurring fires to burn unchecked, as long as they did not threaten lives and property. Between 1972 and 1988, hundreds of these so-called prescribed fires were allowed to burn within Yellowstone Park. (When a fire does not meet these "prescriptions," it is designated as a wildfire, and efforts are made to suppress it.) Most prescribed fires extinguish naturally after burning small areas. Most observers considered this prescribed natural burn policy a success.

Two more recent events have challenged those who manage natural wild areas to re-examine policy regarding the use of fire as a management tool. On May 4, 2000, the National Park Service was managing a prescribed burn to clear underbrush at Bandelier National Monument. High winds quickly whipped it into a wildfire that spread over the town of Los Alamos, New Mexico. The fire burned out of control for over two weeks, burning almost 50,000 acres and destroying 260 homes. Over 25,000 people were required to evacuate their homes. The fire damaged buildings at the Los Alamos Nuclear Weapons Laboratory, birthplace of the atomic bomb and now the nation's major nuclear weapons plant. A report conducted by the U.S. Department of Interior criticized the National Park Service for failing to follow guidelines for such controlled burns. However, Interior Secretary Bruce Babbitt reiterated the Department of Interior's commitment to controlled burns as a management tool for wilderness areas. Secretary Babbitt emphasized that prescribed fires are an important management tool. "We have no choice but to manage these forests to get the fuel loads down. We can't abandon this program." Babbitt said that the U.S. forests are healthier and safer as a result of controlled burns. According to Babbitt, western forests are becoming more "dangerous and explosive" each year, because "the natural fire cycle is no longer present. We've used this prescribed fire program for many years. The fire management agencies have successfully reduced the fuel load, reduced the fire hazard, by burning literally millions of acres every year." This policy will face an immediate challenge in managing the Boundary Waters Canoe Area (BWCA) wilderness following a destructive windstorm during the summer of 1999.

On July 4, 1999, a devastating windstorm moved through the BWCA in northern Minnesota. In a short time, the storm damaged over 400,000 acres of forestland in and around the BWCA. Most trees in a path 30 miles long and 12 miles wide were downed or damaged. The BWCA is a strictly controlled wilderness area in which no motorized vehicles or boats are allowed. Entrance is restricted by a permit system that controls the number of visitors admitted each day. Travel is by hiking or canoe only. By law, these dead and damaged trees within the wilderness area must be left alone, and timber harvesting outside the BWCA in the Superior National Forest is tightly regulated. As a result, millions of dead trees now litter the forest floor. Many observers believe that a major fire throughout the BWCA is inevitable unless significant steps are taken to reduce the buildup of dead timber. Two options have been mentioned as means for doing this. One is a series of controlled burns within the BWCA to burn off excess deadwood and create firebreaks. Another is allowing motorized vehicles, in the form of chain-saws, bulldozers, and trucks, into the wilderness to harvest the downed trees as lumber.

Beyond the fire issue, BWCA authorities recognize that the post-blowdown region will be very different from what existed previously. Many of the trees lost to the storm were red and white pine, some 100 feet tall or more. The species most likely to regenerate will be aspen, a relatively short-lived deciduous tree. It would take many decades for a pine-dominated coniferous ecosystem to return, if in fact it ever did so.

DISCUSSION TOPICS:

1. After a major forest fire, should the U.S. Forest service actively replant trees, or should it "let nature take its course"? Does your answer depend on the cause of the fire? What exactly is the natural course of things?
2. Should fires with a natural cause like lightening be treated differently than human-caused fires?
3. What values would you cite in defending the decision to preserve an area such as Yellowstone National Park? Would those values be different for defending the protection of wilderness areas in the deserts of the American Southwest?
4. The Yellowstone fires did result in the death of wild animals, although many fewer than original estimates. What role should protecting animal life play in decisions to suppress wildfires?
5. As many as 4 million visitors each year travel to Yellowstone Park. How does this affect the park's standing as a "wilderness" area?

7.1 INTRODUCTION

As we noted in Chapter 6, biocentric ethics represents a significant departure from traditional ethical thinking in several ways. By making life itself, and not any particular characteristic of living things, the criterion for moral standing, biocentric ethics greatly expands the moral domain, while avoiding the moral hierarchy implicit in traditional theories. It thus involves a radical shift in ethical thinking by extending moral standing to much of the natural world.

But for many environmentalists, biocentric ethics has not gone far enough in breaking with tradition. Biocentric ethics seems inadequate for addressing a wide range of environmental issues. According to a variety of approaches that we can identify as *ecocentric,* an adequate environmental ethics must also give serious consideration to nonliving natural objects (for example, rivers and mountains), and it must give due consideration to ecological systems. *Ecological ethics* should be holistic in the sense that ecological wholes, such as ecosystems and species, as well as nonliving natural objects and the relationships that exist among natural objects, are seen as deserving ethical consideration.

Ecocentric thinkers argue that biocentric approaches literally fail to see the forest for the trees. They claim that environmental concerns for ecosystems and wilderness areas are not the same as concern for the individual trees, plants, and animals that live within them. Wilderness areas, forests, wetlands, prairies, and lakes are valuable in their own right and deserve moral consideration. According to these critics, biocentric ethics does not or cannot account for the value that we attribute to these ecological wholes. Because ecosystems, species, mountains, rivers, and so forth are not alive in any obvious sense, biocentric approaches seem unable to account for the ethical value that ecocentrists want to attribute to ecological wholes.

Ecocentric ethics owes much to the science of ecology, the study of the interactions of living organisms with each other and with their nonliving environments. *Ecosystems*—forests, wetlands, lakes, grasslands, and deserts—are areas in which a variety of living organisms interact in mutually beneficial ways with their living and nonliving environments. Ecologists seek to understand and explain these systematic interactions and dependencies. Unlike traditional botanists and zoologists, ecologists focus more on interdependencies and relationships than on individual organisms.

Ecocentric philosophies likewise focus more on the ecological communities formed by these interdependencies than on individual organisms. Ecocentric ethics is thus a holistic rather than an individualistic ethics. Ecology plays a major role in each of the ecocentric philosophies examined in the chapters that follow. Each of these philosophies appeals to ecology for help in explaining and defending its conclusions. Unfortunately, challenges arise whenever anyone attempts to use the science of ecology in philosophical and ethical reasoning. First, ecologists do not completely agree on proper scientific methods, models, and conclusions. Ecology has not become a single, unified science. Second, it is unclear what ethical conclusions, if any, can be drawn from scientific observations. It is possible to reason from similar ecological facts to widely different normative conclusions and from different ecological observations to identical normative conclusions. Thus the relevance of ecology to ethics is always an open question.

This chapter offers a general introduction to some important ecological concepts and the ways in which philosophical inferences can be drawn from science. Particular attention will be paid to the ethical and philosophical issues raised by a focus on the value of wilderness areas. As we begin to widen our philosophical and ethical focus to include value questions beyond moral ones, an understanding of the ways in which earlier traditions have thought about and valued the natural world will also prove useful. A good place to start is the various understandings of the term *wilderness*.

Wilderness areas are prominent examples of natural ecosystems, and the preservation of wilderness areas is at the forefront of many environmental disputes. Biocentric approaches seem unable to give direct consideration to wilderness areas. Indeed, any ethical extensionism—arguing for a moral standing for the wilderness, for example—seems unlikely to account for the variety of ways in which we value the wilderness. How we understand the wilderness, how and why we value it, and how we relate to and manage wilderness areas, therefore, are central concerns of ecocentric ethics.

But what principles should guide human interaction with the wilderness? On what ethical basis should we protect the wilderness? Should we actively *manage* the wilderness (if so, how?), or should we be more passive and merely seek to *preserve* or *protect* it? Do we have a responsibility to *restore* wilderness areas that have been developed? If so, what exactly would count as restoration? The Yellowstone fires of 1988 and the resultant controversies regarding fire suppression policy offer a prime example of this debate. Preserving such areas as Yellowstone and the BWCA requires active management—allowing some fires to burn but not others, for example. How should the U.S. Forest Service manage the BWCA after the major blowdown? The post-blowdown wilderness area will be very different from the earlier one. Will it be better, worse, or just different? Would a pine ecosystem restored by human activity be better than an aspen-dominated ecosystem, or just different?

7.2 THE WILDERNESS IDEAL

The *Wilderness Act of 1964* defines wilderness as those areas "where the earth and its community of life are untrammeled by man, where man himself is a visitor who does not remain." The wilderness denotes an area unspoiled and undisturbed by human activity. The *Wilderness Act of 1964* allowed the federal government to set aside large tracts of public land to protect them from development. Wilderness areas are set aside "for the use and enjoyment of the American people in such a manner as will leave them unimpaired for future use and enjoyment as wilderness."[2] Typically, this means that hiking, camping, nonmotorized boating, and some hunting and fishing are allowed. Commercial activities such as mining and timber harvesting and the construction of permanent buildings or roads are prohibited.

The idea of the wilderness is much more complex than it might at first appear. At first glance, a wilderness is much like a river or mountain range. It is a natural object that is just "out there" to be observed. But the *idea* of the wilderness is a much richer concept than this simple example suggests. Wilderness as a natural area set over and against human-inhabited areas such as cities and towns presupposes concepts and values that are far from universal. Indigenous peoples, for example, are unlikely to have a concept of wilderness like the one implied by the Wilderness Act. Agricultural and nomadic people would probably not make as much of a distinction between inhabited and uninhabited areas as urban dwellers might. There are reasons for thinking that the idea of a wilderness is a relatively modern invention.

Few wilderness areas "untrammeled by man" remain on planet Earth, although there are many areas where humans are only visitors. Humans inhabit much of the globe, and human activity affects the entire earth. Global climate change and the atmospheric effects of pollution are just two examples of the way human activity reaches everywhere. Indeed, most "wilderness" areas are human constructs in that constant human activity is necessary to preserve and manage them. Thus even the decision to set aside and preserve a wilderness area involves the active management of the wilderness. A wilderness may be less something that we discover than something that we create. The decision to create, preserve, and manage a wilderness area, therefore, involves ethical questions of how we *should* manage wilderness ecosystems. Should forest fires be suppressed or allowed to burn? Should species be reintroduced to areas where they once lived? Are these policies for the benefit of humans or to preserve some natural state?

Policy decisions about wilderness management depend greatly on how we conceive of and value the wilderness. Part of this understanding, in the minds of many contemporary observers, can be derived from the science of ecology. Part of this understanding also derives from our own history and culture. This section describes several traditional ways in which recent generations, especially Euro-Americans, have conceived of the wilderness.

As the word itself seems to suggest, the term *wilderness* is often taken to refer to a wild or untamed area. In this model, the wilderness is a threat to human survival. It is cruel, harsh, and perilous. This is an ancient view, common to many Judeo-Christian traditions that trace it to biblical discussions of the wilderness.

Both the Old and New Testaments describe the wilderness as a barren and desolate place. Indeed, the arid desert surrounding the ancient settlements of the Middle East was an exceptionally inhospitable place. Humans truly were only visitors there, because prospects for long-term survival outside a settlement were bleak. But the wilderness also has a deeper symbolic meaning.

The Bible states that Adam and Eve were banished from the Garden of Eden into an "accursed" wilderness that "will grow thorns and thistles for you and none but wild plants for you to eat."[3] Moses later leads his people out of slavery and wanders in the wilderness for forty years before entering the Promised Land. In the New Testament, Jesus enters the wilderness to fast for forty days, only to be tempted by Satan.[4] The symbolism is clear. The wilderness not only is dangerous, but it is also home to the devil. It is the antithesis of Eden and the Promised Land.

The views of other cultures provide an interesting contrast. Nomadic cultures, for example, rely too heavily on the wilderness to consider it an enemy. Chief Luther Standing Bear, an Ogallala Sioux, illustrated this point in his 1933 book *Land of the Spotted Eagle.*

> We do not think of the great open plains, the beautiful rolling hills, and the winding streams with tangled growth as "wild." Only to the white man was nature a "wilderness" and only to him was the land "infested" with "wild" animals and "savage" people. To us it was tame.... Not until the hairy man from the East came and with brutal frenzy heaped injustices upon us and the families we loved was it "wild" for us.[5]

To a large degree, the "hairy man from the East"—the European settlers and pioneers—shared the biblical view of the wilderness.

When the *Mayflower* arrived at Plymouth in 1620, the new settlers confronted a "hideous and desolate wilderness," according to William Bradford.[6] Two years later, Michael Wigglesworth described it as:

A waste and howling wilderness
Where none inhabited
But hellish fiends and brutish men
That devils worshiped.[7]

Time and again, Puritan writing and preaching noted the biblical parallels to the Europeans' experiences. Like the Israelites, they had escaped persecution, only to be led into the wilderness where God would test their faith. The wilderness was indeed the "Devil's den," home to "savages" trapped in "the snare of the Devil," "men transformed into beasts," serving as "slaves of Satan."[8]

This *Puritan model* gave rise to an ambiguous attitude toward the wilderness. On the one hand, the wilderness was an area to be avoided and feared. It was the area forsaken by God and home to the devil. Cities and towns were where humans could flourish. Bradford's hideous and desolate wilderness was where they suffered and died.

On the other hand, the wilderness represented an escape from oppression and, if not exactly the Promised Land itself, provided at least a temporary haven in which escapees from persecution could build the Promised Land. The Puritans believed that their faith was being tested in the New England wilderness. The wilderness, after all, was where their God had entered into a covenant with the Israelites. Proof that the Puritans were indeed the new "chosen people" would be manifest in how well they fared in this wilderness. In this way, the wilderness also represented a challenge to be overcome, an enemy to be dominated, and a threat to be conquered.

The Puritan model encouraged an aggressive and even antagonistic attitude toward the wilderness. The wilderness must be tamed. New land must be conquered, and a new Eden must be established. Humans are called to subdue and master the wilderness. The land is developed and improved and its value enhanced when woodlands are cleared, wetlands drained, soil tilled, and permanent settlements established. Like some of the native inhabitants, the Puritans relied on fire as a tool for controlling and conquering the wilderness. Eradication of "pests," "varmints," and "predators" such as wolves, coyotes, and bears is a moral imperative that follows from this perspective.

As these European settlers succeeded in this mission, the early Puritan model gave way to a different understanding of the wilderness. The wilderness could now be seen as a potential source of materials for building the good life. Once conquered, nature becomes identified with natural resources, and wilderness is simply the undeveloped stockpile of supplies. Until it is transformed into resources, the wilderness is a vast wasteland. Once human mastery is ensured, the wilderness is less of a threat and more of a promise. We are reminded of John Locke's image of a great unowned frontier being transformed by human labor into productive and valuable property. This *Lockean model* sees the wilderness as given by God to all people in common, waiting for an individual with initiative and ambition to go out and work it and, in the process, convert it into private personal property.

Thus the Lockean model sees the wilderness as real estate, a commodity to be owned and used. Its value is a function of the human labor with which it is combined. No longer something to be feared, the wilderness represents great potential for serving human ends. The wilderness is relatively passive. It is "just there," serving no purposes other than those of its owners. Unowned and, therefore, unused land literally is a wasteland. Unless and until put to human use, it is wasted potential.

It is fair to say that much of the early conservation movement embraced the Lockean model of the wilderness. Gifford Pinchot and other conservationists identified the wilderness with resources and valued it primarily for the commodities it produced. Of course, the Lockean model also was shared by those who opposed the conservation movement. Those who sought to control and exploit the wilderness in pursuit of personal fortune shared the Lockean assumption that the value of the wilderness is a function of human use. They agreed with the conservationists that the wilderness should be controlled and managed for human use. They disagreed over the range of beneficiaries of these resources.

Unlike the Puritan model, the Lockean model would tend to support a fire suppression policy. Although fires could be employed to clear land for some uses, forest fires represented a loss of resources and potential. The early conservationists guided the fire suppression policy in national forests and national parks. Smokey Bear was a product of the conservation movement. Conservationists could also used the Lockean model to justify eradication of predators, because they competed with humans for "game" and eliminating them would increase the resources available for human use.

A third model of the wilderness, influential among many people in the environmental movement, can also be traced to early European–American roots. The *romantic model* views the wilderness as a symbol of innocence and purity. In this model, the wilderness is the last remaining area of unspoiled and uncorrupted nature. In contrast to the Puritan model, the romantic model identifies the wilderness with Paradise, the Garden of Eden. This is the place to which humans can turn to escape the corrupting influences of civilization. Where the Puritans saw threats and satanic temptations, the romantic sees a sacred purity. Where the Puritans saw the city as home to human flourishing, the romantics see the city as the genuine wasteland.

The philosophical roots of this view can be found in Jean-Jacques Rousseau and in the American writers Ralph Waldo Emerson and Henry David Thoreau. Like Locke, Rousseau spoke in general terms about a "state of nature" that contrasted with the state of life within a society. For Rousseau, nature represented what was genuine, authentic, and virtuous about human existence. Society imposes artificial desires, selfishness, and inequality on human life. Although he did not propose a return to nature, Rousseau did believe that education and politics should be guided by principles derived from an understanding of the natural and intrinsic goodness of human beings. He proposed as a model a life lived in harmony with nature, characterized by self-sufficiency, simplicity of desires, independence from culture and technology, and tranquillity. In this view, the innate goodness of human nature is inseparable from the innate goodness of nature itself, a nature Rousseau often identified with the unspoiled wilderness of the Swiss Alps.

But it was the writings of Emerson and especially of Thoreau that had the earliest philosophical influence on the romantic view of the wilderness. Emerson was influenced by the European romantic movement of the eighteenth and nineteenth centuries. This outlook rejected scientific empiricism and rational analysis as the primary modes for understanding nature. The world of our ordinary experience—the world observed and analyzed by science—is largely a product of human creation and cultural conventions. We see and experience what we are taught to see and experience by our culture. At best, that world only mirrors a deeper reality, a reality unconditioned by human beliefs and values. True understanding comes only when we grasp this deeper, or "transcendent," reality.

The American philosophical movement associated with European romanticism is called New England transcendentalism. Transcendentalists, of whom Emerson and Thoreau are the best known, held that we grasp this deeper reality not by scientific and technological analysis but through intuition and imagination and through poetry and literature. Unspoiled by human activity, the wilderness is the most authentic instance of transcendent reality. It is the purest example of God's creation. The wilderness represents a retreat from the corrupting influences of civilization. The wilderness is the environment in which humans may attain their closest contact with the highest truths and spiritual excellence.

Thus Thoreau retreats to his cabin on Walden Pond. Walking in the wilderness had a tonic effect on his spirit; it was where "my nerves are steadied, my senses and my mind do their office." The wilderness provides the opportunity to "settle ourselves, and work and wedge our feet downward through the mud and slush of opinion, and prejudice, and tradition, and delusion ... till we come to a hard bottom and rocks in place, which we call *reality*."[9]

Perhaps nowhere is this romantic vision of the American frontier more fully observed than in James Fenimore Cooper's "Leatherstocking Tales." In a series of novels beginning with *The Pioneers* and followed by *The Last of the Mohicans, The Prairie, The Pathfinder,* and *The Deerslayer,* Cooper traced the life of Natty Bumpo. Natty—known variously as the Deerslayer, Hawkeye, and Leatherstocking—was the ideal romantic hero. He was raised among the Native Americans of upstate New York and from them learned the ways of the wilderness. He was a simple man, innocent yet wise, honorable, forthright, and virtuous. He was totally without pretense or any of the other vices conditioned by social life. He was at home in the wilderness, living in harmony with it.

As Natty's life unfolded through these novels, he was continuously being pushed farther westward by advancing civilization. He lived always on the border between civilization and the wilderness, a border located in central New York early in his life and on the Great Plains by its end. From this perspective, we can see how the demands and expectations of society turn natural innocence and virtue into greed, destructiveness, and vice. With Natty, we lament the loss of wilderness and, with it, the loss of a simpler life of authenticity and integrity.

7.3 THE WILDERNESS "MYTH":
THE CONTEMPORARY DEBATE

These various models for understanding and valuing the wilderness have had a significant influence on contemporary environmentalism. Obviously, Pinchot's conservationism and its view of the wilderness as a vast warehouse of natural resources have greatly influenced much of twentieth-century environmental policy. But the romantic model has probably had a more pervasive and pivotal influence on contemporary environmentalism. As early as the mid-1800s, the romantic appreciation of the wilderness and the corollary regret over its destruction led to calls for the preservation of wilderness areas. Thus the lines between conservationists and preservationists described in Chapter 3 were drawn six decades before the public debates over Hetch Hetchy. During the first decades of the nineteenth century, John James Audubon, for whom the Audubon Society is named, mourned the "destruction of the forest." He witnessed the "woods fast disappearing under the axe" and concluded that the "greedy mills told the sad tale, that in a century the noble forests should exist no more."[10] In an 1858 essay, Thoreau explicitly called for the creation of wilderness preserves.

> Why should not we have ... our national preserves ... in which the bear and the panther, and some even of the hunter race, may still exist and not be "civilized off the face of the earth"—our forests ... not for idle sport or food, but for inspiration and for our own true recreation?[11]

This transcendentalist conviction that wilderness areas could be the source of inspiration, if not divine revelation, was shared by perhaps the most influential preservationist, John Muir. Muir's writing and organizing contributed significantly to the creation of national and state parks and wilderness preserves. Although the earliest parks, such as Yellowstone, were not established solely for preservationist reasons, Muir's defense of the wilderness clearly underlies much of the contemporary understanding of parks and preserves. To a large extent, this defense is based on the romantic wilderness model as described by Emerson and Thoreau.

Because this romantic model of the wilderness underlies many environmental values, it is important to proceed cautiously. We need to be clear about how much this model is based on an accurate description of wilderness areas. We also need to articulate exactly where the value of wilderness areas lies. Finally, we need to be clear about the reasoning that leads us from a description of wilderness to value-based ethical and policy prescriptions.

Does the romantic model provide an accurate description of wilderness areas? Certainly, many wilderness areas match the beautiful and awe-inspiring images captured by romantic observers. We need only compare the scenic beauty of Glacier National Park with the urban decay of many industrial cities or the tackiness of suburban strip malls to recognize the attractiveness of the romantic model. Nevertheless, the model is not without problems. In recent years many observers, most of whom are sympathetic to the environmental movement, have challenged this "received view" of the wilderness.[12] These critics claim that this view of the wilderness is seriously flawed on scientific, historical, and ethical grounds. A flawed understanding of wilderness, they argue, can lead to misguided and dangerous environmental policies.

On first consideration, the claim that the wilderness is a "myth" might seem bizarre. The wilderness is a place, a natural object. It is "out there," a part of nature. How can a natural place be a myth?

The new critics of this received view of wilderness argue that "wilderness" is a concept best understood within a particular historical and cultural context. Environmental historian William Cronon identifies two primary sources for this idea.[13] Cronon claims that the eighteenth- and nineteenth-century European–American concept of the sublime, a concept central to romanticism, and the particularly American notion of the frontier go a long way toward explaining the modern understanding of the wilderness. For the romantics, a sublime experience was that rare opportunity on this earth to "glimpse the face of God." The sublime implied a sacred, spiritual, otherworldly experience. Such experiences were most likely to be had in places far removed from human contrivances and artifacts—in places where one was overwhelmed by the recognition of one's own mortality and insignificance. Such magnificent places as Yellowstone, Yosemite, and the Grand Canyon come to mind as paradigm cases of sublime environments.

The particularly American experience of the frontier also contributed to the creation of the wilderness myth. The frontier myth of the rugged individual, that independent, creative man of integrity who tested himself against nature, was a powerful force in shaping the American self-image. But as historian Frederick Jackson Turner wrote at the turn of the twentieth century, that frontier was over. It was no accident, according to Cronon, that a culture seeking to hang on to this powerful image would seek to protect the few remaining undeveloped wild areas within its borders.[14]

What are we to make of such claims? It would appear that a society that does not sharply distinguish between nature and culture, and one where individualism, geographical expansion, and conquest play major roles, would be a society where the idea of preserving a wilderness area from human encroachment would mean little.

Although historical explanations of the origins of the idea of wilderness can situate this concept in a historical context, they do not show that the concept is misguided or mistaken. Defenders of wilderness preservation can accept the historical explanation of how the idea arose and still continue to argue that wilderness areas deserve strong protection from human development. The new critics of the wilderness idea, though they are often defenders of wilderness protection themselves, doubt that the traditional understanding of the wilderness can provide sufficient rationale for its protection. Their criticisms of the wilderness *idea* fall into three general categories. Critics charge that the received view of the wilderness is factually and scientifically unsound, that it is ethically suspect, and that it is likely to have unacceptable political and practical implications.

The received view of the wilderness may in fact be an inaccurate model of the world. First, it has a tendency to view the unspoiled wilderness as a relatively benign and temperate place. Many romantic landscape portraits suggest a lush green forest with open meadows, no underbrush, spectacular sunsets, plentiful sources of food and shelter, docile animals, and temperate climate. In reality, of course, the wilderness can be a harsh place. Deserts, Arctic tundra, and rain forests are not at all like the romanticized image of nature that a person forms while walking around Walden Pond. Even the relatively welcoming areas within national parks and forests can be quite inhospitable places in the absence of modern conveniences or in the depths of winter. All too often, we appreciate the sublime wilderness only from a perspective distant and apart from nature—standing on a ridge looking down on the Grand Canyon, for example, rather than sweltering on the canyon floor on a dusty summer day.

Further, the received view can encourage thinking that might be called "pre-Darwinian." This model can see humans as separate from nature, perhaps drawing inspiration from it but nevertheless radically different from it. The human spirit is "transcendent," and although unspoiled nature is our closest contact with transcendent reality, it remains part of a lower physical reality. Many ecocentric ethics, in contrast, stress the Darwinian understanding that humans are much a part of nature, neither transcendent to nor radically different from it. From that perspective, acceptance of a dualism ("man and nature") can encourage moral hierarchies ("man above nature") and conflict ("man against nature").

The received view also has a tendency to identify the wilderness with an idealized image as it existed at one particular point in time. For example, North American and Australian environmentalists sometimes romanticize the land before the arrival of the first European settlers. But many areas "discovered" by the Europeans were of course much used by the native inhabitants. Large human populations were already living in these forests and grasslands when the first Europeans arrived. By systematically ignoring or distorting that fact, this view exhibits more than a small amount of cultural bias, if not outright racism.[15]

Finally, the received view is inclined to see the wilderness as a static, unchanging place. The suggestion is that if we simply leave it alone, the wilderness will be preserved in all its natural, unspoiled wonder. This view is expressed by George Perkins Marsh, a nineteenth-century environmentalist, whose writings influenced both conservationists and preservationists. In his 1864 book *Man and Nature,* Marsh claimed:

> In countries untrodden by man, the proportions and relative positions of land and water, the atmospheric precipitation and evaporation, the thermometric mean, and the distribution of vegetable and animal life, are subject to change only from geologic influences so slow in their operation that the geographical conditions may be regarded as constant and immutable.[16]

But this assumption has problems of its own. Few areas on earth are unaffected by human activity. Even the decision to protect an area as a wilderness preserve makes the wilderness dependent on human actions. But more to the point, as the controversies over the Yellowstone fires imply, the image of an unspoiled "constant and immutable" wilderness is incompatible with the ecological reality of natural processes. Does the commitment to preserving Yellowstone as a wilderness area require that we allow it to be devastated by a fire started by natural events? Lightning fires occur by the dozens every year in Yellowstone. A charred, blackened, treeless landscape might not be the sublime and romantic wilderness envisioned by many environmentalists. To prevent this from happening and, therefore, to "preserve" the wilderness would require substantial human interference with nature. On the other hand, allowing natural processes to unfold may result in a wilderness unlikely to inspire the sort of unity with a transcendent reality suggested by the romantic images of Yosemite and Yellowstone.

Imagine, for example, that you sought to preserve the Boundary Waters Canoe Area wilderness of northern Minnesota in its natural state. What would that look like? Are snowmobiles part of this natural state? Are canoes? Are Native Americans? Would hunting, fishing, and rice harvesting by native peoples be consistent with an unspoiled wilderness? Should Native Americans be allowed to pursue these traditional activities only in the traditional manner, or should they be allowed to use motorized boats? Is the ideal an image of what this area was like before Europeans arrived? Should we seek to reinstate the tundra that characterized the region many centuries ago? Perhaps its natural state is as it was during the last ice age. Is its natural state the coniferous forest of pine, cedar, and spruce, or is it the deciduous forests of aspen and birch that will probably flourish in the wake of the blowdown of July 4, 1999? Questions like these challenge any view of nature as constant and immutable.

Many contemporary ecologists reject the view of an unspoiled and unchanging nature. The wilderness must be understood as more dynamic than static. Change and evolution are often the norm, uniformity and constancy the exception. Ecologist Daniel Botkin makes this point in *Discordant Harmonies* (1990):

> George Perkins Marsh's idea of nature as undisturbed by human influence is the one generally advocated; this point of view is dominant in textbooks on ecology and in the popular environmental literature. Perhaps even more significant, this idea of nature forms the foundation of twentieth-century scientific theory about populations and ecosystems.... Until the past few years, the predominant theories in ecology either presumed or had as a necessary consequence a very strict concept of a highly structured, ordered, and regulated, steady-state ecological system. Scientists know now that this view is wrong at local and regional levels—whether for the condor and whooping crane, or for the farm and the forest woodlot—that is, at the levels of populations and ecosystems. Change now appears to be intrinsic and natural at many scales of time and space in the biosphere.... In at least some cases these changes are necessary for the persistence of life, because life is adapted to them and depends on them.[17]

The challenge for an ecocentric approach is to develop a coherent philosophical ethics that is consistent with ecology's emphasis on biotic wholes and yet recognizes that change is as normal as constancy. Thus we need an explanation of the relationship between parts and the whole and an explanation of the dynamics of change that govern this whole. Again, any ethics that takes ecology seriously must provide a philosophically adequate account of these topics.

Critics also suggest that the received view can encourage an ethnocentric perspective that is ethically suspect. As we have noted, this view often ignores the native people who populated the wilderness before white settlers and colonialists arrived. Once a wilderness is set aside to be preserved, traditional indigenous activities such as hunting and food gathering may no longer be allowed. Not only does such a perspective marginalize native peoples to the point where they can be ignored, but it also has reinforced policies that have lead to the dispossession and even destruction of such people and their cultures.[18]

Finally, according to critics, the received view can have undesirable political consequences. If environmentalists base their defense of wilderness protection on a faulty understanding of the wilderness, then there is a danger that the rationale will no longer be convincing once those faults are exposed. If wilderness areas are "untrodden by man," and if few such areas exist, then the wilderness preservation movement is pursuing an impossible dream, however noble. This exact argument was used, for example, during debates about the original founding of the BWCA wilderness. Wilderness advocates sought to designate over a million acres in Northern Minnesota as a wilderness area. Critics pointed to the homes, cabins, and fishing camps located within the proposed boundary. If a wilderness is an area "where man is a visitor who does not remain" and if there are long-time residents in this area, then it follows that this area is not a wilderness.

Of course, defenders of the wilderness idea have responses to these challenges. Holmes Rolston, for example, argues that such criticisms can gloss over important differences between the wilderness and inhabited regions and between nature and culture.[19] Although humans are part of the natural world, the extent and rate of change due to human activities are significantly different from the extent and rate of natural change. This is particularly true of modern, technological societies with their bulldozers, chainsaws, and machinery. Even when natural change is dramatic and extensive, as with the BWCA blowdown, it is still significantly different from human-wrought change. The changes that humans make are intentional and purposive. Natural change has its own history and causes. The BWCA storm is different—scientifically, historically, biologically, and aesthetically—from a comparably sized clear-cut. Further, even though native peoples populated much of the Americas and Australia before European settlers arrived, the scale and type of habitation changed noticeably with the arrival of European culture. Even though native peoples had complex cultures, they did not have the technology and machinery that could destroy and disrupt entire ecosystems. To say that humans are a part of nature should not imply that all human activities are equally compatible with natural processes. Critics of the wilderness idea are simply not discriminating enough in distinguishing between wild nature and human culture. Defenders claim that there is much to the idea of wilderness that justifies protecting wilderness areas from further human manipulation and habitation.

What are we to make of this debate? Two editors of a major anthology on the wilderness debate, J. Baird Callicott and Michael Nelson, conclude that "the received wilderness idea has been mortally wounded by the withering critique to which it has been lately subjected." Nevertheless, they believe that the wilderness idea is too important to be abandoned. Instead, we must look to a reformed idea of wilderness that can continue to guide environmental policy.[20] These editors offer two alternatives to the received view.

One alternative de-emphasizes the human-centered aspects of the received view. Much of the rationale for the received view was connected to human values; that is, the wilderness was valued as a resource reserve and also for aesthetic, spiritual, and recreational pursuits. Instead, we might focus on the nonhuman values associated with wild areas, particularly their value as habitat for other, often rare and endangered life-forms. Such "biodiversity reserves" should have a valued place as a refuge for diverse life-forms in a world of increasing human population. This alternative understanding can meet the challenges raised against the received view. They are scientifically defensible, because the science of conservation biology can provide solid ground for identifying and managing wilderness as habitat. They are compatible with some human uses, especially the sustainable lifestyles of traditional cultures. They would also broaden our understanding of wild areas by focusing on biodiversity and habitat rather than just on scenery and recreation. Thus biodiversity reserves are compatible with the distinction between nature and culture that Rolston, for example, defends.

Alternatively, we might reconceive that wilderness areas are providing opportunities for humans to live within a natural, sustainable, and symbiotic relationship with wild nature. The preservation of a wilderness area provides humans with their only—and perhaps their last—opportunity to live, learn, or relearn to live in harmony with the natural world. However this debate develops, it seems that a romantic and simple understanding of "the" wilderness is no longer a valid option for environmental policy or ethics.

7.4 FROM ECOLOGY TO PHILOSOPHY

Wilderness areas were examined as a paradigm case of the importance of ecological concepts for environmental ethics. The moral standing debates examined in Chapters 4 through 6 lacked the ecological perspective that many believe lies at the heart of environmental ethics. A central notion for understanding ecocentric ethics is the nature and implications of the biological science of ecology. Because many environmentalists and all of the ecocentric approaches to environmental philosophy that will be examined in the remaining chapters appeal to ecology to explain or justify their conclusions, we must be familiar with some of the models that have guided ecological research. Not only do philosophers disagree about the lessons to be drawn from ecology, but the ecological models of nature from which these lessons are drawn vary widely.

As a distinct science, ecology is little more than one hundred years old. The first use of the term *ecology* is generally attributed to the German biologist Ernst Haeckel in the 1860s. Haeckel combined two Greek words: *oikos,* meaning "household" or "home," and *logos,* meaning "study of." Ecology is the science that studies living organisms in their home or environment. (*Economics* has similar Greek roots: *oikos* plus *nomos,* meaning the "rules of the household.")

One early model invoked to guide ecological science was the *organic model.* In this view, individual species were seen as related to their environment in the same way that organs are related to the body. Just as an organism grows through developmental stages toward a mature level, so do ecological "households" grow, develop, and mature. Ecological environments can therefore be described as healthy, diseased, young, mature, and the like, according to a normal and natural developmental standard. This model, then, explains the parts-to-whole relationship in terms of an organism and construes the nature of change in terms of development or maturity.

This model provides an attractive foundation for many environmental policy recommendations and ethical conclusions. If the natural world goes through a normal and natural developmental process that has evolved over millions of years, we at least ought to proceed cautiously when we interfere with it. With reasoning that is reminiscent of the Aristotelian tradition, we might argue that because ecological systems have a natural telos, we can determine in a scientifically objective manner what is good and proper for those systems. Using this organic model as a guide, some environmentalists reason from the objective facts of ecology to policy and ethical conclusions. Just as we speak of the health and well-being of individual organisms, we can speak of the health and well-being of ecosystems.

This organic model appears in the pioneering work of two late-nineteenth-century American ecologists, Henry Cowles and Frederick Clements. These scientists focused their research on the process of plant succession within a particular geographical area. Working from the University of Chicago, Cowles studied the plant succession along the sand dunes of Lake Michigan. He found that as one makes observations farther and farther from the shore, plants are replaced by other species in a determinate and well-defined progression. Thus the ecologist could describe the normal or natural sequence of plant succession at any given location along the shore.

At the University of Nebraska, Frederick Clements was pursuing similar research on the prairies and grasslands of the western plains. Clements was also taken with the dynamic process of biological change that occurs within a particular habitat. He recognized that through time, various species are introduced into an area and become increasingly prevalent before eventually declining and disappearing. But Clements denied that this plant succession is random or arbitrary. He believed that for any given location and climate, plant succession develops toward a stable and relatively permanent population, what came to be called the climax community. Thus, for any particular location or habitat, ecologists could determine what specific climax community would be most at home there. This community could itself be thought of as a "superorganism" that provides the end point, or telos, for any given location.

In this organic model, the ecologist is like a physician. Just as the physician studies anatomy and physiology to determine the normal and proper function of the body, the ecologist studies a habitat—temperature range, rainfall, soil conditions, and so forth—to determine the normal and proper functioning of that area. The ecologist can then diagnose problems and prescribe treatment to ensure a healthy and balanced organism.

For Clements, this climax community can be understood as itself a "complex organism." It is:

> of a higher order than an individual geranium, robin or chimpanzee.... Like them it is a unified mechanism in which the whole is greater than a sum of

its parts and hence it constitutes a new kind of organic being with novel properties.[21]

Later, Clements claimed that:

> the unit of vegetation, the climax formation, is an organic entity. As an organism, the formation arises, grows, matures, and dies.... The climax formation is an adult organism, the fully developed community, of which all initial and medial stages are but stages of development. Succession is the process of the reproduction of a formation.[22]

According to the organic model, ecosystems strive toward a natural equilibrium, a stable and unified state of balance and harmony. For environmentalists eager to prevent destruction of wilderness areas, the organic model can prove helpful. It provides a seemingly scientific basis for identifying and diagnosing problems and offering advice for solving environmental problems. Not surprisingly, this advice typically faults human intervention and defends preservationist policies.

By the early twentieth century, the organic model had begun to fall out of favor among ecologists. Many ecologists came to believe that the organic model is mistaken on both scientific and philosophical grounds. Natural biotic communities do not always develop toward some one single organic whole. Ecologists began to see that the interaction among species, among plants and animals, and among the biotic and abiotic elements—soil, nutrients, and climate—is more complex and variable than the organic model suggests. The type of unity and stability observed by Clements and Cowles might exist in some locales and over the short term, but it might not persist in other locales and over the long term. The organic model also tends to treat the abiotic elements of a habitat as simply the location or passive environment in which the superorganism grows and lives. Instead, critics wanted to emphasize how this abiotic environment plays an active role in the functioning of ecological processes.

In the mid-1930s, British ecologist Arthur Tansley introduced the concept that would replace the organic model in mainstream ecological thinking. In a 1935 article, Tansley defends the concept of an ecosystem as a more appropriate model for ecological research.

> But the more fundamental conception is, as it seems to me, the whole *system* (in the sense of physics), including not only the organisms-complex, but also the whole complex of physical factors forming what we call the environment of the biome—the habitat factors in the widest sense.

It is the systems so formed which, from the point of view of the ecologist, are the basic units of nature on the face of the earth.

> These *ecosystems,* as we may call them, are of the most various kinds and sizes. They form one category of the multitudinous physical systems of the universe, which range from the universe as a whole down to the atom.[23]

The concept of an ecosystem remains a central scientific concept to this day.

Tansley was seeking to establish ecology as a legitimate scientific discipline. Talk of biotic communities as superorganisms with a life of their own struck many as unscientific and too metaphorical. Tansley wanted to keep ecology connected with the more legitimate physical sciences by replacing the language of complex organisms with the language of physical systems. In this view, ecosystems are no more mysterious than any other physical system and can be understood in the same terms and with the same categories used to describe physical systems ranging from atoms to the solar system.

The concept of an ecosystem has several advantages over the organic concept. First, it eliminates any reference to a superorganism or complex organism, which implies an independent being that is alive. In the 1930s, these ideas seemed to be based more on philosophical or metaphorical thinking than on careful scientific observation. Second, the system concept is well grounded in more mainstream science with analogues in physics, chemistry, and mathematics. Third, the ecosystem concept accommodates the important role that abiotic elements play in ecological processes. These elements contribute much to the structure and function of ecological wholes. This concept unites the physio-chemical processes of the abiotic elements with the biological processes of the living elements. Finally, the ecosystem concept preserves the key ecological idea that ecological wholes are a fundamental part of nature. The individualism that characterizes much of zoology and botany cannot tell the entire story of the biological sciences. Ecology contributes by observing and explaining the integration, connections, and dependencies within and among ecological wholes. The ecosystem concept can be used to explain that nature is not reducible to a collection of independent and isolated parts. Nevertheless, this whole is not itself a being or organism with an independent life but simply a collection of living and nonliving elements organized in a determinate way.

Beginning with Tansley, ecologists began to focus on the structure and function of ecosystems. A system's structure consists of the way its many parts are related. A key concept introduced with the ecosystem idea was the notion of a "feedback loop." Elements within an ecosystem are related not simply in linear and causal ways but also in more complex ways characterized as feedback loops. Essentially, this means that the elements within a system not only are affected by other elements but also produce effects on other elements in a dynamic network of interconnections. This feedback is not random but works to maintain a balance, or equilibrium, within the entire system. The standard example of a feedback loop is the thermostat on a home heating system.

Falling room temperature triggers a reaction by the thermostat, which in turn changes the room temperature by turning on the heating system. This change in room temperature affects the thermostat, which shuts off the heating system until, yet again, room temperature falls and the cycle begins anew.

This approach, then, holds that nature is organized into ecosystems—grasslands, lakes, prairies, and forests—that are structured in such a way that, through the normal functioning of the individual members, the systems maintain a relatively stable equilibrium, much like a heating system maintains room temperature. Both the structure—the network of relationships—and the function—the activities of feedback loops operating to maintain an equilibrium—can be explained in scientific and mathematical terms. Thus the holism of ecology is incorporated into the prevailing physical scientific paradigm.

More specifically, the structure of ecosystems can be explained in terms of the feeding relationships among species within the ecosystem. The network of relationships within an ecosystem is a network of food chains. Species are located at different "trophic levels" (from the Greek work *trophikos,* meaning "nourishment") along the network that reflect what they eat and what eats them. We can further specify the activity among the trophic levels in terms of the energy and biochemical nutrients that they exchange. In this way, ecology is further tied to the physical sciences.

By the mid-twentieth century, the ecosystem had become the standard model for ecological science. The idea of an ecosystem—a structured and identifiable whole that acts to maintain a reasonably unified and stable equilibrium—became an important influence for many environmentalists. We can further identify two strands within this tradition that might suggest different philosophical and ethical implications: the "community model" and the "energy model."

According to the community model, nature is understood as a community or society in which parts are related to the whole as citizens are related to the community in which they live or as individuals are related to their family. Change is viewed less as development or growth and more in terms of food exchanges. Members of a community fill different roles, or "professions," that contribute to the overall functioning of the community. In the community model, ecology truly does study nature's household.

Some early defenders of the community model were motivated by a desire to refute the Darwinian (and, to them, irreligious) emphasis on competition and conflict among species.[24] Nature is designed as a household, with each member cooperating and contributing to the whole. Many of these defenders were more comfortable identifying their project with a phrase older than *ecology.* To study nature's household is to study "nature's economy."

One of the most influential and respected scientists associated with the community model was the English zoologist Charles Elton. Elton described his zoology as "the sociology and economics of animals." His goal was to present a description of nature as an integrated and mutually dependent economy.

Elton's community model, therefore, was a *functional* model: Individual members are identified by the food function that they perform in the system. The system is seen in economic terms. Some members function as producers, some as consumers. The commodity is food, and ecological communities can be described as "food chains" in which individual members fill various occupations. The laws of ecology thus describe the processes of producing, distributing, and consuming food. Accordingly, an individual species' function or role within a food chain—its ecological *niche,* in Elton's terms—is determined by what it eats and what eats it.

The idea of a food chain is perhaps the most familiar concept of the community model. Some organisms, called producers, manufacture their food by producing organic compounds (sugars, starches, and cellulose) from inorganic molecules (carbon dioxide and water) and energy. Photosynthesis is the primary process through which producers manufacture food. Other organisms, called consumers, depend on producers directly or indirectly for their food source. Herbivores, or primary consumers, feed directly and exclusively on plants (producers). Carnivores feed either on plant-eating animals (these carnivores are called secondary consumers) or on other animal-eating animals (in which case they are called tertiary consumers). Omnivores such as pigs, rats, and humans eat plants and animals.

At the far end of the food chain, decomposers (mostly fungi and bacteria) feed on dead organic material, breaking it down into simpler inorganic molecules. These inorganic molecules can again be used by producers, whereas the decomposers are in turn eaten by worms, insects, and other organisms.

Although this community model continues to influence both ecologists and others, it competes with a less metaphorical and anthropomorphic version. In an approach consistent with Tansley's desire to legitimize ecology by connecting it with the physical sciences, some ecologists de-emphasize such qualitative terms as *food, producers, consumers, communities, and occupations* and replace them with the seemingly more objective language of ecosystems and energy.

In this *energy model,* the focus of ecological research is on the ecosystem as an energy system or circuit. Just as the physicist studies the flow of energy through a physical system, the ecologist studies the flow of energy through an ecosystem. The language of a food chain is replaced with the mathematically more precise language of chemistry and physics. The ecosystem appears as just another physical, mechanical system.

Further, the energy model breaks down the distinction between living (biotic) and nonliving (abiotic) components of the system. The abiotic components (such as solar energy, temperature, water, and chemical molecules) are equally important elements in the system. We can trace the flow of energy through an ecosystem in a way that parallels the flow of food through the food chain, but without using economic or household metaphors. Photosynthesis is the process through which solar energy breaks the chemical bonds of carbon dioxide and water molecules, forming new molecules of carbohydrates and oxygen. Respiration transforms carbohydrates and oxygen back into carbon dioxide, water, and energy. The energy released in this process powers the chemical and physical processes of life, growth, reproduction, and so forth. Photosynthesis and respiration are the principles of the carbon and oxygen cycles in ecosystems.

Living organisms also need nitrogen, which provides the chemical basis of proteins, DNA, and other essential molecules. Nitrogen too can be traced through an ecological cycle. Atmospheric nitrogen, which makes up 78 percent of the atmosphere, is converted into water-soluble nitrate ions by various biological and physical processes. Bacteria living in the soil and in the roots of various plants, algae living in water, and even lightning contribute to this conversion. Plants in turn convert nitrates obtained from the soil into more complex nitrogen-based molecules such as proteins and DNA. Animals obtain the nitrogen-based molecules that they need by eating plants or other animals. Finally, when plants and animals die, decomposers eventually break these nitrogen molecules back down into nitrogen gas and nitrate ions. Thus the cycle begins again.

Because the carbon, oxygen, and nitrogen cycles—as well as a similar cycle for phosphorus and the more familiar water cycle—are all ultimately driven by solar energy, ecologists can account for ecosystems in terms of the energy that flows through various chemical, biological, and climatic cycles.[25]

The focus on energy is less a distinct ecological model than it is simply an emphasis within the ecosystem approach. Obviously, not just any energy system is an ecosystem. The energy cycles of interests to ecologists are those that support life and are a part of life cycles. The language of ecological communities remains a part of the ecosystem model. Nevertheless, the different emphases on communities and energy can suggest different normative conclusions. For the most part, all the ecological research mentioned up to this point shares a common assumption. Natural ecosystems tend toward a point of relative stability or equilibrium. When the system is disturbed, natural forces work to return it to a point of equilibrium. A system in equilibrium tends to resist change and stay in equilibrium. Recently, however, some ecologists have challenged this conclusion, arguing instead that natural systems are more chaotic than has previously been thought.[26] This view suggests that ecosystems are constantly changing and, perhaps more important, that this change occurs without direction or any sense of "development." Influenced by chaos theory in mathematics and science, and emphasizing the complex interconnections within ecosystems, this view holds that even small random changes within an ecosystem can have major and unpredictable results. Ultimately, the chaos model denies that any balance or long-term equilibrium exists within natural systems.

7.5 FROM ECOLOGY TO ETHICS

When we consider the ethical and policy implications that many environmentalists wish to draw from ecology, we can see the relevance of the different models. For people interested in bringing holism into the ethical domain, the organic model offers an intriguing option. The organic model suggests that ecosystems are, or at least can be, understood as independent living organisms. Thus we can reason to evaluative conclusions concerning ecosystems with the same scientific confidence that we use in making, for example, medical judgments. These value judgments—healthy, diseased, immature, and developed—are particularly useful if we are seeking to restore an ecosystem, preserve it in its natural form, or manage it for sustainable yields. The organic model would also be useful for those who want to argue for moral standing for ecosystems. If the ecosystem is in fact an organism, it might well meet minimal criteria for moral standing.

In recent years, some observers, led by British scientist James Lovelock and American biologist Lynn Margulis, have suggested that the earth itself can be understood as a living organism.[27] Much of Lovelock's writing uses the ecosystemic concepts of feedback loops and equilibrium, but by giving the entire system a name, *Gaia* (after the Greek goddess of the earth), this view suggests a sympathy for the organic model. Lovelock and other defenders of the Gaia hypothesis use this view to criticize human activities that degrade and pollute the living planet. Whether intended metaphorically or literally, the Gaia hypothesis is a powerful source of ethical arguments in favor of protecting the natural environment.

However, a central challenge to any attempt to ground ethical values in natural facts is the claim that a gap in logic yawns between statements of fact and judgments of value, between what is and what ought to be. Many philosophers reject as fallacious the conclusion, identified in recent decades as the "naturalistic fallacy," that something is good or right based solely on a description of what is natural.

Since at least the time of Plato, philosophers have recognized the problem with such reasoning. In Book I of *The Republic,* Plato showed many of the confusions that underlie the view that identifies justice with the natural property "advantage of the stronger." More recent discussions have focused on the eighteenth-century philosopher David Hume's distinction between *is* and *ought*.[28] The point of these challenges is that the grounds for proving that "this is the way things *are*" are logically distinct from the grounds for proving that "this is the way things *ought* to be." Even after something has been established as natural, whether it is good always remains an open question.[29]

Chapter 2 related how the natural-law–teleological tradition in ethics makes much of the connection between natural activities and the good. From a description of the normal and natural activity of the heart, for example, we reason to an account of a good or healthy heart. From a description of a normal progression of growth from birth through maturity and eventually to death, we also can reason to an account of a good, healthy life. Living systems can be described in teleological terms, and they seem open to evaluations based on this naturalistic description.

If we adopt the organic ecological model and view an ecosystem as an organic whole, then teleological reasoning would seem fitting. From a natural science description of the normal development of the system (its equilibrium and stability), we could reason about what is good or bad, right or wrong, and healthy or unhealthy for elements of that system. Predators are good and ought to be protected, for example, because they contribute to stable populations within the system.

But note that one question always remains: Why *should* we value the overall health of the system itself? If the organism in question is an individual human, we would have fairly standard ways of explaining the value of a healthy heart. But why should we value the integrity and stability of a wetland, desert, or prairie? The teleological model of value is attractive when we are concerned with the relation of parts to whole (the heart) or with the growth and development of a single organism. If, however, ecologists reject the organic model, we seem to be faced with an even greater gap between ecological facts and environmental values.

Perhaps this gap between the natural facts described by ecologists and the values of environmentalists is clearer when we consider the implications of more recent ecological models. For example, the ecosystems approach often concludes that ecosystems have a natural equilibrium and stability. For many environmentalists, this suggests a policy of preservation or protection. Left alone, nature will find its own best way to stability, balance, and harmony. The natural harmony and cooperation within ecosystems guide us toward a policy of respect for nature's way and the preservation of natural systems.

But consider an alternative argument. We might just as well conclude that precisely because nature does work toward balance, we humans can be much more sanguine about our interactions with nature. Further, because we know the mechanisms through which this balance is maintained—specifically, the physiochemical cycles of energy and nutrients—we are in an even better position to manage and control the ecosystem. We can learn to create and manage the harmony of natural processes—perhaps by adding nutrients and fertilizers to the soil, perhaps by killing nonnative species of goats, or perhaps by introducing new predators to prey on the goats.

Similar ambiguity characterizes the implications drawn from a more chaotic view of ecosystems. Imagine that we do conclude that the governing principle of ecology is change rather than stability, that the natural state of things is chaos and flux rather than harmony and equilibrium. What follows? We could use this as evidence to argue against wilderness preservation and restoration, because there is no natural order to preserve or restore. Paralleling the social Darwinists of the nineteenth century, chaos theorists might argue that because all species struggle to survive in a chaotic world, humans also have a natural inclination to manage their environment for their own self-interest.[30] On the other hand, we might argue that the very complexity and chaos of nature mean that we should be even more cautious, rather than less cautious, about our activities. This complexity is more, rather than less, reason to stand in awe of the natural world, to respect it, and to be much more modest about our understanding of and ability to manage nature.

The point of this exercise is to demonstrate that we can draw diverse ethical conclusions from even the most uncontroversial facts of science. Thus, despite the importance of ecology to environmental concerns, the insights gleaned from this science alone are not sufficient to decide among competing environmental policies. We will need to be careful whenever anyone appeals to ecology in defense of some environmental evaluation, ethical judgment, or policy prescription.

7.6 VARIETIES OF HOLISM

At the beginning of this chapter, it was suggested that holism is the unifying idea for ecocentric theories. But this concept, like so many philosophical abstractions, is elusive. At one level, we can grasp it easily enough. The common expression that "the whole is more than the sum of its parts" seems to get at the essence of holism. Yet just below the surface of this ordinary insight lies deep philosophical complexity.

What does it mean to say that the whole is more than the sum of its parts? In one sense—what might be called "metaphysical holism"—this claim can mean that wholes *exist* apart from or as real as their parts. Metaphysical holism claims that wholes are real, perhaps more real than their constituent parts. For our purposes, this would involve the claim that ecosystems have an independent existence beyond the existence of their individual elements. If this were so, the door would be open for arguing that they qualify for moral standing in their own right.

We have seen hints of this before. The organic model, for example, seems to suggest a metaphysical holism. We noted that Frederick Clements referred to the "climax community" itself as a complex organism that "constitutes a new kind of organic being." A similar point is made by J. Baird Callicott, the leading philosophical interpreter of Aldo Leopold's land ethic.

> Ecology is the study of relationships of organisms to one another and to the elemental environment.... The ontological primacy of objects and the ontological subordination of relationships characteristic of classical western science is, in fact, reversed in ecology. Ecological relationships determine the nature of organisms rather than the other way around. A species is what it is, because it has adapted to a niche in the ecosystem. The whole, the system itself, thus, literally and quite straightforwardly shapes and forms its component parts.[31]
>
> From the perspective of modern biology, species adapt to a niche in the ecosystem. Their actual relationships to other organisms (to predators, to prey, to parasites and disease organisms) and to the physical and chemical conditions (to temperature, radiation, salinity, wind, soil, and water [acidity]) literally sculpt their outward forms, their metabolic, physiological, and reproductive processes, and even their psychological and mental capacities.[32]

This seems to suggest that individual organisms do not constitute their ecosystems, but that ecosystems create individuals. Callicott's "ontological primacy" would seem equivalent to metaphysical holism.

A second sense of holism might be called "methodological or epistemological holism." Unlike metaphysical holism, this version is not concerned with claims about what exists or what is real. Methodological holism focuses instead on how best to understand or come to know various phenomena. In this view, we would have an inadequate and incomplete understanding of an ecosystem even if we knew everything about its constituent parts.

In some ways, we could see the ecosystem model as suggesting methodological holism. In offering *functional* explanations for individual organisms, the ecosystem model implies that an adequate understanding comes only when we view individuals relative to the system of interdependencies in which they exist. The food chain, for example, identifies individuals in terms of the role they play in the chain.

Finally, what we can call "ethical holism" would suggest that moral considerability should be extended to wholes. Just as we recognize that corporations, for example, have a legal standing independent of the legal standing of their individual members, the ethical holist argues that ethical standing can also be extended to relevant kinds of nonindividuals.

There is perhaps no better example of such a view than Aldo Leopold's statement.

A thing is right when it tends to preserve the integrity, stability, and beauty of the biotic community. It is wrong when it tends otherwise.[33]

Right and wrong are functions of what is good or bad for the whole community, not for its constituent members.

This is not the place to review the philosophical debates concerning holism. Serious philosophical challenges can be raised against each type of holism. Indeed, we will see specific versions of these criticisms raised in the chapters that follow. But this should indicate the challenges that lie ahead for ecocentric environmental philosophies.

7.7 SUMMARY AND CONCLUSIONS

Ecocentric approaches to environmental ethics develop from the conviction that ecology must play a primary role in our understanding and valuing of nature. The primary shift of the ecocentric approach involves an emphasis on ecological wholes and moves away from individual plants and animals. However, as we have seen in this brief survey, the science of ecology is evolving. Thus ecocentric philosophies are environmental approaches that are not yet fully formed. We need to pay particular attention to what specific ecological facts are being used in these philosophies and to how well that use is explained and justified.

NOTES

1. For a discussion of the Kirtland's warbler and its dependence on the jack pine, see Daniel Botkin, *Discordant Harmonies* (New York: Oxford University Press, 1990), pp. 68–71.

2. *Wilderness Act of 1964*, 16 U.S.C. 1131(a).

3. Gen. 3:17–19.

4. Gospel of Matthew 4:1.

5. Luther Standing Bear, *Land of the Spotted Eagle* (Boston: Houghton Mifflin, 1933), as quoted in T. C. McLuhan, ed., *Touch the Earth: A Self-Portrait of Indian Existence* (New York: Promontory Press, 1971), p. 45.

6. William Bradford, *Of Plymouth Plantation, 1620–1647* (Boston: Wright and Potter, 1899), p. 62, as quoted in Roderick Nash, *Wilderness and the American Mind* (New Haven, Conn.: Yale University Press, 1967), p. 24. Much of this section relies on Nash's superb history of the notion of wilderness.

7. Massachusetts Historical Society, *Proceedings of the Massachusetts Historical Society* 83 (1871–1873), as quoted in Mark Sagoff, *Economy of the Earth* (New York: Cambridge University Press, 1990), p. 125.

8. John White, *The Planter's Plea* (1630), as quoted in Peter Carroll, *Puritanism and the Wilderness* (New York: Columbia University Press, 1969), p. 11.

9. Henry David Thoreau, *Walden* (1854; New York: Library of America, 1985), as quoted in Nash, *Wilderness and the American Mind*, pp. 89–90; the emphasis is in the original.

10. John James Audubon, *Delineations of American Scenery and Character*, ed. Francis Hobart Herrick (New York: Baker, 1926), pp. 9–10, as quoted in Nash, *Wilderness and the American Mind*, p. 97.

11. Henry David Thoreau, *The Maine Woods*, in *The Writings of Henry David Thoreau*, vol. 3 (Boston: Houghton Mifflin, 1894), pp. 212–13, as quoted in Nash, *Wilderness and the American Mind*, p. 102.

12. *The Great New Wilderness Debate*, J. Baird Callicott and Michael P. Nelson, eds., (Athens: University of Georgia Press, 1998) provides the best single resource for central writings of this debate. I follow Callicott and Nelson in adopting the language of the "received view" here.

13. "The Trouble with Wilderness, or Getting Back to the Wrong Nature" by William Cronon, in *Uncommon Ground: Toward Reinventing Nature*, ed. William Cronon (New York: Norton, 1995).

14. Ibid.

15. James Fenimore Cooper's "Leatherstocking Tales" are a perfect example of the connection between the romantic wilderness myth and culturally biased and racist attitudes toward Native Americans. Throughout these books, natives are described as fitting one of two stereotypes. Either they are heroic and noble or they are dangerous savages.

16. G. P. Marsh, *Man and Nature*, ed. D. Lowenthal (1864; Cambridge, Mass.: Harvard University Press, 1967), pp. 29–30, as quoted in Botkin, *Discordant Harmonies*, p. 8.

17. Botkin, *Discordant Harmonies*, p. 9.

18. One of the first contemporary authors to call attention to the bias implicit in American understandings of the wilderness was Ramachandra Guha, "Radical American Environmentalism and Wilderness Preservation: A Third World Critique," *Environmental Ethics* 11 (Spring 1989): 71–83. See also "Indian Wisdom," in *Land of the Spotted Eagle* by Chief Luther Standing Bear (Boston: Houghton Mifflin, 1933). A fine collection of similar critiques of the wilderness idea can be found in Part Two of *The Great New Wilderness Debate*, edited by J. Baird Callicott and Michael Nelson (Athens: University of Georgia Press, 1998).

19. "The Wilderness Idea Reaffirmed" by Holmes Rolston, originally published in *The Environmental Professional* 13 (1991): 370–77.

20. "Introduction" by J. Baird Callicott and Michael Nelson, pp. 1–20 of *The Great New Wilderness Debate*, op. cit.

21. As quoted in Donald Worster, *Nature's Economy* (Cambridge, England: Cambridge University Press, 1985), p. 211.

22. Ibid.

23. Alfred Tansley, "The Use and Abuse of Vegetational Concepts and Terms," *Ecologist* 16 (1935): 284–307, quoted in Frank Golley, *A History of the Ecosystem Concept in Ecology* (New Haven, Conn.: Yale University Press, 1993), p. 8; the emphasis is Tansley's. I rely on Golley's book for much of the section that follows.

24. See Worster, *Nature's Economy*, Ch. 14.

25. A very readable summary of these topics can be found in David Gates, "The Flow of Energy in the Biosphere," *Scientific American* 224 (September 1971): 89–100.

26. For an excellent review of this more chaotic approach to ecology, see Donald Worster, "The Ecology of

Order and Chaos," in *The Wealth of Nature* (New York: Oxford University Press, 1993), Ch. 13.

27. James Lovelock, *Gaia: A New Look at Life on Earth* (Oxford, England: Oxford University Press, 1979); *The Ages of Gaia: A Biography of Our Living Planet* (Oxford, England: Oxford University Press, 1988); and Dorian Sagan and Lynn Margulis, "The Gaia Perspective of Ecology," *Ecologist* 13 (March–April): 160–67.

28. David Hume, *A Treatise on Human Nature* (London: Oxford University Press, 1740), book 3, pt. 1, sec. 1.

29. The classic twentieth-century discussion of the naturalistic fallacy appears in G. E. Moore, *Principia Ethica* (London: Cambridge University Press, 1903). Perhaps the best critical commentary on Moore is William Frankena, "The Naturalistic Fallacy,"

Mind 48 (1939): 464–77. A helpful collection of analytic essays on this topic is W. D. Hudson, *The Is/Ought Question* (New York: St. Martin's Press, 1970).

30. Donald Worster discusses this "ideological" attribution of social Darwinism to chaos theory in "Ecology of Order and Chaos," pp. 165–70.

31. J. Baird Callicott, "The Conceptual Foundations of the Land Ethic," in *In Defense of the Land Ethic* (Albany: State University of New York Press, 1989), p. 87.

32. J. Baird Callicott, "The Metaphysical Implications of Ecology," in *In Defense of the Land Ethic*, p. 110.

33. Aldo Leopold, "The Land Ethic," in *A Sand County Almanac* (New York: Oxford University Press, 1949), p. 262.

DISCUSSION QUESTIONS

1. If you were responsible for managing a national park such as Yellowstone, would you support or oppose road-building plans designed to give more people access to the backcountry? Should national parks be made more accessible to RVs and campers? To elderly and disabled people?

2. Should the U.S. Forest Service take steps to prevent a major fire within the Boundary Waters Canoe Area wilderness? Should the U.S. Forest Service replant the red pine and white pine trees that were destroyed in the blowdown, or should they "let nature take its course" even if the result would be a forest of short-lived aspen and birch?

3. What images come to mind when you think of wilderness? What is the origin of those images? What adjectives would you use to describe the wilderness?

4. Can aesthetic appreciation and value be taught? Could you persuade someone that a mountain vista is beautiful if he or she did not already appreciate it? What considerations would you cite in your argument?

5. What model should guide policies aimed at restoring a wilderness area? Should it be restored to the point at which it was found by the first white settlers? Should it simply be left alone, even if this means that nonnative species will populate the area?

6. What role should the science of ecology play in the management of wilderness areas? What decisions is it not appropriate to make in terms of ecological considerations?

7. Is the good for some collective such as a team or country identical to the good of its individual members? Can the good for an individual become identical to the good of the group? Are there any rules to follow in resolving conflicts between collective goods and individual goods?

GLOBAL ENVIRONMENTAL ETHICS WATCH

For more information on Wilderness, Ecology, and Ethics, please see the Global Environmental Ethics Watch. Updated several times a day, Global Environmental Ethics Watch is a focused portal into GREENR—our Global Reference on the Environment, Energy, and Natural Resources—an ideal one-stop site for current events and research. You will have access to the latest information from trusted academic journals, news outlets, and magazines as well as access to statistics, primary sources, case studies, videos, podcasts, and much more.

To gain access please use the access code that accompanies your book. If you do not have an access code, visit cengagebrain.com to purchase one.

8

The Land Ethic

DISCUSSION: Hunting, Ethics, and the Environment

Is hunting an environmentally responsible activity? On one hand, concern and care for the natural world would seem to count against a practice that intentionally kills animals for sport. On the other hand, hunting can play a role in wildlife management that seems to contribute to healthy ecosystems. While some defenders of animal rights and biocentric ethics argue that hunting is always unethical in all forms, other critics challenge hunting along several dimensions: which animals are hunted, and how, when, why, and with what they are hunted.

Consider the range of animals that are commonly hunted for recreation and sport: deer, ducks, geese, quail, pheasants, and turkey. So-called "trophy" hunting targets big-game animals such as bear, wolves, elk, moose, tigers, lions, elephants, rhinoceros, and buffalo. When fishing is added to the mix, hunting also involves marine species from trout to sharks. Marine mammals such as seals and

whales are also hunted. Indeed, it would be difficult to find a species of animal or fish that is not hunted.

People hunt for many reasons. Recreational or sports hunting is the most common form of hunting and is done for the sport and enjoyment of the hunt. Subsistence hunting is done to acquire food for the hunter. Commercial hunting is done to sell all or parts of the killed animal. Some hunting is done for "trophies" such as tusks, heads, skins, antlers, or entire animal bodies that can later be displayed. Some animal body parts, for example elephant tusks, rhinoceros horns, and shark fins, are valued as delicacies, as medicinal compounds, and as artistic objects. Some animals are hunted for scientific purposes. Some people hunt to eradicate unwanted or invasive species. Some hunting is done for ecological reasons, as when deer are hunted to regulate overpopulation.

A variety of methods are used in hunting. Some hunters stalk and track their prey through wilderness areas. Some hunt in game preserves, supported by professional guides. Some wait for the animals to approach them. Some hunting involves dogs that flush the prey. Some bear hunters use dogs to tree the bear where it is then shot. Some hunting is done from vehicles which can track and chase the prey while providing protection. Whaling ships and ocean trawlers can track ocean-going animals across the globe. Some hunters use airplanes and helicopters to hunt wolves and other wild animals from the air. Most commonly, recreational hunters use rifles, shotguns, bows and arrows, and traps. Subsistence and commercial hunters use a wide variety of technologies to hunt, including automatic and semi-automatic weapons, motorized vehicles, and satellite tracking. It is even possible to hunt on-line, using a remote-controlled camera and gun that shoots with the click of a mouse.

There is also a code of ethics for hunters, which governs proper and appropriate ways to hunt. Hunting out of season, trespassing to hunt, inflicting undue pain on the animal, not tracking wounded animals, poaching, hunting from cars, and being careless with firearms are among the actions that are considered unethical by hunters. Baiting animals or using other means that do not seem to give the animal a fair chance of escape is considered unethical by many hunters.

In some areas for some species, there is also a hunting "season" which determines when hunting is allowed. The hunting season typically corresponds to the mating and birth seasons of the prey, allowing the species the capacity to reproduce. Hunting limits also aim to conserve the number of animals available for future hunts.

Some hunting has been criticized on ethical grounds, because it is perceived as excessively cruel. Fox hunting, bear baiting, and seal hunts are notable examples. Some hunting has been criticized because the species itself is considered to have moral standing; primates, whales, and dolphins come to mind. People also protest the hunting of endangered species, as with great apes, rhinoceros, and leopards.

But hunting and killing animals for ecological reasons has also generated significant controversies, both in the public and among environmentalists.

The lack of predators, restrictions on hunting, and reduction or restriction of its range has created many situations in which a species exceeds the carrying capacity of its habitat. The overpopulation of white-tail deer in many suburban and urban areas in the United States is an obvious example. Culling, or hunting animals for ecological reasons, is a long-established practice to reduce animal populations to a level in balance with the carrying capacity of the animal's habitat. In many ways, much of the regulation of hunting that exists through the establishment of seasons, and the issuance of licenses and permits, is done in accord with scientific understanding of how many animals are needed to maintain a sustainable population size.[1]

DISCUSSION TOPICS:

1. When might hunting be justified, or unjustified, on environmental grounds?
2. Is it ironic that there is a code of ethics for hunting, when the entire aim of the hunt is to kill, and this aim is supposed to meet an ethical code?
3. By the middle of the twentieth century, wolves had been hunted to near extinction in many parts of the western United States, because they were seen as a threat to domestic animals like cattle and sheep, and competition for game animals such as deer and elk. After reintroduction in recent years, the wolf has grown to the point where wolf hunting is again allowed. Under what conditions would you support hunting wolves?
4. Some animals such as coyote, rodents, prairie dogs, and starlings are considered pests, or varmints, and hunted indiscriminately. Are there some species that you would support hunting even to the point of eradicating the entire species?
5. Do you consider fishing ethically on a par with hunting? Why or why not?

8.1 INTRODUCTION

Aldo Leopold (1887–1948) is the single most influential figure in the development of an ecocentric environmental ethics. The science of ecology developed during his lifetime, and he was the first person to call for a radical rethinking of ethics in light of this new science. He made the effort to integrate ecology and ethics his life's work. Leopold was an eloquent and prolific writer, and the collection of essays published posthumously as *A Sand County Almanac* (1949) is a classic text of the environmental movement. The definitive essay of this book, "The Land Ethic," is the first systematic presentation of an ecocentric ethics. This chapter focuses on Leopold's land ethic as the best example of an ecocentric ethics.

The development of Leopold's thinking parallels the change in thinking about predators. In many ways, Leopold is the person most responsible for this change. In his early research, Leopold was to game management what Pinchot was to forestry. He introduced scientific techniques and principles to the management of natural resources—in this case, to the management of game. Leopold was trained at the Yale Forest School, and his book *Game Management,* published in 1933, became the classic text in the field. It was also a classic conservationist text: game species such as deer and quail were "resources" or "crops" that should be managed to increase their harvest. "Like all other agricultural arts, game management produces a crop by controlling the environmental factors which hold down natural increase, or productivity, of the seed stock."[2] One environmental factor that "holds down" game resources, of course, is the existence of predators.

In an early essay published in 1915, Leopold set out the conservationist position regarding predators, or, as they were labeled, varmints. Regretting the antagonism that seemed to exist between ranchers and hunters, Leopold advises in "The Varmint Question" that ranchers, hunters, and game protectionists are "mutually and vitally interested in a common problem. This is the reduction of predatory animals." In a passage that today would outrage most ecologists and environmentalists, Leopold explains:

> It is well known that predatory animals are continuing to eat the cream off the grower's profits, and it hardly needs to be argued that, with our game supply as low as it is, a reduction in the predatory animal population is bound to help the situation. If the wolves, lions, coyotes, bob-cats, foxes, skunks, and other varmints were only decreasing at the same rate as our game is decreasing, it might at least be said that there was no serious occasion for worry.... Whatever may have been the value of the work accomplished by bounty systems, poisoning, and trapping, individual or governmental, the fact remains that varmints continue to thrive and their reduction can be accomplished only by means of a practical, vigorous, and comprehensive plan of action.[3]

But as his own ecological understanding developed as a result of his field experiences and research, Leopold began to see problems with this conservationist approach to nature. Specifically, the conservationist approach tends to view nature mechanically, as a mere object that can be manipulated for human ends without repercussions. Leopold recognized that this conflicts with a more ecological perspective in at least two ways. First, it seriously underestimates the interconnectedness of nature. Manipulating one part of nature by exterminating predators, for example, surely has significant implications elsewhere—for example, the overpopulation of deer herds. Further, unlike a mechanistic model, ecology teaches us that we never know with any certainty what consequences will follow from these manipulations. Second, the mechanistic approach treats the earth as "dead" when, in fact, ecology recognizes that even a handful of dirt contains an abundance of living organisms. Less than ten years after writing "The Varmint Question," Leopold discussed conservation as a "moral issue" that transcends the utilitarian economic calculations of earlier conservationism.

> Many of the world's most penetrating minds have regarded our so-called "inanimate nature" as a living thing, and many of us ... have felt intuitively that there existed between man and the earth a closer and deeper relation than would necessarily follow the mechanistic conception of the earth....
>
> Philosophy, then, suggests one reason why we cannot destroy the earth with moral impunity; namely that the "dead" earth is an organism possessing a certain kind or degree of life, which we intuitively respect as such.[4]

This new perspective, what we might call an "ecological conscience," developed over decades and was presented most fully in the late 1940s as the land ethic. This ecological conscience represents a shift from a view of nature as having only instrumental value to one that recognizes an intrinsic worth in natural systems. We can see this shift in Leopold's own thinking in his short essay, "Thinking Like a Mountain," published in *A Sand County Almanac*. Leopold recalls a time when, "young and full of trigger-itch," he shot a wolf and reached it in time to watch it die, "to watch the fierce green fire dying in her eyes."[5] At the time, he believed that fewer wolves meant more game. But on seeing the wolf die, he began to recognize that from a broader perspective, what we would call ecological perspective, this was not true. In fact, our short-sightedness was more likely to harm than to help the balance of nature. Until we learn to "think like a mountain" and understand nature from a wider and longer-term perspective, we are doomed to mismanage natural ecosystems.

8.2 THE LAND ETHIC

Leopold opens "The Land Ethic" by retelling the story of Odysseus, who, upon returning from the Trojan War, hanged a dozen of his women slaves for misbehavior. Because slaves were understood as property, Odysseus's action was not seen as unethical or inappropriate. Since that time, ethics has evolved to a point where moral standing is extended to all human beings. "The Land Ethic" is Leopold's call to continue this extension of ethics to include land, plants, and animals. At mid-century, land, like Odysseus's slaves, was understood as mere property. We had privileges in respect to the land but no obligations to it.

An ecological understanding of land rebuts the Lockean view of land as property. We can no longer treat the land as a mere object, as dead matter that can be used and shaped in any way that humans desire. Land should be viewed as a living organism that can be healthy or unhealthy, injured or killed. "Land, then, is not merely soil; it is a fountain of energy flowing through a circuit of soils, plants, and animals," Leopold writes.[6]

Thus Leopold opens "The Land Ethic" by suggesting the sort of moral extensionism presented in earlier chapters. He speaks of the "extension of ethics" and tells us that "the land ethic simply enlarges the boundaries of the community to include soils, waters, plants, and animals, or collectively, the land." Although "we have no land ethic yet, we have at least drawn nearer the point of admitting that birds should continue as a matter of biotic right."[7] His suggestion seems to be that we should extend moral consideration—"biotic rights"—to birds, soils, waters, plants, and animals.

However, Leopold never abandons his belief that these natural objects can and should be used as "resources" that can be managed for human benefit. As a result, it would be difficult to read Leopold as a defender of animal and plant rights, in the style of Singer, Regan, or Stone.[8] It is difficult to reconcile granting moral rights to animals with being willing to treat them as resources. Leopold's own long-standing practice of hunting also suggests that he cannot be placed in the animal rights camp.

This apparent inconsistency is resolved when we view the land ethic *holistically*. It is the "land community" that is granted moral standing. Individual members of that community can still be treated as resources as long as the community itself is respected. The "ecological conscience" teaches that humans are but members of the biotic community, "biotic citizens," rather than conquerors of nature. Ecology shifts the focus of moral consideration away from individuals and to biotic wholes.

Accordingly, the moral extensionism that is at work in Leopold's writing does not ask that we simply make room in our moral deliberations for yet another type of individual moral subject. Leopold asks that we make a radical category shift away from individuals. We now ought to grant moral standing to communities, symbolically represented as the land.

This aspect of the land ethic is concisely summarized in Leopold's most celebrated and controversial statement.

> A thing is right when it tends to preserve the integrity, stability, and beauty of the biotic community. It is wrong when it tends otherwise.[9]

When combined with some basic ecological observations, this principle can be used to generate specific normative conclusions.

Leopold uses the image of a "biotic pyramid" or "land pyramid" to help us understand the nature of the biotic community. This is an important image, because it shows how Leopold has adopted many elements of Tansley's ecosystem approach to ecology. The land pyramid is a "highly organized structure" of biotic and abiotic elements through which solar energy flows. This structure can be represented as a pyramid, with soil on the bottom, followed by a plant layer, an insect layer, a bird and rodent layer, "and so on up through the various animal groups to the apex layer, which consists of the larger carnivores."[10]

Thus species are arranged in layers, or "trophic levels," according to the food that they eat. Because the members of a prey species must be more numerous than the members of a species that preys upon it (otherwise the predators would soon starve), "each successive layer decreases in numerical abundance," forming the pyramidal shape of the system. The "lines of dependency for food and other services are called food chains."

> Each species, including ourselves, is a link in many chains. The deer eats a
> hundred plants other than oak, and the cow a hundred plants other than
> corn. Both, then, are links in a hundred chains. The pyramid is a tangle
> of chains so complex as to seem disorderly, yet the stability of the system
> proves it to be a highly organized structure. Its functioning depends on the
> co-operation and competition of its diverse parts.[11]

With this, we can begin to reach some general normative prescriptions. Given the complexity of this "highly organized structure," only a "fool would discard seemingly useless parts." Preservation of life-forms in all their diversity is the first general rule that we ought to follow, because not even ecologists understand how this complex system operates.

Because this complex structure has developed through millions of years of evolution, human interference with it ought always to be humble and constrained. Any change in the system requires that many other elements adjust themselves to it. When this occurs slowly, as it does through evolution, the system is self-regulating. When change is introduced abruptly and violently, as it typically is through human intervention, the potential for disaster is genuine. Thus we should tread lightly on the ecosystem. It is also wise to assume that native plants and animals are best suited for a particular locale. We can speculate that Leopold would support the decision to reintroduce wolves into Yellowstone, but would conclude that introducing non-native species is courting disaster.

More generally, a portrait of a stable and harmonious ecological relationship emerges from *A Sand County Almanac*. The many images of Leopold living on his Sand County farm depict a healthy relationship with the land. We feel that if only we could generalize from life on a small, self-sustaining farm, we would be close to the ideal ecological and environmental lifestyle.

One image that is particularly moving is the almanac entry for February.

> There are two spiritual dangers in not owning a farm. One is the danger of
> supposing that breakfast comes from the grocery, and the other that heat
> comes from the furnace. To avoid the first danger, one should plant a gar-
> den, preferably where there is no grocer to confuse the issue. To avoid the
> second, he should lay a split of good oak on the andirons, preferably where
> there is no furnace, and let it warm his shins while a February blizzard tosses
> the trees outside. If one has cut, split, hauled, and piled his own good oak,
> and let his mind work the while, he will remember much of where the heat
> comes from, and with a wealth of detail denied to those who spend the
> weekend in town astride a radiator.[12]

Leopold then lets his mind work as he traces the life cycle of an oak tree. The oak now used as firewood was killed by lightning during a July storm. The lightning "put an end to woodmaking by this particular oak" and "bequeathed to us three cords of prospective fuel wood." Leopold mourns the loss of the old tree but is satisfied to know that a dozen of its progeny have already set down roots in the nearby woods. After a year of drying, he cut the oak by hand, each pull of the saw cutting through years of the oak's life as captured in its annual rings. Leopold traces the life of the oak with each pull, rehearsing the changes in the local environment back through the years to the time around the Civil War when the oak first sprouted from an acorn. At the other end of the cycle, the oak is reduced to ashes in the fireplace, while providing heat for the farmhouse. Eventually, the ashes will be returned to the land as compost, only to reappear, in time, as a red apple or a "fat squirrel bent on planting acorns."[13]

Thus the death of a single magnificent oak tree, however sad in itself, can be viewed from a broader perspective. All living things, including humans, must be viewed as members of the ecological community. The oak is honored as a member, even as it is used as firewood. One oak dies, and other species benefit by consuming it. Yet in a harmonious and stable relationship, every member of the community is a resource for the continuation of the lives of others. An oak dies, but oaks live on. Resources are used but never without being recycled through the system. The community is characterized by countless of these interdependencies. Its health is characterized by its long-term integrity and stability.

At this point, there are several elements of the land ethic that make it an attractive philosophical option. First, the land ethic offers a fairly comprehensive perspective. At first sight, it appears to offer a decision process for most, if not all, environmental and ecological issues. Unlike the animal welfare movement, it can offer normative guidance for issues as diverse as wilderness preservation, pollution, conservation, energy, and resource depletion.

Second, it also can avoid many of the counterintuitive conclusions that burden the individualistic biocentric approach. We do not need to be overly concerned with such seemingly insignificant issues as killing a mosquito, cutting a tree, or tearing up a lawn. The continued healthy functioning of the system is the primary concern.

Finally, the land ethic is thoroughly nonanthropocentric. Humans are said to have no privileged status in the ecological community. They are reduced from conquerors to mere members. Not only does this shift accord natural objects and systems moral standing, but it also is more consistent with the teachings of ecology. For many environmentalists, this is the single most important prerequisite for a sound environmental perspective.

8.3 LEOPOLD'S HOLISM

Before we assess the land ethic, it is important that we understand the nature of Leopold's version of holism. The summary statement quoted earlier clearly suggests that Leopold is committed to a form of *ethical holism*. Right and wrong are a function of the well-being of the community, not of its constituent members.

In this view, we could argue that it is ethically permissible to kill individual deer as long as the "integrity, stability, and beauty" of the deer population were preserved. In fact, in the many cases in which deer overpopulation threatens the stability of the herd or the integrity of an entire ecosystem within which the deer live, we might well have an obligation to selectively kill individual deer.

But why is it reasonable to adopt ethical holism in regard to ecological communities? We can find traces of three answers in Leopold's writings. First, ethical holism is the most *practical* approach to take when making decisions about resource management. Second, ethical holism is implied by an *epistemological* holism implicit in ecology. Finally, ethical holism acknowledges the *metaphysical reality* of ecological wholes.

A practical reason for adopting ethical holism stems in part from the failure of more individualistic thinking. History supplies ample evidence that when we think only in terms of individual plants and animals, we adopt misinformed and risky land management policies. We have more than ample evidence for the abuse and destruction that follow from ignoring the interdependencies within an ecosystem. As an example, Leopold cites the effects that the destruction of predators can have on the population of deer. Therefore, treating ecosystems as though they had moral standing, "thinking like a mountain" in Leopold's words, would be a significant corrective to these errors. When Leopold writes to ranchers, farmers, hunters, and policy makers, he tends to adopt this more pragmatic approach to ethical holism.

Epistemological holism follows from the claim that an adequate understanding of ecology can come only from holistic or functional explanations. A full understanding of a wolf, for example, must include an account of how that species functions within the ecosystem. As a member of the biotic community, the wolf plays a role in the overall stability and integrity of the system. This functional community model of the ecosystem, in turn, provides a basis for ethical holism. The value of an individual organism is derived in part from its function, role, operation, relationships, and the like. Ecological understanding, therefore, gives reasons for adopting an ethical perspective that grants moral consideration to factors other than individual organisms.

We have also seen Leopold, in passages quoted here, suggest that the land might be regarded as a living thing. The metaphysical holism that is implied by the organic model provides further reasons for accepting ethical holism. Quoting the Russian philosopher Ouspensky, Leopold tells us that it is possible "to regard the earth's parts—soil, mountains, rivers, atmosphere, etc.—as organs, or parts, of a coordinated whole." Our belief that the earth is dead matter arises in part from our inability to recognize the "enormously slow, intricate, and interrelated functions" of its life processes. In a passage that makes the connection between metaphysical and ethical holism explicit, Leopold says:

> Philosophy, then, suggests one reason why we cannot destroy the earth with moral impunity; namely that the "dead" earth is an organism possessing a certain kind and degree of life, which we intuitively respect as such.[14]

If the earth itself is alive and if we can attribute to it such attributes as health, sickness, growth, and death, we can argue along familiar lines that the earth itself deserves moral consideration.

But to say that there are various reasons for adopting ethical holism is not yet to explain the nature of the biotic wholes in question. As we saw in Chapter 7, ecologists have relied on several different models of ecological systems, and all of these models can have different ethical implications. How exactly should the biotic community be understood? Which model best describes the activities of ecosystems?

Because Leopold's life spanned the early years of ecology, we should not be surprised to find various ecological emphases in his writing. We have already seen quotations in which Leopold refers to the earth as a living organism. Throughout much of "The Land Ethic," Leopold relies on the community model of ecology. The crucial image of the food pyramid has strong ties to Elton's functional community model. But even in the midst of this, Leopold also emphasizes the language of the energy model: "Plants absorb energy from the sun. This energy flows through a circuit called the biota which may be represented by a pyramid consisting of layers."[15] Whether we are concerned with food flowing through food chains of producers and consumers or with energy flowing through circuits may make an ethical difference.

Take, for example, the images of land health and death. Leopold often emphasizes our duty to preserve the health of the land and often laments those cases in which the land has died. But whereas the terms *health* and *death* can be applied straightforwardly to organisms, they can be applied only metaphorically to communities and energy circuits. Most of us would be willing to defend the intrinsic value of health, but what is its value when the concept is used metaphorically? Again, the "integrity and stability" of an organism may mean one thing, and the integrity and stability of a community or energy circuit may mean quite another. These are crucial questions for the land ethic. Clearly, Leopold reasons from ecological factors to normative ethical conclusions. Those conclusions attribute "integrity, stability, and beauty" to ecosystems. Two major challenges emerge: Can such properties be attributed to ecosystems, and how do ecological facts support the ethical conclusions?

What, exactly, was Leopold's model for understanding ecological wholes? The honest answer is probably that he was not as finely attuned to the nuances of these various models—and perhaps especially to the ethical nuances—as we might like. Leopold seems largely to abandon the organic model in his later writings.[16] But if we take "The Land Ethic" as his most mature work, we must conclude that he either did not see or did not think it important to make a clear and constant distinction among the various models.

8.4 CRITICISMS OF THE LAND ETHIC: FACTS AND VALUES

We will separate challenges to Leopold's land ethic into two general sections: the move from the facts of ecology to the values of ethics, and the ethical implications of Leopold's holism. The first type of challenge focuses on what philosophers have called the "naturalistic fallacy," the second on the nature of ecological wholes.

As outlined in previous chapters, a central challenge to any attempt to ground ethical values in natural facts is the claim that a logical gap exists between statements of fact and judgments of value—between *is* and *ought*. Identified in recent decades as the naturalistic fallacy, concluding that something is good or right solely on the basis of a description of what is natural is rejected by many philosophers as fallacious. Leopold's famous dictum, "A thing is right when it tends to preserve the integrity, stability, and beauty of the biotic community. It is wrong when it tends otherwise," would seem to be an example of exactly this type of reasoning.

At first glance, if Leopold adopts the organic model, one way to bridge this gap might be to use the type of teleological reasoning defended by the Aristotelian tradition. The organic model presents a view of ecosystems as distinct wholes and develops toward a point of stable equilibrium. From such a natural scientific description of the normal development of an organic whole, with its own identifiable integrity and stability, we could reason about what is good or bad, right or wrong, and healthful or unhealthful for elements of that system. Predators are good and ought to be protected, for example, because they contribute to stable populations within the system and, thus, to its health. Eliminating exotic species (such as the mountain goat in Olympic National Park) or reintroducing native species (such as the Yellowstone wolves) is right, because it maintains the natural integrity of the ecosystem.

But note that one question, described in Chapter 7, always remains: Why *should* we value the overall integrity or stability of the system itself? We could appeal to the role that particular ecosystems play in the overall stability and integrity of some larger organic whole. Thus, like a heart, a wetland performs a function for some organic whole. Accordingly, we ought to preserve the integrity and stability of an ecosystem because, in doing so, we are promoting the good of some larger whole of which the ecosystem is a part. Following this line, we would eventually argue, as Leopold sometimes does, that the earth itself should be considered an organic whole. But even if this were scientifically valid (and as we have seen in our survey of ecological models, that is far from clear), this line of reasoning simply pushes the open question back a step. Why value the integrity and stability of this larger organic whole? Because instrumental and individualistic reasons (for example, that the larger whole should be valued, because it preserves the well-being of its constituent parts, such as human beings) are not part of the land ethic, we would have to argue that some teleological goal exists for the entire system. Here the teleological model seems to break down. Neither ecology nor philosophy has produced a plausible account of what the earth's telos might be.

The other option is for the land ethic to argue that an ecosystem, like an individual organism, goes through developmental stages. The normal developmental progression would thereby provide a basis, as it does in human medicine, for evaluating the health and well-being of that system. Unfortunately, this is logical only if we assume the validity of the organic model, wherein every locale has a single climax stage toward which ecological succession aims and wherein each ecosystem is separate and unique. But given that most ecologists have moved away from the organic model, use of this option is weak. There may well not be a single ecosystem that develops through time. For example, over time the populations of a field might go through a series of ecological transformations from weeds to perennials and grasses, to shrubs, to pine forests, to oak forests. What would the "integrity and stability" of this system be? Should we seek to preserve the field as home to prairie grasses and shrubs, preserve the locale once it reaches the stage of a pine forest, or stay out altogether and let whatever happens happen? The important point is that we can meaningfully ask these questions. Hence, the leap from ecological fact to ethical value remains an open question.

Abandoning the organic model in favor of the more mainstream ecosystem model also does not resolve this problem. In the community model, individuals are related to each other functionally (as members of a food chain), but there is little reason to assume a function for the chain itself. We might be able to give a functional evaluation of the roles of individual organisms and species in the food chain—for example, that my garden's abundance of aphids is good for ladybugs. But why any particular food chain or, more to the point, any particular arrangement of the food chain should be valued in itself is yet to be answered. We have even less reason to assume a normative account of energy circuits. Why is the preservation of the integrity and stability of a food chain or energy circuit good or right?

We can summarize the philosophical point of these challenges. Leopold's normative conclusion ("a thing is right when it tends to preserve the integrity, stability, and beauty of the biotic community") seems to be derived, in some way, from the facts of ecology. Even assuming that a factual and meaningful basis exists for attributing integrity, stability, and beauty to ecosystems (and, as we have seen in the discussion on ecological models, that is far from established), how these facts are connected to the value conclusion remains an open question.[17]

If we spoke of ecological functions in an Aristotelian teleological sense as aiming toward some goal, either as parts within a larger whole or as a whole with its own goals, we might have some basis for reaching normative conclusions. But, as we saw in Chapter 2, the Darwinian account of natural selection casts serious doubt on the meaningfulness of teleological explanations in biology. In this account, members of an ecosystem do not function the way they do because of some forward-looking goal or purpose toward which they are aiming. Components of an ecosystem function the way they do, because functioning in this way has, in the past, proved adaptive.

Consider the example of large predators such as wolves within an ecosystem such as Yellowstone. When we speak of how predators "function" within an ecosystem, it is easy to think that wolves exist *in order to* prey on elk and other species and thus to maintain a natural stability and equilibrium. But the Darwinian explanation suggests that wolves prey on elk and other species, simply because in the past this behavior has proved adaptive and wolves that have done it have survived to reproduce. Note that this backward-looking explanation of ecosystem function gives us much less reason to conclude that this functional activity is right or good. In the phrase used in Chapter 2, "nature is neither good nor bad; it just is."

We should be careful to avoid overstating the force of these criticisms. The point is not that we cannot support ethical judgments by appeal to naturalistic facts. The point is that in defending something as right or wrong, we need to do more than simply say that it is normal or natural. Ecological facts, in and of themselves, do not "prove" that ecological integrity and stability are ethical values.

We can find indications in "The Land Ethic" of how Leopold might respond to these challenges. Leopold suggests that the ethical revolution implicit in his extension of ethics to the land can come about only alongside a radical change in human psychology. This change in psychology, brought about through moral and ecological education, might bridge the gap between is and ought.

> It is inconceivable to me that an ethical relation to land can exist without love, respect, and admiration for land, and a high regard for its value. By value, I of course mean something far broader than mere economic value; I mean value in the philosophical sense.[18]

This passage suggests that ethical holism, extending direct ethical consideration (the "philosophical sense" of value) to ecological wholes, can come about only when humans change their attitudes toward the land. Only when humans come to love, respect, and admire the land will they have reasons to act in ways that benefit it. But how will humans come to love, respect, and admire the land? "One of the requisites" for an ecological valuing of land "is an understanding of ecology."[19] Thus the natural facts of ecology do not lead directly to ethical conclusions. They lead instead to a change of attitude that can in turn lead to a change in ethical evaluations. Accordingly, we value the preservation of an ecosystem not simply because it is natural or normal but because, given what we have learned of it from ecology, we love it, respect it, and admire it.[20] In this interpretation, the role of ecology is concentrated more in moral education than in normative ethics.

Unfortunately, however, when we take this approach, the "integrity and stability" principle loses some of its force. In this view, the principle is not a straightforward normative principle ("Act in ways that tend to preserve the integrity, stability, and beauty ... "). Rather, it is an exhortation to get people to think in a certain way ("Stop thinking solely in economic and instrumental terms; try thinking this way: a thing is right when ... "). The principle becomes, as Leopold suggests, a challenge to the logjam preventing the "evolutionary process" from extending ethical consideration to land. It provides an alternative and a challenge to the economic way of thinking. But it provides no independent reason for acting on behalf of the land.

8.5 CRITICISMS OF THE LAND ETHIC: HOLISTIC ETHICS

A second group of challenges to the land ethic centers on its holism. Two general concerns underlie these challenges: Can a meaningful account of ecological wholes be defended, and are its ethical implications acceptable?

The most serious ethical criticism of the land ethic's holism is that it condones sacrificing the good of individuals to the good of the whole. If we do define right and wrong in terms of the biotic community, it would seem possible to sacrifice individual members—for example, individual human beings—for the good of the community. For example, Leopold seems willing to condone hunting individual animals to preserve the integrity and stability of the biotic community. But because he also describes humans as equal members of that community, he would seem to be committed to the permissibility of hunting humans, if doing so would preserve the integrity, stability, and beauty of that community.

Various critics have offered versions of this challenge. Marti Kheel, a writer and activist, has called ethical holism totalitarian, and philosopher Eric Katz has claimed that it subverts respect for individuals.[21] Another criticism was voiced by Tom Regan, who labeled Leopold's approach "environmental fascism."

> The difficulties and implications of developing a rights-based environmental ethic ... include reconciling the *individualistic* nature of moral rights with the more *holistic* view of nature.... Aldo Leopold is illustrative of this latter tendency.... The implications of this view include the clear prospect that the individual may be sacrificed for the greater biotic good, in the name of "the integrity, stability, and beauty of the biotic community." It is difficult to see how the notion of the rights of the individual could find a home within a view that ... might be fairly dubbed "environmental fascism."[22]

These are serious charges. If they cannot be answered by defenders of the land ethic, we will have good reason to look elsewhere for a satisfactory environmental ethic.

One approach might develop the suggestion concerning practical holism. Given the history of human destruction of natural environments, we would be well advised to act as though ecosystems had moral standing. The problem with this approach is that it merely postpones the question of fascism. What ought we to do when the good of an ecological community conflicts with the good of an individual human? Either we act as though the community itself has standing and override the interests of the human, or we abandon the pretense and allow the human interest to take precedence. With the first option, we face the fascism charge, and with the second, we abandon holism.

Philosopher Don Marietta suggests another response.[23] He points out that ethical holism can have a variety of implications. A statement such as Leopold's integrity and stability claim might imply that the *only* source of right and wrong is the good of the biotic community. It might imply that the *most important* source lies with the good of the community, or it might imply simply that *one* source of right and wrong lies with the good of the community.

Marietta goes on to argue that we cannot justify treating the good of the biotic community as the only, or even necessarily the most important, source of right and wrong. These extreme positions are reductionistic in that they treat human beings as though they were *only* biological entities. Humans are more than that, of course, and a satisfactory ethics must take into account the wide range of morally relevant factors about humans. This includes, but is not limited to, humans' biological role in nature.

Thus Marietta concludes that ethical holism should be seen as introducing one new source of right and wrong into ethics. Only if we assume that it introduces the only or the most important source does holism fall victim to the charge of fascism. As it stands, we should recognize that we face complex moral situations with few specific and overriding rules that dictate exactly what we should do. Holism calls our attention to some complexity that we may have missed otherwise. It does not necessarily commit us to environmental fascism.

Can Leopold's holism be defended in this way? At first glance, it cannot. Leopold's principle that "a thing is right when … it is wrong when it tends otherwise" would seem to suggest exactly the sort of overriding rule that Marietta rejects. This principle suggests that something is either right or wrong, and hence it leaves no room for the type of moral pluralism that Marietta accepts. But perhaps there is a way to synthesize these two views.

First, we can follow Marietta's suggestion and recognize that in a morally complex world, certain acts might be both right in one way and wrong in another way. Thus it might be both right and wrong for a farmer to fill in a wetland in order to increase the land available for agriculture. From the ecocentric point of view, it might be wrong. From the point of view of the farm family that is facing bankruptcy, it might be right. In this case, right or wrong would simply mean that good and plausible reasons can be given for both sides.

Philosopher Jon Moline suggests yet another approach.[24] Moline's interpretation focuses on the word *thing* in Leopold's account of right and wrong. If by thing we mean an individual *action,* Leopold would be open to the fascism charge. But if we interpret thing to mean a *type* of action, rule, or attitude, the fascism charge is less plausible. Moline calls the first option "direct holism" and the second option "indirect holism" and suggests that Leopold ought to be read as an indirect holist.

> I argue that Leopold, by contrast, is an *indirect* holist, i.e., one who applies holistic criteria not directly to acts, but only indirectly to these through criticisms of practices, rules, predilections, and attitudes. He criticizes above all our manner of thinking and wishing, seeing that all our actions flow from this.[25]

We can integrate Moline's suggestion with the discussion of an ethics of character discussed previously. Leopold's integrity and stability principle should be viewed as normative for human character: our attitudes, dispositions, and "our manner of thinking and wishing." It proposes the type of person we should be, a trait of character, not the specific acts we should perform.

Moline acknowledges that some critics will charge that direct and indirect holism ultimately are indistinguishable.[26] In any particular instance, either the indirect principle will have exactly the same prescription as the direct version, or it will not. If it does, there is no practical difference between the two (if the direct holism is fascistic, so is the indirect version). If it does not, the indirect version is not, after all, holistic (because in tough cases, it abandons the holistic conclusion).

But this criticism is valid only if we assume that any particular case always has one unambiguous and knowable prescription. And time and again, Leopold points out that even the ecologist does not know exactly what will preserve the integrity and stability of the biotic community.

> The ordinary citizen today assumes that science knows what makes the community clock tick; the scientist is equally sure that he does not. He knows that the biotic mechanism is so complex that its workings may never be fully understood.[27]

Given the complexity of ecosystems, and given the realization that they undergo constant change, we should not presume that we ever know with certainty what will or will not preserve integrity or stability in any particular case. Thus, as a direct guide for action, Leopold's principle would be empty and irrelevant.

We now can see a way to integrate Leopold's appreciation of the ecological complexity of nature, Marietta's appreciation of the moral complexity of our world, and Moline's indirect holism. Ecology teaches that natural biotic systems are extremely complex. We need to abandon the mechanistic view of nature and be suspicious of any abrupt and human-wrought changes to it. Marietta cautions us to be sensitive to moral complexity as well. Combine these two perspectives, and we would conclude that ecological ethics is fundamentally indeterminate. That is, we just might never be able to know, in any particular case, what the ethically correct act is. We often will not know enough about an ecosystem to understand the consequences of our actions, and competing values might be pulling us in different directions. But it is exactly in such a situation that a second-order principle of the type Moline describes can help us.

In these situations, we should be guided by those attitudes, dispositions, and practices that have tended to preserve the integrity and stability of ecosystems. In general, these are attitudes of love, respect, and admiration. In practice, this would imply a relatively conservative approach to natural systems: presumptions in favor of natural evolutionary changes (rather than human-wrought changes), native plants and animals, slow rather than rapid change, and biological rather than mechanical, artificial, and manufactured solutions to environmental problems.

In this view, Leopold's ethics is focused less on rules that guide action and more on moral dispositions or virtues. We may be unable to specify in any detail what the correct act or decision is, but we can determine whether a person is acting responsibly. If a person acts out of a "loving and respectful" character, then the decision will be a responsible one. Both the world of ecology and the world of morality make it unlikely that any specific moral rule will be able to offer us unambiguous practical advice. In such a situation, the best we can do is to rely on the best judgment of a particular type of person. This would be a person who loves, respects, and admires the biotic community. Whatever this person decides will be the ethically responsible thing, even though we have no way of independently and antecedently specifying what that ought to be.

Before turning to a final consideration of Leopold's holism, consider one further point. Philosophical critics may not find the foregoing line of reasoning persuasive. After all, they might charge that implicit in whatever act the virtuous person performs will be a rule (or maxim) that could be made explicit. Either that maxim should be followed in relevantly similar situations, or it should not. If it should, then we do after all have a rule to guide our actions, and we can proceed with the philosophical examination of that rule. If it should not, then we have abandoned ethics completely in favor of an arbitrary decision process.

Perhaps an example arising in medical ethics can help illustrate the alternative. We have all become familiar with cases in which individuals who are suffering from major physiological damage are kept alive (or at least their bodies are kept functioning) only by complex technological devices. Many states have responded to these tragedies by enacting legislation that recognizes the validity of "living wills." In such cases, an individual can specify, while still competent, the conditions under which she or he would choose to have life-support technology removed. We seem, as a society, to have accepted the principle of self-determination. Competent individuals may decline any medical procedures.

The problem that living wills pose is not unlike that facing the ecologist. Science—in this case, medicine—is often indeterminate. Given the complexity of the human organism, physicians simply never know with certainty a patient's prognosis. Thus, when writing a living will, people are faced with extreme uncertainty about what their condition might be, their prognosis, the technology that might be available in the future, and so forth. But they are also faced with moral uncertainty. Strong reasons can be given both for and against the decision to discontinue life support.

In the face of this deep complexity, we might argue that a living will should be an *indirect,* not a *direct,* guide. The will should specify *who* should be empowered to make the decision, not the conditions under which a specific decision should be made. Thus, we might decide that a loved one—spouse, parent, or child—should have the authority to decide for us. The view is that whatever such a person decides will be the correct decision. Our justification for this judgment lies in the character of this person. While writing the living will, I might reason as follows. Because this person loves me and is generally a reasonable, thoughtful, and sensitive person, this person will make the best decision in a complex situation. I recognize that this is a decision that even I cannot make in the abstract, and I also recognize that good reasons can be given for and against whatever that decision turns out to be.

This interpretation makes Leopold sound like a modern Aristotelian. Like Aristotle's ethics, the land ethic would focus on the formation of an ethical character rather than on the defense of some ultimate moral rule or principle. Like Aristotle, moral education and moral psychology have an important role to play in the development (evolution?) of ethics. Whether this is a plausible reading can be left for another time. At this point, we should acknowledge that the land ethic faces serious challenges but is not without resources for answering these challenges.

We now turn to a final challenge to Leopold's holistic ethics. Is a meaningful account of ecological wholes defensible? We have seen that ecologists have defended different models of an ecosystem: the organic, community, and energy circuit models. Which, if any, can be made compatible with the land ethic?

We know that Leopold at times adopts an organic model of ecosystems. The land itself is seen as a living organism. In some ways, this is the model best suited for the land ethic. We seem most able to move between the facts of ecology and the values implicit in such concepts as integrity and stability, health, and well-being, when we treat ecosystems as organic wholes.

Human and veterinary medicine provide a powerful example of how this reasoning could develop. Given a scientific understanding of the normal growth and development of an individual organism, medical science has proved capable of diagnosing ills and promoting health. If it turns out that ecosystems are relevantly similar to these individual organisms, then the potential exists for a similar synthesis of science and values.

But we have already seen that ecologists have moved beyond this organic model. The very science that Leopold relied on to present the holism of ecosystems has concluded that the organic model of ecological systems is inadequate. The classical refutation of the organic model is found in the writings of Arthur Tansley.[28]

Tansley argued that ecosystems can be viewed as organisms only in a metaphorical way. They are not literally organisms, because individuals within an ecosystem, unlike the individual organs of a body, could exist outside the organism. Ecosystems do not have the "unity and definiteness" of real organisms, and their constituent parts are quite capable of moving into other systems and becoming full members of them. This independence means that members of an ecosystem are quite unlike the organs of a body.

Perhaps, then, Leopold's holism should be understood within the functional community model. Here, members of an ecosystem are not understood as related to that ecosystem in the same way as parts to a whole or as organs to a body but are construed as functionally dependent on each other. An individual organism is identified as part of the biotic community or the food chain by reference to what it eats and what eats it. The arrangement of individual organisms and their relations to one another are what constitute the system.

But can this account of an ecosystem provide what is required of it in Leopold's ethics? Leopold makes it clear that at least one object of our moral consideration (our love, respect, and admiration) is the community itself, not its constituent members. The well-being of this community consists of its integrity and stability. But what can integrity and stability mean if we are talking about food chains and not organisms?

Consider what is being asked. In the reading of Leopold offered so far, human beings are encouraged to act out of a love, respect, and admiration for the biotic community. This seems possible only insofar as this community has some good or interests of its own. (Otherwise, we would be acting for the good of the community only as a means for attaining the good of its constituent members. This would be to abandon the holistic perspective.) But is it reasonable to hold that we can love and respect a biotic community? Leopold's principle suggests that it is. A community can be loved and respected, because it has interests, and its interests rest on its integrity and stability. But are biotic communities the kinds of things that possess integrity and stability?

At any given time, it might appear that they do. A small pond, for example, can be said to possess integrity and stability if it is not drained, its various biotic populations remain stationary, the climate remains constant, artificial or non-native elements are not added, and so forth—in short, if its structure and functional relationships can be maintained. But as we have noted, ecosystems do not remain stable over time. Through natural biological, chemical, geological, and climatic forces, biotic communities evolve into different types of ecosystems. Thus we are faced with a choice: either interfere with these natural processes in order to preserve a particular integrity and stability or allow these natural processes to continue and abandon the most obvious sense of integrity and stability. The example of Yellowstone wolves raises these questions rather dramatically.

But perhaps the term *biotic community* can be understood to refer not to the particular members of the community or to a particular arrangement of those members but to the conditions under which the biological processes and relationships can be preserved. An ecosystem, which now means something more akin to a locale, has integrity and stability to the degree that it is capable of sustaining biological processes. Thus a healthy community has topsoil that is rich in nutrients and not eroded, has rain that is not acidified, is free of pesticides and herbicides, does not suffer from an overpopulation of any species, and so forth.

Unfortunately, this answer has several problems. First, this concept of ecosystem health may be too open-ended. Certain biological processes have shown themselves quite capable of surviving in the most ecologically blighted areas. For example, the HIV, bubonic plague, and polio agents seem to thrive in conditions of something less than the ecological ideal. We would need some further standard to decide which biological processes contribute to a system's health and which do not.

More important, this answer also seems to base the land ethic on instrumental and nonholistic values. In effect, this answer says that we ought to preserve the integrity and stability of a system or community not because it has value in itself, but because it contributes to the well-being of other things that have intrinsic value.

8.6 CALLICOTT'S REVISIONS

Since the mid-1970s, the American philosopher J. Baird Callicott has written extensively in defense of Leopold's land ethic.[29] Callicott offers valuable insights into Leopold's thinking and provides a creative interpretation of the land ethic. Callicott's work demonstrates that Leopold's approach remains a rich resource for continued work in environmental ethics.

Underlying the challenge identified as the naturalistic fallacy is the assumption that a gap in logic exists between statements of fact (is) and statements of value (ought). Facts are objective and independent of human judgment. Values are subjective and dependent on human judgment. A primary goal for normative ethics, in this view, is to reason from facts to values. But the facts themselves are never sufficient for drawing normative conclusions.

Callicott seeks to bridge this gap by locating Leopold within an ethical tradition extending from David Hume and Adam Smith through Charles Darwin. According to Callicott, this tradition places moral sentiments at the center of ethics. In this view, ethics arises out of human sentiments, what we might variously call feelings, attitudes, dispositions, or affections. For David Hume, sympathy is one of the most fundamental human sentiments. Human beings can identify with and feel sympathy for other human beings. This feeling for the other is at the origins of ethics. Thus the oughts of ethics arise not from simple facts about the world (it was, after all, Hume who so clearly identified the gap between is and ought) but rather from facts about us. To figure out the moral wrong with willful murder, for example, Hume tells us to look within ourselves, and we will find a "sentiment of disapprobation." The evil is a matter of fact, but "it lies in yourself, not in the object."

Consider an example of how moral sentiments help bridge the gap between is and ought. We can begin with purely descriptive, factual "is" statements. In the yard is a young child who has fallen and scraped his knee. He is crying. He is my son. From these statements, I conclude that I ought to rush outside to comfort and care for this child. To the question of why I ought to rush to that child, Hume would answer, "Because he is your son, and you love him." Accordingly to Hume, the fact that he is my son, in and of itself, does not logically lead to the "ought" statement. It does so only when conjoined with additional (also factual) statements about my own and (more generally) human psychology: parents love their children. Thus judgments of value are rooted in fundamental elements of human psychology.

Callicott believes that this approach is further developed in Darwin and later picked up by Leopold and incorporated into the land ethic.

> Darwin's account, to which Leopold unmistakably (if elliptically) alludes in "The Land Ethic," begins with the parental and filial affections common, perhaps, to all mammals. Bonds of affection and sympathy between parents and offspring permitted the formation of small, closely kin social groups, Darwin argued. Should the parental and filial affections bonding family members chance to extend to less closely related individuals, that would

permit the enlargement of the family group. And should the newly extended community more successfully defend itself and/or more efficiently provision itself, the inclusive fitness of its members severally would be increased, Darwin reasoned. Thus the more diffuse familial affections, which Darwin (echoing Hume and Smith) calls the "social sentiments," would be spread throughout a population.[30]

Thus the sentiments of affection and sympathy, sentiments that bridge the gap between facts and values, can be extended from the individual to include a wider social universe. In Leopold's words, "The land ethic simply enlarges the boundaries of the community to include soils, waters, plants, and animals, or collectively: the land."[31]

In Callicott's interpretation, Leopold is part of this Hume–Darwin tradition. Leopold encourages us to extend our recognition of family and community bonds to include all other members of the biotic community. Thus, reasoning from an "is" statement to an "ought" statement, from the facts of ecological destruction to the oughts of environmental activism, is logically the same as reasoning from the facts of a child's suffering to the conclusion that I ought to help. According to Callicott, the logic of the land ethic:

> is that natural selection has endowed human beings with an affective moral response to perceived bonds of kinship and community membership and identity; that today the natural environment, the land, is represented as a community, the biotic community; and that, therefore, an environment or land ethic is both possible, the biopsychological and cognitive conditions are in place, and necessary, since human beings collectively have acquired the power to destroy the integrity, diversity, and stability of the environing and supporting economy of nature.[32]

Although this interpretation may place Leopold within a distinguished intellectual tradition, it is not without problems. Perhaps the most serious challenge is that sentiments are a notoriously unstable foundation, on which to build an ethics. It would seem that for every case in which humans act out of sympathy, affection, or cooperation, we can find a case of someone acting out of selfishness, hatred, or competition. Human psychology seems just as capable of building barriers between people as of building bonds. Thus the open question remains: Why should I extend my sympathy rather than my animosity to the land? We still need reasons to develop positive rather than negative sentiments.

This challenge may gain some practical weight, when we recognize that at least some environmental issues arise from cases in which humans destroy the integrity, stability, and beauty of an ecosystem in the name of family or community well-being. For example, in many areas of the world, people destroy rain forests, wilderness areas, and endangered species so that they can provide a basic living for their families. In such cases, moral sentiments would seem to provide an incentive to destroy rather than protect the ecosystem. If we base the land ethic on moral sentiments, we have little moral answer to those who would destroy the land in the name of those very sentiments.

This problem echoes the challenge that Immanuel Kant raised against Hume's ethics. Human psychology is an insufficient basis for ethics, because it can offer only hypothetical imperatives. If you care about others, you should not harm them. Ethics, for Kant, must supply categorical imperatives, normative judgments that are inescapable for any rational person. Oughts should not depend on the feelings, attitudes, or sentiments of the individual.

It may well be unfair to ask more of Leopold than we ask of philosophers. Despite Kant's best efforts, philosophers still actively debate this point. Callicott has offered a thoughtful and provocative account of the ethical foundations of the land ethic. Mainstream Western philosophy has no doubt judged that foundation to be unstable, at least when compared to the possibility of a more categorical imperative. Perhaps Western philosophy has asked too much of ethics. Perhaps the best we can hope for is an ethics based on sympathy, compassion, and love.

Callicott also offers an interpretation of Leopold that responds to the challenge raised against holism. In this interpretation, the land ethic adopts a metaphysical holism, with ethical implications following from this. We encountered Callicott's interpretation of Leopold's metaphysical holism in Chapter 7. Using the "functional energy" language of ecosystems ecology to explain Leopold's food pyramid, Callicott argues for the metaphysical primacy of relations and wholes.

> Ecology is the study of relationships of organisms to one another and to the elemental environment…. The ontological primacy of objects and the ontological subordination of relationships characteristic of classical western science is, in fact, reversed in ecology. Ecological relationships determine the nature of organisms rather than the other way around. A species is what it is, because it has adapted to a niche in the ecosystem. The whole, the system itself, thus, literally and quite straightforwardly shapes and forms its component parts.[33]

In another place, Callicott tells us that:

> from the perspective of modern biology, species adapt to a niche in the ecosystem. Their actual relationships to other organisms (to predators, to prey, to parasites and disease organisms) and to the physical and chemical conditions (to temperature, radiation, salinity, wind, soil, and water [acidity]) literally sculpt their outward forms, their metabolic, physiological, and reproductive processes, and even their psychological and mental capacities.[34]

Guided by modern ecological science, Callicott reasons that relationships are "prior to," in the sense of being more real than, the things related, and that "ecosystemic wholes are logically prior to their component species, because the nature of the part is determined by its relationship to the whole."[35] Thus ecological holism points us toward the underlying nature of reality. Callicott believes that ecology not only has implications for metaphysics but leads to ethical conclusions as well.

Since individual organisms, from an ecological point of view, are less discrete objects than modes of a continuous, albeit differentiated, whole, the distinction between self and other is blurred.... As one moves, in imagination, outwardly from the core of one's organism, it is impossible to find a clear demarcation between oneself and one's environment.... The world is, indeed, one's extended body.[36]

Thus "the relational view of self ... transforms egoism into environmentalism." Because we are one with nature, it is in our self-interest (egoism) to preserve and protect the natural world (environmentalism). Accordingly, Callicott reasons from ecology to metaphysics to ethics, once again providing a bridge from ecological facts to ethical value.

We are left with two questions: Does ecology provide reasons to adopt the type of holism Callicott defends, and does that holism commit us to a defensible environmental ethics?

Both issues encounter serious problems. First, as the review of ecological models in Chapter 7 suggests, ecologists have not agreed that the functional energy model that Callicott attributes to the land ethic offers the most accurate description of nature. More important, we need to be careful with any attempt to draw metaphysical conclusions from scientific observations. Indeed, most philosophers would probably argue that metaphysics and epistemology precede science, not the other way around. Scientific claims and observations presuppose a set of assumptions about what is real and what can be known. It begs the question to derive philosophical conclusions from science, because science cannot begin without philosophical assumptions.[37]

More relevant to our present concerns, perhaps, is the move from metaphysical holism to an ethics of environmentalism. Callicott reminds us that the intrinsic value of individuals is taken as a given in much Western philosophy. Earlier chapters noted that the question of intrinsic value is a key question in the move away from animal welfare rights and a more general ethical extensionism toward a broader environmental ethics. Callicott answers this question by telling us that ecological holism outflanks the problem of attributing intrinsic value to natural objects other than humans. Because humans are assumed to possess intrinsic value (and if they do not, what does?), and because we cannot make a clear distinction between self and nature, we are justified in attributing intrinsic value to nature.

But this (alleged) synthesis of self and nature is a metaphysical one, not a psychological one. Whatever Callicott claims to be true metaphysically, it nevertheless remains true that for most of us, the distinction between self and nature is an obvious, immediate, and lived one. I certainly do not believe (or feel, if we wish to remain consistent with the Humean ethics of Leopold and Callicott) that I am one with nature. The claim that no firm divide (metaphysical or natural) exists between self and other is not in itself enough to establish what we ought to do. In effect, the naturalistic fallacy challenge has risen again.

Consider an alternative conclusion that might be drawn from Callicott's metaphysical holism. Assume that the self does become merged psychologically as well as metaphysically with the natural world. What ought "I" to do? Callicott suggests that, driven by a new "enlightened self-interest," I ought to extend the intrinsic value previously reserved for the self to the natural world. But why do this rather than extend the mere instrumental value previously reserved for nature to the self? Why should I not always be willing to sacrifice the self for the good of the whole? More generally, might we lose the intrinsic value of humans in the name of the greater good? The specter of fascism has returned.

Remember that a major challenge to ethical holism is that in service to the well-being of the whole, one will sacrifice the well-being of individuals. As the intrinsic value originally reserved for the individual is transferred to the whole, the possibility arises that the individual would be left without intrinsic value. As we begin to extend our affections from the self to the land, the self may become totally merged into the whole and be deprived of its moral standing.

Callicott surely has resources to answer this challenge. At times, he speaks of our existing within "nested and overlapping communities," suggesting a model of concentric circles in which our affections are extended first to self and family and later to broader communities.[38] In this model, we extend moral considerability to the land without disavowing an initial and prior value that characterizes the inner circles. But, again, what do we do in cases in which conflict exists between responsibility to the innermost circle—that is, to myself and my family—and responsibility to outer circles, which include ecosystems and wilderness areas? If we favor the objects in the outermost circles, we are open to charges of fascism. If we favor ourselves and our families, holism seems not to have advanced the ethical standing of the nonhuman natural world.

What are we to make of these debates? It seems that we have gone far afield from the elegance of Leopold's inspiring and original work. Seeking to defend it from challenges, we find ourselves enmeshed in philosophical debates that seem quite removed from environmental and ecological concerns. But perhaps this is testimony to the continued need for philosophy. As we have seen throughout this textbook, environmental concerns raise fundamental questions about how we ought to live. We should not expect that these fundamental questions will be easily answered.

8.7 SUMMARY AND CONCLUSIONS

Serious philosophical challenges to the land ethic remain. Nevertheless, Leopold's work holds promise for philosophical reflection on the environment. Without question, his writing provides inspiration for everyone concerned with environmental ethics. Perhaps his greatest contribution lies in focusing attention on ecosystems and relationships—in short, in taking ecological wholes as worthy of serious moral consideration. Whether this consideration turns out to be in the form of direct or indirect moral standing, Aldo Leopold has ensured that this issue can no longer be ignored.

NOTES

1. For an early defense of hunting from an environmental perspective, see Robert Loftin, "The Morality of Hunting," Environmental Ethics, Vol. 6, No. 3, Fall 1984, pp. 241–50.

2. Aldo Leopold, *Game Management* (New York: Scribner's, 1933), p. 179.

3. Aldo Leopold, "The Varmint Question," reprinted in *The River of the Mother of God and Other Essays* by Aldo Leopold, eds. Susan Flader and J. Baird Callicott (Madison: University of Wisconsin Press, 1991), pp. 47–48.

4. Aldo Leopold, "Some Fundamentals of Conservation in the Southwest" (1923), reprinted in Flader and Callicott, eds., *River of the Mother of God and Other Essays*, pp. 47–48.

5. Aldo Leopold, "Thinking Like a Mountain," in *A Sand County Almanac* (1949; New York: Ballantine, 1970), p. 138.

6. Leopold, "The Land Ethic," in *A Sand County Almanac*, p. 253.

7. Ibid., pp. 253, 239, 247.

8. Callicott argues this point forcefully in "Animal Liberation: A Triangular Affair," *Environmental Ethics* 2 (Fall 1980): 311–38. Callicott tempers his claims a bit in later essays, but he does not abandon the essential point that Leopold's views are incompatible with the animal rights movement. See J. Baird Callicott, *In Defense of the Land Ethic* (Albany: State University of New York Press, 1989). Jon Moline makes a similar point in "Aldo Leopold and the Moral Community," *Environmental Ethics* 8 (Summer 1986): 99–120.

9. Leopold, "The Land Ethic," p. 262.

10. Ibid., 252.

11. Ibid., 252–53.

12. Leopold, *A Sand County Almanac*, pp. 6–7.

13. Ibid., 6–19.

14. Leopold, "Some Fundamentals of Conservation in the Southwest," p. 95.

15. Leopold, *A Sand County Almanac*, p. 252.

16. For a discussion of this point, see J. Baird Callicott, "The Conceptual Foundations of the Land Ethic," in *In Defense of the Land Ethic*, pp. 87–90.

17. For a sustained and sophisticated defense of the use of integrity in this context, see Laura Westra, *An Environmental Proposal for Ethics: The Principle of Integrity* (Lanham, Md.: Rowman & Littlefield, 1994).

18. Leopold, "The Land Ethic," p. 261.

19. Leopold, *A Sand County Almanac*, p. 262.

20. Callicott develops this defense in greater detail in "Hume's Is/Ought Dichotomy and the Relation of Ecology to Leopold's Land Ethic," reprinted in *In Defense of the Land Ethic*, pp. 117–27. Callicott's interpretation and defense of the land ethic are always worth reading, even if it is not always clear where Leopold's work leaves off and Callicott's begins.

21. Marti Kheel, "The Liberation of Nature: A Circular Affair," *Environmental Ethics* 7 (Summer 1985): 135–49, and Eric Katz, "Organicism, Community, and the 'Substitution Problem,'" *Environmental Ethics* 7 (Fall 1985): 241–56.

22. Tom Regan, *The Case for Animal Rights* (Berkeley: University of California Press, 1983), pp. 361–62; the emphasis is Regan's.

23. Don E. Marietta, Jr., "Environmental Holism and Individuals," *Environmental Ethics* 10 (Fall 1988): 251–58.

24. Jon Moline, "Aldo Leopold and the Moral Community," *Environmental Ethics* 8 (Summer 1986): 99–120.

25. Ibid., 105.

26. Ibid., 106. This criticism is best known as having been directed against act-and-rule utilitarianism. See, for example, David Lyons, *Forms and Limits of Utilitarianism* (Oxford, England: Clarendon, 1965), p. 118.

27. Leopold, "The Land Ethic," pp. 240–41.

28. Arthur Tansley, "The Use and Abuse of Vegetational Concepts and Terms," *Ecology* 16 (1935): 284–307. See also an earlier Tansley article, "The Classification of Vegetation and the Concept of Development," *Journal of Ecology* 8 (1920): 118–49. For a general history of ecology, see Donald Worster, *Nature's Economy* (Cambridge, England: Cambridge University Press, 1985).

29. Many of Callicott's most important essays are collected in *In Defense of the Land Ethic.*

30. Callicott, "Conceptual Foundations of the Land Ethic," p. 79. Callicott cites Darwin's *Descent of Man*, especially Ch. 4, as the source for these claims.

31. Leopold, "The Land Ethic," p. 239.

32. Callicott, "Conceptual Foundations of the Land Ethic," p. 83.

33. Ibid., 87.

34. Callicott, "The Metaphysical Implications of Ecology," in *In Defense of the Land Ethic*, p. 110.

35. Ibid., 110–11.

36. Ibid., 112–13.

37. Two insightful and convincing sources that advance this claim are Andrew Brennan, *Thinking about Nature: An Investigation of Nature, Value, and Ecology* (Athens: University of Georgia Press, 1988), and Karen Warren and Jim Cheney, "Ecosystem Ecology and Metaphysical Ecology: A Case Study," in *Environmental Ethics* 15 (Summer 1993): 99–116.

38. This view is seen most clearly in Callicott's "Animal Liberation and Environmental Ethics: Back Together Again," in *In Defense of the Land Ethic*, Ch. 3.

DISCUSSION QUESTIONS

1. Should farmers and ranchers be allowed to kill wild predators such as the coyote and wolf in order to protect their herds? How should government balance these competing interests?

2. Do you support reintroducing wolves into the Yellowstone ecosystem? Respond to those who would oppose your conclusions.

3. How might Singer and Regan differ from Leopold on the question of hunting deer? How relevant would such factors as herd size and ecosystem condition be? Would these thinkers have different views on the value of domestic animals compared to wild animals?

4. Do you support the view that humans are equal moral citizens of the biotic community? Is there a middle ground between humans as masters of nature and humans as equal biotic citizens?

5. Leopold suggests that the "dead earth" is an organism that does possess a certain kind of life. What exactly is the difference between a

living organism and a nonliving object? Is the earth itself alive?

6. Can land or an ecosystem really be characterized as healthy or unhealthy in anything other than a metaphorical way? What exactly would a healthy ecosystem be?

7. Return to a question asked at the end of Chapter 1. Are all things that are "natural" also good? Has your thinking on this question changed since you read Chapter 1?

GLOBAL ENVIRONMENTAL ETHICS WATCH

For more information on The Land Ethic, please see the Global Environmental Ethics Watch. Updated several times a day, Global Environmental Ethics Watch is a focused portal into GREENR—our Global Reference on the Environment, Energy, and Natural Resources—an ideal one-stop site for current events and research. You will have access to the latest information from trusted academic journals, news outlets, and magazines as well as access to statistics, primary sources, case studies, videos, podcasts, and much more.

To gain access please use the access code that accompanies your book. If you do not have an access code, visit cengagebrain .com to purchase one.

9

Radical Environmental Philosophy: Deep Ecology and Ecofeminism

DISCUSSION: Environmental Activism or Ecoterrorism?

For many observers, environmental destruction is the result not of individual action but of deeply ingrained social, economic, and cultural values and practices. To the degree that this is true, acting on behalf of the environment will require broad social changes and not mere individual adjustment and reform. Thus, environmental ethics becomes more a matter of environmental politics than personal morality.

But if environmental problems are connected to deeply held social positions, then opposition to change will also be deeply ingrained and change to current policy will require various degrees of political and social activism. Lobbying for legislation, writing letters, supporting political candidates, attending rallies and celebrations, holding protest marches, filing lawsuits, and staging economic boycotts have all, to various degrees, influenced contemporary environmental policy. Underlying these actions is the shared assumption that change can effectively be brought about by working within existing political and economic systems.

But what happens if you believe that a political and economic system itself is responsible for environmental problems? The economic and political influence of polluters and developers, lax enforcement of the law, biased or deficient media coverage, an economic system that rewards selfishness, competition, and consumption, and a system of private property rights that allows private owners almost total control over their property are just some of the factors that diminish the effectiveness of working within the system.

In light of this, are illegal means ever justified in the pursuit of environmental and ecological goals?

We can distinguish between two extralegal strategies for environmental protection. The first is a variation on a long tradition of civil disobedience, and the second has been called "ecosabotage" or "ecoterrorism."

Civil disobedience has roots in the lives and writings of such diverse thinkers as Henry David Thoreau, Mohandas Gandhi, and Martin Luther King. In general terms, civil disobedience is the intentional refusal to obey a law on moral grounds as a means of protesting or thwarting government policy. As a form of protest, civil disobedience often but not always protests the very law that one disobeys. Thus, American civil rights protestors, following Gandhi's lead, protested segregation and apartheid laws by refusing to sit in segregated sections of public facilities. Thoreau, on the other hand, refused to pay taxes not to protest taxation, but to protest government support for slavery. The leading defenders of civil disobedience typically are committed to nonviolence and accept public responsibility (and punishment) for the act.

In this vein, we recognize that numerous actions of environmental activists can be classified as acts of civil disobedience. The environmental group Greenpeace is perhaps best known for its activities that fit the civil disobedience model. Some Greenpeace members have been known to sail their ships into restricted nuclear testing zones, climb smokestacks to hang banners denouncing pollution, harass and ram whaling and fishing vessels, and the like. Typically, these acts involve criminal trespass and other minor offenses but pose little or no danger to humans or property.

Defenders of these acts argue that they can be justified in the same ways that civil rights activists in twentieth century America have justified their civil disobedience.

Essentially, we could argue that we live in a culture and at a time in which people are slow to recognize the serious wrongs being committed. The normal political and legal processes are unlikely to change things, because much of the public is unaware of or has failed to appreciate the extent of the harms. Public acts of civil disobedience, especially if they are covered in the media and result in well-publicized arrests and trials, can be an effective means for focusing public attention and stimulating public action. If done in such a way as to minimize the detrimental effects that can accompany breaking the law, which often means if done respectfully and nonviolently, the beneficial consequences can justify civil disobedience.

Some activists believe that such political protests, even if strictly speaking illegal, do not go far enough in defense of the environment. Some believe that the dire environmental consequences of political inaction justify something more than civil disobedience. Some have argued that acts of sabotage against property, what is often called "monkey wrenching," is morally justified in defense of the environment. Some have even claimed that violence against individuals and property, what has been called "ecoterrorism," is morally justified.

Monkey wrenching was popularized in a series of publications originating with Edward Abbey's novel *The Monkey Wrench Gang*. The publications of the radical environmental group Earth First! have described and encouraged, if not advocated, monkey wrenching. As defined by sociologist Bill Devall, monkey wrenching is the "purposeful dismantling or disabling of artifacts used in environmentally destructive practices at a specific site—dismantling fishing gear or logging equipment, for example." Devall goes on to define "ecosabotage" or "ecotage" as "disabling a technological or bureaucratic operation in defense of one's place." Typical examples of monkey wrenching include tree spiking (driving large metal spikes into trees to discourage logging), pouring sand into the gas tanks of construction and logging vehicles, pulling up survey stakes, and cutting down power lines. Similarly destructive acts against property have been performed by animal liberation groups that break into and sometimes destroy laboratories to save animals from experimentation.

Unlike classic instances of civil disobedience, monkey wrenching and ecosabotage are often performed under the cover of darkness with the intent of escaping detection. For example, a group called the Sea Shepherd Conservation Society sank two Icelandic whaling boats while they anchored in harbor in 1986. These saboteurs secretly entered the boats at night and opened seacocks to flood and sink the ships. Unlike well-established cases of civil disobedience, these activities usually involve destruction of property and, if not themselves acts of violence, hold the potential of injuring or killing people. Loggers have been injured when their saws hit a spike driven into a tree.

The Sea Shepherd Conservation Society refused to sink a third ship when they found a night watchman aboard. They had pledged not to injure human beings. This decision stands in contrast to the actions of the French government against Greenpeace protesters in 1985. Greenpeace members intended to sail their vessel, *Rainbow Warrior,* into restricted waters where the French were planning to conduct nuclear weapons testing. The French government sent intelligence agents into New Zealand with false passports to sink the *Rainbow Warrior.* A crew member aboard the ship at the time of the sinking was killed. In the fall of 1995, the French military again forcibly seized several Greenpeace ships that were protesting French nuclear tests in international waters.

The Earth Liberation Front (ELF) is a loosely connected group that has also claimed responsibility for numerous acts of ecosabotage. Among the acts attributed to ELF was an arson at a ski resort in Vail Colorado in 1996, explosive devices left at labs at universities in Michigan and Washington, and arson at a condominium complex and at a SUV dealership in San Diego in 2006.

In March 2001 the Federal Bureau of Investigation identified ELF as a "terrorist threat" and made ecoterrorism the highest priority domestic terrorist threat in the United States. In 2005 and 2006, the FBI launched an investigation called "Operation Backfire" that resulted in indictments against 30 people on charges of domestic terrorism.

DISCUSSION TOPICS:

1. Would civil disobedience in defense of the environment ever be justified? If so, when and why? Which laws would you break in defense of the environment?

2. Is tree spiking a defensible means for preventing logging of old-growth forests? Is tree spiking a nonviolent form of civil disobedience?

3. Throughout much of the Western tradition, governments have often justified violence and killing in pursuit of important social goals. The just war theory and self-defense are two ways that violence has been ethically justified. Sometimes, our culture has accepted violence, if it is a last resort and a way to protect innocent life. Might violence against individuals ever be justified in order to protect nonhuman life? Could rationales like the just war or self-defense arguments be extended to ecological issues?

4. Would dire environmental consequences of political inaction ever justify illegal acts directed against private citizens or private businesses? Are acts of sabotage against property, setting fire to unoccupied housing developments or SUVs for example, ever morally justified?

5. Would you characterize acts of ecosabotage such as arson as acts of terrorism? Why or why not?

9.1 INTRODUCTION

Social and cultural critics can be categorized into two general groups: those who believe that the status quo needs only reform, and those who believe that radical change is necessary to adequately address the problems. All of the environmental philosophies that we have examined so far can be classified as reformist: we should reform economics, extend our present understanding of moral standing, create a better integration of science and ethics. This chapter will consider environmental philosophies that advocate more radical social change to address present environmental challenges.

Both believers in deep ecology and ecofeminism think that the cause of environmental and ecological destruction lies with cultural and social factors that are deeply entrenched in the contemporary world. Only by addressing these deeply ingrained causes, only by making radical change rather than mere reform, can we hope to fully address the present environmental crisis. A simpler description could be made in terms of symptoms and underlying causes. By focusing on issues such as pollution and resource depletion, the reform approach looks only at the immediate effects of the environmental crisis. Just as a sneeze or a cough can disrupt a person's daily routine, pollution and resource depletion disrupt the lifestyle of modern industrial societies. However, it would be a mistake for medicine merely to treat sneezing and coughing and not to investigate their underlying causes. So, too, it is a mistake for environmentalists to be concerned only with pollution and resource depletion without investigating their social and human causes. Thus, deep ecology and ecofeminism are radical environmental philosophies in the sense that they espouse that significant social change is necessary to get to the root of environmental problems.

But proponents of deep ecology and ecofeminism disagree in identifying those underlying causes. Deep ecology identifies the roots of ecological destruction in a general philosophy or worldview, which they believe dominates contemporary thinking. This dominant worldview includes a narrow human-centeredness to all our thinking. Thus a cure for the crisis can come only with a radical change in our philosophical outlook about human beings and their place in nature. This change involves both personal and cultural transformations and would "affect basic economic and ideological structures."[1] In short, we need to change ourselves as individuals and as a culture.

Ecofeminists think that this analysis is too abstract and too general, arguing instead that specific human institutions and practices—*unjust* institutions and practices—are more critical. Specifically, ecofeminists believe that the domination and degradation of nature arise from social patterns of domination and hierarchy, patterns of social life in which some humans exercise control or domination over others. Rosemary Radford Reuther, one of the first feminist thinkers to address ecological issues, has written,

> Women must see that there can be no liberation for them and no solution to the ecological crisis within a society whose fundamental model of relationships continues to be one of domination. They must unite the demands of the women's movement with those of the ecological movement to envision a radical reshaping of the basic socioeconomic relations and the underlying values of this society.[2]

In this view, environmental and ecological destruction is best understood as a form of human domination, in this case the human domination of nature. To understand this crisis fully, we need to understand more general patterns of human domination of other humans.

9.2 DEEP ECOLOGY

Unlike the land ethic, deep ecology has not developed out of one primary source, nor does it refer to one systematic philosophy. Deep ecology has been used to describe a variety of environmental philosophies, ranging from a general description of all nonanthropocentric theories to the highly technical philosophy developed by the Norwegian philosopher Arne Naess.[3] For many people involved in radical environmentalism as a political movement (members of Earth First! and the Earth Liberation Front, for example), deep ecology also provides the philosophy that legitimizes their form of activism. In recent years, the phrase *deep ecology* has come to refer primarily to the approach to environmental issues developed in the writings of academics Naess, Bill Devall, and George Sessions, which is how it is used in this chapter.[4]

Deep ecologists trace their philosophical roots to many of the people and positions that this textbook has already examined. The debate between Gifford Pinchot and John Muir examined in Chapter 3 was an early version of the tension between shallow (Pinchot) and deep (Muir) approaches. Rachel Carson's critique of anthropocentrism in *Silent Spring* and Lynn White's critique of western Christianity, along with the nineteenth-century romanticism of Thoreau, were precursors of deep ecology.[5]

Arne Naess first introduced a distinction between deep and shallow environmental perspectives in 1973.[6] Naess characterized the shallow ecology movement as committed to the "fight against pollution and resource depletion." He maintained that it is an anthropocentric approach with the primary objective of protecting the "health and affluence of the people in developed countries." Deep ecology looks to more fundamental issues, at what it calls the "dominant worldview," which underlies such issues as pollution and resource depletion. Their critique is based on two positions we have examined: ecocentrism and nonanthropocentrism. Deep ecologists attempt to work out an alternative philosophical worldview that is holistic and not human-centered.

But any call for a radical change in people's philosophical worldview immediately faces a major challenge. How do we even begin to explain the alternative if, by definition, it is radically different from the starting point? How do we step outside our personal and cultural worldview or ideology to compare it with something radically different?

Deep ecologists use a variety of strategies to meet these challenges, including reliance on poetry, Buddhism, spiritualism, and political activism via civil disobedience and ecosabotage. Perhaps the best way to begin exploring this movement is to consider the practical principles that Naess and Sessions drew up to articulate the ideas on which all its adherents agree. This platform serves as a core around which the diverse deep ecology movement can be unified.

9.3 THE DEEP ECOLOGY PLATFORM

Deep ecologists are committed to the view that solutions to the current grave environmental crisis require more than mere reform of our personal and social practices. They believe that a radical transformation in our worldview is necessary. Naess and Sessions developed the deep ecology platform as a statement of shared principles. The platform is intended to be general enough to allow for a diversity of philosophical interpretations and specific enough to distinguish the deep from the shallow approach to practical matters.[7] As developed by Naess and Sessions, the platform includes these principles:

(1) The flourishing of human and nonhuman life on earth has intrinsic value. The value of nonhuman life-forms is independent of the usefulness they may have for narrow human purposes.

(2) The richness and diversity of life-forms are values in themselves and contribute to the flourishing of human and nonhuman life on earth.

(3) Humans have no right to reduce this richness and diversity except to satisfy vital needs.

(4) Present human interference with the nonhuman world is excessive, and the situation is rapidly worsening.

(5) The flourishing of human life and cultures is compatible with a substantial decrease of the human population. The flourishing of nonhuman life requires such a decrease.

(6) Significant change of life conditions for the better requires changes in policies. These affect basic economic, technological, and ideological structures.

(7) The ideological change is mainly that of appreciating *life quality* (dwelling in situations of intrinsic value) rather than adhering to a high standard of living. There will be a profound awareness of the difference between *big* and *great*.

(8) Those who subscribe to the foregoing points have an obligation directly or indirectly to participate in the attempt to implement the necessary changes.[8]

We can see how these principles could serve to explain and support a wide range of specific positions on practical environmental controversies. In working against the continued destruction of rain forests, for example, we could appeal to the first three principles. Principles 5 and 7 would be important in developing an energy policy that would address such issues as resource conservation, population growth, consumer demand, and nuclear energy.

An important point is that the platform also reflects the ways in which the science of ecology influences deep ecology. In some sense, ecological science would provide direct support for principles 4 and 5. Ecology would also be relevant in explaining and defending principles 1 and 2. But ecology is also important for deep ecology in that it provides a model for a nonreductionist, holistic worldview.

More specifically, the conclusions reached in ecology and conservation biology are often "statements of ignorance." "Only rarely can scientists predict with any certainty the effect of a new chemical on even a single small ecosystem," Naess writes. Given this pervasive scientific ignorance, the burden of proof should rest with anyone who proposes a policy that intervenes in the natural environment.

> Why does the burden of proof rest with the encroachers? The ecosystems in which we intervene are generally in a particular state of balance which there are grounds to assume to be of more service to mankind than states of disturbance and their resultant unpredictable and far-reaching changes. In general, it is not possible to regain the original state after an intervention has wrought serious, undesired consequences.[9]

Accordingly, ecology contributes to deep ecology in the same ways in which scientific understanding has often contributed to ethical analysis. We gain a better understanding of the world, and on the basis of this understanding, we are in a better position to offer ethical evaluations and prescriptions. Because ecological understanding offers new insights, an ethics that relies on ecology can be expected to offer new evaluations and prescriptions.

9.4 METAPHYSICAL ECOLOGY

Like the land ethic, deep ecology relies on the science of ecology in a variety of ways. Ecology provides a good deal of information about how natural ecosystems function. Ecology helps us to diagnose environmental disorders and to prescribe policies that can resolve these disorders. Ecology provides us with an understanding of natural ecosystems, and this understanding in turn is the basis from which we can make evaluations and recommendations. Ecology also cautions against any quick-fix technological solution to environmental problems. Echoing a theme found in Aldo Leopold's work, Naess argues for a humble and constrained approach to environmental change.

But Naess also is aware of the limits of science and warns against too great a reliance on ecology. There are dangers in what Naess calls "ecologism," the view that takes ecology as the ultimate science. The danger arises when we rely too heavily on ecology for solutions to specific problems. To treat ecology as just another science that can offer scientific answers to specific problems is to be tempted by the standard shallow hope for a technological quick fix. As is consistent with his commitment to deep ecology, Naess believes that environmental issues such as wilderness destruction and species extinction point to fundamental questions about how we ought to live. The fear is that the recent development of an "ecological conscience," will be used simply to substitute one shallow quick fix for another. In this view, ecology would simply be a new means for treating only the symptoms. Thus it would subvert attempts to probe more deeply into the underlying causes of the environmental crisis. Ecology might then become a diversion from these more fundamental issues. The risk is that ecology will be used as part of a political strategy to derail movements that question the fundamental assumptions of our culture. In Naess's words, we need to "fight against depoliticization" to stay focused on the political nature of the deep ecology movement.[10]

Scientific ecology provides a model for thinking about the deep fundamental issues that underlie the environmental crisis. Inspired by ecology, deep ecologists seek to develop alternative worldviews that echo ecological insights into such issues as diversity, holism, interdependencies, and relations. Deep ecology traces the roots of our environmental crisis to fundamental philosophical causes. Solutions can come only from a transformation of our worldview and practices and from our answers to fundamental questions. What is human nature? What is the relation of humans to the rest of nature? What is the nature of reality? These questions are traditionally identified as *metaphysical* questions. Deep ecology, therefore, is as concerned with questions of metaphysics and ontology (the study of what is) as it is with questions of ethics. Deep ecologists trace the cause of many of our problems to the metaphysics presupposed by the dominant philosophy of modern industrial society. Deep ecology is concerned with a *metaphysical ecology* rather than a scientific one.

The dominant metaphysics that underlies modern industrial society is *individualistic* and *reductionistic*.[11] This view holds that only individuals are real and that we approach a more fundamental level of reality by reducing objects to their more basic elements. These most basic elements, whatever they turn out to be, are related according to strict physical laws. But this dominant worldview also sees humans as essentially different from the rest of nature. Individual human beings possess a "mind" or "free will" or "soul" that exempts them from the strict mechanical determinism characteristic of the rest of nature. Thus the dominant worldview rejects the position identified in Chapter 7 as metaphysical holism.

Rejection of these dominant beliefs is central to the metaphysics of deep ecology. Taking its cue from ecology, the metaphysics of deep ecology denies that individual humans are separate from nature. Humans are fundamentally a part of their surroundings, not distinct from them. Humans are constituted by their relationships to other elements in the environment. In an important sense, the environment—by which the deep ecologists mean both the biotic and the abiotic constituents—determines what human beings are. Without the relationships that exist among humans and between humans and nature, human beings would literally become different sorts of beings. A philosophy that "reduces" humans to "individuals" that are somehow distinct from their social and natural environment is radically misguided.

This point has been expressed by Warwick Fox, an Australian philosopher and deep ecologist.

> It is the idea that we can make no firm ontological divide in the field of existence: that there is no bifurcation in reality between the human and the non-human realms ... to the extent that we perceive boundaries, we fall short of Deep Ecological consciousness.[12]

Thus, echoing the metaphysical holism of Callicott described in Chapter 8, deep ecologists deny the reality of individuals—at least as they are typically understood in Western philosophy. There are no individuals apart from or distinct from relationships within a system. Human "nature" is inseparable from nature. Viewing human beings as individuals is how the dominant worldview has understood humans and has broken up reality, but it is a dangerous and misleading metaphysics.

No doubt, thinking like this tempts many people to relegate deep ecologists to the fringe of environmental philosophy. These views certainly represent a radical shift from mainstream Western thinking. But any call for a radical shift in perspective faces difficulties in being understood. We can, perhaps, approach deep ecology in a variety of ways in the hope that we can begin to understand this alternative outlook.

In the spirit of deep ecology, we might begin by taking a hint from scientific ecology. If we think of ecosystems as energy circuits through which solar and chemical energy flow, we might begin to think of individual organisms as less permanent and less real than the chemical and biological processes themselves. Individual organisms come and go, but the process goes on as long as environmental conditions permit. Individual organisms can be thought of as the location at which these chemical processes occur.

Another way of approaching this conclusion is to consider what it means to say that an individual organism is alive. Minimally, an individual organism is alive only if certain chemical and biological processes are occurring. When these processes cease to occur, the organism ceases to live. Thus the processes are necessary for the existence of the organism. On the other hand, when the processes are occurring, life exists. Thus the processes are sufficient for life. Because chemical and biological processes are both necessary and sufficient for the existence of life, we have some reasons for saying that the processes are at least as real as, if not more real than, individual living organisms.

Biophysicist Harold Morowitz makes a similar point.

> Viewed from the point of view of modern [ecology], each living thing is a dissipative structure, that is, it does not endure in and of itself but only as a result of the continual flow of energy in the system…. From this point of view, the reality of individuals is problematic because they do not exist per se but only as local perturbations in this universal energy flow…. An example might be instructive. Consider a vortex in a stream of flowing water. The vortex is a structure made of an ever-changing group of water molecules. It does not exist as an entity in the classic Western sense; it exists only because of the flow of water through the stream. If the flow ceases the vortex disappears. In the same sense the structures out of which the biological entities are made are transient, unstable entities with constantly changing molecules dependent on a constant flow of energy to maintain form and structure.[13]

Finally, we might better appreciate metaphysical ecology by considering the language of "individualism." Ordinarily, we seem confident that we know what we refer to when we speak of individuals. But although we often use *individual* as a noun (*an* individual, *the* individual), the word is perhaps more precisely used as an adjective (an individual person, an individual tree, and the like).

Imagine being asked to go out and count the individuals that you see. We might assume that the assignment involves individual humans, or we would be well advised to ask, "Individual what?" This suggests that when we speak of individuals, we have already adopted a worldview or metaphysics that has divided our experiences up in one way rather than in another way. Our ordinary language seems to presuppose a metaphysics in which separate and isolated organisms are most real. But note that we might just as well refer to individual communities, individual ecosystems, individual species, and individual chemical cycles. We might just as well refer to individual body parts, individual organs, individual cells, individual molecules, individual atoms, and so forth. The individual human person can be seen either as a part of some larger individual (such as a species or an ecosystem) or as a collection of other individuals (such as organ systems or cells).

The implication of this is that the world does not come already broken down into categories such as individuals and wholes. Rather, particular ways of understanding the world and the particular needs served by understanding it in those ways determine what is to count as an individual and what is to count as a whole. Deep ecology argues that the dominant worldview assumes an artificial distinction between individuals and their surroundings. The ecological and environmental devastation that has followed from this particular metaphysics has proved it to be dangerous. An alternative metaphysics, one inspired by scientific ecology, can offer an opportunity for reversing this devastation.

9.5 FROM METAPHYSICS TO ETHICS

Perhaps the most philosophically challenging aspect of deep ecology involves connecting the metaphysical views to the normative prescriptions derived from them. The early chapters of this textbook examined a variety of ways in which standard ethical theories were extended and applied to environmental problems. In those chapters, we mentioned recent critics who claim that traditional ethics has been stretched beyond the breaking point by environmental challenges. With deep ecology, we now see how radically different the alternatives to traditional ethics can be.

Environmental challenges require not just new ethics but a new metaphysics as well. This section considers how deep ecologists move from metaphysical ecology to ethical and political concerns.

One of the most common and fundamental distinctions made within the Western philosophical tradition is between *objectivity* and *subjectivity*. Mainstream Western metaphysics, particularly the field of ontology, investigates the nature of reality. The *real* world is taken to be that which exists independently of human beings and human understanding. This is the objective world, and it is the goal of science to comprehend this reality. Insofar as it does this, scientific claims are "true" and "objective," because they correspond to reality. On the other hand, human beings ("subjects") interpret the world, make judgments about it, perceive it, value it, and have feelings about it. These human factors are *subjective* because they depend on the human subject. Because they depend on human subjects, they should not be mistaken for objective "truths" about the real world.

In general terms, this distinction between objectivity and subjectivity has had significant implications for mainstream epistemology and ethics. Deep ecologists believe that the distinction has had a detrimental influence on both how we understand and on how we value nature.

Epistemologically, objective descriptions of nature can be measured, tested, verified, and the like. Subjective judgments about nature, on the other hand, are arbitrary, unpredictable, biased, and unverifiable. Objective descriptions can be rational and true. Subjective judgments cannot. In ethics, subjective judgments of value ("oughts") cannot be derived from objective descriptions of fact ("is").

To elaborate this distinction, philosophers in the seventeenth century relied on a contrast between the *primary* and the *secondary* qualities of physical objects. An object's primary qualities existed in the object and were taken to represent what the object truly and really was. Size, shape, mass, extension, and movement were understood as examples of an object's primary qualities. They existed in the object itself. On the other hand, secondary qualities were said to exist as a result of the interaction between an object and an observer. An object's color, texture, taste, and smell were secondary qualities in that they existed only insofar as there existed a perceiver who experienced them. Because secondary qualities depended on a perceiver, they were subjective and not really a part of the object itself.

Continuing with this seventeenth-century perspective, the role of science is to fully describe an object's primary qualities. Because all these primary qualities can be fully described in mathematical terms, the real world turns out to be the world of mathematical physics and mechanics. Real trees, for example, have no color. They merely reflect light waves. If our eyes were constituted differently, they would appear differently. Trees are not heavy. They have mass that is subject to the force of gravity. Were we larger, stronger beings, trees would be less heavy than they now appear. Therefore, descriptions of natural objects that refer to secondary qualities such as color, weight, and taste are scientifically irrelevant. They are not really true, rational, or objective.

Further, more complex descriptions of natural objects in terms of *tertiary* qualities are even less objective and true than judgments about secondary qualities. For example, to describe a tree as "majestic," "beautiful," or "awe inspiring" is to say something that is merely personal opinion. Although color may exist as an interaction between object and subject (reflected light waves reacting with nerve cells), beauty is totally in the eye of the beholder.

Note how these distinctions and the value conclusions that flow from them depend greatly on a clear distinction between subject and object. When the human subject is viewed as essentially one with the natural world, as deep ecologists argue that it should be, the rationale for clinging to a strict distinction between objective and subjective, between real and perceived, and between fact and value is weakened. We can still make these distinctions and they can be useful for us, but they lose their metaphysical priority. The real world ceases to exist "out there," separate and apart from us. We exist in the real world. Our perceptions, judgments, and evaluations are as real as the abstract judgments of science. Just as important, these judgments and evaluations can be as rational, true, and objective as the judgments of science.

Note also how these distinctions can play a significant role in debates about environmental controversies. Often, environmentalists are dismissed as sentimentalists who allow their emotions to cloud their reason. A stand of oak really is only a collection of primarily carbon and water molecules that play a role in cycling carbon, oxygen, nitrogen, and other elements through the ecosystem. Rationally, we might just as well put the carbon to a more useful purpose, such as furniture or firewood, especially if we can find the technological means for replacing the oaks' function in the carbon, oxygen, or nitrogen cycles. To fight against development for the sake of a "majestic" stand of oak trees is mere emotion and sentiment. When environmental positions are cast as emotional and sentimental, they can be dismissed as irrelevant. According to the dominant worldview, they are not rational, objective, or scientific.

Naess makes a similar point.

> Confrontations between developers and conservers reveal difficulties in experiencing what is real. What a conservationist sees and experiences as reality, the developer typically does not see, and vice versa. A conservationist sees and experiences a forest as a unity, a gestalt, and when speaking of the heart of the forest, he or she does not speak about the geometrical centre. A developer sees quantities of trees and argues that a road through the forest covers very few square kilometers compared to the whole area of trees, so why make so much fuss? And if the conservers insist, he will propose that the road does not touch the centre of the forest. The heart is saved, he may think. The difference between the antagonists is one rather of ontology than of ethics.... To the conservationist, the developer seems to suffer from a kind of radical blindness. But one's ethics in environmental questions are based largely on how one sees reality.[14]

According to many deep ecologists, as long as we maintain a strict distinction between individuals and nature, we can make an equally strict distinction between objective and subjective judgments. This distinction provides a rationale for taking the judgments of science and technology as epistemologically justified while dismissing the evaluative judgments of ethics and aesthetics. But when deep ecologists challenge the distinction between individual and nature, they also are challenging the strict distinction between the objective and subjective. This leaves open the possibility that evaluative judgments about the value and beauty of a wilderness, for example, can be shown to be as rationally justified as the judgments of science.

Naess is careful to recognize that mere spontaneous feelings or emotional reactions and outbursts are not rational arguments. The mere expression of a feeling does not advance rational dialogue and debate. However, we need to be equally clear in recognizing that evaluative judgments "motivated by strong feelings" do have "a clear cognitive function." The *feeling* of anger produced by the destruction of a forest or the imperative to "stop that destruction" is neither true nor false in itself. But the judgment that "this mountainside has been destroyed and ruined" is open to rational assessment and might well be true.

The challenge to deep ecologists is to specify the conditions under which such environmental judgments can be demonstrated as true and rational. Naess phrases his approach to such challenges in terms of relational properties and gestalts. Properties such as "being destroyed" and "being ruined" can be understood only within a context that Naess calls a gestalt or totality. The conservationist and the developer experience different realities. Their concepts and perceptions occur within different contexts and are related to many different concepts and perceptions. Given these contexts, and given that each of their judgments makes sense, each is in that way "rational." At the same time, neither can claim a privileged status as better reflecting reality.

But the point remains that conservationists and developers disagree radically about what we should do. Their respective practical recommendations are embedded in their different gestalts. However, if each gestalt makes sense and if neither enjoys a privileged status, we are left without means for deciding which course of action, if either, is more reasonable. In general terms, how do we judge between the conservationist's and the developer's worldviews?

In some sense, rational discourse breaks down at this point. Each worldview has its standards of rationality, values, and reality. But Naess believes that continued discussion is possible and that we eventually can attain substantiation of one side or the other. Naess suggests that this is possible if we avoid "absolutism" and take care in clarifying our norms, while remaining open to honest and nonviolent communication with our opponents.

> If a speaker's norm pronouncement, "It is right to deny X," is answered from the audience, "It is not right to deny X," there is nothing to get in a fuss about. The situation begs to be debated. A debate requires clarification of value priorities.[15]

At this point, other deep ecologists rely on stories, poetry, narrative, myths, and ritual. The goal is to make the deep ecology worldview understandable to people who do not yet view reality in this way. Because, by definition, these people do not share the concepts, norms, values, and metaphysics of deep ecology, straightforward linguistic explanation typically is unsuccessful. The epistemology of deep ecology involves the search for ways to encourage people to make radical shifts in their worldviews. In addition to poetry and ritual, the religious concept of "bearing witness" in the way that we live our lives is a method for communicating the deep ecology worldview. Another method of communicating this is the "forceful announcement" of our values and living in accordance with those values. Civil disobedience is another means of demonstrating, rather than explaining, the depth of difference between worldviews.

9.6 SELF-REALIZATION AND BIOCENTRIC EQUALITY

The practical ethics of deep ecology is best seen in the platform discussed earlier. These are the principles we can directly apply to concrete situations to explain and justify environmental activism. But at a more abstract and philosophical level, the ethics of deep ecology focuses on two "ultimate norms." These norms are ultimate in the sense that they are not derived from any further or more basic principles or values. They are the point at which ethical justification ends. We can perhaps best think of them as connecting deep ecology's abstract metaphysics with its more specific ethical platform.

The two ultimate norms of deep ecology are *self-realization* and *biocentric equality*. Self-realization is a process through which people come to understand themselves as existing in a thorough interconnectedness with the rest of nature. A sense of biocentric equality is the recognition that all organisms and beings are equally members of an interrelated whole and, therefore, have equal intrinsic worth.

Although self-realization grows out of a tradition that is as old as philosophy itself, the particular version developed within deep ecology represents perhaps its most original insight. The ancient Greek directive to "know thyself" and Socrates's claim that "the unexamined life is not worth living" imply that the good life involves a process of self-examination and self-fulfillment. The teleological understanding of the good as the actualization of internal potentialities provides a similar insight. The suggestion from these traditions is that as we go through a process of self-examination, we become able to separate trivial, superficial, and temporary interests from deeper, more central, and lasting interests.

To understand the concept of self-realization, we can start with a general distinction that we used earlier in this textbook for *needs, interests,* and *wants*. Needs can be understood as those elements that are necessary for survival. Food, clothing, shelter, and nontoxic air and water are obvious examples of needs. A person's interests are those factors that contribute to well-being. It is in a person's interest to have friendships, education, and good health. Wants are the immediate desires and goals toward which a person is inclined. I want a vacation, a glass of juice, or a free lunch.

Note that these categories can overlap. Nutritious food and clean air are things that I need, have an interest in getting, and in fact want. But there can also be tensions and conflicts between these categories. Although it is in my interest to improve my education and, toward that end, to stay home and read, what I want is to go out to a party with my friends.

Wants seem to be a matter of individual psychology. They are those factors that provide a motive for acting. Wants come to be developed, chosen, learned, created by advertising, and the like. Interests are not a matter of immediate psychological states. They are connected to what is good for a person and, therefore, are not a matter of choice. (Even if being free is in a person's interest, the fact that freedom is in that person's interest is not a matter of individual choice.) Interests can be understood and determined but not chosen.

Wants are typically seen as a product of individual choice, culture, or society. They are superficial and temporary in the sense that they are dependent on an individual's personal background, history, and culture. Various ethical traditions encourage humans to separate these transitory wants from their basic interests as rational beings. The good life is a life spent in pursuit of basic and true interests. Self-interest, properly understood, is the good for human beings.

Thus, in effect, these traditions see two "selves" in every person. One is the self constituted by the conscious beliefs, wants, and intentions of the ego. The other self is the true nature that underlies this person's ego. "Know thyself" is the injunction to get beyond this surface self to figure out and realize our true underlying nature. Thus traditions as diverse as Greek philosophy, Christianity, Buddhism, romanticism, and Marxism all see a process of self-realization as central to the good life.

Self-realization plays a similar role in deep ecology. But for deep ecologists, the underlying self is the self that is one with the natural world. Self-realizing is a process of self-examination in which people come to understand themselves as part of a greater whole. It is a process through which a person comes to understand that "there is no firm ontological divide between humans and nonhumans," between self and other. It is the process through which we come to know ourselves not as individuals separate and distinct from nature but as a part of a greater "self." This self is the self described within metaphysical holism. If what we are as human beings—our nature—is constituted by our relationships with other parts of the natural world, self-realization is a coming to understand and fully appreciate this oneness.

For many in the Western philosophical tradition, self-realization would be a means for developing a person's separate, individual, and personal nature. Deep ecologists retain a commitment to self-realization, self-interest, and self-fulfillment, but they deny this individualistic understanding of the self. To distinguish their holistic and relational view of the self from the more individualistic model, deep ecologists typically use "Self" to refer to the holistic view and "self" for the individualistic view. Thus "Self-realization" is a process through which "self comes to understand itself as Self" and "self-interest" comes to be seen as "Self-interest."

Devall and Sessions summarize these points.

> In keeping with the spiritual traditions of many of the world's religions, the deep ecology norm of Self-Realization goes beyond the modern Western self which is defined as an isolated ego striving primarily for hedonistic gratification.... This socially programmed sense of the narrow self or social self dislocates us, and leaves us prey to whatever fad or fashion is prevalent in our society.... Spiritual growth, or unfolding, begins when we cease to understand or see ourselves as isolated and narrow competing egos and begin to identify with other humans from our family and friends to, eventually, our species. But the deep ecology sense of self requires a further maturity and growth, an identification which goes beyond humanity to include the nonhuman world.[16]

The second ultimate norm is that of biocentric equality. Devall and Sessions explain this intuition as follows:

> All things in the biosphere have an equal right to live and blossom and to reach their own individual forms of unfolding and self-realization within the larger Self-realization. This basic intuition is that all organisms and entities in the ecosphere, as parts of the interrelated whole, are equal in intrinsic worth.[17]

At one level, biocentric equality is the same insight described in Chapter 6 as biocentrism. Taylor's *Respect for Nature,* for example, also defends a biocentric ethics based on the notion of equal inherent worth. However, Taylor's biocentrism is well rooted within traditional Western philosophy. It develops out of an individualism that views organisms as centers of individual lives. The biocentric equality of deep ecology grows out of metaphysical holism with equally old Western roots. Members of the biotic community possess equal moral worth, not because as individuals they have intrinsic worth, but simply because they are members of that community.

Is there a significant difference? If there is any, it seems that deep ecologists are less willing to make trade-offs between human and nonhuman interests. When human interests conflict with nonhuman interests, deep ecologists are less inclined to favor the human interests. Taylor goes to some lengths to work out a means for rationally resolving conflicts. For deep ecologists, this is likely to result in hierarchies that inevitably have human interests at the top. Deep ecology seeks a more democratic and less hierarchical equality.

Deep ecologists are committed to promoting lifestyles that tread lightly on the earth. This means that humans ought to live in simple, relatively nontechnological, self-reliant, decentralized communities. Second, and by analogy to the concept of an ecosystem, communities ought to be organized regionally, existing as "bioregions" rather than as more traditional political organizations. Our lifestyles ought to be simple in the sense that our consumer or material desires should be kept to a minimum. We need to recognize material wants as artificial products of human society. The ideal seems to be a situation in which local communities exist in a harmonious and self-regulating relationship with their surroundings. This ideal has been called an "ecotopia"—a community that seeks harmony with nature rather than dominance over it.

9.7 CRITICISMS OF DEEP ECOLOGY

It sometimes seems that deep ecology acts as a lightning rod for environmental criticism and backlash. Because deep ecology does critique the dominant worldview, we should not be surprised to find significant critical reaction. As mentioned at the start of this chapter, the term *deep ecology* does not refer to one specific and systematic philosophy. It refers to an assortment of philosophical and activist approaches to ecological issues that share some fundamental ecocentric and nonanthropocentric assumptions. It is perhaps best thought of as a movement that encompasses both philosophical and activist sides.

Given this diversity, it is difficult to offer any precise criticisms of deep ecology. A critique of, for example, the tactics of Earth First! could be rebuffed by deep ecologists as beside the point, because not all deep ecologists agree with these tactics. Likewise, a critique that accuses deep ecology of being too abstract and vague on issues such as "Self-realization" might be rejected by deep ecologists who are more inclined toward political activism.

Of course, this ambiguity itself can be grounds for criticism. In some ways, the claims of deep ecology are so sweeping and general as to become empty. A "movement" that can claim inspiration from such diverse sources as Taoism, Heraclitus, Spinoza, Whitehead, Gandhi, Buddhism, Native American cultures, Thomas Jefferson, Thoreau, and Woody Guthrie is certainly eclectic at best. At worst, it becomes unintelligible.

This ambiguity can be frustrating for critics as they try to focus on specific claims, only to find their target shifting. It can also lead to an end of dialogue because critics can be dismissed as missing the point, as irrelevant, or as misrepresenting deep ecology.[18]

Another criticism echoes the fascism charge raised against holistic and nonanthropocentric ethics in earlier chapters. Biocentric equality would seem to suggest treating human interests as equal to the interests of other living things, as well as of the more general biotic community. However, when this equality is combined with the metaphysical claim that individuals are not real and with the charge that humans alone are responsible for significant environmental destruction, deep ecology can seem misanthropic (as hating humanity). Humans are no better than other living things and, in fact, are guilty of great environmental malevolence. Thus human well-being is not a moral priority. Some of the better-known examples of misanthropic remarks include Edward Abbey's claim in *Desert Solitaire* that he would rather shoot a human than a snake[19] and Dave Foreman's suggestion that we should not aid starving Ethiopians and should allow them to die.[20]

Deep ecologists disavow such claims. Fox, for example, points out that deep ecologists criticize "not humans per se (i.e., a general class of social actors) but rather human-centeredness (a legitimating ideology)."[21] This claim amounts to the view that deep ecologists do not deny intrinsic value to humans. They simply deny that only humans have intrinsic value.

But the same challenge can be issued here that was raised in Chapter 6. What is to be done when human interests conflict with the interests of elements of the nonhuman natural world, as so often is the case with environmental issues? In such cases, if we favor humans, we seem to abandon nonanthropocentric holism. If we favor the nonhuman world, we approach the misanthropic position that deep ecologists want to deny. Again, this requires deep ecologists to work out a clear hierarchy of vital needs.

Another challenge is raised in various forms by a diverse group of critics. The problem with deep ecology, in their view, is that it has overgeneralized in its critique of human-centeredness, anthropocentrism, and the dominant worldview.

From this point of view, not all humans and not all human perspectives are equally at fault for environmental problems. When deep ecologists critique "the" dominant worldview, they fail to acknowledge that many humans are not part of that dominance. Thus deep ecologists are too broad in their critique and, consequently, too broad in their positive program.

One version of this critique is raised by the Indian ecologist Ramachandra Guha.[22] Guha argues that despite its claims to universality, deep ecology is uniquely an American ideology, essentially a radical branch of the wilderness preservation movement. In Guha's view, if it were put into practice, deep ecology would have disastrous consequences, especially for the poor and agrarian populations in underdeveloped countries. Describing India as a "long settled and densely populated country in which agrarian populations have a finely balanced relationship with nature," Guha reasons that a policy of biocentric equality and wilderness preservation would effectively result in a direct transfer of wealth from poor to rich and a major displacement of poor people.

Applying the deep ecology platform to societies in underdeveloped countries smacks of Western imperialism. "We (environmentalists in the West) know what is best for you. Let us generalize from our experiences and our culture and tell you why you should live in ways that we suggest. Stop treating nature as resources, even if you are living at a mere subsistence level. Preserve and respect nature for its own sake."

Guha also faults deep ecology for its appropriation of Eastern philosophies and traditions. Citing Hinduism, Taoism, and Buddhism as though they were a single consistent Eastern worldview and one that is more in tune with environmentalism "does considerable violence to the historical record." Eastern cultures, as well as Western cultures, have manipulated nature and caused significant ecological destruction.

Accordingly, deep ecology is not very helpful to the environmental concerns of peoples of underdeveloped countries. At best, it is irrelevant. At worst, it can be harmful to the very people who already are victimized by social and political dominance.

Similar critiques of deep ecology have been offered by thinkers associated with *ecofeminism*. This perspective agrees that in the search for the "deep" underlying causes of the environmental crisis, deep ecologists have focused their attention at too abstract a level. The more significant causes can be located at a much more localized level: the social, economic, and patriarchal structures of contemporary societies. In faulting anthropocentrism, deep ecologists fail to recognize important distinctions between people. If there is "a" dominant worldview, deep ecology must recognize that many humans are also oppressed by it. Not all humans are equally at fault for environmental destruction, and not all humans were included in the "human-centered" dominant worldview. Instead of looking at some abstract dominant worldview, these critics seek to specify the particular practices and institutions that dominate both human and nonhuman alike. Guha calls our attention to the perspective of people, especially poor people, in underdeveloped countries. Ecofeminists suggest that the causes of environmental domination and the oppression of women are connected. We turn now to an examination of ecofeminist environmental philosophies.

9.8 ECOFEMINISM: MAKING CONNECTIONS

Ecofeminism comprises a variety of approaches that also see a connection between social domination and the domination of nature. Since the term was first used by Françoise d'Eaubonne in 1974, ecofeminism has generated a significant amount of interesting writing and research.[23] As described by Karen Warren, the connections between feminism and ecological concerns have been studied in fields from literature to religion and from science to philosophy. Ecofeminism is a recent development among environmental philosophers, and as a result, much work is still concerned with simply exploring the connections between the feminist and ecological movements.

Because feminists offer a wide variety of viewpoints concerning the nature and analysis of women's oppression, they also have diverse views concerning the connections between the domination of women and the domination of nature. What follows is a review of some of these connections and an overview of their philosophical and environmental significance.

We begin with a discussion of the most general features of any system of domination, or what Warren has called the "logic of domination."[24] The logic of domination is a pattern of thinking characterized as follows: two groups (for example, men and women) are distinguished in terms of some characteristics (for example, men are rational and women are emotional); a value hierarchy is attributed to these characteristics (for example, reason is superior to emotion); and the subordination of one group is justified by its lack of this superior characteristic (for example, men ought to be in positions of authority because they are more rational and less emotional than women). This is the most general pattern of thinking that feminists reject. Different feminisms can be distinguished in terms of their analyses of this logic of domination.

One early framework for organizing feminist thinking that has influenced many ecofeminists was developed by philosopher Alison Jaggar.[25] Jaggar distinguishes liberal, Marxist, radical, and socialist forms of feminism. Each offers an account of the oppression of women and an alternative social philosophy. *Liberal feminists,* for example, deny that any relevant difference between men and women exists. Liberals (such as the utilitarians, Kant and Rawls) argue that all humans possess the same nature as free and rational beings and that any unequal treatment of women would deny this moral equality and would therefore be unjust. As a result of this analysis, liberal feminists devote much of their energy to locating discrimination and fighting for equal rights and equal opportunity.

Marxist feminists argue that women are oppressed, because they are relegated to domestic and, therefore, dependent forms of labor. These feminists argue, for example, that the Lockean theory of private property rights makes sense only within a context in which women's labor is ignored. A necessary precondition for a "man" to "mix his labor" with some unowned land is that there exist women who are performing full-time domestic labor, allowing the man the free time necessary to accumulate land. Domestic labor, of course, did not give women property rights of ownership over the home. Only by becoming full participants in independent and productive forms of labor do women become liberated from economic and political exploitation.

Socialist feminists reject the strict class analysis offered by Marxists and claim that a complex web of social relationships underlies the oppression of women. These relationships include both economic factors and the traditional patterns of gender roles and identities.

Radical feminists believe that biological and sexual differences between men and women have been made the basis of women's oppression. This type of feminism is "radical" in the sense that it denies that women's oppression can be reduced to some other, more basic form of oppression. Women have been culturally defined in terms of their biology. This biological difference has been used to justify a wide-ranging gender system that ensures that women remain dominated by men, primarily by being cast exclusively in roles of mother, wife, and sex object. Because of their roles in childbearing, child raising, and human sexuality, women have been characterized as more controlled by their bodies, more passive, and more emotional than men. Given the logic of domination, it is a short step from these gender distinctions to the conclusion that men, by virtue of being more reasonable and active than women, ought to be in positions of authority over women.

Recognizing this pattern of thinking, some radical feminists conclude that women can escape oppression only when traditional gender roles are abolished. Some early radical feminists argued that women should strive for a "unisex," or androgynous, culture, whereas others advocated a separation between women and men. Still other radical feminists turned this logic of domination on its head. Rather than denying biological, sexual, and gender differences between men and women, these feminists seek instead to encourage and celebrate the female. Accepting the view that women do experience, understand, and value differently than men, some radical feminists seek to develop an alternative feminist politics, culture, and ethics.

A significant amount of work on ecological issues has come from this branch of radical feminism. What has been called cultural ecofeminism[26] accepts the view that there do exist authentic and particular "women's ways" of experiencing, understanding, and valuing the world. Cultural ecofeminism holds that women's perspectives historically have been and today remain closely identified with nature and that women, like nature, have been systematically oppressed in the process. But rather than denying the link between women and nature (as liberal ecofeminists, for example, might), cultural ecofeminists aim "to remedy ecological and other problems through the creation of an alternative "women's culture" … based on revaluing, celebrating, and defending what patriarchy has devalued, including the feminine, non-human nature, the body, and the emotions."[27]

The connections between alternative women's cultures and ecological concerns have been explored in a number of ways. We will briefly consider two: an ecological ethics based on care and relationships and a women's spirituality movement.

One contrast between masculine and feminine that has been a part of the oppression of women views men as rational and objective, while viewing women as emotional and overly concerned with the personal. As is consistent with this contrast, the dominant models in ethics construe the moral realm in terms of abstract, rational, and universal principles. The traditional theories of natural law, utilitarianism, and deontology are prime examples of ethics perceived in this way. The domestic roles of women as mothers and wives meant that those values important to women—caring, relationships, love, responsibility, and trust—remained outside of mainstream ethical theorizing.

In recent decades, some feminists have brought many of the values traditionally associated with women's roles, summarized as an "ethics of care," into the forefront of ethical theorizing. Drawing on the work of Carol Gilligan, Nel Noddings, Sara Ruddick, and others, these feminists seek to articulate and defend a perspective that de-emphasizes abstract rules and principles in favor of a contextualized ethics focused on caring and relationships.[28] Traditional ethical concepts such as moral laws, rights, duties, obligations, and justice presuppose a world in which interests conflict, the demands of justice restrict and limit human freedom, and morality battles egoism. An ethics of care begins with a moral universe in which cooperation replaces conflict, relationships replace confrontation, and caring for the other replaces rights and duties. It is a moral universe in which mothering and friendship, rather than abstract principles such as individual autonomy and freedom from interference, serve as moral ideals.

Feminists offer different explanations on why an ethics of care is particularly a women's perspective. In general, feminists such as Noddings and Ruddick understand an ethics of care as more compatible with the life experiences of women, specifically as those experiences follow from both reproductive biology and mothering. Abstract ethical principles and rules seem irrelevant in a life of childbearing and child rearing. The vocabulary of rights and duties, autonomy and justice, and rules and laws is highly artificial and inappropriate in the context of a mother–child relationship.

Some cultural ecofeminists build on these observations concerning an ethics of care. These thinkers acknowledge that women historically have been portrayed as closer to nature than men. But rather than criticizing this portrayal as the basis for much of the violence done to women, as feminist Susan Griffin has, some ecofeminists build on this identification as a basis for a benevolent relationship between humans and nature.[29] From this perspective, the ethics of care covers human–nature relationships as appropriately as it covers mother–child relationships. Women, who are taught to experience this caring more directly and more immediately than men, are the more appropriate voices for nature's interests.

To briefly develop this description of an ethics of care, reflect on some issues of virtue and character discussed earlier in this book. The care perspective moves beyond an ethics conceived of as abstract universal rules that we can apply to specific problems and from which we can deduce what decisions we should make. The moral person is not construed as a free and independent individual who must answer "What should I do?" The care perspective focuses on specific relationships in all their detail, seeking to uncover the full nature of these relationships and affiliations. In such particularity, an ethics of character or an ethics of virtue appropriately replaces abstract and general principles. The good person—for example, the loving mother—is what an ethics of care seeks to describe. Moral actions would be those performed by the good person rather than those that conform to abstract general principles.

How might this be relevant to environmental issues? Again, reflect on some earlier issues. Many philosophers have challenged the claim that we have duties to future generations by asserting that people of the future do not meet certain abstract and general conditions for moral standing. An ethics of care can shift our focus away from such abstract questions and start from the simple reality that many people do in fact care about what happens to people of the future. So, too, an ethics of care does not get encumbered with abstract questions concerning the moral standing of animals that characterizes so much of the animal liberation discussion. Rather more central for ethics are certain other questions: Do we care about animals? Do we have relationships to them? What is the basis for our attachments to animals?[30] The discussion of moral standing and moral considerability is similar. We can and do exist in relationships with our natural surroundings, and any abstract ethical theory that ignores that will be inadequate. A view consistent with an ethics of care is Leopold's injunction that we must first come to "love, respect, and admire the land" before applying the more abstract principles of the land ethic.

The women's spirituality movement is another area in which cultural ecofeminists have explored a bond between women and nature.[31] Within much mainstream Western religion, God is seen as outside of, or transcending, nature. Nature is mere matter: passive, inert, shapeless, and dead. God created, formed, and breathed life into the dust. In much of this tradition, women again are associated with nature, because they are so dependent on their bodies and are so passive. Thus organized religion often sees women as lacking the special spirituality that would qualify them to be priests, rabbis, ministers, popes, and so forth. Thus, within much of this mainstream, we again witness the dual denigration of women and nature.

Many cultural ecofeminists seek a spiritualism or theology that reverses these trends.[32] We should instead observe and honor the identification of women, nature, and the divine. Often looking to ancient religions, in which God was identified both as the earth itself and as a woman, some cultural ecofeminists honor a spirituality that views the Goddess as immanent in nature and the natural world as revealing the divine. Thus the earth itself is worshipped as divine, and caring for or loving the earth is a spiritual as well as an ecological responsibility. Celebrating Mother Nature or the Greek goddess Gaia, for example, becomes the way for women's spirituality to rejoice in the sacredness of women and nature.

9.9 ECOFEMINISM: RECENT DEVELOPMENTS

Despite these developments, many feminists are reluctant to accept the strategy of those who embrace the view that distinctive and separate "women's ways" of understanding, experiencing, and valuing the world do exist. They fear that by accepting the dualism implicit in viewing women as "closer to nature" than men, these feminists only reinforce the way of thinking that underlies hierarchies and the logic of domination. Philosopher Val Plumwood calls this "the feminism of uncritical reversal" and sees it as "perpetuating women's oppression in a new and subtle form."[33] Ynestra King suggests that an "unwitting complicity" in a patriarchal mind-set underlies the culture–nature split that this view assumes.[34]

In place of cultural ecofeminism, with its roots in radical feminism, Plumwood and Warren seek a "third wave" of feminism that "is an integrative and transformative feminism, or that moves us beyond the current debate over the four leading versions of feminism and makes a responsible ecological perspective central to feminist theory and practice."[35]

The view that we are considering can be found in the writings of Warren and Plumwood.[36] To introduce this third wave of feminism, it will be helpful to follow Plumwood's review of the first two waves. Feminism's first wave, typified by liberal feminism, seeks to end discrimination and attain equality for women. The problem with this view is that in a culture in which masculine traits and characteristics dominate, equality for women can amount to little more than requiring women to adopt these dominant male traits. In effect, women can be equal to men only if they become masculine, and to the degree that strong cultural forces work against this, women always fall just a little short of full equality. (This point parallels the critical discussion in Chapter 5 concerning animal liberation. Only those animals fortunate enough to resemble humans are granted moral standing.) The ecological implications of this first wave can be devastating. Women can liberate themselves from an oppressive identification with nature only if they, like men, become oppressors of nature.

The second wave of feminism is represented by the "uncritical reversal" of some feminists. This perspective promotes and celebrates a distinctive female point of view. However, as suggested earlier, this perspective risks being co-opted by the dominant male culture through accepting the dualisms that male culture has used, via the logic of domination, to justify women's oppression.

The third wave seeks an alternative to both liberal and radical versions of feminism. This alternative sees the domination of nature and the domination of women as inextricably connected. They are connected in more ways than simply being two types of a more general pattern of domination. Women have been identified as closer to nature, and nature has been identified as feminine. These identifications have mutually reinforced the oppression of each. Thus environmental philosophy and feminism need to develop in unison, each recognizing the parallel character of their interests.

Plumwood and Warren suggest that at the most general level, both feminism and the ecological movement need to address a cluster of dualisms and dualistic ways of thinking that underlie the logic of domination. This is not to suggest, of course, that distinctions are not to be made nor differences recognized. But we should challenge those distinctions that are designed to reinforce superior–inferior, oppressor–oppressed frameworks. This type of ecofeminism challenges feminists and environmentalists alike to uncover the patterns of domination common to the oppression of women and of nature and to begin exploring alternative and nondualistic ways of thinking about both human and nonhuman nature. This type of ecofeminism is also quite similar to Bookchin's more general analysis of hierarchies and domination.

Some of these dualistic ways of thinking that are especially relevant to ecofeminism involve the split between masculine and feminine, human and nature, reason and emotion, mind and body, and objectivity and subjectivity. Each dualism typically is used within our culture in contexts that support domination: masculine over feminine, human over nature, reason over emotion, mind over body, and objectivity over subjectivity. The goal, therefore, is to weed out dualisms and develop alternative patterns of thinking.

One of the most interesting directions in which this type of analysis has proceeded concerns science, technology, and a scientific understanding of nature. As we have noted, a number of feminist scholars have chronicled the many ways in which culture has identified women with nature. But much interesting research has also been conducted on how that identification has influenced Western science.[37] Science has typically been identified with the dominant part of these dualisms—masculine, human, rational, mental, and objective. Feminist scientist Evelyn Fox Keller has detailed the ways in which a particular manner of understanding nature, women, and even marriage has also helped shape the early development of Western science.[38]

Fox quotes the early scientist Francis Bacon to show how many of the models and metaphors of early science betrayed an aggressive attitude toward both women and nature. According to Bacon, science seeks to "establish a chaste and lawful marriage between Mind and Nature…. I am come in very truth leading to you Nature with all her children to bind her to your service and make her your slave." Science and technology do not "merely exert a gentle guidance over nature's course; they have the power to conquer and subdue her, to shake her to her foundations."[39] Bacon's images are clear. Nature is a woman, and she is to become married to man, who will subdue her and turn her into a slave. Bacon associates nature not only with women and marriage but also with a particularly dominating and abusive type of marriage.

Sensitivity to these kinds of images should alert us to similar attitudes within modern science. Typically, scientific theories are judged by their ability to explain and predict natural phenomena. But all too often the ability to predict natural phenomena is simply the first step in developing a technology to control natural phenomena, to "conquer and subdue her" and "make her your slave." This is a science and technology that sees value only in instrumental terms. How can we humans use nature for our own interests? Seldom does this science and technology consider noninstrumental values in nature; rather, it typically rejects these values as a matter of "emotion" or "feelings" and, therefore, "subjective" and scientifically irrelevant.

Recent feminist scholarship alerts us to many of these subtle but oppressive patterns of thinking and acting. This scholarship also offers suggestions for alternatives. Keller has written a biography of the geneticist Barbara McClintock. In *A Feeling for the Organism: The Life and Work of Barbara McClintock*, Keller describes an approach to science that exhibits this "feeling for the organism," an approach that is often called and then dismissed as "a woman's way of thinking." Keller does not suggest that mainstream science be abandoned in favor of this more particularized approach to knowing, but she insists that science done from the control-and-dominate perspective alone will miss much that is important. One need only review many of the discussions presented in this book to find situations in which little feeling is exhibited toward nature by a science bent on domination and control. Look particularly at the science and technology involved in creating pesticides, harnessing nuclear energy, developing wilderness areas, experimenting on animals, conducting agribusiness, and eliminating varmints and predators. For alternatives, consider the science that would support sustainable agriculture.

A second direction for further environmental thinking encouraged by this type of ecofeminism develops from a much more modest conception of human action, ethics, and understanding. This third wave of ecofeminism encourages thinking that is "contextualist," "pluralistic," "inclusive," and "holistic."[40] It is contextualist in that it seeks to avoid abstract and universal ethical pronouncements. This process of abstraction can prevent us from recognizing the rich diversity within both human and nonhuman nature. Too often, this process of abstracting to the universal has simply taken characteristics of the dominant group and turned them into ethical and philosophical ideals. We have already seen how this can reinforce oppression of women, animals, and the rest of the natural world.

This third wave of ecofeminism is pluralistic and inclusive in that it respects diversity and difference. Perhaps the key aspect of a dominating ideology is the belief that there is only one right way of being, thinking, and acting. A philosophy that self-consciously avoids hierarchies and domination will celebrate diversity and resist attempts to establish one "correct" environmental theory.

Finally, this ecofeminism is holistic in that it encourages us to understand human beings as essentially a part of their human and natural communities. (Note that this common way of speaking already assumes a dualism, as though human communities were somehow not "natural.") This ecofeminism rejects the view that humans are abstract individuals, fully constituted by their private consciousness, thoughts, and choices. Humans are created by and remain an inextricable part of their social and natural environments.

9.10 SUMMARY AND CONCLUSIONS

The opening chapters of this book described philosophical ethics as involving a process of stepping back and abstracting oneself from the customary beliefs, attitudes and values of one's culture. Viewed from within the culture, this process of abstraction can appear quite radical and strange. After all, thinking outside of customary beliefs and acting outside of accepted values is, by definition, abnormal. Both deep ecology and ecofeminism challenge customary ways of thinking and acting in order to advocate for radical social change to address present environmental challenges.

Any radical social movement faces similar challenges. The radical changes that supported believe is necessary requires that society think and act in very different ways than what is customary. Yet, the beliefs and values cannot be so different that few will even understand the proposed alternative. The earliest writings of deep ecology and ecofeminism occurred in the 1980s and a plausible case can be made that their call for radical social change has not fallen on fertile ground. These movements seem not to have had lasting influence among environmentalists. Perhaps the times have been such that the "dominant worldview" described by deep ecologists was not ready for their message. Perhaps the "basic economic and ideological structures" that they sought to change were too entrenched. Or, perhaps the messages themselves lacked depth and enduring insight. Whatever the explanation, environmentalism in the past decade has seemed to take on a more pragmatic shift. Environmentalism of the twenty-first century seems to have focused more on balancing environmental goods with the demands of economics and social justice. We turn to these themes in the remaining two chapters.

NOTES

1. Arne Naess, "A Defense of the Deep Ecology Movement," *Environmental Ethics* 6 (Fall 1984): 264.

2. Rosemary Radford Reuther, *New Woman/New Earth* (New York: Seabury, 1975), p. 204.

3. See, for example, the distinction between "deep" and "shallow" offered by Donald VanDeVeer and Christine Pierce in *People, Penguins, and Plastic Trees* (Belmont, Calif.: Wadsworth, 1986), pp. 69–70. Here "shallow ecology" is taken as the view that "nature has no value apart from the needs, interests, and good of human beings," and "Deep Ecology holds that nature has value in its own right independent of the interests of humans."

4. See Arne Naess, *Ecology, Community, and Lifestyle*, trans. and rev. David Rothenberg (Cambridge, England: Cambridge University Press, 1989), and Bill Devall and George Sessions, *Deep Ecology: Living As If Nature Mattered* (Salt Lake City, Utah: Peregrine Smith Books, 1985).

5. For these citations and others, see *Deep Ecology for the Twenty-First Century*, ed. George Sessions (Boston: Shambala Publications, 1995), p. ix.

6. Arne Naess, "The Shallow and the Deep, Long-Range Ecology Movement," *Inquiry* 16 (1973): 95–100.

7. This description relies heavily on David Rothenberg's introduction to Naess's *Ecology, Community, and Lifestyle.*

8. This platform is presented in Devall and Sessions, *Deep Ecology: Living As If Nature Mattered*, Ch. 5, as the "basic principles" of Deep Ecology. These principles are also presented as a "platform" in Naess, *Ecology, Community, and Lifestyle*, Ch. 1.

9. Naess, *Ecology, Community, and Lifestyle*, pp. 26–27.

10. Ibid., 130–33.

11. For one sustained account of the "dominant modern worldview," see Devall and Sessions, *Deep Ecology: Living As If Nature Mattered*, Ch. 3.

12. Warwick Fox, "Deep Ecology: A New Philosophy for Our Time?" *Ecologist* 14 (November-December 1984): 194–200, as quoted in Devall

and Sessions, *Deep Ecology: Living As If Nature Mattered*, p. 66.

13. Harold Morowitz, "Biology as a Cosmological Science," *Main Currents in Modern Thought* 28 (1972): 156. This material is quoted and discussed in J. Baird Callicott, "Metaphysical Implications of Ecology," *Environmental Ethics* 9 (Winter 1986): 300–15. Callicott's essay suggests that a "consolidated metaphysical consensus" might be emerging from ecological science that would supplant the mechanical model that emerged from seventeenth-century physics.

14. Naess, *Ecology, Community, and Lifestyle*, p. 66; the emphasis is in the original.

15. Ibid., 70–71.

16. Devall and Sessions, *Deep Ecology: Living As If Nature Mattered*, pp. 66–67.

17. Ibid., 67.

18. For example, George Sessions dismisses a range of critics in less than one page in his preface to *Deep Ecology for the Twenty-First Century*, pp. xii–xiii. Criticism of Deep Ecology is "based on misinterpretation and misunderstanding." It seems to me that this is a theme in many deep ecologists' responses to critics.

19. The Edward Abbey quote is "I'm a humanist; I'd rather kill a man than a snake." And is taken from *Desert Solitaire: A Season in the Wilderness*. (New York, McGraw-Hill, first ed.) 1968.

20. The Foreman quote is taken from *Confessions of an Eco-Warrior* (New York Crown Publishers), 1991. "An individual human life has no more intrinsic value than does an individual Grizzly Bear life. Human suffering resulting from drought and famine in Ethiopia is tragic, yes, but the destruction there of other creatures and habitat is even more tragic."

21. Warwick Fox, "The Deep Ecology—Ecofeminism Debate," in Sessions, ed., *Deep Ecology for the Twenty-First Century*, p. 279. This is a version of an essay of the same title previously published in *Environmental Ethics* 11 (Spring 1989): 5–26.

22. Ramachandra Guha, "Radical American Environmentalism and Wilderness Preservation: A Third World Critique," *Environmental Ethics* 11 (Spring 1989): 71–84.

23. Françoise d'Eaubonne, *Le féminisme ou la mort (Feminism or Death)* (Paris: Pierre Horay, 1974). Among the most recent philosophically helpful sources are *Hypatia* 6 (Spring 1991), the special issue on ecological feminism, and the *American Philosophical Association Newsletter on Feminism and Philosophy* 90 (Fall 1991) and 91 (Spring 1992). In addition to articles and interviews, the APA's newsletters contain helpful course syllabi and bibliographies.

24. See Karen J. Warren, "Feminism and Ecology: Making Connections," *Environmental Ethics* 9 (Spring 1987): 3–20, and "The Power and Promise of Ecological Feminism," *Environmental Ethics* 12 (Summer 1990): 125–46. In the earlier article, Warren takes the logic of domination as characteristic of patriarchal frameworks, whereas in the more recent paper, she has revised her views to include all "oppressive" frameworks. In this respect, the second article seems to parallel more closely Bookchin's general discussion of hierarchies. These discussions are developed in *Ecofeminist Philosophy*, especially in Chapter 3.

25. This classic discussion of liberal, Marxist, radical, and socialist feminisms can be found in Jaggar, *Feminist Politics and Human Nature*. For a discussion of these models as they are related to ecological issues, see

Warren, "Feminism and Ecology"; Carolyn Merchant, "Ecofeminism and Feminist Theory," in *Reweaving the World*, eds. Irene Diamond and Gloria Feman Orenstein (San Francisco: Sierra Club Books, 1990), pp. 100–105; and Val Plumwood, "Feminism and Ecofeminism," *Ecologist* 22 (January-February 1992): 8–13.

26. This follows the usage of Val Plumwood, "Current Trends in Ecofeminism," in *The Ecologist* 22, no. 1 (January-February 1992): 10.

27. Ibid.

28. Carol Gilligan, *In a Different Voice: Psychological Theory and Women's Development* (Cambridge, Mass.: Harvard University Press, 1982); Nel Noddings, *Caring: A Feminine Approach to Ethics and Moral Education* (Berkeley: University of California Press, 1984); Sara Ruddick, *Maternal Thinking* (New York: Ballantine, 1989).

29. Two of the earliest and best sources that explore the connections between women and nature and the oppression and violence against women are Susan Griffin, *Women and Nature: The Roaring Inside Her* (New York: Harper & Row, 1978), and Carolyn Merchant, *The Death of Nature: Women, Ecology, and the Scientific Revolution* (New York: Harper & Row, 1980).

30. A helpful bibliography, "Women and Animals," is part of the thorough bibliography, "Feminism and the Environment," eds. Adams and Warren, that appears in the *American Philosophical Association Newsletter on Feminism and Philosophy*.

31. Diamond and Orenstein, eds., *Reweaving the World*, contains several articles on women's spirituality and includes another helpful bibliography. See also Carol Christ, *Laughter of Aphrodite: Reflections on a Journey to the Goddess* (San Francisco: Harper & Row, 1987); Reuther, *New Woman/ New Earth;* and Starhawk, *The Spiral Dance: A Rebirth of the Ancient Religion of the Great Goddess* (San Francisco: Harper & Row, 1986).

32. Two classic sources for exploring the more general issue of women's spiritualism are Reuther, *New Woman/ New Earth*, and Mary Daly, *GYN/ Ecology: The Metaethics of Radical Feminism* (Boston: Beacon, 1978). Neither Reuther nor Daly subscribes to the particular overview of spiritualism described here, however.

33. Plumwood, "Feminism and Ecofeminism," p. 12.

34. Ynestra King, "Feminism and the Revolt against Nature," *Heresies* #13: *Feminism and Ecology* 4 (1981): 15.

35. Warren, "Feminism and Ecology: Making Connections," pp. 17–18. The phrase *third wave of feminism* is from Plumwood, "Feminism and Ecofeminism," pp. 12–13.

36. For Warren's views, see the citations in notes 2 and 9, as well as *Ecological Feminism* (New York: Routledge, 1994). Plumwood's more recent thinking appears in her *Feminism and the Mastery of Nature* (London: Routledge, 1993).

37. See especially Merchant, *The Death of Nature: Women, Ecology, and the Scientific Revolution*, and Evelyn Fox Keller, *Reflections on Gender and Science* (New Haven, Conn.: Yale University Press, 1985).

38. See especially Keller's "Spirit and Reason at the Birth of Modern Science," Ch. 3 in *Reflections on Gender and Science*.

39. Ibid., 36.

40. Adopted from Warren, "The Power and Promise of Ecological Feminism," pp. 141–45.

DISCUSSION QUESTIONS

1. Classical economists such as those discussed in Chapter 3 claim that humans are always motivated by self-interest. In light of the discussion of the "self" and "Self" in this chapter, do you agree with that view of human motivation? Would the deep ecology view of "Self-realization" require that human nature be rewired as Baden and Stroup claim in Chapter 3?

2. Is there enough uniformity and consistency in human cultures for talk of a "human-centered" worldview to make sense? Which specific beliefs and values are particularly anthropocentric?

3. What is an individual? What is an individual living thing? Does the meaning of the word *individual* change in different contexts? What implications for ethics follow from your answer?

4. Is the statement "This is a tall tree" any more objective than the statement "This is a majestic tree"? Explain how both might be defended as true.

5. Review the common dualisms (for example, mind–body, reason–emotion, and objectivity–subjectivity) mentioned in this chapter. Discuss and evaluate the value hierarchies that are implicit in them.

6. In Chapter 1, we quoted scientist Amory Lovins as saying that the answers you get depend upon the questions you ask. What "different questions" might someone taking a feminist approach to science and technology ask about such issues as nuclear energy, population policy, pesticide use, and animal agriculture?

GLOBAL ENVIRONMENTAL ETHICS WATCH

For more information on Deep Ecology and Ecofeminism, please see the Global Environmental Ethics Watch. Updated several times a day, Global Environmental Ethics Watch is a focused portal into GREENR—our Global Reference on the Environment, Energy, and Natural Resources—an ideal one-stop site for current events and research. You will have access to the latest information from trusted academic journals, news outlets, and magazines as well as access to statistics, primary sources, case studies, videos, podcasts, and much more.

To gain access please use the access code that accompanies your book. If you do not have an access code, visit cengagebrain.com to purchase one.

10

Environmental Justice
and Social Ecology

DISCUSSION: Environmental Refugees

The United Nations High Commission on Refugees (UNCHR) was founded in 1949 with the mission "to provide, on a non-political and humanitarian basis, international protection to refugees and to seek permanent solutions for them." Originally founded to help the millions of European refugees following World War II, UNCHR expanded in the following decades to support millions of additional refugees in post-colonial Africa, in the Middle East, and in such places as Bangladesh, China, Viet Nam, Rwanda, and Somalia.

UNCHR defines refugees as "a person who owing to a well-founded fear of being persecuted for reasons of race, religion, nationality, and membership of a particular social group or political opinion, is outside the country of his nationality and is unable or, owing to such fear, is unwilling to avail himself of the protection of that country." Under the UN convention, refugees have internationally recognized rights to asylum, and to basic goods such as food, shelter, protection, and medical care.

The United Nations has been careful to distinguish refugees from people fleeing poverty, or what are sometimes called economic migrants. The humanitarian rationale that justifies the rights of refugees does not extend to people who flee their home country to escape poverty. As such, economic migrants do not have internationally recognized rights to asylum.

Beginning in the 1970s, claims were made for a new type of refugee—what are variously called "environmental refugees," "environmental migrants," and more recently, "climate change migrants." An environmental refugee would be someone displaced from his home as a result of changes in local environment such as water shortages, sea level rises, desertification, drought, pollution, or natural disasters such as floods, hurricanes, earthquakes, or tsunamis.

The threat of global climate change has led many observers to predict that in coming years tens of millions of people will become environmental refugees. In areas such as sub-Saharan Africa, millions of people already face water and food shortages that will only be intensified by higher temperatures and droughts. A long-standing drought and famine in Somalia has resulted in hundreds of thousands of people fleeing their homes to neighboring countries, including Kenya, where 400,000 people live in the world's largest refugee camp. In Bangladesh where more than 150 million people live in low-lying areas just above sea level, or the Marshall Islands where the entire population live on low-lying atolls, even a slight rise in sea levels could make these lands uninhabitable for millions of people.

Refugees are those people who have no other choice than to leave their homes to increase their chances of survival. In virtually every case, the burden of environmental problems falls overwhelmingly on the poorest countries, and the poorest citizens within those countries. Wealthy countries have more opportunities to adapt to change, and wealthy individuals will always find countries willing to welcome them.

But neither the United Nations, the United States, nor the European Union recognize environmental degradation as creating a legitimate class of refugees. From this perspective, people fleeing environmental harms are more akin to economic migrants fleeing poverty than they are to political refugees fleeing persecution. As such, environmental refugees or migrants are not extended the same legal status for asylum and humanitarian aid as are political refugees.

The 400,000 refugees, at least half of whom are children, living in the Dadaab refugee camp in Kenya are a case in point. The refugees have come to Dadaab from neighboring Somalia, as a result of more than twenty years of civil war exasperated by a long-term drought and famine. In July 2011, it was estimated that as many as 1,000 new refugees arrive each day, mostly women and children who have traveled hundreds of miles. But are they political refugees, escaping the war-torn Somalia that has not had a central government in decades, or are they environmental refugees escaping drought and famine? Would there be less of a case for humanitarian aid if Somalia had a functioning central government and no civil war?

DISCUSSION TOPICS:

1. How would you distinguish economic migrants from political refugees? Is there a moral difference between them that would justify asylum rights for one but not for the other? In what ways are people fleeing environmental threats similar to economic migrants and political refugees?

2. Economic or environmental migrants would claim that their right to life justifies immigrating to other countries. Likewise, countries that close their borders to such immigrants also do so in defense of their own lifestyles and property. Is there a rational way to resolve conflicting rights in such cases, or is it simply a matter of who has the power to enforce their views on others?

3. Do wealthy countries have a special responsibility to help the victims of environmental disasters? Is it more a matter of duty or charity?

4. A common saying is that "poverty anywhere endangers prosperity everywhere." In what ways, if any, is the prosperity of the United States and Western Europe endangered by poverty in such places as sub-Saharan Africa and south Asia?

10.1 INTRODUCTION

Earlier chapters described ethics as addressing this fundamental question: How should we live? But we noted that this question is ambiguous in that "we" can refer either to each of us individually or to all of us collectively. In the first case, ethics is sometimes referred to as *personal morality,* whereas in the second case, ethics refers to *social justice.* This chapter will examine theories of social justice and their implications for environmental ethics.

Living together in a community creates benefits and burdens that exist only within community, and we cannot account for community benefits and burdens solely in terms of personal morality, or individual rights and responsibilities. Further, social institutions and practices influence individuals, so the desires and beliefs of individuals are sometimes dependent on the society in which they live. Addressing social issues solely in terms of personal morality will miss this important fact. Social justice must address these questions: How should the benefits and burdens of society be distributed? How should social institutions treat people? What do people deserve from society? How are individuals shaped and conditioned by various social structures and institutions? What is the ethically proper structure of society?

Justice is the fundamental governing norm of society, providing the rules and principles by which we live together in community. In his influential book, *A Theory of Justice,* philosopher John Rawls explained that "Justice is the first virtue of social institutions, as truth is of systems of thought." In more general terms, we can say that justice is concerned with giving every person what they deserve, or as is commonly said, to each his due. But theories of justice differ in determining exactly what people deserve.

One way to approach the question of what people deserve is to create a list of goods that each person should receive. This was the basis for common theories of justice in the Western philosophical tradition during the classical and medieval periods. What people deserve was interpreted in terms of those goods that humans need to survive and flourish. Thus, with this view, justice is concerned with getting what is required to live a good, meaningful human life.

But widespread doubt and disagreement about what are needs and what the good, meaningful human life is, led modern theories of justice to move away from basing justice on a theory of the good life. In practice, few societies are uniform enough to have a single and widely accepted understanding of what a good and meaningful human life is. Instead, modern theories of justice have emphasized respecting the rights of individuals to pursue their own conception of what is good. Contemporary theories of justice therefore tend to focus less on *what* people are due, and more on *how they ought to be treated.*

In general terms, justice demands that people ought to be treated with respect. In particular, contemporary theories of justice explain this concept of respect in terms of two fundamental human values: liberty and equality. To respect individual human beings is to leave them to make their own decisions as far as possible (liberty), and to recognize that each individual deserves respect equally.

10.2 PROPERTY RIGHTS AND LIBERTARIAN JUSTICE

One influential approach to social justice that has significant impact on environmental issues begins with the individual right to liberty. Libertarian justice holds that respect for individual liberty, the right to be left alone, is the most fundamental way that society can respect individuals. Libertarians respect equality by recognizing that each individual enjoys an equal right of liberty. Thus, liberty is best understood not as the right to do whatever one wants—that would surely jeopardize the freedom of others—but as freedom from interference by others. Put another way, libertarians understand liberty as the right to choose what one wants as long as it does not interfere with the equal rights of others, or the right to maximum freedom compatible with equal freedom for all.

Libertarian justice has long held that individual property rights and free markets are crucial elements of individual liberty. Free market exchanges represent the essence of personal liberty. Private property is both necessary for personal liberty, and a manifestation of what it means to be free from interference by others.

Many argue that numerous environmental concerns, from wilderness preservation to pollution controls to carbon emission regulations, and from wetlands protection to the Endangered Species Act, run afoul of the liberty and property rights of individuals. According to these critics, these rights lie at the heart of social justice, and if environmental initiatives violate that right, they are unjust. It is fair to say that advocates for strong property rights and individual liberty are among the strongest critics of environmental legislation. The recent Tea Party movement in the United States has a strong philosophical grounding in libertarian justice and private property rights.

The political arrangements of a constitutional democracy are a useful framework for examining the connections between ethical theory, individual rights such as property, and social justice. A commitment to majority rule can be seen as serving the utilitarian goal of maximizing happiness. If we seek to attain the greatest happiness for the greatest number, we do not go far wrong by taking a vote and following the will of the majority. On the other hand, constitutional protections of civil rights and civil liberties can be seen as serving the Kantian goal of respecting individual autonomy. Thus constitutional rights serve as a check on and limit to the majoritarian decisions of legislature. Following a long tradition of deontological ethics, individual rights trump the will of the majority.

The challenge, of course, is to explain which rights are important enough to trump majoritarian decisions. Too broad a conception of rights would allow a single individual to exercise veto power over every social decision. Too narrow a view would allow the majority to tyrannize individuals. According to some, the individual right of property is significant enough to trump overall social and environmental welfare.

Few individual rights have played a more important role in Western political and philosophical traditions than the right of private property. Unquestionably, no right is more crucial in a wider variety of environmental issues. Property and the related concepts of ownership and land are fundamental to many debates that we examine in this textbook.

Contemporary Western understanding of property rights is often traced to the seventeenth-century English philosopher John Locke.[1] Locke's political philosophy begins by speculating about a "state of nature," the situation in which humans would exist if there were no government. In this original natural state, all land is unowned (or, more in line with seventeenth-century thinking, is owned by God). This unowned land becomes owned, becomes *private* property, when an individual "mixes his labor" with the unowned land. In essence, Locke's argument is as follows:

1. People have exclusive rights over—that is, they "own"—their bodies and their labor.

2. Land, in its natural state, is unowned; no one individual can rightfully claim exclusive control of it.

3. Therefore, when someone's labor, which is owned, comes to be "mixed" with land that is unowned, that person's exclusive rights over his or her labor are transferred to the land. The person comes to own the land.

For example, when people travel into the wilderness, clear some land, build homes, till the soil, and grow crops on this land, they come to have a legitimate claim to it. This legitimate claim is the establishment of private property rights.

Once rights to private property are established, libertarian justice looks for market exchanges as the only just means for the exchange of property. Any interference with the free and uncoerced exchange of property, such as the government regulation of the market, or any coerced taking of property, such as government taxation or the confiscation of private property for public use, constitutes a violation of justice.

Two general criticisms of this strong conception of private property have emerged. First, many argue that the specific Lockean conception of private property has fatal logical and philosophical flaws. Second, many argue that no conception of property rights is so strong that it ethically overrides all other environmental values.

A number of powerful objections have been raised against this Lockean view of private property. Some objections stem from the vagueness of the "mixing" metaphor. If I do mix something owned with something unowned, why assume that I come to own what was previously unowned? Why not assume that I lose ownership of what was previously owned—in other words, that I lose my labor in the mixing? Why not assume that I gain ownership over only the improvements that I make, so that I can own the crops that I grow but not the land itself? Suppose that my labor worsens rather than improves the land? What if the goal of the first people on the land is to preserve it, and they therefore make a conscious decision not to mix their labor with it? Must all land be developed to be valued and owned?

Other problems arise when we realize that Locke's seventeenth-century European image of some vast unowned wilderness does an injustice to historical fact. The image of early American settlers, mixing their labor with the western frontier and laying claim to it, ignores the native peoples who had been using that land for millennia. In effect, the Lockean view of property presupposes an agricultural or industrial conception of property. Nomadic cultures, for example, might travel over broad expanses of land as they follow changing seasons or migrating herds. The idea of laying a private and exclusive claim on the land would be quite outlandish in such a culture.

Finally, according to Locke's ethical principles, private ownership can be justified only when "enough and as good" land remains for others. Lockean property rights are derived from a more fundamental right of personal liberty ("the exclusive rights over one's own body"). Thus I can justify *my* ownership only when it does not violate the liberty of other people. This violation will not happen, according to Locke, so long as sufficient land is left in common for others. But in the modern world, with a population of almost 7 billion people, it is difficult to see how this condition can be met.

Whether or not we adopt Locke's specific justification of private property, other critics point out that private property rights cannot override all other ethical considerations. Within the Western philosophical tradition, private property has been defended on three broad grounds: utility, liberty, and fairness. Most observers believe that none of these justifications is sufficient to show that private property always overrides environmental protection.

The utilitarian defense of property argues that allowing individuals to acquire private ownership of property will produce greater social benefits— through incentives, productivity, and the like. However, because this defense of private property is made in terms of beneficial consequences, we would always have to calculate *all* the consequences of any limitation on property rights. There seems no reason to assume that in each and every case, strong private property rights would produce more beneficial social consequences than environmental regulation. A second defense of property is made in terms of its value in protecting individual liberty and autonomy. Private ownership of property allows individuals to be free from dependence on others or on the state for the material conditions necessary to life. However, because some environmental regulations also are aimed at protecting the freedom of individuals (such as freedom from pollution), we cannot assume that private property rather than environmental protection is always the preferred means for protecting liberty. Finally, defenders of private property often invoke principles of fairness. Much as Locke argued, denying someone ownership of the goods and value that they have produced through their labor would seem to be unfair to those individuals. However, as we shall see in the following section, many argue that this same value of fairness is often the precise goal of environmental regulation. Thus, according to many, private property cannot provide sufficient justification for the claim that environmental policies violate social justice by denying private property rights.

Difficulties such as these have led more contemporary interpretations to view private property as involving not a single right, but a bundle of associated rights. These include the right to possess, control, use, benefit from, dispose of, and exclude others from the property. The "bundle view" is thought necessary because of the complexity that follows from any attempt to specify the implications of property rights. For example, surely it will not do to say that my right to property means that I can do anything I want with it. The rights of other people restrict my property rights in a number of ways. I cannot turn my backyard into a toxic waste dump, for example. Zoning laws restrict the type of building that I can construct on my property and the uses to which I can put that building. Similarly, owning stock in a corporation entitles me to receive certain benefits from ownership of that stock in the form of dividends and appreciation. However, stock owners may not have the right to manage the corporate property or to exclude others from using it, nor in some cases can they even sell the stock to anyone they choose.

When property rights are viewed as a bundle of rights, they can no longer be seen as an all-or-nothing entitlement. Just as zoning laws restrict but do not violate my property rights, much legislation aimed at protecting the environment will restrict only some rights in the bundle. Keep this in mind while reviewing contemporary environmental debates such as those surrounding the wise-use movement and the Tea Party's critique of environmental policy. The debate is seldom couched in all-or-nothing terms: either the environment is harmed or I lose my property rights. Most debates involve the degree and type of control that property owners are allowed to exercise over the various aspects of their interests.

10.3 JUSTICE AS FAIRNESS

The American philosopher John Rawls developed one of the most powerful and influential contemporary accounts of justice.[2] Rawls account of justice balances personal liberty with a commitment to equality, and he grounds justice in the principle of fairness. Rawls's theory of justice consists of two major components: a method for deciding on the principles of justice, and the specific principles derived from that method.

Rawls's method is a version of the hypothetical social contract used earlier by Locke and Kant. Imagine rational and self-interested individuals having to choose and agree to the fundamental principles for their society. To ensure that the principles are fair and impartial, imagine further that these individuals do not know the specific details of their own lives. They do not know their abilities or disabilities, their talents or weaknesses. They are, in Rawls's terms, behind a "veil of ignorance" and must choose principles that they will abide by when they come out from behind the veil. To ensure that each individual is treated as an end and not as a means, imagine finally that these individuals must unanimously agree on the principles. These initial conditions of impartiality—what Rawls calls the "original position"—guarantee that whatever principles chosen will be fair to all.

The idea of this "original position," of having to make decisions behind a veil of ignorance, is at the heart of Rawls's theory that fairness is the central element of a just decision or just organization. He contends that our decisions *ought* to be made in such a way, and our social institutions *ought* to be organized in such a way, that they would prove acceptable to us *no matter whose point of view we take*. A fair decision is an impartial decision. Rawls would argue that the only way we can reach this conclusion is to seek out the original perspective from behind a veil of ignorance, to imagine ourselves ignorant with regard to our position and strive toward impartiality.

Rawls derives two fundamental principles of justice from this original position. The first principle states that each individual is to have equal rights to the most extensive system of liberties. Individuals in the original position would demand as much freedom as they can get, but rational and self-interested individuals would not be willing to sacrifice their own equality simply to secure more liberty for others. The second principle holds that social and economic benefits and burdens should be distributed equally unless an unequal distribution would benefit the least advantaged members of society, and even then only if those benefits are attached to positions that all persons have an equal opportunity of occupying.

These two specific principles of justice are also valuable tools for thinking about economics and environmental policy. The first principle states that each individual is to have an equal right to the most extensive system of liberties. No one has a right to personal liberty without qualification. This first principle argues that disproportionate burdens should be alleviated, even if this requires the loss of personal freedom to some.

The second principle holds that benefits and burdens of a society should generally be distributed equally. No person in the original position would accept additional burdens so that others can receive more benefits. An unequal distribution could be justified only if it would benefit the least advantaged members of society and only if those benefits derive from positions for which each person has an equal opportunity. Thus Rawls's justice as fairness would imply specific conclusions regarding such issues as environmental refugees and victims of environmental tragedies.

Rawls believes that people would accept these principles because rational people would follow a "maximin" strategy. That is, if you did not already know your position in society, and you had to agree to a distribution of benefits and burdens, you would adopt the conservative strategy of trying to minimize your potential harms rather than trying to maximize your potential benefits. Consider: Is it more rational to take a great risk for the possibility of a great benefit—using all your savings to buy lottery tickets—or a slight risk for a slight gain—keeping your money in an insured savings account?

Some would see a philosophical basis for the precautionary principle in this account of rational decision making. The precautionary principle is often used in environmental policy making. It holds that in the face of uncertainty, if an action has a possibility of causing great harm, it is only rational to demand a strong justification before proceeding. Some would apply this to the threat of global climate change. Even if we don't know for certain that increasing atmospheric carbon dioxide will result in global warming, the harmful consequences of global warming are so serious that we demand greater proof from skeptics than from others.

Given this brief discussion of justice, let us return to the questions of environmental justice: How are the benefits and burdens of society distributed? Who gets the benefits? Who bears the burdens? Are the current distributions of benefits and burdens fair? Further, what kinds of people—what character traits, values, and attitudes—are being reinforced by society?

More specifically, what are the environmental benefits and burdens? Consider some of the topics mentioned in this book: air and water pollution, toxic waste dumps, pesticide poisoning, overpopulation, wilderness loss and development, and global warming. Who carries the burdens of environmental harms, and who benefits from the practices that cause them? Who would benefit from the policies promoted by environmentalists? Who would bear the burdens created by these policies? While it might be tempting to answer these questions in terms of some general humanity, as in "Humans suffer from environmental destruction" or "Humans would benefit from wilderness preservation," such general claims miss important distinctions among people. We need instead to examine more precisely who benefits from, and who pays the price for, environmental problems and environmentalist solutions. In the case of environmental problems, we must also examine who is at fault.

10.4 ENVIRONMENTAL JUSTICE AND ENVIRONMENTAL RACISM

Environmental justice investigates the social distribution of environmental benefits and burdens. A society that distributes these benefits and burdens unequally is prima facie unjust. According to many observers, all too often society places the burdens on people in the least advantaged positions—the poor and people of color, for example. Thus these policies are more accurately described as examples of environmental racism.

Consider the distribution of health and safety risks associated with pollution and toxic wastes. Since the mid-1970s, a number of researchers and activists have called attention to the disproportionate risks faced by communities of color. Sociologist Robert D. Bullard has been at the forefront of this research. Time and again, Bullard finds toxic waste dumps, landfills, incinerators, and polluting industries being located in communities and neighborhoods with a high density of poor and minorities. Bullard cites a 1992 study conducted by the *National Law Journal,* which concludes,

> There is a racial divide in the way that the U.S. government cleans up toxic waste sites and punishes polluters. White communities see faster action, better results, and stiffer penalties than communities where blacks, Hispanics, and other minorities live. This unequal protection often occurs whether the community is wealthy or poor.[3]

From prevention to cleanup to punishment of offenders, this study found that enforcement of environmental laws is systematically lax when it concerns minority communities.

This research confirmed the results of an earlier study conducted by the United Church of Christ Commission on Racial Justice. This 1982 study, *Toxic Wastes and Race in the United States,* concluded that race is the best predictor in identifying those communities and neighborhoods most likely to be the location of toxic waste sites. The evidence is strong. If you are a person of color, you are much more likely to live in an area where toxic dumps, landfills, incinerators, and polluting industries are or will be located. It is also less likely that the pollution will be cleaned up, and polluters probably will face lighter punishments than if they were located in white neighborhoods.[4]

Similar results are found at the international level. Poor countries are more likely to suffer environmental degradation—deforestation, desertification, and air and water pollution—than wealthy countries, and the poorest residents of those countries, the poorest of the poor, are likely to suffer most. Part of the explanation for this is the historical legacy of colonialism. During the past few centuries, many countries that today are underdeveloped were governed as colonies or near colonies, supplying the natural resources to fuel the industrial growth and living standards of Europe and the United States. The colonists exploited the resources of these countries with little or no regard for the environmental costs to the local community.

But the legacy of such injustices live on, often implicit in the economic thinking examined in Chapter 3. If we conduct a cost–benefit analysis, we find that distributing environmental risks to people and places with the "least value" is more efficient. It simply costs less. For example, if we are planning to build a trash incinerator, it makes economic sense to build it in an area with low property values. In this way, costs are minimized.

Philosopher Laura Westra finds a clear example of such reasoning in a World Bank memo written in the 1990s. Westra quotes the World Bank's chief economist, Lawrence Summers, as arguing the following:

> The measurement of the costs of health-impairing pollution depends on the forgone earnings from increased morbidity and mortality. From this point of view a given amount of health-impairing pollution should be done in the country with the lowest cost, which will be the country with the lowest wages. I think the economic logic behind dumping a load of toxic waste in the lowest-wage country is impeccable and we should face up to that.[5]

When we understand that the World Bank effectively controls the administration of international debt and thus exercises tremendous influence over the economies of most underdeveloped nations, we can see some real problems with this attitude. Except, perhaps, within the most crude form of utilitarianism, it would be difficult to find any theory of justice that would accept any of these examples as just or fair. Certainly, most would fail Rawls's restriction that inequalities can be justified only if they benefit the least advantaged members of society. Because the people burdened by these decisions seldom even have a voice in making them, these examples may well violate Rawls's first principle as well.

We do not need to look far to find other policies that would reinforce environmental injustice and environmental racism. Many prescriptions for controlling population growth strike a number of people as disproportionately burdening the poor and minority communities. Those who target population growth as a major cause of environmental destruction often ignore cultural and economic factors that encourage the poor, especially poor women, to value more rather than fewer children. Given the history of oppressive population control policies targeted against minorities—a history that includes slavery, Nazism, and apartheid—minority people have reason to be skeptical of population policies advanced by wealthy white environmentalists.

In a classic article on world hunger and population growth, ecologist Garrett Hardin argued that overpopulation is a serious threat to the survival of all humans.[6] Using the metaphor of a lifeboat, Hardin claims that overpopulation is threatening to sink all of us as population surpasses the carrying capacity of the earth. Hardin discourages providing food relief to victims of famine and other starving people. Such help will only lead to a greater population explosion among the poor and place a greater burden on the earth's productive capacity.

Critics point out that such policies harm the most disadvantaged human beings, the people least able to protect themselves. Such a policy would also protect the interests of the most advantaged peoples (those already aboard the lifeboat). A policy such as Hardin's implies that people in developed countries, especially those in positions of power and privilege, can maintain their comfortable standard of living while the least advantaged human beings are allowed to starve. It is not just that we are in the lifeboat and they are not. There is less room in the lifeboat because we have brought with us all the creature comforts of our consumerist society. Again, it would be difficult to find a theory of justice willing to claim that such policies give people what they deserve.

Many preservationist policies also appear to benefit social elites while harming the most vulnerable. We have already seen a version of this in Guha's critique of deep ecology in Chapter 9. This issue was a major theme at the 1992 Earth Summit in Rio de Janeiro. Many environmentalists from the industrialized countries of Europe and North America promoted policies at the summit that would limit development and population growth while preserving wilderness areas, rain forests, and biological diversity. Of course, these policies were most often aimed at less developed countries. To many people from countries in the less industrialized Southern hemisphere, such policies seemed to serve the interests of the industrialized North at the expense of the less advantaged in the South. It sounded as though northern environmentalists were saying, "Our culture wreaked environmental havoc so that we might attain a comfortable and healthy lifestyle. Now that we have that, you should not seek a comparable standard of living, because that would jeopardize the remaining wilderness areas, rain forests, and biological diversity. We did not value these things more than our own economic development, but you should."

Finally, some observers point out that in most of these examples of environmental injustice, the least advantaged people, often women and children, actually bear the brunt of the harms. The potential harms caused by exposure to pollutants, pesticides, and toxins fall disproportionately on women.[7] Consider, as an example, how the tragic drought and famine in Somalia described in the opening Discussion Case has impacted women and children disproportionately.

Throughout much of the developing world, women have a threefold responsibility. They are primarily responsible for domestic chores such as cooking and maintaining the home, they have primary responsibility for the care of children, and they work outside the home, typically being responsible for tending domestic crops and livestock. Worldwide, women have less mobility than men to escape pollution and unsanitary conditions. Women have greater responsibility for the nonmechanized harvesting of crops and thus face risks associated with exposure to pesticides. Women have primary responsibility for gathering fuel wood and water. Thus they suffer acutely from loss of access to forestlands and from water pollution. One estimate suggests that 34.6 percent of all childhood deaths in underdeveloped countries result from the lack of access to clean water.[8] Environmental destruction and development in many underdeveloped countries inflict particular burdens on women. Of course, population policies also typically burden women in ways not experienced by men. Women and children suffer more from the harms of overpopulation, and women are typically thought to be responsible for controlling population growth.[9]

10.5 MURRAY BOOKCHIN'S SOCIAL ECOLOGY

Murray Bookchin is a social theorist, who has been writing about the connections between social domination and the domination of nature for more than four decades. His views have been characterized in a number of ways, including "libertarian social ecology," "ecoanarchism," and, most commonly, "social ecology." In what follows, we will use the phrase *social ecology* to refer specifically to the social philosophy developed in Bookchin's writings.

Social ecology has its roots in a variety of philosophical traditions, including Marxian socialism, libertarian anarchism, and the "Western organismic tradition" associated with philosophers such as Aristotle and Hegel. Although a full description of these diverse traditions is well beyond the scope of this textbook, we need to consider them in order to understand social ecology.

First, we must examine what Bookchin means by social domination and how this is connected to ecological problems. Specifically, Bookchin is concerned with *hierarchies,* which he explains as

> the cultural, traditional, and psychological systems of obedience and command, not merely the economic and political systems to which the terms class and State most appropriately refer. Accordingly, hierarchy and domination could easily continue to exist in a "classless" or "Stateless" society. I refer to the domination of the young by the old, of women by men, of one ethnic group by another, of "masses" by bureaucrats who profess to speak of "higher social interests," of countryside by town, and in a more subtle psychological sense, of body by mind, of spirit by a shallow instrumental rationality.[10]

This view is reminiscent of the "logic of domination" that was described in the previous chapter's discussion of ecofeminism. Hierarchies imply the existence of at least two groups, one of which holds power over the other. This power enables the "superior" group to command obedience from the "inferior" group. Hierarchies promote social systems of domination in which the superior group is able to manipulate the inferior group to serve the purposes of the superiors, while preventing the inferiors from pursuing their own true ends.

In this quotation, Bookchin distinguishes his views from those of traditional Marxists and traditional anarchists. Unlike the Marxists, Bookchin does not believe that the primary form of social hierarchy and domination rests with economic classes. In addition, unlike the anarchists, Bookchin does not believe that the modern nation–state is the primary agent of social domination. In his view, we are likely to find structures of domination within societies that lack economic classes and the bureaucratic nation–state.

This quotation also suggests that physical domination and power are not the only means of social control. Hierarchy "is also a state of consciousness" as well as a social condition. People can be oppressed by their consciousness, their understandings and beliefs, as much as by external forces. Thus Bookchin speaks of people who "internalize" social structures of hierarchy and learn to accept a life of "toil, guilt, and sacrifice" while their "superiors" enjoy a life of pleasure and satisfaction.[11] As this quote from Bookchin suggests, human freedom involves more than just the absence of external controls. In his classic book *The Ecology of Freedom,* Bookchin offers a history of the diverse forms of hierarchy and domination that have existed in societies from the Paleolithic era to the modern world.

But the most pertinent aspect of Bookchin's views concerns his assertion that the domination of nature "stems from" these patterns of social hierarchy and domination. How exactly should we understand this claim?

An initial point to note is that Bookchin essentially has reversed a standard Marxist interpretation. In the view of many Marxists, the human ability to dominate nature in the appropriation of private property allowed the creation of wealth and class structures that in turn led to class conflict and oppression. Bookchin suggests that social structures of domination preceded the domination of nature.

Bookchin also distinguishes his views from a Marxist view by denying any necessity or determinism to the connection between social domination and the domination of nature. He allows for the possibility that hierarchical societies might actually have rather benign relationships to nature and that nonhierarchical societies might abuse their natural environment.[12] Rather, he seeks to uncover how patterns of social domination can foster "a broad cultural mentality" or "ideology" that supports the domination of nature.

In summary, societies characterized by a high degree of hierarchy are also likely to abuse and damage their natural environment. Social hierarchies provide both the psychological and the material conditions—the motivation and the means—for exploiting and dominating nature. In hierarchical societies, social institutions and practices (which would include, for example, forms of agriculture and technology) are designed in ways that facilitate control. You might think of the concept of economic efficiency as one such social ideal. In such a society, success is understood in terms of dominance and control. The more people who work for you, the more wealth, power, and status that you have, the more successful you are. Such a society also identifies human success with the domination and control of nonhuman nature. To understand the analysis further, it will help to discuss briefly another facet of social ecology, what Bookchin refers to as the "organismic tradition."

The organismic tradition in social philosophy focuses on the relations between individuals and their society. It seeks a middle ground between those who believe that individuals are simply the products of their society and those who believe that society is nothing more than a collection of individuals. An organic society, or what is more often called a community, exists in what philosophers call a "dialectical relationship" with individual human beings. That is, communities are created by human actions and human decisions, but humans are also created by their community. Social institutions, practices, values, and beliefs all influence the person I become. My identity is constituted to a large extent by my social roles, social history, and social circumstances. But the organic tradition does not reify the society, making it some "thing" out there that shapes and controls humans. Society is a product of human action and human decisions. Thus the dialectical relationship sees humans as creating their society while being created by it.

Given this understanding of social history, we can now understand Bookchin's primary social and ethical value. Humans cannot help but be shaped and created by their social history. But this can occur in two ways. Humans can go through life being created by and in turn creating their social world without fully recognizing this reality, or they can be fully conscious of and responsible for this history. The preeminent human value is fully conscious, "self-determining activity," because it is only through this type of action that humans most fully attain their natural potential as conscious, thinking beings. This value is Bookchin's anarchist conception of freedom.

How is fully conscious self-determining activity possible? It is possible only when humans are free from all forms of external control and domination, which include not only physical but social, legal, psychological, intellectual, and emotional forms of coercion. Thus, the only truly just society is one in which humans are free from all forms of control or domination. This, then, is the goal of Bookchin's "libertarian anarchism." Philosophical anarchism holds that no coercive authority is ever justified. Put another way, philosophical anarchism maintains that all claims of authority are simply disguised forms of power or coercion.

In this model, the just community is one that is created to serve common needs and goals. It is a community that eschews domination in any form, whether domination of humans or nature. It would be a community in which democratic values such as full participation and freedom are the norms. Bookchin characterizes this just community as one that avoids institutions and customs that place one person or group of people in positions of authority over others. It would be a community in which decision-making authority is decentralized, where individuals complement and cooperate with each other but do not dominate each other. Indeed, the ideal "anarchistic community would approximate an ecosystem; it would be diversified, balanced, and harmonious."[13]

Given these philosophical goals, we can see how such practices as sustainable agriculture would play a central role in Bookchin's ideal social and ecological community. He sees sustainable agriculture not as a collection of solutions to specific farming problems but as part of a lifestyle in which both humans and their natural surroundings can live free from dependence on dominating institutions and practices. Sustainable agriculture decentralizes and diversifies decision-making authority.

In this sense, it is truly a democratic practice. Decisions are made directly by the people most affected by them. Sustainable agriculture reinforces a lifestyle in which local communities become sustainable and self-sufficient. In this type of world, humans experience true freedom, and only in this type of community are humans able to live in harmony with their natural environment. It is not coincidental, according to Bookchin, that nature's freedom from human domination can come about only in a world in which humans are also free from domination.

10.6 CRITICAL REFLECTIONS

Several challenges can be raised against Bookchin's social ecology. One concerns the alleged connection between social domination and the domination of nature.[14] A second focuses on the role that humans play in guiding the evolutionary development of nature.[15]

Bookchin explicitly denies that there is any necessary connection between social hierarchies and social domination on the one hand and attempts to dominate nature on the other. The former does not *cause* the latter. But what *is* the relationship? Bookchin's answer is not always clear. Yet without a clear answer, social ecology loses much of its persuasive force, especially when we consider its practical implications.

A strong causal connection between social domination and the domination of nature would suggest that we will be unable to meet environmental challenges unless we first abolish social hierarchies. In this interpretation, our policy demands are clear. We must address social questions before ecological ones. Yet if the connection is less clear, then so, too, should be our policy priorities. If we can address ecological problems first and independently of addressing social hierarchies, the very relevance of social ecology is open to question.

In fairness to Bookchin, his view is more subtle than this challenge allows. As he sees it, the connection is less than a necessary causal connection but more than a mere accident. Bookchin speaks of the historical connection between real social hierarchies and the *idea* of dominating nature.[16] This suggests that, as a matter of historical fact, hierarchical societies encourage humans to identify social progress with control of and domination over nonhuman nature. Eventually, the connections can be thought of as mutually reinforcing. By implication, we need to address both, and to address one is also to address the other. Changing to a more benign relationship with the natural world will provoke changes in social arrangements (as the discussion of the political nature of sustainable agriculture might suggest). Changing our social relationships to less hierarchical, more decentralized associations will encourage a more felicitous relationship with nature (as the discussion of sustainable agriculture might suggest).

A second challenge to Bookchin focuses on the role that he allows humans in guiding natural evolution. Bookchin casts humans as "stewards" of evolution, capable of consciously serving and directing natural evolution. To some critics, this suggests a willingness to privilege human interests over nonhuman interests, to allow humans to "seize the helm of evolution" and direct nature to human ends.[17] Critics reject such anthropocentrism as being exactly the attitude that created much ecological destruction in the first place.

This criticism grows out of Bookchin's description of human rationality and human society as products of natural evolution, a "nature-rendered self-conscious." On this basis, Bookchin rejects any view that calls for humans to remove themselves from the natural world or that "denies or degrades the uniqueness of human beings." He lists both biocentric ethics and deep ecology among the philosophical views that degrade the rational abilities of human beings. He describes social ecology as "humanistic in the high Renaissance meaning of the term," which requires "a shift in vision from the skies to the earth, from superstition to reason, from deities to people—who are no less the products of natural evolution than grizzly bears and whales."[18]

Bookchin distinguishes "second nature," which includes such features of human evolution as rationality, communication, culture, and society, from "first nature," which consists of the nonhuman natural world. Although he emphasizes that this is a distinction of degree rather than kind, it also suggests that humans are not simply the "equal biotic citizens" described in biocentric ethics, the land ethic, and deep ecology. The implications of this position trouble critics, especially when Bookchin elaborates as follows:

> Natural evolution has not only provided humans with the *ability,* but also the *necessity* to be purposive interveners into "first nature," to consciously *change* "first nature" by means of a highly institutionalized form of community we call "society."... Taken together, all of these human traits—intellectual, communicative, and social—have not only emerged from natural evolution and are inherently human; they can also be placed at the *service* of natural evolution to consciously increase biotic diversity, diminish suffering, foster the evolution of new and ecologically valuable life-forms, [and] reduce the impact of disastrous accidents or the harsh effects of mere change.[19]

Bookchin explicitly denies that he is suggesting that humans should take command of nature and control it for anthropocentric ends. As it exists today, second nature is thoroughly shaped by social hierarchies and ideas of domination. Hence it would be a mistake simply to pass control of the natural world over to this type of thinking and reasoning. Further, in a spirit reminiscent of Leopold's, Bookchin emphasizes the complexity of first nature and strongly recommends a conservative and prudent approach to any activity that changes nature. Nonetheless, he does not shy away from the ramifications of his initial claim. Humanity as a part of natural evolution—and the only part capable of sophisticated, rational thought—has a responsibility to act as steward of the natural evolutionary process.

During the late 1980s, an acrimonious debate developed on this issue between Bookchin and several deep ecologists. Deep ecologists accused Bookchin of anthropocentrism and attributed to him the view that "human beings are a *higher* form of life."[20] Bookchin, for his part, had accused deep ecology of advocating an oppressive and misanthropic philosophy.[21] A short review of this debate can provide a helpful summary of Bookchin.

Bookchin's critique of deep ecology can be generalized to apply to any bio-centric or ecocentric ethics that attributes "equal moral worth" to human and nonhuman life-forms. During this debate, Bookchin highlighted the extreme views of members of Earth First! and several deep ecologists. These views sug-gested that famine and AIDS, for example, were "nature's revenge" for overpop-ulation and ecological destruction. The implication was that starving children in places such as Ethiopia and Somalia should be allowed to die in the name of some natural ecological law concerning carrying capacity and population dynam-ics. Bookchin forcefully rejected these views as unjust, claiming that they fol-lowed straightforwardly from the philosophy of biocentrism.

> If the deep ecology principle of "biocentrism" teaches that human beings are no different from lemmings in terms of their "intrinsic worth" and the moral consideration we owe them, and if human beings are viewed as being subject to "natural laws" in just the same way as any other species, then these "extreme" statements are really the *logical* conclusion of Deep Ecology philosophy.[22]

One problem with the principle of biocentric equality is that it tends to treat all humans as equally responsible for ecological destruction. The cause of the ecological crisis is attributed to "anthropocentrism," a human-centered ethics. As an alterna-tive, a biocentric or life-centered ethics is developed. But Bookchin rejects the view that "humanity" is at fault and that "we" are destroying the natural world.

> But, I have to ask, who is this "us" from which the living world has to be protected? ... Is it "humanity"? Is it the human "species" per se? Is it people, as such? Or is it our particular society, our particular civilization, with its hierarchical social relations ...? One of the problems with this asocial, "species-centered" way of thinking, of course, is that it blames the victim. Let's face it, when you say that a black kid in Harlem is as much to blame for the ecological crisis as the president of Exxon, you are letting one off the hook and slandering the other.[23]

We can see the central insight of Bookchin's philosophy in these challenges to deep ecology and biocentrism. To understand the roots of our ecological cri-sis, we need to look to how societies are organized. Society is a human creation, and some forms of society can lead to an attitude that encourages humans to dominate and destroy the natural world. But because society is a human creation, human beings can also change it. Bookchin reminds us that although human decisions and human values have played a major role in ecological destruction, they can be a major part of ecological solutions as well.

10.7 SUMMARY AND CONCLUSIONS

The shift from individualism to holism within ecology is a helpful reminder that ethical issues arise both at the level of individual people and at the level of social institutions and practices. Environmental ethics must address questions of social justice as well as individual rights and duties. Like deep ecologists, advocates for environmental justice and the social ecologists call our attention to the social and cultural roots of environmental destruction. But unlike the deep ecologists, environmental justice movements are more specific in identifying the social and cultural roots. They see the domination of the natural world as part of a more general pattern of social domination and control. Addressing environmental issues adequately requires that we also address wider issues of social justice.

But the environmental justice movement does face challenges, both practical and philosophical. Pragmatically, the movement must confront priority questions when issues such as jobs and economic growth seem to conflict with environmental protection. As a matter of fact, it can often be the case that the very people benefited by environmental destruction are the people who social justice advocates identify as marginalized and oppressed. Philosophically, environmental justice must also address challenges that arise when such rights as private property, individual freedom, and self-determination conflict with the goals of environmental protection. A complete account of environmental justice will take us deep into topics of social and political philosophy.

Nevertheless, the environmental justice movement has already made significant contributions to environmental ethics and environmental philosophy. No longer can these issues be discussed independently of discussions of social justice and social domination. By calling our attention to such issues, these movements stimulate our thinking about the connections between environmental and ethical justice, two of the three pillars of sustainability that will be described in Chapter 12.

NOTES

1. This memo exists in places in the public domain after having been leaked to the press, apparently from an internal World Bank source.

2. When the memo reprinted here was circulated, Lawrence Summers was chief economist of the World Bank. In 1999 he was appointed secretary of the treasury by President Clinton. After the memo was leaked to the public, Mr. Summers apologized and explained that it was intended as ironic. Later reports suggested that Mr. Summers had not even written the memo, although it was circulated with his name attached.

3. John Rawls, *A Theory of Justice* (Cambridge, Mass.: Harvard University Press, 1971).

4. For Locke's defense of private property, see his *Second Treatise on Government*, ed. C. B. Macpherson (Indianapolis, Ind.: Hackett, 1980), especially Ch. 5. For a helpful collection of essays on property rights and economic justice, see Virginia Held, *Property, Profits, and Economic Justice* (Belmont, Calif.: Wadsworth, 1980). For an excellent collection on land use policy and ethics, see Lynton Caldwell and Kristin Shrader-Frechette, *Policy for Land* (Lanham, Md.: Rowman & Littlefield, 1993).

5. Marianne Lavelle and Marcia Coyle, "Unequal Protection," *National Law Journal,* September 21, 1992, as quoted in *Unequal Protection,* ed. Robert Bullard (San Francisco: Sierra Club Books, 1994), p. 9.

6. Bullard's work is a solid resource for these claims. In addition to the anthology mentioned in note 5,

see Robert D. Bullard, *Dumping in Dixie: Race, Class, and Environmental Quality* (Boulder, CO: Westview, 1990). Other sources include *Environmental Justice,* ed. Bunyan Bryant (Washington, D.C.: Island Press, 1995), and *Faces of Environmental Racism,* eds. Laura Westra and Peter Wenz (Lanham, Md.: Rowman & Littlefield, 1995). Bullard and Bryant emphasize policy and activist readings, and Westra and Wenz are philosophers. For a general introduction to a justice perspective on environmental issues, see Peter Wenz, *Environmental Justice* (Albany: State University of New York Press, 1988). See also United Church of Christ Commission for Racial Justice, *Toxic Wastes and Race in the United States* (New York: United Church of Christ, 1987).

7. Laura Westra, "A Transgenic Dinner? Ethical and Social Issues in Biotechnology and Agriculture," *Journal of Social Philosophy* 24 (Winter 1993): 215–32. Quoted in Westra and Wenz, eds., *Faces of Environmental Racism,* p. xvi.

8. Garrett Hardin, "Lifeboat Ethics: The Case against Helping the Poor," *Psychology Today* 8 (September 1974): 38–126. Reprinted in *World Hunger and Morality,* 2d ed., eds. William Aiken and Hugh LaFollette (Upper Saddle River, N.J.: Prentice Hall 1996), pp. 5–15.

9. Leonie Caldecott and Stephanie LeLan, eds., *Reclaim the Earth* (London: Women's Press, 1983); Vandana Shiva, *Staying Alive: Women, Ecology, and Development* (London: Zed Books, 1988).

10. This estimate is from UNICEF, *State of the World's Children* (1988) as quoted in Vandana Shiva, "The Impoverishment of the Environment," *Ecofeminism,* eds. Maria Mies and Vandana Shiva (London: Zed Books, 1993), p. 81.

11. See Annabel Rodda, *Women and the Environment* (London: Zed Books, 1991), pp. 68–80, for extended discussions of these claims.

12. Murray Bookchin, *The Ecology of Freedom* (Palo Alto, Calif.: Chesire Books, 1982) p. 4. For more of Bookchin's views, see also *The Philosophy of Social Ecology* (Montreal: Black Rose Books, 1990).

13. Ibid., 4–8.

14. Much of what follows is taken from Murray Bookchin, "Recovering Evolution: A Reply to Eckersley and Fox," *Environmental Ethics* 12 (Fall 1990): 253–73.

15. Bookchin, "Ecology and Revolutionary Thought," in *Post-Scarcity Anarchism* (Berkeley, Calif.: Ramparts, 1971), p. 80. This essay originally was published in 1965.

16. See, for example, Robin Eckersley, *Environmentalism and Political Theory* (Albany: State University of New York Press, 1992), pp. 148–54.

17. Ibid., 154–60. See also Eckersley's "Divining Evolution: The Ecological Ethics of Murray Bookchin," *Environmental Ethics* 11 (Summer 1989): 99–116.

18. Murray Bookchin, "Social Ecology versus Deep Ecology," *Socialist Review* 18, nos. 1–2 (1988): 27–28.

19. Ibid., 28; the emphasis is in the original.

20. Judi Bari, "Why I Am Not a Misanthrope," *Earth First!,* February 2, 1991, p. 25. For other deep ecology critiques of Bookchin, see Christopher Manes, *Green Rage: Radical Environmentalism and the Unmaking of Civilization* (Boston: Little, Brown, 1990), and Warwick Fox, *Toward a Transpersonal Ecology* (Boston: Shambhala, 1990). An excellent overview of these debates can be found in Steve Chase, ed.,

Defending the Earth: A Dialogue between Murray Bookchin and Dave Foreman (Boston: South End Press, 1991).

21. See Bookchin, *Social Ecology versus Deep Ecology* (Burlington, Vt.: Green Program Project, 1988), reprinted in

Socialist Review 18, nos. 1–2 (1988): 27–28.

22. Chase, ed., *Defending the Earth: A Dialogue between Murray Bookchin and Dave Foreman,* p. 125.

23. Ibid., 30–31.

DISCUSSION QUESTIONS

1. Must a public policy intentionally discriminate before it can be described as racist or sexist? Is discrimination always a matter of intent? In your opinion, what is the intent behind decisions on where to locate waste dumps?

2. In his book *Earth in the Balance,* former Vice President Al Gore described the infamous nineteenth-century Irish potato famine as resulting from mono-culture farming techniques. That is, because the Irish relied almost entirely on a single imported species of potato, a single infestation destroyed their entire food supply. This brings to mind the claim of some deep ecologists that famines often are "nature's revenge" on humans for their abuse of nature. In his book, Gore also notes that other foodstuffs, including wheat and sheep, were being exported to England even as Irish people were starving. How might a social ecologist analyze the causes of the Great Hunger in Ireland?

3. The United States Constitution prohibits the government from taking private property for public use without just compensation.

Do you think that this clause should protect developers when they seek to build housing or a commercial development in an environmentally sensitive area? Do environmental laws that restrict land use violate this constitutional protection? If so, should developers be compensated for the price they paid for the land? Or should they be compensated for the "loss" of what they could have received if they had been allowed to develop the land?

4. If the price of land in a rural area is less than that of comparable land in an urban area, is this land less valuable? If not, how do you determine the value of land?

5. Nomadic peoples on many continents travel great distances following migrating herds of animals. Such people never settle permanently on one section of land. How might their understanding of ownership and property differ from yours? Can a concept of "private property" even exist in such a culture?

GLOBAL ENVIRONMENTAL ETHICS WATCH

For more information on Environmental Justice and Social Ecology, please see the Global Environmental Ethics Watch. Updated several times a day, Global Environmental Ethics Watch is a focused portal into GREENR—our Global Reference on the Environment, Energy, and Natural Resources—an ideal one-stop site for current events and research. You will have access to the latest information from trusted academic journals, news outlets, and magazines as well as access to statistics, primary sources, case studies, videos, podcasts, and much more.

To gain access please use the access code that accompanies your book. If you do not have an access code, visit cengagebrain.com to purchase one.

Pluralism, Pragmatism, and Sustainability

This book opened with a discussion on global warming and global climate change. Perhaps like no other environmental issue, global warming has become a focus of vitriolic partisan debates that seem to divide people into irreconcilable camps. Because of this, global warming is often characterized as an all-or-nothing issue: global climate change is a catastrophic event that will inevitably occur in the near future, or climate change is a hoax perpetrated on the public.

Against this backdrop it is easy for environmentalists to think that we need to find *a* solution, *a* strategy, *a* policy to solve the problem. Given the size of the challenge, various radical proposals have been proposed, including nuclear fusion, space-based solar panels, and geo-engineering techniques to increase oceanic photosynthesis, block sunlight from reaching the earth, increase cloud cover, and sequester carbon beneath the earth. Such revolutionary proposals

face exactly the type of challenges discussed in Chapter 1. History seems to show that reliance on technological fixes for environmental problems has often caused as many problems as it has solved. Yet, failing to identify a single solution to global warming, can easily lead to despair. There is nothing we can do to address this challenge, so why bother?

Scientists, engineers, and policy experts working at the Carbon Mitigation Institute (CMI) at Princeton University believe that they have identified more than a dozen separate strategies and technologies that, together, can level off global carbon emissions and keep it level for fifty years. These well-established and presently available tools can buy enough time for alternative energy sources to mature to the point that we can replace carbon-based fuels. Importantly, this approach can be adopted without causing major economic or social upheavals, and they do not rely on radical geo-engineering projects.

Current trends predict a doubling of carbon emissions from the fossil fuel use in the next fifty years. The Carbon Mitigation Institute strategy begins with the goal of leveling off carbon emissions to present levels while still meeting the growing global demand for energy. Meeting this goal will require a reduction of about 8 billion tons of carbon emissions annually through 2060. The Carbon Mitigation Institute uses a concept of "stabilization wedges" to explain their strategy.

The trend line for carbon emission follows a steep upward slope from the beginning of the industrialized age well into the future. The goal of leveling off emissions would follow a flat line from the present through 2060. The Carbon Mitigation Institute calls the gap between the upwardly sloping trend line and the level line the "stabilization triangle." The size of this stabilization triangle shows the daunting task facing any single strategy to eliminate this entire gap. But, if we divide the entire triangle Into eight distinct parts, each representing a reduction of 1 billion tons each year, the challenge appears less daunting. These eight sections of the stabilization triangle, what would appear as wedges slicing through the triangle, are identified as "stabilization wedges."

The Carbon Mitigation Institute believes that more than a dozen presently available tools could each be capable of reducing carbon emissions by 1 billion tons annually. No single tool alone will be enough to turn the trend, but together this portfolio of tools is capable of entirely eliminating the stabilization triangle and, optimally, even reducing carbon emissions below present levels. These tools include the following: efficiency in auto fuel mileage, public transportation usage, in home and building energy use, and in power plant production; carbon capture and sequestration; switching from coal to natural gas for electricity generation; replacing some coal plants with nuclear power; increasing wind, biofuel, and solar energy production; creating natural carbon sinks by reducing deforestation and improving conservation in agriculture.

Critics have faulted this approach on several grounds. Some believe that CMI has seriously underestimated the economic costs of their strategies. While the technologies might exist, ramping up to the level needed to produce the carbon reductions required will be significantly expensive. Other critics suggest that some of the technologies are not mature or safe enough to be so widely used. But some critics from within the environmental community focus on challenges that we have seen previously in this book.

This carbon mitigation strategy relies almost exclusively on technological fixes to global warming. This is reminiscent of problems described in Chapter 1 where scientist Amory Lovins was quoted as saying that the "answers you get depend on the questions you ask." Lovins explained that if we define our energy problem as a supply problem, we can easily conclude that we are running out of energy and need new energy sources rather than considering that our energy problem might instead be more of a demand problem. So, too, some environmental critics fault CMI for taking as a given the increasing demand curve that drives increasing carbon emissions. Finally, critics also point out that CMI has been funded in part by both Ford Motor Company and BP, two of the world's largest beneficiaries of a carbon-based economic system.

DISCUSSION TOPICS:

1. Do you think that increasing global carbon emissions is more a demand problem (humans are demanding too much energy from fossil fuels) or a supply problem (we do not have sufficient technologies to produce alternative energy or control carbon)?

2. Are you skeptical of CMI because of its association with and support from Ford and BP?

3. Review the CMI tools to reduce carbon emissions (more information can be found on their website: http://cmi.princeton.edu/). Which tools would you support? Which tools would you oppose? Is there a combination of the tools that you would support?

4. Chapter 9 distinguished approaches that seek to reform society from those that seek radical changes. CMI clearly is a reformist approach. What radical criticisms of CMI could you envision?

11.1 INTRODUCTION: AGREEMENT AND DISAGREEMENT IN ENVIRONMENTAL ETHICS

At the conclusion of this intellectual journey through a variety of environmental philosophies, an obvious question arises. Which, if any, is right? Describing theories such as biocentrism, the land ethic, deep ecology, social ecology, and ecofeminism is only half of the philosophical task. Should we not now determine which theory is ethically and philosophically the most valid or true? Which should guide our decisions? If we do not reach a clear conclusion, are we not left with disarray, disagreement, and contradiction? We return to the skeptical question raised in Chapter 1: Who is to say what is right or wrong?

At this point, the relativist's answer might seem attractive. We have looked at a variety of environmental philosophies and have seen much disagreement among them. Animal rights philosophers disagree with the land ethic, Deep ecologists disagree with social ecologists, and social ecologists disagree with ecofeminists. Further, the field of environmental ethics seems to be entirely defined in terms of a variety of conflicting dualisms: anthropocentrism versus nonanthropocentrism, holism versus individualism, and intrinsic versus instrumental value. Environmental ethics seems to offer little more than disagreement and controversy. If we cannot determine a single right answer, then—as the relativists have claimed all along—ethics has no objectivity. Environmental ethics should then be relegated to the domain of mere opinion.

Before drawing such skeptical conclusions, however, we should recognize that agreement among these theories also exists. It may be helpful to step back and review some areas in which a strong consensus does exist—the diagnosis of environmental problems and some guidelines that need to be followed when addressing these problems.

Environmental philosophers have reached a strong consensus that the narrow worldview of classical economics and the preference utilitarianism that underlies it must be rejected. We should not allow consumer demand alone to decide environmental policy and determine environmental value. Valuing the natural world as a mere resource to be manipulated and consumed to satisfy the short-term consumer preferences expressed in economic markets has resulted in much environmental destruction. We would find wide agreement on this among anthropocentric and nonanthropocentric approaches, biocentric and ecocentric theories, those concerned with future generations, those concerned with animal welfare, and those concerned with social justice for the poor and marginalized.

Different environmental philosophies would offer different explanations of why this approach is wrong. Some would point out that it misunderstands or ignores important human values. Some would argue that it distorts and ignores the interests of human beings in the near and distant future. Others would argue that people at society's margins—the poor, the oppressed, and minorities—are systematically excluded from markets. Still others would point out that preference utilitarianism is contemptuous of the respect due for plants, animals, and other parts of the natural world. All might insist tenaciously on the validity of their own unique criticisms. Nevertheless, they would all agree that the assumptions and values of the economic worldview are philosophically and ethically incomplete.

Further, although these various philosophies offer differing prescriptions for what needs to be done, a consensus is emerging around several ecological judgments. All environmental philosophies recognize that there are limits to the capacity of natural ecosystems to produce essentials such as clean air and water, food, fertile topsoil, and a stable climate. All recognize that natural ecosystems have a limited capacity to assimilate wastes and pollutants and to rebound from disruptions and destruction. The natural world and natural ecological processes—at least those necessary for human survival—are more fragile and more interdependent than we previously understood.

We humans need to undertake our activities with less arrogance and more humility for our own sake, if not also for the sake of future generations and other living beings. Even those who endorse a narrow anthropocentrism that attributes only instrumental value to the natural world acknowledge this.

11.2 MORAL PLURALISM AND MORAL MONISM

Nevertheless, the lack of agreement among environmental philosophies is troubling. Certainly, there are good reasons to seek a unified ethical perspective. Chapter 1 introduced ethics with Socrates's call to examine what we are saying so that we might come to know what is true. Irresolvable conflict about important matters does seem to threaten the foundations of an ethical life and our ability to know what is true. Without a determinate procedure for making decisions, we seem to lack any guide for making them. Further, to live without a unified and consistent ethics seems to be to live a life without integrity, principles, and commitments.

Within moral philosophy, these questions are part of a debate between moral monism and moral pluralism. Monists claim that there can be only one valid or correct moral theory. Pluralists accept the possibility that more than one basic approach can be legitimate. Because of the wide-ranging disagreements over environmental policy and the diversity of environmental perspectives, the debate concerning moral pluralism has intensified among environmental philosophers in recent years.[1] Pluralism is a useful theme for some final reflections for this textbook.

One strong motivation behind moral monism is the fear of the alternative. Without a single unified and coherent ethical theory, we seem relegated to ethical relativism. The alternatives seem to be embracing a single ethical theory or abandoning the quest for a rational ethics.

But this either–or dualism is what moral pluralists deny. Pluralism is an alternative to monism *and* to relativism. Rejecting the monist view that there is only one correct answer in ethics, pluralists also reject the relativist claim that there can be no right answer. Instead, moral pluralists maintain that there is a plurality of moral truths that cannot (perhaps unfortunately) be reconciled into a single principle. According to monists, this posture is the same as relativism.

We have observed a plurality of environmental values at many points in this textbook. Indeed, the very structure of the book suggests a continuing expansion of ethical values. Some issues, such as water pollution and pesticide contamination, directly threaten human beings and thus raise familiar ethical concerns. Other issues, such as the storage of nuclear waste and global warming, extend these familiar concerns to future generations. Issues such as wilderness preservation increase our concern for aesthetic, spiritual, historical, and symbolic values. Other topics challenge us to consider the moral value of nonhuman natural objects such as animals, plants, and even ecosystems and the earth itself. The landscape of environmental ethics appears to be populated by a value diversity that rivals the biological diversity of natural landscapes.

We have also examined several strategies for maintaining a monistic approach in the face of diverse values. The distinction between basic and nonbasic interests that characterizes the animal welfare debates is one attempt to bring unity to a diversity of values. Paul Taylor's set of procedural rules for resolving conflicts in the interests of living beings is a similar project. J. Baird Callicott's image of concentric circles of moral sentiment is yet another. Each project attempts to bring unity and consistency to a range of values that, at least at certain points, seem to conflict. These strategies share the assumption that an ethical theory is incomplete unless we can find a single way to reconcile conflict and prioritize competing values.

But perhaps a diversity of values is not as bad as it appears. Chapter 1 also warned us not to be misled by scientific models when making ethical judgments. Science and mathematics may require certainty and unambiguous answers as their standard of rationality. But perhaps it is a mistake to apply scientific and mathematical standards to ethics. Perhaps we are asking too much when we seek clear, unambiguous, and certain decisions on ethical matters. Perhaps can be rational about ethical matters without having unequivocal, definitive answers.

Christopher Stone uses such strict standards in his recent writings on moral pluralism and environmental ethics. Stone tells us that a monistic theory involves "a single coherent set of principles capable of governing all moral quandaries" and yielding "for each quandary one right answer." Because all traditional ethical theories seem incapable of doing this, and because relativism is unacceptable, Stone concludes that pluralism is the answer.[2]

Why should we expect ethics to be so mechanical in generating answers? With the exception of mathematics, logic, and perhaps the mathematical sciences and engineering, few intellectual disciplines produce certain results. When we confront a problem in mathematics, we know that if we apply the relevant rules in the correct way, we will arrive at a single correct answer. (This is what computers are so good at doing.) But consider a science such as medicine. Although medicine can sometimes provide a single right answer for diagnostic or prognostic questions, several alternative answers often are equally valid. Good doctors have many diverse tools in their black bags: surgery, a wide variety of medications, exercise, rest, nutrition, and counseling. Medicine is not a mechanistic science of applying unambiguous rules to specific situations and seeking one right answer. Deciding when and where to apply which tool is the essence of being a good physician. On the other hand, it is also important to note that the alternative to determinate rules is not chaos. There is still a big difference between a good physician and a quack.

Suppose we were to ask the doctor this question: Of all the diverse treatments in your repertoire, which is the best for protecting and preserving good health? The best answer surely is none and each. No one answer is the best in all situations, but each is, in particular situations, the best. Perhaps this is how we ought to think about the diverse environmental philosophies considered in this book. No one has all the right answers in every situation, but each has something important to contribute to environmental ethics. Each provides a different perspective from which we can understand the value of humans and their place within nature.

When we think about ethical issues in general and environmental controversies more specifically, we should consider whether ethics is more like mathematics or medicine. Perhaps it would be nice if we could get unambiguous answers in both medicine and ethics. But it would appear that neither health nor the good life is open to such determinations.

Here, again, we might learn something from the history of philosophy. At the beginning of his writing on ethics, Aristotle reminds his readers not to demand more precision and accuracy than a subject matter allows. It is one thing to demand rigorous proof of a mathematician and another to demand such proof of a rhetorician. "Virtue and justice—the subject matter of politics—admit of plenty of differences and uncertainty, so much so that some have thought them to be matters of convention rather than being natural and true."[3] Lacking rigorous scientific proof is not a sign that ethics is merely a matter of convention. It may reflect the fact that ethics involves complex and subtle matters. In this case, it may be irrational to insist on unequivocal answers. Aristotle reminds us that ethics involves practical reason, with which we judge not what is true but what we should do. Often, practical decision making is exclusive. If we do one thing, we are precluded from doing another. This, of course, is the real appeal of monism. Because I can do only one thing, ethics should give specific and unequivocal advice. But pluralism resists that attraction, holding that several different actions may be equally rational and equally justified.

Consider what is involved in being a good parent. Parents are constantly confronted with decisions, some easy and some difficult. It would be peculiar to insist that good parents must hold to "a single coherent set of principles" that would yield "for each quandary one right answer." Obviously, some acts are ruled out. A good parent is not abusive. But just as obviously, some quandaries have no single right answer. For example, good parents try to encourage self-confidence in their children, yet they also should provide comfort and a safe haven. Sometimes these principles may offer conflicting advice. Being a good parent sometimes requires backing away to allow a child to face difficulties alone. But sometimes it requires stepping in to provide comfort and support.

There is no mechanical way to decide this (and it certainly is not the sort of thing a computer could do). Pluralism acknowledges this complexity and characterizes the ethical life as involving many situations in which diverse, equally important values must be balanced. According to Aristotle, such situations are best left to older, more mature people who have had greater and more diverse experiences. His theory relied on the judgments of the "good man." For ethical guidance in the face of uncertainty and complexity, we should rely on the judgment of the person with experience, wisdom, and moral character. This is not unlike how we might proceed when faced with complex medical or parental decisions. Perhaps the best we can hope for is to rely on the judgments of experienced, knowledgeable, and caring people.

In this way, we can think of the theories considered in this textbook as the various tools that we find in a doctor's repertoire. They are resources that we can use to diagnose and treat environmental illness. Although no single approach provides all the right answers, we need them all. A responsible citizen should be familiar with the values that each articulates, as well as with the limitations of each. Especially in a democracy, we should be prepared to encounter a variety of values and points of view. This perspective, along with important virtues such as courage, humility, and care, may be the best for which we can hope.

11.3 ENVIRONMENTAL PRAGMATISM

In recent years, some environmental philosophers have turned their attention to a more pragmatic approach to environmental issues.[4] Environmental pragmatism takes moral pluralism seriously and articulates a middle ground between a single monistic theory and an "anything goes" relativism.

The words *pragmatic* and *pragmatism* have two related meanings in ordinary usage. On the one hand, to be pragmatic is to be practical and aim for what can be achieved rather than for some unattainable ideal. A pragmatic person is realistic, sensible, down-to-earth, and willing to compromise. A pragmatic person rejects ideology—the commitment to a single idea or principle that is never questioned or doubted. The diverse carbon mitigation strategies developed by CMI is a clear example of this pragmatic approach.

On the other hand, pragmatism is the particular philosophical tradition developed by American philosophers such as William James and John Dewey in the nineteenth and early twentieth centuries. Philosophical pragmatism is skeptical of monistic theories in both epistemology and ethics. Instead, pragmatism focuses on context-dependent practical accounts of both truth and value. Pragmatism is sometimes described as a radical empiricism. Empiricism holds that all knowledge is derived from experience. Pragmatism emphasizes the particularities of experience. If we take experience seriously, we must recognize that the world of experience is a world of diversity, change, and pluralism.

These two meanings of pragmatism can be found in recent discussions among environmental philosophers. Some believe that environmental philosophy is so focused on abstract conceptual issues that it has become irrelevant to the pressing concerns of environmental policy. In this view, it is time for philosophers to be more concerned with real-world practical issues such as pollution, environmental destruction, and environmental justice. Philosophers should come down out of the clouds (to use Aristophanes' ☐ image of Socrates) and become more pragmatic. Some of these observers also believe that the explicit philosophy of American pragmatists can be useful in contemporary environmental debates.

Pragmatism echoes some of the themes discussed previously. Like physicians, pragmatists recognize that what methods and tools are appropriate will depend on the specifics of each situation. No single approach can be known to be correct in the abstract, apart from the particular context. Like Aristotle, pragmatists shift attention in ethics from what is *true* to what is *practical,* and they understand that practical reasoning may not always offer unambiguous advice. Pragmatism also supports democratic values such as tolerance and respect for diverse opinions and the commitment to engaging in free and open procedures for deciding rather than seeking the single "true" decision.

Relating a recent personal experience may help in understanding environmental pragmatism. Some years ago, I was a member of a local task force appointed by our mayor and charged with drafting an environmental ordinance to govern economic development and the preservation of environmentally sensitive natural areas. Our city had recently merged with a surrounding township. The land within the original city limits was mostly developed, and the land in the surrounding township was mostly agricultural and rural. The challenge to this task force was to decide how this rural land should be developed. As one might expect, members were appointed to represent the various constituencies: landowners, farmers, real estate developers, builders, representatives from the Sierra Club and the Audubon Society, and officials from local and state government agencies.

In some ways, this was not a diverse group at all. All of the members were white, European Americans, most came from the middle- and upper-middle economic classes, many had college degrees, and slightly more than one-half were men. Yet in terms of their environmental philosophy, this was a very diverse group. Several members believed that developers already faced adequate environmental regulation; for this reason, they opposed any new regulation at all. Some members argued that 50 percent of any new development should be set aside as open space. Some thought that economic markets and the demand for new housing should determine what land would be developed and how. One person even argued that every available piece of land should be developed and brought onto the tax rolls to benefit the entire community. Of those who wished to preserve open spaces, some argued that wild animals and trees deserved protection, and others argued that wild spaces should be preserved as habitat for hunting and fishing. Some argued that ecologists should decide what areas would remain protected, and others thought the City Council should decide.

For the first two years of its work, the task force resembled much of the field of environmental ethics. Most participants thought that their own theories (seldom explicitly articulated) should determine the policy. Each brought a particular "theory" and principles to the table, applied them to this specific case to determine what ought to be done, and then tried to convince others to accept these conclusions. For the first two years of its work, the task force got nowhere. Not only did people disagree (and they did, significantly), but some had a difficult time even understanding the opposing side. This time was chaotic, frustrating, and totally unproductive. In the meantime, of course, development continued under the old regulations, which meant that no land was being protected.

At a certain point, several members sought to revitalize the group by listing the issues on which there was general agreement. Many were surprised by the result. There was widespread agreement that several natural areas within the city ought to be preserved, even if the city needed to purchase them to do it. Likewise, several areas were acknowledged to be prime sites for commercial development. There was also wide agreement that more housing developments, especially affordable housing, were needed within the city. And there was agreement that open spaces ought to remain in those areas being developed. People agreed that ecologically trained naturalists and scientists should be consulted in deciding boundaries for the protected areas. The task force then created development guidelines for achieving these goals and was able to complete its work within a few months. In effect, agreement on principles followed agreement on practice.

This experience captures many of the insights of environmental pragmatism. Disagreement reigned when people approached the challenge seeking to apply preconceived theories and principles. The diversity and abstractness of these starting points effectively prevented agreement and understanding—and also led to animosity and frustration among participants. Further, while we were debating the efficiency of markets or the moral status of a rare northern cactus, unregulated development continued. The alternative began with the practical matter of getting things done, and it did this by starting with specific issues on which people agreed. Ultimately, "theory" followed practice in the sense that the final governing principle was developed out of the agreed-upon starting points. In effect, the task force was monistic in terms of its practical conclusions but remained very pluralistic in terms of its theories about why we ought to adopt these conclusions. Members agreed on what should be done but disagreed on why. In this sense, pragmatism has elements of both monism and pluralism. Of course, a different community might have begun with different agreements and, therefore, would probably have ended with a different policy.

The solution was a practical compromise. The new ordinance creates a process that each planned development must go through. An initial survey identifies all the natural areas that are ecologically sensitive and historically significant. Native prairies, rare woodlands, riparian corridors, and habitat of rare species top the list. If a planned development will affect one of these areas, the developer and city planners enter negotiations aimed at preserving the natural area. As part of the bargaining, the city is legally empowered to offer compromises on other zoning regulations (for example, street width and housing density) in order to minimize the financial impact of preserving the natural area. The procedure offers no guarantees to either side and relies a great deal on the good-faith efforts of many people. So far, it seems to be working.

No party got all it had originally desired, and neither side "won." Yet as one member pointed out, the real winner was democratic citizenship. People came together, argued, debated, and eventually found common ground. The compromise "worked" in the sense that most everyone concluded that they could live with it. In a democracy—indeed, in any situation in which diverse perspectives conflict—it is unrealistic, unreasonable, and perhaps unfair to expect or desire one side completely to triumph over others. This is, in many ways, the "pragmatic" solution.

Consider the example of CMI's approach to reducing carbon emissions. Some would see this as a capitulation to vested interests in the present energy policy. Others would view it as a sensible and pragmatic approach. Or consider recent debates within the United States over tax policy, debt limits, and budget deficits. Some see these political debates as a matter of principle and believe that to compromise is to betray one's principles. More pragmatic politicians believe that finding a common ground, even when no one gets all that they desire, is a victory for democracy.

Although environmental pragmatism has many articulate defenders, criticisms remain. In the opinion of critics, the practical compromise that characterizes pragmatic solutions can be little more than a wishy-washy capitulation to the status quo. If we test environmental policy against what "works" and what is "practical" in a specific situation, we may be doing little more than conforming to the expectations and values that shaped the status quo. Assuming that we do face real environmental challenges that have arisen in part from that very status quo, this pragmatic approach might prove counterproductive at best. Critics of CMI's carbon mitigation strategy level this charge against an approach supported by Ford and BP. A second criticism holds that the context-dependent nature of pragmatic solutions means that pragmatism never fully escapes ethical relativism.

In response to the first challenge, pragmatists would point out that a pragmatic solution does not privilege the status quo in the way suggested by this criticism. In the words of Anthony Weston, values and practices "co-evolve."[5] Neither has an absolute priority over the other. As values are brought in line with practices, they evolve to guide future practices, which in turn shape future values. Our practices elevate some values and principles and discount others. In my community, for example, it would be very difficult to defend an "environment-be-damned" attitude after the compromises reached by the task force. The consensus has legitimized certain values that no doubt will shape future development. The criticism, then, inaccurately assumes that practices never change and never progress.

Pragmatists also have a response to the challenge of relativism. Pragmatic solutions are relativistic only if we assume that ethical evaluations must fit an either–or, true–false dichotomy. But pragmatism rejects this monistic view of value. We can return to Aristotle's reminder that ethics involves practical reason that judges not what is true but what we should do. The criterion in ethics is not truth so much as reasonableness. For the pragmatist, two incompatible ethical judgments might both be equally reasonable. Only for the monist must at least one be wrong. Because only one judgment can be left standing, there is a tendency among ethical monists to seek confrontation, conflict, and triumph. If, as pragmatists hold, many competing views can be equally reasonable, the tendency will be toward tolerance, respect, compromise, and getting along. Pragmatists argue that there are standards for reasonableness—intellectual and moral openness, intellectual and moral care, and attention to detail—and that these standards prevent the collapse of pragmatism into relativism.

11.4 CONCLUSION: SUSTAINABILITY REVISITED

Given these pluralistic and pragmatic conclusions, a legitimate question is "Where, exactly, do we go from here?" Assuming that there is no unambiguous and dominant theory of environmental ethics to guide us, does the pluralistic and pragmatic solution provide any guidance? Are we left simply to muddle our way into the future? By way of an answer, I would like to return to the discussion of sustainable development in Chapter 4.

It is easy, in a textbook or class on environmental ethics, to lose sight of the fact that environmental concerns are only one among several areas of ethical focus. As the social ecologists and ecofeminists remind us, environmental destruction must be understood within broader ethical contexts. Issues of social justice should not be ignored by environmentalists. Neither should economic and political factors. We can begin to approach the question of future direction by recognizing that in planning for an adequate social and political future, it is necessary to address ethical and economic, as well as environmental, challenges. Many writers who address sustainable development refer to these connections as the "three pillars of sustainability." A sustainable future must be sustainable on three related grounds: economic, environmental, and ethical. Instability or inadequacy of any of the three will undermine a society's ability to sustain itself over time.

Consider the perspective of policy makers in Kenya. Kenya is a relatively poor country with an expanding and increasingly urban population. Poverty and homelessness are a fact of life for millions. Millions of people in Kenya and neighboring Somalia are suffering from the effects of long-term droughts. As in many countries of sub-Saharan Africa, the AIDS epidemic is an ever-present threat. Estimates are that almost 15 percent of the population are HIV positive and that as many as a million children have been orphaned as a result of AIDS. Any hope for addressing problems of this magnitude will require significant economic resources.

Social justice and ethical challenges are just as formidable. Besides the ethical challenge of addressing poverty and AIDS, justice toward the Maasai and other indigenous cultures demands that people not be displaced or destroyed as a means to such socially desirable ends as wilderness and wildlife preservation. Corruption within Kenya's political structures continues to present barriers to reforms and policy initiatives.

Against this background, calls to protect wildlife, to preserve vast areas of land, and to displace indigenous peoples in the process might seem more than a little heavy-handed. When such preservationist proposals are voiced by people from countries in the economically developed Western world, they are particularly offensive.

Yet no one should dismiss the destructive capacity, both environmentally and ethically, of rampant economic growth and industrialization. Unfettered economic growth has been ecologically and socially destructive throughout history, from nineteenth-century Europe to present-day China. Sustainable development—economic development that is guided by both ethical and ecological principles—is a plausible alternative. Programs such as community-based conservation seem in step with the principles of sustainable development. Helping people understand that their well-being, both short-term and long-term, is connected to the health of their own ecosystem would appear to be a reasonable strategy for protecting those ecosystems. Doing so in a way that involves local people in decision-making seems to be both good strategy and good ethics.

However (and here's the rub), sustainable practices offer no guarantees to reassure those committed to a single environmental principle or theory. Trade-offs are inevitable. When people disagree and when diverse values are at stake, democratic decision making requires compromise. The goals of sustainable development suggest that such compromises are not open-ended. Not just any practice or policy is consistent with sustainable development. Yet sustainability does seem committed to using natural goods as resources, a conclusion that some monistic theories of environmental ethics reject in principle.

Where, then, do we go from here? Allow me to offer a concluding metaphor. Although many different paths are open, I suggest that there are two basic directions. One direction encompasses several distinct paths, each of which heads toward a single environmental endpoint. The endpoint may be clear to some, but the exact path to follow in getting there is more obscure, because there will be many obstacles to overcome. The other direction has a broader path and, although it has a clear direction, its ultimate endpoint is undetermined. There are guidelines to prevent decision makers from going too far astray in any direction, but once the path is established, they must compromise, sometimes emphasizing one direction, sometimes another.

This is by no means to suggest that theorizing about environmental ethics is without merit—far from it. But in light of this discussion of pluralism, pragmatism, and sustainability, we need to exercise care in our final evaluation of the relevancy of philosophical ethics. Ethical theory and analysis have important roles to play in environmental issues, but perhaps, as the pragmatists advise, they should not be regarded as independent principles to be imposed from on high to resolve environmental controversies. However, this is not the only way for abstract theoretical thinking to guide our lives. Without carefully analyzing and consistently being mindful of the detailed and sophisticated theories of environmental ethics, we can hope for little more than an opinionated and biased environmental ethic. By providing clear and intellectually rigorous principles, environmental philosophies establish the intellectual boundary conditions for both thinking and deciding. An environmentally sustainable future, as well as our own intellectual integrity, demands more than just earnest opinion and good feelings. The path to the future must not be paved only with good intentions. My hope is that this survey of environmental philosophies can contribute to a reasoned and considered first step along the path to a sustainable—economically, ethically, *and* ecologically sustainable—future.

NOTES

1.   Much of this recent debate was provoked by Christopher Stone's book *Earth and Other Ethics: The Case for Moral Pluralism* (New York: Harper & Row, 1987), and by his later essay "Moral Pluralism and the Course of Environmental Ethics," *Environmental Ethics* 10 (Summer 1988): 139–54. Stone's view was soon challenged by J. Baird Callicott, "The Case against Moral Pluralism," *Environmental Ethics* 12 (Summer 1990): 99–112. My own thinking on these issues owes much to Peter Wenz, "Minimal, Moderate, and Extreme Pluralism," *Environmental Ethics* 15 (Spring 1993): 61–74, and to Bryan Norton, *Toward Unity among Environmentalists* (New York: Oxford, 1991).

2.   Christopher Stone, *Earth and Other Ethics: The Case for Moral Pluralism* (New York: Harper & Row, 1987), p. 116.

3.   Aristotle, "Nicomachean Ethics," in *Basic Works of Aristotle*, ed. Richard McKeon (New York: Random House, 1941), book 1, Ch. 3, 15–17.

4.   The single best resource for environmental pragmatism is *Environmental Pragmatism*, eds. Andrew Light and Eric Katz (New York: Routledge, 1996). Several of the essays reprinted there were originally published in the journal *Environmental Ethics*.

5.   Anthony Weston, "Before Environmental Ethics," *Environmental Ethics* 14, no. 4 (Winter 1992), reprinted in Light and Katz, eds. *Environmental Pragmatism*, pp. 139–160.

GLOBAL ENVIRONMENTAL ETHICS WATCH

For more information on Pluralism, Pragmatism, and Sustainability, please see the Global Environmental Ethics Watch. Updated several times a day, Global Environmental Ethics Watch is a focused portal into GREENR—our Global Reference on the Environment, Energy, and Natural Resources—an ideal one-stop site for current events and research. You will have access to the latest information from trusted academic journals, news outlets, and magazines as well as access to statistics, primary sources, case studies, videos, podcasts, and much more.

To gain access please use the access code that accompanies your book. If you do not have an access code, visit cengagebrain.com to purchase one.

Glossary

altruism motivation that is focused on the best interests of others and is contrasted with egoism, or motivation out of self-interest.

anthropocentric ("human-centered") ethics a theory that only human beings have moral value. Thus, although we may be said to have responsibilities *regarding* the natural world, we do not have direct responsibilities *to* the natural world.

biocentric ethics a theory that views all life as possessing intrinsic value. The word *biocentric* means "life-centered."

BP Deep Water Horizon the oil drilling platform that caused the catastrophic oil spill in the gulf of Mexico during the summer of 2010.

Brundtland Commission named for its chair, Prime Minister Gro Harlem Brundtland, this United Nations commission studied long-term strategies that might help nations achieve economic development without jeopardizing the earth's capacity to sustain all life.

carbon mitigation refers to any of a number of strategies aimed at moderating global climate change by reducing the amount of carbon dioxide in the atmosphere.

categorical imperative within Kantian moral philosophy, this expresses both the logic and the content of the fundamental ethical duty. An imperative is a command (an "ought" or "should" statement) and can be expressed hypothetically ("You should do this *if...*) or categorically ("You should do this"). Kant argued that moral commands must be categorical; they depend on no other consideration to be binding on all rational beings. According to Kant, the fundamental moral duty is to act only in those ways that could be willed to be a universally binding law. Other Kantian formulations of the categorical imperative are as follows: treat persons as ends and never as means only, and treat persons as subjects, never as objects.

community-based conservation (CBC) an approach to conservation that pursues a balance of development and preservation, seeking both simultaneously. CBC shifts the focus of conservation from centralized state control to localized control and management. CBC holds that any adequate protection of an ecosystem must be based within the local community and must address the social, economic, and political needs of local people.

community models the view that ecosystems are on a par with a social community, wherein each individual member plays a functional role within that community.

deontological ethics   certain fundamental duties that require us to act in certain ways and to refrain from acting in others.

ecofeminism   the idea that there are important connections between the domination of women and the domination of the natural world. These connections have been examined in disciplines from philosophical ethics to literature and from religion to science.

ecological ethics   the view that environmental ethics should be holistic in the sense that ecological wholes, such as ecosystems or species, as well as nonliving natural objects and the relationships that exist among natural objects, deserve ethical consideration. Ecocentric ethics is holistic in a sense in which biocentric ethics, which focuses on individual living things, is not.

ecology   the science that studies living beings in relationship with their biotic and abiotic environments.

environmental ethics   a systematic account of the moral relationships between human beings and their natural environment. Environmental ethics is a branch of philosophy involving the systematic study and evaluation of the normative judgments that are so much a part of environmentalism.

environmental philosophy   the broader philosophical questions raised by environmental issues. Such topics might be the focus of other disciplines such as metaphysics (the nature of "nature," the concept of personhood, reality of ecosystems and individuals), epistemology (the distinction between objective and subjective, knowledge of intrinsic value, the nature of scientific knowledge), and social-political questions (the just society), as well as ethical questions.

environmental refugees   also referred to as "environmental migrants" or "climate change migrants" are people displaced from their homes as a result of changes in their local environments such as water shortages, sea level rises, desertification, drought, pollution, or natural disasters such as floods, hurricanes, earthquakes, or tsunamis.

epistemology   the branch of philosophy that studies questions of knowledge and truth.

ethical egoism   an ethical theory making the normative claim that humans ought to strive for their own self-interest. Most varieties of ethical egoism distinguish perceived self-interest, or the actual wants and desires of people, from their ethical or true best interests.

ethical extensionism   the practice of extending traditional ethical theories and concepts to previously unnoticed objects and topics, such as animals and future generations.

ethical relativism   the view that it is not possible to make objective ethical judgments. The relativist holds that ethical standards depend on, or are *relative to*, an individual's feelings, culture, religion, and so forth. A relativist would claim that ethics is merely and exclusively a matter of what is customary. Therefore, relativists deny that there can be objective norms by which we can evaluate ethical behavior and judgments.

ethical theory   any attempt to provide systematic answers to the philosophical questions raised by descriptive and normative approaches to ethics. These questions are raised from both an individual moral point of view and the point of view of society or public policy.

ethics   in a purely descriptive sense, ethics consists of the general beliefs, attitudes, values, or standards that guide behavior. In a normative sense, ethics consists of those beliefs, attitudes, values, and standards that *ought to* guide behavior. As a discipline within philosophy, ethics is the systematic study of those beliefs, attitudes, values, and standards. Ethics is sometimes divided into questions of personal morality and questions of social and public justice.

ethics of care the explication of morality in terms of cooperation and relationships rather than confrontation and conflict. Care ethics often emphasizes particular personal relationships rather than abstract moral principles. Many feminist philosophers believe that this approach is particularly compatible with the life experiences of women, especially giving birth to and raising children.

global climate change the various climatic changes that result from a build-up of atmospheric greenhouse gases, such as carbon dioxide, that result in an increase in overall global temperatures.

holistic ethics the idea that we have moral responsibilities to collections of (or relationships between) individuals rather than (or in addition to) responsibilities to those individuals who constitute the whole. For example, holistic environmental ethics might allow selective hunting of individual animals so long as the population of that species is not endangered.

instrumental value a function of usefulness. An object with instrumental value possesses that value because it can be used to attain something else of value. The instrumental value of an object lies not in the object itself but in the uses to which that object can be put.

intrinsic (or inherent) value a value that is to be found or recognized rather than given. To say that an object is intrinsically valuable is to say that it has a good of its own and that what is good for it does not depend on outside factors or judgments. It has value in itself and is not to be valued simply for its uses. The value of such things is intrinsic to them.

metaphysics the branch of philosophy that studies questions about the nature of ultimate reality.

moral standing or moral considerability concerns questions of what things count, morally. An object has moral standing or deserves moral consideration if it is the type of thing that rationally must be factored into any moral deliberation.

natural law ethics the idea that there are natural rights and principles. In one version these are derived from God's commands, which direct ethical behavior.

nonanthropocentric ethics moral standing granted to such natural objects as animals and plants.

normative ethics ethical judgments, advice, and evaluations of what ought to or should be. This first level of abstraction is the type of ethical reasoning that most people associate with ethics. Normative judgments prescribe behavior.

organic models in ecology view the relationship between an individual and its ecosystem as similar to the relationship between an organ and the body; both are parts of a greater independent and separate whole.

philosophical ethics a higher level of generality and abstraction in which normative judgments and their supporting reasons are analyzed and evaluated. This is the level of the general concepts, principles, and theories to which we appeal in defending and explaining normative claims.

pluralism in contrast to ethical monism, accepts the possibility that more than one basic approach to questions of value can be legitimate. Monists argue that all questions of ethics and values can be reduced to a single fundamental ethical principle, theory, or truth.

pragmatism a philosophical perspective that focuses on context-dependent practical accounts of both truth and value. Pragmatism is sometimes described as a radical empiricism. Empiricism holds that all knowledge is derived from experience. Pragmatism emphasizes the particularities of experience. If we take experience seriously, we must recognize that the world of experience is a world of diversity, change, and pluralism.

psychological egoism   an empirical claim about human motivation, holding that human beings are motivated solely by self-interest. It is often used as support for certain economic theories that presuppose self-interest. Psychological egoism should be distinguished from ethical egoism, which holds that humans should strive for their own self-interest, properly understood.

sustainable development   development that meets the needs of the present without compromising the ability of future generations to meet their own needs. Development, which involves improving the quality of life, is often distinguished from economic growth, which simply means increasing the overall size of economic activity.

teleology   an approach in metaphysics, which holds that there are natural ends or characteristic activities for all natural objects. As an approach to science and epistemology, teleology holds that a natural object is not fully explained without reference to its natural end or activity. As an approach to ethics, teleology holds that attaining its natural end is the good for each natural object.

utilitarianism   an approach to ethics that advises us to act in ways that maximize overall social benefits

virtues and virtue ethics   the virtues are character traits or habits of an ethically good person. Virtue ethics emphasizes the importance of the virtues and of questions such as "What type of person should I be?" It can be contrasted with such ethical theories as utilitarianism and deontology, which emphasize ethical rules and principles that guide behavior.

Index